SCANDINAVIAN IMMIGRANTS
IN NEW YORK
1630-1674

NOVA BELGICA sive NIEUW

NEDER LANDT

MAP OF NEW NETHERLANDS,
With a view of New Amsterdam, (now New-York) A. D. 1656.

Reduced from a copy in the Lenox Library, New York City.

Scandinavian Immigrants

IN

NEW YORK
1630—1674

WITH APPENDICES ON

SCANDINAVIANS IN MEXICO AND SOUTH AMERICA, 1532—1640
SCANDINAVIANS IN CANADA, 1619—1620
SOME SCANDINAVIANS IN NEW YORK IN THE EIGHTEENTH CENTURY
GERMAN IMMIGRANTS IN NEW YORK, 1630—1674

BY

JOHN O. EVJEN, Ph. D.
(LEIPZIG)

PROFESSOR OF CHURCH HISTORY IN AUGSBURG [THEOLOGICAL]
SEMINARY, MINNEAPOLIS, MINN.

ILLUSTRATED

MINNEAPOLIS, MINN.
K. C. HOLTER PUBLISHING COMPANY
1916

Notice

In many older books, foxing (or discoloration) occurs and, in some instances, print lightens with wear and age. Reprinted books, such as this, often duplicate these flaws, notwithstanding efforts to reduce or eliminate them. The pages of this reprint have been digitally enhanced and, where possible, the flaws eliminated in order to provide clarity of content and a pleasant reading experience.

Scandinavian Immigrants in New York 1630-1674

Originally published
Minneapolis, Minnesota
1916

Reprinted by:

Janaway Publishing, Inc.
732 Kelsey Ct.
Santa Maria, California 93454
(805) 925-1038
www.janawaygenealogy.com

2017

ISBN: 978-1-59641-394-8

TO MY REVERED TEACHER
ALBERT HAUCK, Ph. D., D. Th., D. Jur.
PROFESSOR IN THE UNIVERSITY OF LEIPZIG
THIS BOOK IS DEDICATED
ON HIS 70th BIRTHDAY
DECEMBER 9, 1915
IN SINCERE GRATITUDE AND AFFECTION

PREFACE.

This volume is a collection of biographic articles on Norwegian, Danish, and Swedish immigrants who settled in New Netherland, or the present state of New York, between the years 1630 and 1674. It is the result of research work begun seven years ago while I was teaching in Pennsylvania College, Gettysburg, Pennsylvania.

The most elementary, but also the most difficult, task connected with this work was to establish by documentary evidence which persons in the materials examined were Dutch or German, and which persons were Scandinavian. The English and French names were easily recognized. But the more strictly Teutonic names appeared to be fully as much Scandinavian as Dutch. In most instances the Dutch and Scandinavian nomenclature — especially the ending "szen" or "sen" in surnames — necessitated my making excursions into the personal history of the candidates for septentrional glory until their nationality was established.

Hundreds of possible Scandinavian names were traced in the documents until they proved to be the property of other Teutons than the Scandinavians. Some of them turned out to be the property of members belonging to the Celtic, to the Mongolian, and to the Ethiopian stock. Thus, a Jan Andersen and a Hendrick Hendricksen were two promising Scandinavian candidates until I discovered that they were Irish. Jan Swaen was one of my Swedish candidates until I had traced him to his original home, Africa. Promising candidates for my volume were also Emanuel Pieterszen, Lucas Pieterszen, and the latter's wife, Anna Jans. But these, too, proved to be of negro stock. Less promising were the candidates Hans and Hendrick, both without a surname, but Hans proved to be a Mohawk Indian, and Hendrick a plain Indian.

My field would have been more inviting, if it had been better cultivated. Judging by a statement made by Professor George T. Flom, it had hardly seen a plow as late as 1909, when he published his valuable "A History of Norwegian Immigration to the United States," which says:

"In the early days of New Netherlands colony, Norwegians sometimes came across in Dutch ships and settled among the Dutch. The names of at least two such have been preserved in the Dutch colonial records." Professor Flom then gives the names of Claes Carstensen and Hans Hansen. In addition he refers to Anneke Hendricks and Helletje Hendricks as Norwegian immigrant women. However, Helletje had the surname Noorman, not because she was a Norwegian, but because she was married to Claes Carstensen. But Anneke, the first wife of the ancestor of the Vanderbilts, was from Norway.

Professor Flom's phrase "at least two," coming, as it does. from a careful scholar of recognized ability, a graduate of Columbia University (which has derived some of its wealth from a parcel of the farm of two of the earliest Norwegian immigrants, Roelof Jansen and his wife Anneke Jans), may be taken as an index of the knowledge which the average public, six years ago, had of the first Norwegian immigrants in New York, of whom I have registered in the present volume no less than fifty-seven.

Mr. Hjalmar Rued Holand, M. A. (Wisconsin) unknowingly corroborates my statement regarding the knowledge the public has of Scandinavian immigration in the seventeenth century. In "De norske Settlementers Historie" (1909) he gives the names of twenty persons in early New York, who, in his opinion, were Scandinavians. Only eight of these, however, prove to be that, while the total number of Scandinavians treated in the present work is 187.

"Danske i Amerika" (1908f), published by C. Rasmussen Publishing Company, Minneapolis, has devoted considerable space (e. g. pp. 39—43, 358—384) to Danish immigrants. However, the sources used are not primary, but secondary at the best. And the treatment is uncritical. A number of immigrants are mentioned. as Danes, though they belonged to other nationalities. And a great number of real Danish immigrants have escaped the notice of "Danske i Amerika," otherwise in many respects a work of which the Americans of Danish ancestry can be proud.

Less ambitious but far more scholarly than the endeavors in

"Danske i Amerika" are two articles by Mr. Torstein Jahr, in "Symra" (V., 2, 1909; IX, 1, 1913), a magazine in Norwegian, published at Decorah, Iowa. They are chiefly based upon the "Van Rensselaer Bowier Manuscripts" published in Albany, 1908. Mr. Jahr's articles in "Symra" tell in some forty pages about the Norwegian immigrants who came to Rensselaerswyck. He dwells especially on the family of Bratt and of Anneke Jans, devoting some twenty-five pages to the latter. He makes good use of the well-known Anneke Jans literature, but offers nothing new to scholars beyond the claim—and this is important—that Anneke Jans and her husband Roelof Jansen were Norwegians. Mr. A. J. F. van Laer, the editor of the "Bowier Manuscripts," had called attention to the fact that Anneke and her husband did not come from Holland, as it had been supposed, but from Marstrand, "an island of the coast of Sweden." It would then appear that they were Swedes. Mr. Jahr, however, called attention to the fact that Marstrand was a Norwegian town, founded by the Norwegian king Haakon Haakonsson about the year 1230, and that it became a Swedish possession in 1658. And hence Anneke and her husband were, in all probability, Norwegians.

As for the Swedish immigrants in New York, but little appears to have been written concerning them, the Swedish settlement on the Delaware having engaged the attention of the more capable writers on Scandinavian immigration to our country, whose efforts have been crowned in the elaborate work of Dr. Amandus Johnson.

Sporadic statements concerning Scandinavian immigrants have not been wanting in general works on New York (state and city), but the attention bestowed upon these early pioneers from Northern Europe is almost insignificant. J. Riker's "Harlem, Its Origin and Early Annals" (revised edition, 1904) and J. H. Innes' "New Amsterdam and Its People" (1902), particularly the latter, belong to the exceptions. They avoid the common error of making every resident of New Amsterdam or New Netherland Dutch or English. However, the number of Scandinavians they mention is very limited, and the treatment accorded them meagre.

The present volume is in the main based on *primary* sources The most important of these sources, at least for genealogical data and personal history, are the lists of passengers which the immigrant ships of the seventeenth century kept; parish records, or church registers, kept in New York, Brooklyn, Albany, etc., records stating whence the several immigrants came, whom they married, the date of their marriage, the names of the children, the date of the baptism of the children, the names of the sponsors; court records, legislative records, municipal protocols, municipal orders; deeds; marriage contracts, and general contracts; petitions and proclamations; wills; private account books, inventories; lists of soldiers; war dispatches; letters; rent rolls and tax rolls, general business papers and accounts, etc.

Some of the material is published in Dutch, but most of the other published material is available, to the general public, only in English translations. Some of these translations are excellent, e. g., that of the "Van Rensselaer Bowier Manuscripts." But many of them are admittedly poor, a fact that the New York State Library is trying to remedy. It planned some five years ago (see: Educational Department Bulletin, No. 462, Albany) to translate and publish the manuscript Dutch records of the government of New Netherland 1638—74. According to the plan adopted, three or four volumes of this projected publication should have appeared by this time. But the Albany Capitol fire of March 29, 1911, did havoc, destroying not only the first volume of the records but also a copy of the Dutch text and the translations which Mr. van Laer had prepared.

My aim in writing "Scandinavian Immigrants in New York, 1630—1674" has been to present facts, in detail and chronological order. Wherever I have found it feasible, I have used the words of published sources. I have given verbatim many excerpts from the court records. I have quoted at length public and private documents, in order to illustrate or illumine certain facts, in the selection of which I have been guided by various considerations, which it would be useless to enumerate.

My biographies are concerned with the *immigrants*. The information they give in regard to the descendants of these immigrants is secondary. To trace the descendants beyond the seventeenth century would require many volumes of genealogy and personal history. I have, however, endeavored as much as possible to give important data bearing on the history of the children born of Scandinavian parents in New Netherland prior to 1674. But these children, not being immigrants, of course receive no treatment in special articles, as do the 188 immigrants. They are mentioned in connection with their parents.

As to the length of the articles, those treating of the well-known personages like Hans Hansen from Bergen, Laurens Andriessen van Buskirk are briefer than those dealing with less known characters like Dirck Holgersen and Pieter Jansen Noorman. I am conscious of gaps in these articles, but this is due to the nature of the source material. The historian is concerned with facts, and it is not his, nor in fact anybody's, business to fill gaps with fiction.

The articles also vary in the quality of matter. But this, too, is due to the nature of the sources. Unfortunately such sources as court records—and I have drawn heavily upon them—are quite silent about many of the nobler deeds of men, in regard to which we should like to be fully as well informed as we are concerning the role these men played in litigations. I have endeavored to leave no stone unturned in order to obtain all the facts possible relative to the history of the immigrants, and I have made esthetical considerations entirely secondary to the "micrology" of facts. For in a pioneer volume like "Scandinavian Immigrants in New York," which in some degree shifts the emphasis in treating immigration to our country in the seventeenth century, it is necessary to register even what appears to be pure trivialities. Only those who are acquainted with the nature of the sources of the early history of New York can appreciate what it means to trace a deed to the author of the deed, especially when the author has a number of namesakes or is known by several different names.

Such a work, packed with details and bristling with names and dates, does, of course, not claim to be a contribution to belles-lettres. In some places it resembles the court docket or an abstract of title. Nevertheless it claims to make a distinct contribution to a hitherto almost entirely neglected field in colonial history. As a reference work it may modestly pave the way for further research in this field and be of some use to the general historian.

Of special use it should be to such Americans of Scandinavian ancestry as in their school-days were taught a little about the Swedes on the Delaware, more about the Dutch in New York, most about the sons and daughters of New England, but nothing about the Scandinavians, particularly the Danes and Norwegians, along the Hudson. There are many Scandinavian descendants in the eastern section of the United States who are mistaken as to the original home of their forebears. It suffices to mention some of the descendants of the famous Anneke Jans. There are many in New York who do not know that the Episcopal Trinity Church, famed in the courts for its great wealth, owes some of it to an old Norwegian farm. There are many who do not know that the Bronx of New York was the property of Jonas Bronck. a Dane, and that the ancestor of the Vanderbilts married a Norwegian woman. No doubt, there is much abuse of the study of genealogy in our country, and there is much false pride connected with it. But this should not prevent us from trying to find out to what extent countries like Norway, Denmark, and Sweden, had a share in populating the Empire State in early days.

Why the Empire State and not any other states? *All* the known Norwegian and Danish immigrants up to 1674 settled in New York and adjacent territory. They did not go to the New England states nor to those in the South. And the Swedish immigrants settled either in New York or at the Delaware. The only Scandinavians in "New Sweden" were Swedes, whose history is already more or less known.

My work is divided into three parts. The first part treats of the Norwegians. They were numerically inferior (fifty-seven biographies) to the Danish immigrants. But many of them immigrated earlier than the Danes and, on the whole, receive more attention in the early records. They came from such places as Fredrikstad, Holme, Langesund, Sande, Flekkerö, Hellesund, Stavanger, Bergen, Tönsberg, Selbu, Marstrand, and many other places in Norway.

The second part of this work treats of the Danes (ninety-seven biographies), who were numerically as strong as the Swedes and Norwegians together. They emigrated from places like Copenhagen, Roskilde, Ribe, Svendborg, Aalborg, Christianstad, Nordstrand, Frederikstad (Friedrichstadt), Glückstadt, Husum, Varberg, Dithmarschen, Oldenburg, Hassing, Helsingör, and several other towns or districts of Denmark, which in earlier days included Schleswig and Holstein.

The third part is devoted to the Swedes (thirty-four biographies). At first sight this may seem strange, as there were fully as many Swedes in America in the seventeenth century as Danes and Norwegians. But the Swedes had, as has already been stated, their own settlement, New Sweden, or the present Delaware. They were very little concerned about New York proper, both before and after the conquest of their settlement by Governor Stuyvesant, in 1655. The Swedes that are noticed in this volume are, therefore, with the possible exception of one or two, only such as came to New Netherland direct from Sweden. The Swedish immigrants came from Stockholm, Göteborg, Helsingborg, Vesterås, Vexiö, Vintjern, Åbo (Finland), etc.

The biographical part is followed by a Retrospect.

I have added four Appendices, one of which, "German Immigrants in New York, 1630-1674," may not seem pertinent to the theme of my book. My reasons for including this Appendix is given elsewhere. Suffice it here to state, the German New Netherlanders were the religious allies of the Scandinavian, they were on par with these in numbers, and they have, like these, been a *terra incognita* to historians. A famous work, published as late as 1909, registers only four Germans who settled in New York before 1674; the present volume gives information concerning 186 of them.

As to the occupation of the early immigrants from Norway, Denmark, and Sweden, the biographies will show that they were engaged in various walks of life, representing the farmer, the miller, the wood-sawyer, the tobacco-planter, the carpenter, the smith, the mason, the trader, the merchant, the soldier (captain, sergeant), the mariner (captain, skipper, etc.), the boatbuilder, the shoemaker, the gauger, the tapster, the brewer, the surgeon, the fisher, the firewarden, the drayman, the land owner, the council member, the capitalist, the policeman, the judge, etc. The nobleman as well as the peasant is represented.

The orthography of proper names has caused some difficulty. There was much "phonetic" spelling in polyglot New Netherland.

This highly variable species of spelling makes it difficult, in many
instances, to adhere to iron-rule uniformity. I have retained the
more or less Dutch way (for Dutch was the official language) of
spelling foreign names, sometimes even at the expense of con-
sistency. When we know that one of New York's former archivists, Dr. E. B. O'Callaghan, in his "Documents Relative to the
History of New York" "invariably substituted English equivalents
for Dutch given names"; and when we notice that reputable
writers on the history of New York spell the Indian word "seawan" in a half dozen different ways, it is, for the present, nigh
hopeless either to attain or to observe uniformity in the orthography
of foreign proper names. I shall specify one instance of "phonetic"
orthography. Jochem Kalder, treated in this volume, has his surname spelled in the records as follows: Kalder, Calder, Calser, Caljer, Calker, Kayker, Kier, Callaer. The various forms may be
due to the misreading of documents in transcribing them, but also
to the niceties of pronunciation, which a scribe, unfamiliar with a
foreign language, would not be able to record on paper. The so-
called "tykke l" (thick l) in certain parts of Norway no doubt
puzzled the scribes of New Amsterdam.

The Dutch distinction in terminating patronymics with "sz"
or "sen" for men, and "s" or "se" for women has not been much
observed in this volume, where the termination "sen" has been
used indiscriminately, more in accord with Scandinavian usage.

For my material I am indebted to the Congressional Library,
in Washington; the Pennsylvania State Library, in Harrisburg;
the State Historical Library, St. Paul, Minnesota; University of
Minnesota Library, Minneapolis Public Library; the libraries of
Pennsylvania College and Gettysburg Theological Seminary, Gettysburg Pennsylvania. I wish to express my sincere thanks to
the administrators of these libraries; to Messrs. A. J. F. van Laer
and Mr. Peter Nelson, Archivists of the Manuscripts Section of
the New York State Library; and to Mr. J. H. Innes, author of
"New Amsterdam and Its People."

For permission to use illustrations from specified works on
the history of New York I am grateful to Charles Scribner's
Sons; G. P. Putnam's Sons; Mr. J. A. Holden, N. Y. State
Historian; the Hon. John H. Finley, President of the University
of the State of New York. The New York Public Library has

supplied me with reproductions of certain views of early New York. Also to this institution my thanks are due.

In offering this volume to the public, it is my hope that those who peruse its pages may feel a little of the *Entdeckerfreude* which I experienced in collecting the data, which have made "Scandinavian Immigrants in New York, 1630-1674" possible.

JOHN O. EVJEN.

Minneapolis, 1915.

CONTENTS

PART II

DANISH IMMIGRANTS IN NEW YORK, 1630-1674

PART III

SWEDISH IMMIGRANTS IN NEW YORK, 1630-1674

ILLUSTRATIONS

LIST OF PLATES

LIST OF ILLUSTRATIONS IN THE TEXT

SCANDINAVIAN IMMIGRANTS
IN NEW YORK
1630-1674

NEW AMSTERDAM, about 1630. Reversed and reduced from the view in Hartgers' "Beschrijvingh van Virginia," Lenox Library, New York City.

INTRODUCTION.*

The history of New Netherland, later called New York, does not begin with the year 1524, when the Bay of New York was first visited by a European navigator; but with the year 1609, when Henry Hudson, an Englishman in the employ of the East India Company, ascended the river which now bears his name. During the next four years sundry Dutch merchants who were interested in the reports of Hudson's exploration fitted up small ships for themselves which carried glass beads, strips of cotton, and diverse other articles to the natives of Manhattan and in exchange brought back skins of beaver, otter, and mink. In 1614 they formed the United New Netherland Company, and obtained from the General States a charter granting them the right of trading along the coasts and rivers which their navigators had explored. This charter, however, did not claim New Netherland as a Dutch possession nor deny the right of other nations to traffic with the natives. It merely prohibited other Hollanders from interfering with the rights of the patentees.

The name of New Netherland occurs first in 1614, in the instrument just mentioned. In this and in all subsequent documents where the name is used, it occurs in the singular and never in the plural. There was only one New Netherland. The Netherlands of Europe are plural because they are an aggregation of small states, as Professor John Fiske says. The southern limit of New Netherland was the South River, later called Delaware River, the northern limit the forty-fifth parallel, the eastern lay between the Hudson and the Connecticut rivers, the western never extended many miles west of the Hudson.

In 1618 the charter of the United New Netherland Company expired. The company tried to get an extension of it, but encountered opposition. It nevertheless went on with its trade, and

---

* In the preparation of this sketch, I have found much help in Mr. Dingman Versteeg's article, "The City of New Amsterdam," in the Year Book of the Holland Society of New York, 1903.

prospered. As it was a mercantile, and not a political, organization, it was felt that a stronger organization, somewhat like that
of the East India Company, was needed. Accordingly, the Dutch
West India Company was formed, in 1621. The charter which
it received gave it exclusive jurisdiction over Dutch navigation and
trade on the barbarous coasts of America and Africa. The West
India Company was authorized to found colonies and govern them
under the supervision of the States General, to wage war, but
not to make a formal declaration of war without the consent of
the States General, which was to aid it with soldiers and warships.

In 1623 New Netherland became a political entity. Its
government was vested in the West India Company. In colonial
matters it possessed all legislative, executive and judicial powers,
with the restriction that the States General should confirm the
appointment of the highest officials and the instructions given them;
that the Roman-Dutch law of the fatherland should prevail when
special laws did not meet all needs; and that persons convicted
of capital crimes should be sent home with their sentences.

In the same year New Netherland received its first genuine
settlers who came not simply to traffic but to live, to establish
farms and towns. No less than thirty Dutch and Walloon families
came to this country that year. Some settled on Manhattan, some
went north towards Albany, others went as far south as to Delaware River, near what was later called New Sweden. In 1625
two shiploads of cattle, horses, swine, and sheep followed.

In 1626 Manhattan island, twenty-two square miles in extent,
was purchased for sixty guilders in beads and ribbons. Sixty
guilders are equivalent to about twenty-four gold dollars. In our
day this sum, the purchasing value of gold being considered, would
amount to $120.

Manhattan was yet no colony. It was more like a colonial
farm. No individual person had yet obtained land in his own
name or engaged in transmarine commerce in his own interest.
But a change soon took place.

In 1629 the first step was taken to give the province of New
Netherland self-government. For the purpose of encouraging immigration the system of patroons was established. The condition
of the patroon's grant of land was that he should bring fifty
grown-up persons to New Netherland and settle them along the
Hudson River. The most famous of these patroons was Kiliaen

Van Rensselaer, a jeweler in Amsterdam. In the present work he is often mentioned as the patroon of the region around Albany. He caused several Scandinavians to immigrate and settle on his manor.

In spite of the new system of colonizing the country, the current of immigration was weak. In order to stimulate it the West India Company renounced and abolished all previous monopolies. The effect was marked. Immigration increased and the country began to attain prosperity. But now the Indian wars followed, in which many colonists perished and much property was destroyed. These wars were at their worst during the rule of Director-General William Kieft (1638–1647), whose predecessors in office were Cornelis Jacobsen May (1624–1625), William Verhulst (1625–1626), Peter Minuit (1626–1632), Sebastian Jansen Krol (1632–1633), Wouter van Twiller (1633–1638), and whose only successor was Petrus Stuyvesant (1647–1664).

The colonists of New Netherland were much dissatisfied with the rule of Kieft. This dissatisfaction brought about, on August 29, 1641, the election of a board of Twelve Men, the first "representative" body in New Netherland. But as this body had only advisory power, and Kieft continued to rule as he pleased, new grounds for dissatisfaction were given, and, on February 18, 1642, the Twelve Men were summarily dismissed. Circumstances, however, forced Kieft again to consult the people. As a consequence the board of Eight Men was elected in September, 1643, which in September, 1647, was succeeded by the board of Nine Men. The latter body served until February, 1653, when the city of New Amsterdam was incorporated. The incorporation, however, was accompanied by so many restrictions that the newly appointed municipal authorities exercised very little power. The Director-General and Council, therefore, often provoked opposition on the part of the local administration, to which, after much correspondence with the authorities in Holland, Stuyvesant and his Council were obliged to make a number of concessions.

There were two governing bodies in New Amsterdam: (1) the Director and Council whose jurisdiction extended over entire New Netherland, and (2) the local government. Both of these bodies are frequently referred to in the present work.

The local government consisted of two Burgomasters — the administrative representatives, so to speak; several Schepens, who had judicial power; one Schout, who was city attorney and "head of police." Strictly speaking there was no police department. The schouts and underschouts and two court messengers were expected to preserve order and to make arrests. Other city officers were the Secretary, the City Treasurer, the Vendue Master, the City Marshall, Gauger of Weights and Measures, Jailer etc. The local government or "Court of Schout, Burgomasters and Schepens," as it was called, was handicapped from the very beginning. For its most important officer, the schout, was at the same time the fiscal of the Company. He was entirely independent of the burgo-masters and the schepens. Mr. Dingman Veersteg aptly says that the city government was practically an inferior court of justice without much political significance, being in a large measure de-pendent upon the higher court, much like the board of Nine Men had been. All the city's officers from city clerk down to the com-monest porter were appointed by the Director-General and Council.

The supreme government was at the Fort. It consisted of the Director-General and three or four members of the Council of New Netherland, whose chief officers were the Fiscal, the Pro-vincial Secretary, the Comptroller of the Finances, the Receiver-General, and the Surveyor-General with their staff of bookkeepers, clerks and messengers. This council not only framed the laws of the province, but also formed its supreme court, uniting in itself the legislative, judicial and executive authority of the colony.

The city authorities were in financial matters entirely depend-ent upon the good will and pleasure of the Director-General and the Council. Their constant striving for the right to levy taxes, to appoint officers and to extend their judicial authority was not without result. They gradually approached their goal: absolute communal autonomy for themselves and a representative govern-ment for entire New Netherland. But the final conquest of New Netherland by the English, in 1674, put a stop to political initia-tive which was revived a century later when the yoke of the English was thrown off.

The liberty which was coveted in political life was desired by the churches also. For New Netherland was not so tolerant in matters of religion as European Netherlands. The ideal of Governor Stuyvesant and his Council was a state church of the Dutch Reformed confession. As early as 1628 New Am-sterdam had received its first Dutch Reformed minister, and in

THE FORT IN KIEFT'S DAY. From "Historic New York," edited by M. W. Goodwin.
By Permission of G. P. Putnam's Sons, New York.

1631 built its first church. The Lutherans in New Amsterdam, the majority of whom were Scandinavians and Germans, and not Dutch, experienced great difficulty in securing the right of public exercise of their "religion." It really seems as if they did not get this right until after the conquest of New Netherland in 1664. The vast majority of parents in New Amsterdam and in its vicinity had their children baptized by Dutch Reformed ministers, but only a minority of these parents were or became members of the Dutch Reformed Church. In 1686 the population of the city of New York was 3,800 while the Dutch Reformed Church at the same time numbered 354 adults and 702 children. From 1649 to 1701 it had baptized 5,700 infants, but received only 1812 communicants. As the present work treats of Scandinavians, it may be proper to state here that the larger number of those who signed the petition of the Lutherans in New Amsterdam in 1657, were Germans and Scandinavians. They requested that Rev. J. E. Goetwater, the newly arrived Dutch Lutheran minister, might be permitted to remain in the city instead of being deported, as the colonial government, actuated by zeal for the Reformed "religion," had ordered. The fact that the minister of these Lutherans was Dutch needs no explanation. Dutch was the language of New Netherland and easily learned by the Germans and Scandinavians, who, moreover, as a rule intermarried with the sons and daughters of Netherlands. Even an Englishman like Charles Bridges became so thoroughly Teutonized that he called himself by the Dutch equivalent of his name — Carel van Brugge. The real leader of the Lutheran church in New Amsterdam, before it received a clergyman, was Paulus Schrick, a well-to-do German, from Nürnberg.

The progress of the people of New Amsterdam was, naturally, more marked in economic fields than in the ecclesiastical. Between 1630 and 1640 many ships were constructed in New Amsterdam. In 1641 a commodious tavern was built, which later became the city hall. In 1642 a new church was erected, supplanting the one built in 1631. In 1648 a general fair was established to continue ten days each year, likewise a weekly market to be held on Monday. The city, as it was stated above, was incorporated in 1653. In the same year it was enclosed by palisades. In 1657 a "burgherrecht", or citizenship, was established; the city was surveyed; the streets were regulated and named; several of the streets were

THE RIVER AND DOCK FRONT, about 1642. From "Historic New York," edited by M. W. Goodwin. By Permission of G. P. Putnam's Sons, New York.

also paved. In 1658 the General and Council gave the city permission to build a pier, to charge wharfage and to trade with other countries. In 1661 the first regularly appointed revenue cutter was put into commission.

The leading industries centered in saw mills and grist mills, boat and yacht building, sail-making, soap-boiling, tanning, lime-burning, pot-baking, stone-quarrying, brick-making.

New Amsterdam had the first public Latin and Greek school in our country. It drew pupils even from New England. "It would be honor enough for this stock (Dutch) to have been the first to put on American soil the public school, the great engine for grinding out American citizens, the one institution for which Americans should stand more stiffly than for aught others." (Speech by Theodore Roosevelt, 1896).

As to the protection of the colonists, New Netherland had a garrison of 180 men who were employed on distant expeditions to Delaware River, Bergen, Esopus, Beverwyck, Long Island, Staten Island and other threatened points. They were also utilized as custom house employees and put aboard every incoming ship to guard against smuggling. New Amsterdam had its own guard — the burgher's guard, consisting of three companies. After the Indian surprise of 1655 the city was patrolled on Sundays during service by a corporal's guard.

As to the population, it has been estimated that there were 270 people in New Amsterdam in 1628, 1000 in 1642, but only 800 in 1653 on account of the Indian wars. In 1660 New Amsterdam had a population of about 1800 and about 350 houses, of which 300 were inhabited. In 1664 its population was about 2,400, its number of houses 500, of which 400 were dwellings.

Entire New Netherland had a population of 1,500 in 1647, of 2,000 in 1653, and of 10,000 in 1664.

The official language of New Netherland, as has been stated, was Dutch, though more than a score of languages were spoken in the city of New Amsterdam long before the English conquest. As it will be shown, those who spoke Danish, Norwegian, and Swedish contributed their share in making the metropolis of the West cosmopolitan in speech and tolerant in religion. The earliest library of which any record survives in the annals of New York was the polyglot collection owned by Jonas Bronck, the Dane after whom the Bronx in New York has been named.

Most of the books in this little library were Danish, several of them were celebrated works on Lutheran theology. The effort of the Lutherans to get religious liberty has already been noted.

The Scandinavians of early New York also taught, it would appear, our country a new form of architecture, the clapboard construction of buildings. It is the merit of Mr. J. H. Innes to have called attention to this fact. His work "New Amsterdam and Its People," which on account of its painstaking investigation of the topography of New Amsterdam, will prove a most valuable guide to the readers of my volume, does not discuss this new form of architecture. But in a reply to a letter of mine, in which I had asked for permission to use certain views contained in his book on New Amsterdam, he makes the following very instructive statements, which he permits me to quote.

"It is perhaps proper to caution you not to lay too much stress on the views, for you will understand that they are only enlargements of the Danckers and Visscher views, both of which are on a pretty small scale. The artist however, aided by myself, has collated pretty faithfully the two views, and introduced the distinctive features of buildings, so far as we could inform ourselves from any source; nevertheless, much is to be wished for. At the time of the views, I suppose, the original bark-lined or log houses of the earliest settlers had about all disappeared. What form of architecture took their places? Well, about this period the Dutch began to talk a good deal about houses "van Steen". Now this in the mouth of a Dutchman just from the old country would almost invariably mean brick, or "gebakken Steen," and we may fairly assume that all houses with narrow gable end and more than two stories high were at least fronted with Holland brick. These houses were comparatively few, however. The same assumption would not do for the smaller Dutch houses, because the vicinity of New Amsterdam was abundantly supplied with boulder stones from the glacial drift. These as a rule were so easily workable by mere unskilled labor, — requiring nothing more than a stout man with a good sledge-hammer, — that they were immediately put into requisition, not only for the foundations but for the construction of the walls themselves where they were not too high. Perhaps half of the ancient Dutch farm houses around New York, many of which remained within my personal recollection, were constructed of these boulder stones, squared by the hammer to some extent.

"The greater number of houses were undoubtedly of wood and to a certain degree foreign to Dutch ideas, but they adopted its use from economical reasons, and about this period the corrupted term "Klabbaude" began to appear in the records. This was our familiar "clapboards," by which we mean of course the boards nailed horizontally and overlapping one another. I am informed, however, that such method of construction is foreign to Holland, that the term "Klap hout" has no such meaning as the above, but is applied to strips of wood nailed up and down, such as we see in small constructions, such as sheds, board fences etc.

"Where did the Dutch get this clapboard construction from at New Amsterdam? Certainly not from the English, for when they, the English, commenced to build their first permanent houses in New England, and on the Eastern End of Long Island, they almost invariably made use of shingles in siding their buildings. . .

"Now in my copy of George Braun's monumental work, "De Praecipuis Totius Universi Orbis Urbibus," Cologne 1572," I find in the large folio water color of Bergen in Norway almost exactly the clapboard construction of buildings to which we became accustomed in America, and I am therefore inclined to believe that we owe this to Scandinavian influences, and that where the "Noormans" built themselves at New Amsterdam or vicinity, they are quite likely to have adopted this method. . . ."

The present volume gives a good view of Bergen in the sixteenth century. The clapboard construction appears in it, but most of the boarding is horizontal. I have seen pictures of clapboard construction on the Faroe Islands, inhabited by people of Scandinavian stock. And a prominent Faroese, Jonas Bronck, may have put up this form of building on his plantation in New York, 1639. That Scandinavian influences have been at work in the early colonial architecture of the Empire State of the North is quite evident.

Thus much in general about New Netherland and New Amsterdam.

This introduction would be far too lengthy if it were to dwell on the regions about Albany, on the villages along the Hudson, on the settlements on Long Island, and many other places in New

York state mentioned in this work. We must refer the reader, for more detailed information, to John Fiske's "The Dutch and Quaker Colonies in America" (1899); to "The Memorial History of the City of New York," edited by James Grant Wilson (1892); to J. H. Innes' "New Amsterdam and Its People" (1902); and to Mrs. Schuyler Van Rensselaer's "History of the City of New York in the Seventeenth Century" (1909), which contains an extensive bibliography.

Readers will ask, Why does this volume stop at the year of 1674? We answer, New Netherland surrendered in that year to England. It had been taken in possession for the English as early as 1664, by Col. Richard Nicolls, when both New Netherland and New Amsterdam received the name of New York. But the language of the colony continued, in the main, to be Dutch, though English was used officially. Dutch was again introduced as the official language in 1673, when the province saw "the last flash of Dutch rule". Anthony Colve, taking advantage of the war between England and the Netherlands, captured New Netherland in the name of the Dutch Republic. The city of New York once more received a new name: New Orange. It always retained its adjective "New". The old form of local government by schout, schepens, etc., was reinstituted. From August 9, 1673, to November 10, 1674, New York was again under Dutch rule. Then the English came and made the second and ultimate conquest of the province.

After 1664, the Scandinavian immigration decreased perceptibly, and still more after 1674, though it probably never ceased entirely.

Why this decrease?

The Scandinavians, especially the Norwegians and the Danes, had, for many years, been accustomed to see their sons and daughters go, for a longer or shorter time, to Holland. The commerce between Norway and Holland was large. The vast forests of Norway furnished the Dutch with timber. And Norwegians and Danes joined the Dutch fleet in great numbers. It was Holland that taught Norway that her future was on the water. For Norway was not a sea-faring nation about the year 1600, as it was in the days of the vikings. Holland was the mistress of the seas. In 1650 her tonnage as compared to that of England, was as five to one. And at the close of the seventeenth century, after the

Navigation Act, Holland still maintained the ruling of the seas. She had a tonnage of 900,000 to England's 500,000, while the combined tonnage of the other nations together was only 200,000.

Years ago England, becoming a great colonial power, overtook the supremacy on the ocean, though her fleet during our civil war was not greater than that of the United States. Norway soon came second on the list. Her fleet is still superior to that of the United States, which counts inland tonnage to make a good showing; but of late she has come down to the fourth place, still outdistancing, however, her former mistress, Holland.

During the period our book covers, Amsterdam was *the* emporium of the world. According to Erik P. Pontoppidan, a Dane, later bishop in Norway, there assembled some 8,000 or 9,000 Norwegian, Danish and Holstein sailors every year, about fall time, when the fleets were returning from East India, West India, Greenland and other places. Pontoppidan, who lived for some time in Holland, gives this estimate in his anonymous work "Menoza" (1743).

Of Norwegians who attained fame in the service of the Dutch fleet, mention may be made of the marine hero Curt Adelaer (originally Sivertsen), who was born in Brevik, Norway, and at the age of fourteen (1637) joined the Dutch fleet. In 1642–1661 he fought in the Venetian fleet against the Turks. His achievements were remarkable. Returning to his home, he was appointed General-Admiral of the Danish-Norwegian fleet. He also received the title of nobility. Soon he built and organized a large and powerful fleet.

In 1670, the Danish-Norwegian envoy at the Hague, Marcus Gjøe, reported to the government in Copenhagen that a large number of the subjects of the [Danish-Norwegian] King were in Dutch service, and that the majority of them were Norwegians. He added, that on account of the jealousy of the Dutch, they were, for the most part, common sailors. The Dutch were averse to making them lieutenants and captains.

An English statesman, Robert Molesworth, in "An account of Denmark as it was in the year 1692," states that the best sailors who are subjects of the Danish king are Norwegians, but the majority of them are in Dutch service. He also adds that many sailors from Scandinavian countries had settled with their families in Holland.

Some of the noteworthy Norwegians who served in the Dutch
fleet were, according to the Norwegian historian L. Daae,* Zeiger
Peters; Mickel de Voss, born in Soggendal, 1640; Mickel Tennissen, born at Lister, 1642; Evert Tennissen; Morten Pedersen, born
in Skien, 1652; Hans Schønnebøl, a nobleman, born 1654 in Nord-
land; Thomas Dideriksen Seerup, born 1638 in Bergen; Hans
Garstensen Garde, born in Spangereid; Iver Tønnesen Huitfeldt
from Throndstad in Hurum, died 1710; Frederik Bolling, who
went as Adelbors to East India in 1669–1673; Michel Caspar Lund;
Anders Christensen from Christiania, who returned to his home
after twenty-seven years of foreign service.

Those were sea-faring men. As to the settled Scandinavian
population in Holland, an idea may be got from the fact, that the
Danes and Norwegians in 1663 organized a Danish-Norwegian
church at Amsterdam. They issued a special hymnal, as their
church was a union church which was to adhere to the Reformed
and the Lutheran confessions. Their first pastor was Christian
Pedersen Abel, from Aalborg, Denmark. Their sexton was Didrik
(Erik) Meyer, from Søgne, in Norway. In Amsterdam was also
Anders Kempe, from Trondhjem, Norway, who had become a
Schwenkfeldian.

As there were many Scandinavians in Holland, so there were
quite a number of Hollanders in Norway and Denmark. Their
influence was felt in many directions, and not least in the fields
of art and architecture.

There was, in other words, much reciprocity in the seventeenth
century between the Dutch and the Scandinavians. Such a reciprocity did not exist in the same century between the English and

* For what I state in regard to Scandinavians dwelling in Holland or serving
in the Dutch fleet in the seventeenth century, I am indebted to L. Daae's carefully written booklet "Nordmænds Udvandringer til Holland og England i nyere
Tid." (1880). Of the Scandinavians mentioned by Dr. Daae, not a single one, at
least to my knowledge, immigrated to New Netherland. He knows, of course, about
the Swedish colony in Delaware. But he seems to know nothing about Danish and
Norwegian Immigration to our country in the seventeenth century. He says, "It
is reported that also some Norwegians (and Danes) settled in North America in
New Jersey in the seventeenth century; and that they, in 1664—1676, founded a
city there, which they called Bergen, after its (Norwegian) namesake, and that the
surrounding district got the name of Bergen county. But this report is apocryphal
. . ." (Underscoring mine). He adds, that Nicolai Wergeland, in 1816, used this
report as an argument against the tyranny that Denmark had subjected Norway to,
in the days of their union.
    It is indeed true, that Bergen in New Jersey was no Norwegian colony. Its
name is derived not from Bergen in Norway, but from Bergen op Zoom. But if
Daae had heard the mere statement, thirty-five years ago, that there were at least
150 Norwegians and Danes who emigrated to New York 1630—1674, he would
possibly again have resorted to the apocryphal explanation. Fortunately we now
have, what we did not have in 1880, an abundance of published source material,
which is ever increasing.

the Scandinavians, though the Norwegians exported much timber to England, particularly after the great fire in London.

Naturally, Scandinavian immigration to New York after the Dutch had surrendered, began to decrease. To what extent, we can not say. The Dutch were very painstaking in keeping their records, even in the New World; the English were not. Data which could have established the nationality of new immigrants, and which would have been recorded by the Dutch, are wanting in the English records.

We therefore stop at the year 1674, with the end of the second period of Dutch rule in New York.

When Stuyvesant in 1666, after the English had made the first conquest of New Netherland, was on his way to Holland, he came first to Bergen. He had left New Amsterdam for Curacao, where he in his younger days had lost his leg. He was so short of powder that he was obliged to borrow from a ship "lying in her harbor of Bergen" "three muskets, a parcel worth about 12 lbs. of powder, to be used on the voyage from Bergen aforesaid to Holland."

The ex-governor may have thought of former days, when he was bent upon keeping his subjects in political and religious bondage. Had he acted differently, he might have been spared the journey to Bergen and the borrowing of powder in northern waters. But who can ascertain all the facts, and forecast the exact course of history? History is not the result of chance. It is the sum of necessity and liberty.

PART I

NORWEGIAN IMMIGRANTS
IN NEW YORK
1630-1674

ALBERT ANDRIESSEN.

Albert Andriessen, or Albert Andriessen Bradt [Bratt], was one of the earliest Norwegian settlers in New Netherland. He came from Fredrikstad, a town at the mouth of the Glommen, the largest river in Norway. In the early records he is often called Albert the Norman. After 1670 he became known as Albert Andriesz Bradt. Whether he was related to the Bratts of Norwegian nobility, can not be ascertained. The Bratt family lived in Bergen, Norway, before the early part of the fifteenth century, when it moved to the northern part of Gudbrandsdalen. It had a coat of arms until about the middle of the sixteenth century. Since that time the Bratts belong to the Norwegian peasantry. They have a number of large farms in Gudbrandsdalen, Hedemarken, Toten, and Land.[1] In the state of New York there are many families of the name of Bradt, descendants of the pioneer from Fredrikstad.

The name of Albert Andriessen occurs for the first time in a document bearing the date August 26, 1636, an agreement between him and two others on the one hand, and the patroon of the colony of Rensselaerswyck, Kiliaen van Rensselaer, on the other.[2] The agreement was made and signed in Amsterdam. It states that Andriessen was a tobacco planter. He may have learnt the cultivating of tobacco in Holland, where tobacco was raised as early as 1616.

As Andriessen was twenty-nine years of age when he made the agreement with Kiliaen Van Rensselaer, he must have been born about 1607. Pursuant to the stipulation in the agreement, he sailed, accompanied by his wife, Annetje Barents of "Rolmers,"

---

[1] Illustreret norsk konversations leksikon, Christiania, 1907 ff. Vol. I., Article ''Bratt.''

[2] Van Rensselaer Bowier Manuscripts. Translated and edited by A. J. F. van Laer, Archivist, Albany, 1908, p. 676.

and as it would seem by two children, October 8, 1636, on the "Rensselaerswyck," which arrived at New Amsterdam March 4, 1637.

On this voyage, which was very stormy, his wife gave birth to a son, who received the name of Storm and who in later records is frequently called Storm from the Sea. The log of the ship ("Rinselaers Wijck") contains under the date of November 1 and 2 [1636], the following interesting entries which are given in facsimile in the "Van Rensselaer Bowier Manuscripts," 360 f.:

(Reduced size.)

The translation is as follows:

Novemb[er]

Sa[turday] 1. In the morning we veered toward the west and drifted north. The Wind S. W. with rough weather and high seas. The past half day and entire night.

Su[nday   ] 2. Drifted 16 leagues N. E. by E.; the wind about west, the latitude by dead reckoning 41 degrees, 50 min. with very high seas. That day the overhang above our rudder was knocked in by severe storm. This day a child was born on

the ship, and named and baptized in England *stoerm;* the mother
is *annetie baernts.* This day gone.

Inasmuch as there were eight children born to Andriessen and
his wife, Storm being the third, two of their children, Barent
and Eva, were likely with their parents on this voyage. Five
of their children were born in the new world: Engeltje, Gisseltje
Andries, Jan, Dirck.[3]

Eva was married in October, 1647, to Anthony De Hooges,
since 1642 superintendent of the colony of Rensselaerswyck, and
later on August 13, 1657, at Fort Orange, to Roeloff Swartwout,
who on January 27, 1661, was made sheriff, thus completing the
organization of the first council of justice in the present county
of Ulster.[4]

Engeltje was married to Teunis Slingerland, of Onisquathaw.

Gisseltje was married to Jan van "Eecheten"(?).

Storm Albertsz is mentioned in a list of settlers in Esopus.
The list was prepared 1662. His will, in which we learn the name
of his wife, Hilletje Lansinck, probably Dutch, and which mentions that he had children, but does not give their names, is dated
February 24, 1679.[5]

Dirck or Hendrick is mentioned in a list of settlers in Esopus
(1664).

Andriessen and his partners were to operate a mill. But not
long after his arrival he took the liberty of dissolving partnership
and established himself as a tobacco planter. Van Renssselaer
had sent greetings to him in a letter dated September 21, 1637,
(addressed to the partner of Andriessen, Pieter Cornelisz, master
millwright) but in a subsequent letter, of May 8, 1638, to Cornelisz
he wrote: "Albert Andriessen separated from you, I hear that he
is a strange character, and it is therefore no wonder that he could
not get along with you."[6]

Nevertheless, Van Rensselaer entertained the hope that Albert
Andriessen would succeed as a tobacco planter. On December 29,
1637, he wrote to Director William Kieft that he should assign
some of the young men on board the "Calmar Sleutel", commanded
by Pieter Minuit and sailing in the same month, to tobacco plant-

3 E. B. O'Callaghan, History of New Netherland (1848), II., p. 437.
4 Van Rensselaer Bowier Manuscripts, p. 825.
5 B. Fernow, Calendar of Wills on File and Recorded in the Offices of the
Clerk of the Court of Appeals, New York, 1896, p. 444.
6 Van Rensselaer Bowier Manuscripts, pp. 851, 406.

ing with Andriessen "if he has good success," otherwise they were to serve with the farmers. These young men were inexperienced, it seems. One, Elbert Elbertz, from Nieukerck, eighteen years old, was a weaver; Claes Jansen, from the same place, seventeen years old, was a tailor; Gerrit Hendricksz, also from the same place, fifteen year old, was a shoemaker. Gerrit must have served Andriessen for a term of at least three years; for his first three years' wages, from April 2, 1638 to April 2, 1641, are charged to Andriessen.[7]

In a letter of May 10, 1638, Van Rensselaer advised Andriessen that he had duly received his letter stating that the tobacco looked fine. But he was desirous to get full particulars as to how the crop had turned out, and to get a sample of the tobacco. He expressed dissatisfaction at Andriessen having separated from Pieter Cornelisz, and liked to know the cause of his dispute with the officer and commis Jacob Albertsz Planck and his son. He informed Andriessen that he was obliged to uphold his officers, and promised him to stand by him and cause him to be "provided with everything." But he would not suffer bad behavior. He also informed him that it was apparent from the news he had received from several people that he was "very unmerciful to his children and very cruel" to his wife; he was to avoid this "and in all things have the fear of the Lord" before his eyes and not follow so much his own inclinations. But there was also another matter for which Van Rensselaer censured him: he had traded beaver furs with Dirck Corszen Stam, contrary to contract, defrauded and cheated him. For seven pieces of duffel he had given him only the value of twenty-five merchantable beavers.[8]

Van Rensselaer also addressed a letter, of the same date, to Jacob Albertsz Planck, informing him that he had written to Andriessen that he should have more respect for the officers. Planck was instructed to notify Andriessen and all others living in the colony not to engage in "such detrimental fur trade," for he did not care to suffer in his colony those who had their eyes mainly on the fur trade.[9]

Notwithstanding, it was Dirck Corszen that was an unfaithful supercargo. And Van Rensselaer requested, in a letter of May 13, 1639, of Andriessen, that he should write him the truth of the

7 Ibid., 395 ff.
8 Van Rensselaer Bowier Manuscripts, p. 409.
9 Ibid., p. 411.

matter and pay him what he still owed Corszen. If he saw that Andriessen acted honestly herein, he would do all in his power to help him. Andriessen should go to the superintendent of the colony, Arent van Curler, and purchase necessaries for himself and his own people at an advance in price of 50 per cent. He should get merchandise for the Indian trade at an advance of 75 per cent. In return he was to furnish Van Curler with skins at such a price that he could make something on the transaction.

Van Rensselaer also informed Andriessen that he would try to sell his tobacco at the highest price and furthermore give him 25 per cent more than his half of the net proceeds would amount to. He would moreover grant him 25 per cent discount on the grain which he bought. In fact, Van Rensselaer's confidence in Andriessen seemed to be increasing. For he not only acknowledged that he had received several letters from him, but also wished to say to his credit that he had received returns from no one but him. He complained, however, of the tobacco which had been sent to him in barrels. It was a great loss to both that the "tobacco was so poor and thin of leaf that it could not stand being rolled." This, he thought, was likely due to Andriessen having left too many leaves on the plants. But not this alone: the weight was short. One barrel, put down at 292 lbs., weighed but 220 lbs. This was perhaps due to deception on the part of a certain Herrman, a furrier. But anything like this should be avoided in the future. The tobacco amounted to 1,156 pounds net, which was sold for 8 st. (16 cents) a pound. Had it not been so bad and wretched, it could have been sold for twenty cents a pound. A higher price could be obtained if Andriessen would be more careful in the future and leave fewer leaves on the plants. He should try to grow "good stuff", for the tobacco from St. Christopher, an island in the West Indies, was so plentiful in Netherland that it brought but 3 stivers a pound. Andriessen should also each year make out a complete account of all expenses and receipts from tobacco, so Van Rensselaer could see whether any progress was made.[10]

But Andriessen was a poor accountant. Neither Van Rensselaer nor his nephew, the former Director Van Twiller, could understand his accounts.[11] Van Rensselaer therefore gave him directions to follow in making his entries and statements, claiming

10 Ibid., 446.
11 Ibid., p. 500.

that any other procedure would "leave everything confused and mixed up." [12]   He complained that Andriessen laid certain transactions before the patroon, which should be laid before the commis.   He expressed the sentiment that Andriessen was making him his servant when he wrote to him "about soap and other things." He also complained that Andriessen caused great loss by making him hold the tobacco too high: it was safest to follow the market price in Netherland.   Finally he censured him for buying unwisely: he had paid f. 200 for a heifer, "which is much too high." [13]

The patroon and Andriessen had several disagreements.   The latter, with his brother Arent Andriessen, whom we shall later get acquainted with, sent to the patroon sometime in 1642, 4,484 lbs. of tobacco.   It was sold on an average of eight and one half st. a lb.   Deducting 270 lbs. for stems, the net weight brought a sum of f. 1790:19.   But the duty, freight charges, and convoy charges amounted to f. 629:15.   The patroon said he would deduct only half of this if Andriessen compensated him according to his ordinance for his land on which the tobacco grew.   But as long as he was in dispute with him he would deduct the whole sum. [14]

Andriessen did not suffer.   Van Rensselaer complained in letter of March 16, 1643, to Arent van Curler that he did not know what privilege Albert Andriessen had received, since "his cows are not mentioned in the inventory sent him."   He stated he would not want any one, no matter who he was, to own any animals which were not subject to the right of pre-emption.   Therefore, Curler should include Andriessen's animals in the inventory, or make him leave the colony and pay for pasturing and hay during the past year.[15]

On September 5, 1643, the patroon stipulated the following with respect to Andriessen, whose term had long before expired without his having obtained a new lease or contract.

He "shall . . . be continued for the present but shall not own live stock otherwise than according to the general rule of one half of the increase belonging to the patroon and of the right of preemption and, in case he does not accept this, his cattle shall immediately be sent back to the place whence they came, with the un-

12 Ibid., p. 506.
13 Ibid., p. 514.
14 Ibid., p. 661.
15 Ibid., p. 662.

derstanding, however, that half of the increase bred in the colony shall go to the patroon in consideration of the pasturage and hay which they have used; and as to his accounts he shall also be obliged to close, liquidate and settle the same; and as far as the conditions after the expiration of his lease are concerned, the patroon adopts for him as well as for all others this fixed rule, of which they must all be notified and if they do not wish to continue under it must immediately leave the colony, namely, that every freeman who has a house and garden of his own shall pay an annual rent of 5 stivers per Rhineland rod and for land used in raising tobacco, wheat or other fruits 20 guilders per Rhineland morgen, newly cleared land to be free for a number of years, more or less, according to the amount of labor required in such clearing. . . ."[16]

Andriessen not only cultivated tobacco. He operated "two large sawmills," run by a "powerful waterfall," worth as much as f. 1000 annual rent, but the patroon let him have them for f. 250 annual rent. [17] From May 4, 1652, to May 4, 1672, Andriessen is charged with the annual rent for these two mills and the land on Norman's Kill. [18] Originally this Kill was called Tawasentha, meaning a place of the many dead. The Dutch appelative of Norman's Kill is derived from Andriessen.

In New Amsterdam he had acquired a house and lot from Hendrick Kip, August 29, 1651. It lay northeast of fort Amsterdam.[19] Under date of October 5, 1655, we find that he was taxed fl. 20 for this house and lot.[20]

The acquirement of property is not seldom followed by litigation, as is also seen in the case of Andriessen.

In May, 1655, before the court of the Burgomasters and Schepens in New Amsterdam, Roeloff Jansen, a butcher, appeared and made a complaint against Christiaen Barentsen, attorney for Andriessen. Jansen had leased a house and some land belonging to Andriessen who was to give him some cows. But the house was "not tight" and "not enclosed," and the cows were missing. He claimed the interest and damage which he had suffered or

16 Ibid., p. 696.
17 Ibid., p. 742.
18 Ibid., p. 810.
19 Calendar of Historical Manuscripts in the Office of the Secretary of State Albany, 1865. Edited by E. B. O'Callaghan. I., p. 54.
20 The Records of New Amsterdam from 1653 to 1674. Ed. by Berthold Fernow, I., p. 374.

might still suffer. The defendant, as attorney for Andriessen, replied that it was not his fault that the demand had not been complied with according to the contract. He requested time to write to his principal about it. The Court granted him a month's time in which to do this. In due time, however, the court ruled that Andriessen should make the necessary repairs.[21]

Some years later, Simon Clasen Turck started a suit against Andriessen, of which we shall let the court minutes of New Amsterdam speak:

[August 19, 1659]. "Simon Turck, pltf., vs. Dirck van Schelluyne as att'y of Albert Andriessen, deft. Deft. in default. Symon Turck produces in Court in writing his demand against Albert Andriessen concluding, that the attachment on the two cows grazing with Wolfert Webber shall stand good and have its full effect, until the said Albert Andriessen shall have paid him his arrears to the amount of fl. 2, sent to him by Joris Jans Rapalje Ao. 1649, the 3d Septr. in the absence of Pieter Cornelissen, millwright, decd., not accounted for nor made good by him." The attachment on the cows is declared valid by the Court.[22]

[August 19]. "Dirck van Schelluyne in quality as att'y for Albert Andriessen Noorman, answers demand of Symon Clasen Turck. The court orders copy to be furnished to party to answer thereunto at the next Court day."[23]

[September 2]. "Symon Clasen Turck replies to answer of Dirck van Schelluyne, att'y of Albert Andriessen. Court orders copy to be furnished to party to rejoin at the next court day,"[24]

[September 23]. "Tielman van Vleeck as att'y for Turck requests by petition, that Sybout Clazen shall be ordered to deliver by the next Court day his papers used against the abovenamed Symon Turck; also that Dirck van Schelluyne, att'y of Albert Andriessen, shall be ordered to rejoin to Symon Turck's reply. Apostille: Petitioner's request is granted, and parties shall be ordered to prosecute their suit by the next court day."[25]

"On date 17th January 1660, has Dirck van Schelluyne furnished me Secretary Joannes Nevius, his rejoinder and demand in reconvention, as attorney of Albert Andriessen against Tielman van Vleec, att'y of Symon Clazen Turck, also rejoinder of Abra-

---

21 Ibid., I., p. 326; II., p. 248.
22 Ibid., III., p. 24 f.
23 Ibid., III., p. 32.
24 Ibid., III., p. 37.
25 Ibid., III., p. 57.

ham Verplanck against ditto Van Vleeck as substitute of Anthony Clasen More: Whereupon the President of the Burgomasters and Schepens ordered: Copy hereof to be furnished to party, and parties are ordered to exchange their papers with each other and to produce their deductions and principal intendit by inventory on the next Court day."

On January 22, 1660, the Burgomasters and Schepens dismissed the "pltfs. suit instituted herein" and condemned him to pay the costs incurred in this suit.[26]

But a few days later, on January 28, 1660, it rendered the following decision: "Burgomasters and Schepens of the City of Amsterdam in N: Netherland having considered, read and reread the vouchers, documents and papers used on both sides in the suit between Tielman van Vleeck attorney of Simon Clasen Turck, (as husband and guardian of Merretje Pieters, daughter of the dec[eas]d Pieter Cornelissen, millwright, and his lawful heir, as well for himself as representing herein the orphan child of Tryntie Pieters, deceased daughter of said Pieter Cornelissen) pltf. against Dirck Van Schelluyne, attorney of Albert Andriessen Noorman, residing at Fort Orange, deft. relative to and concerning two hundred guilders, which Symon Clasen Turck is demanding from Albert Andriesen for so much, that Albert Andriesen has received from Jorsey in the absence of Pieter Cornelissen, millwright, dated 3rd September, 1649, gone to Virginia and not computed by him nor made good as appears by contract made between Albert Andriessen and Symon Clasen Turck by the intermediation of — Corlear and Dirck van Schelluyne according to acte thereof executed before D: V. Hamel, Secretary of the Colony of Reinselaars Wyck, dated 27th September, 1658; and whereas the words of the contract read as follows:— 'Firstly, Symon Turck shall collect, receive, retain and dispose of as his own according to his pleasure, all outstanding debts receivable, wherever they be; all effects and goods found in the house of the deceased Pieter Cornelissen, whether belonging to him individually or to his Company or Association; On the other hand, Albert Andriesen assumes himself all the debts payable where and to whomsoever they may be, relating to their partnership, whether these stand in the name of Pieter Cornelissen or his own name, promising to release Symon Turck from all claims relat-

26 Ibid., III., pp. 102, 108.

ing hereunto.' — Having looked into, examined and weighed everything material, Burgomasters and Schepens find it right, that the pltf's demand be dismissed, inasmuch as they find, that the two hundred guilders were not to be received, but were paid several years since to Joris Rapalje, who sent the same to Albert Andriesen Noorman and are accordingly not payable to the estate of Pieter Cornelissen, but whenever Symon Turck or his attorney can prove that, at the time of the settlement of a/cs and writing of the contract, Albert Andriesen Noorman notified Symon Turck, that he should receive the fl. 200., hereinbefore in question, from Sybout Clasen, then Albert Andriesen shall give and pay the above mentioned fl. 200., with costs, and in default of proof the pltf. is condemned in the costs of the suit.   Regarding the demand in reconvention about certain planks, no disposition can be made therein as the same is moved according to the *Lites Contestatio*.   Thus done and adjudged by the Burgomaster and Schepens of the City of Amsterdam in New Netherland as above.

"Adj. as above

"Martin Kregier."[27]

The court minutes under date of June 8, 1660, regarding this litigation, state:

"On petition of Tielman Van Vleeck, attorney for Symon Clasen Turck, wherein he requests that the Court may not only examine, but also expedite the solution given by him relative to the fulfillment of the interlocutory judgment pronounced 28th January last, it is ordered:—Copy of the solution shall be furnished to party to answer thereunto at the next Court day."[28]

And under date of January 29, 1661, the minutes pertaining to this case read: "On the petition of Tielman van Vleeck, agent of Symon Clasen Turck, wherein he requests, as Albert Andriesen Noorman remains in default, to answer the solution given in to Court on the 8th of June 1660, that the above named Albert Andries(e)n shall in contumacy be condemned to pay him petitioner the computed two hundred guilders remaining due to him; Whereupon was ordered: The petitioner shall notify his party hereof according to law."[29]

Albert Andriessen was married twice. His first wife died

---

27 Ibid., III., pp. 117 ff.
28 Ibid., III., p. 168
29 Ibid., III., p. 256 f.

before June 5, 1662. His second wife, Pietertie Jansen, died about the beginning of 1667 in New Amsterdam, leaving an insolvent estate. Her son-in-law was Ebert Benningh.[30]

Albert Andriessen died June 7, 1686.[31]

To show how certain documents were drafted in the days of our pioneers, we append the following exhibits, in which Albert Andriessen is one of the parties.

(A)

"In the name of the Lord, Amen. On conditions hereafter specified, we, Pieter Cornelissen van munnickendam, millwright, 43 years of age, Claesz jans van naerden, 33 years of age, house carpenter, and albert andriessen van fredrickstadt, 29 years of age, tobacco planter, have agreed among ourselves, first, to sail in God's name to New Netherland in the small vessel which now lies ready and to betake ourselves to the colony of Rensselaers-wyck for the purpose of settling there on the following conditions made with Mr. Kiliaen Van Rensselaer, as patroon of the said colony, etc.

"Thus done and passed, in good faith, under pledge of our persons and property subject to all courts and justices for the fulfillment of what is aforewritten, at Amsterdam, this 26th of August [1636].

'In witness whereof we have signed these with our own hands in the presence of the undersigned notary public . . . .

"Kiliaen Van Rensselaer

"Pieter Cornelissen
"albert andriessen . . .
"Claes jansen.

"J. Vande Ven, Notary."[32]

(B)

"Appeared before me Robert Livingston, secretary etc., and in presence of the honorable Messieurs Philip Schuyler and Dirck Wessells, commisaries etc., Albert Andriese Bratt, who acknowledged

80 Ibid., VI., pp. 56 ff. Mr. A. T. F. van Laer says he married Geertruy Pieters Vosburgh, Van Rensselaer Bowier Manuscripts, p. 810.
81 Jonathan Pearson, A History of the Schenectady Patent, 1883, p. 93.
82 Van Rensselaer Bowier Manuscripts, p. 676 ff. In reproducing translations of originals we retain the phonetic orthography, the use of small letters instead of capitals, and other peculiarities that fall short of the demands of the ordinary school "Rhetoric." — Claes Jansen Ruyter failed to accompany his partners in the "Rensselaerswyck" in 1636. He arrived at New Amsterdam by "den Harinck" on March 28, 1638. This late arrival may have been the reason for Andriessen's dissolving partnership in the mill company.

that he is well and truly indebted and in arrears to Mr. Nicolaus Van Renselaer, director of colony of Renselaerswyck, in the sum of 3,956 guilders, as appears by the books of the colony of Renselaerswyck, growing out of the part rent for the mill and land; which aforesaid 3,956 guilders the mortgagor, to the aforenamed Mr. Director or to his successors, promise to pay, provided that whatever he, the mortgagor shall make appear to have been paid thereon shall be deducted: pledging therefor, specially, the produce of his orchard, standing behind the house which the mortgagor now possesses, from which produce of the orchard he promises to pay in rent during life twenty guilders in patroon's money in apples, and generally pledging his person and estate, personal and real, present and future, nothing excepted; submitting the same to the force of all laws and judges to promote the payment thereof in due time, if need be, without loss or cost.

"Done in Albany, without craft or guile, on the 30th of October, 1677.

"Aalbert Andriess Brat.

"Philip Schuyler.
"Dirck Wessels.
"Acknowledged before me,

"Robt. Livingstone, Secr."[33]

EVA ALBERTSE.

Eva Albertse [Andriessen] was the daughter of Albert Andriessen of Fredrikstad, Norway. She arrived, in company with her parents and two brothers, one of whom was born on the sea, at New Amsterdam, March 4, 1637. She lived with them in the vicinity of the present Albany, where she in October, 1647, was married to Antony de Hooges, one of the leading men in the colony of Rensselaerswyck. He was a widower with several children.

After his death she was married August 13, 1657, to Roeloff Swartwout who became sheriff of the present county of Ulster, New York.

A concise record of the occupation of Eva's first husband in

33 Early Records of the City and County of Albany and Colony of Rensselaerswyck 1656—1675. Translated from the original Dutch, with notes. By Jonathan Pearson, 1969, p. 165.

the colony of Rensselaerswyck is given in the Van Rensselaer Bowier Manuscripts, which state:

Antony de Hooges was engaged as underbookkeeper and assistant to Arent van Curler, and sailed from the Texel by den Conick David, July 30, 1641. He reached New Amsterdam Nov. 29, 1641, but apparently did not arrive in the colony (Albany and vicinity) till April 10, 1642, being credited from that date till April 10, 1644, with a salary of f. 150 a year. From van Curler's departure for Holland, in Oct., 1644, till van Schlichtenhorst's arrival on March 22, 1648, he was entrusted with the business management of the colony; from the latter date till his death, on or about Oct. 11, 1655, he held the office of secretary and *gecommitteerde*. In the accounts, he is credited, from May 11, 1652, to Oct. 11, 1655, with a salary of f. 360 a year as secretary, and for the same period with a salary of f. 100 as *gecommitteerde*, also with f. 56 for salary as voorleser (reader in the church) during two months and one week in 1653.

As our book contains a facsimile of the log registering the birth of Eva's brother, Storm, so it reproduces a facsimile of an order in regard to the transport of her first husband.

The translation of this Order of the West India Company to Job Arisz, skipper of den Conick David, to transport Antony de Hooges and other, July 10, 1641, is, according to the version in "Bowier Manuscripts" as follows (The written parts of the manuscript are printed in italics):

"The directors of the West India Company, Chamber of Amsterdam order and direct *Job Arissen,* skipper of the ship named *d' Co. David* to transport in said ship under his command and to permit to sleep and eat in the cabin the person of *Anthony de Hogus in the service of Mr renselaer and Johan Vᵣbeeck with his wife and daughter and maid servant, and Geertgen nanninx, with son and little daughter,* provided he bring with [him] a musket or firelock and sword of [his] own, with *his* accompanying baggage specified below and marked with the mark of the Company; and for transporting these the skipper shall upon [declaration] signed by said *Anthony de Hogus,* be paid for board — stivers a day, *according to the amount agreed upon with Mr renˢ for board of his colonists.* Done at Amsterdam, *the 10th of July 1641.*

"[signed] *Fredᵣ: Schulenbᵣ:*

"*S. blomaert*

"I   went on board the *23rd* day of the month of *July*
and left the ship the   day of the month of
Done at   the

"*The above named having with them four chests large and
small containing their apparel, clothes, linen and other effects,
further some furniture and miscellaneous articles, shall pay upon
arrival for freight twenty-eight guilders, I say, must pay for freight
f28:   Done at Amsterdam this 19th of July 1641.*

"[signed] J: Eincklaen

"For *Anthonij de hooges* ———————————————————— f 8

For *Jehan Verbeeck, his wife, child and maidservant* ———— f 10

For *Gurtgen Nanninx and two children* ———————— f 10

——————
f 28

"[Endorsed]   *Renselaer"*

To this interesting document we shall append a copy of the
marriage contract between Eva and her second husband Roeloff
Swartwout.

"In the name of the Lord, Amen, be it known by the contents
of this present instrument, that in the year 1657, on the 13th day
of the month of August, appeared before me Johannes La Montagne, in the service of the General Privileged West India Company, deputy at Fort Orange and village of Beverwyck, Roeloff
Swartwout, in the presence of his father, Tomas Swartwout, on
the . . ., and Eva Albertsen (Bratt), widow of the late Antony De
Hooges, in the presence of Albert Andriessen (Bratt), her father
of the other side, who in the following manner have covenanted
this marriage contract, to wit, that for the honor of God the said
Roeloff Swartwout and Eva Albertsen after the manner of the
Reformed religion respectively held by them shall marry; secondly,
that the said married people shall contribute and bring together all
their estates, personal and real, of whatsoever nature they may be,
to be used by them in common, according to the custom of Holland, except that the bride, Eva Albertse, in presence of the orphanmasters, recently chosen, to wit, Honorable Jan Verbeeck and
Evert Wendels, reserves for her a hundred guilders, to wit, for
Maricken, Anneken, Catrina, Johannes, and Eleonora De Hooges,
for which sum of one hundred guilders for each child respectively
(she) mortgages her house and lot, lying here in the village of

ORDER OF THE WEST INDIA COMPANY TO JOB ARISZ, skipper of den Coninck
David, to transport Antony de Hooges and others, July 10, 1641.
From Van Rensselaer Bowier Manuscripts, 1908.
(About one-half of original size.)

Beverwyck; it was also covenanted, by these presents, by the mutual consent of the aforewritten married people, that Barent Albertse (Bratt) and Teunis Slingerland, brother and brother-in-law of the said Eva Albertse, and uncle of said children, should be guardians of said children, to which the aforesaid orphanmasters have consented; which above written contract the respective parties promise to hold good, on pledge of their persons and estates, personal and real, present and future, the same submitting to all laws and judges.

"Done in Fort Orange, ut supra, in presence of Pieter Jacobsen and Johannes Provost, witnesses, for that purpose called.

"Roeloff Swartwout.

"This is the mark of + Eva Albertse.

Thomas Swartwout.

Albert Andriessen.

Jan Verbeeck.

Evert Wendel.

Teunis Cornelissen.

"Johannes Provoost, witness
"This is the mark of + Pieter Jacobsen.

"Acknowledged before me,
        "La Montagne, Deputy at Fort Orange." [84]

Signature of Roelof Swartwout, husband of Eva Albertse.

ARENT ANDRIESSEN.

Arent Andriessen was a brother of Albert Andriessen, and, like him, a tobacco planter. He was from Fredrikstad, Norway. He appears to have come over with his brother on the "Rensselaerswyck," which sailed from Texel, October 8, 1636, and arrived at New Amsterdam, March 4, 1637. He also appears to have re-

---

84 Ibid., p. 50.

mained with his brother in the colony for one year. His wages — fl. 75 a year — began April 2, 1637. However, he soon acquired a plantation of his own.

The tobacco he raised on his own farm was "extraordinary," judged from the sample he had sent to Kiliaen Van Rensselaer, the patroon whom he served, but it had "a strange aftertaste." The patroon wrote in 1640 that he was willing to grant him a plantation on the basis of that of 1639, but not at all to share expenses.[35]

Between 1638 and 1646 Arent Andriessen is various times credited with tobacco furnished to the superintendent van Curler and Anthony de Hooges.

On April 23, 1652, he got a lot in Bewerwyck, and on May 1, 1658, he obtained a lease from Jan Baptiste van Rensselaer on all the tilled land on the island opposite the center of the village of Bewerwyck, that is opposite the fort, apparently what is known as Boston or Van Rensselaer Island; also on all the land which he could further obtain from the natives, with the exception of the land already cultivated by van Rensselaer. The rent should be 100 guilders a year besides tithes and two fowls as "toepacht," to be paid in good wheat and oats at four guilders a "mudde." If the lessee should be prevented from using the land by the savages or otherwise, he should be free from the obligation of the lease and pay for such a period as he did not have the use of said land. The lease was to expire May 1, 1662.[36]

Arent was one of the first white men to settle Schenectady, a portion of the Mohawk valley, which is sixteen miles long and eight miles wide. Here he became a proprietor, but died soon afterward leaving a widow and six children. His wife was Catalyntje, daughter of Andries De Vos, deputy director of Rensselaerwyck.[37] After the death of her husband, the grants of land allotted to him were confirmed to her. The children Arent Andriessen had by her were: Jesie (Aeffie), Ariantje, Andries, Cornelia, Samuel, Dirk. Their ages at the father's death were 13, 11, 9, 7, 3, 1 years, respectively.

In 1664 his widow was married to Barent Jansen Van Ditmars. Her ante-nuptial contract with the "orphan masters," for

35 Van Rensselaer Bowier Manuscripts, p. 513.
36 Ibid., p. 758.
37 February 27, 1656, Arent and his father-in-law, Andries de Vos, were appointed curators of the estate of Cornelia Vedos, wife of Chris. Davids, at Fort Orange. See: Calendar of N. Y. Historical Manuscripts in the Office of the Secretary of State. Edited by E. B. O'Callaghan, p. 312. Jonathan Pearson, A History of the Schenectady Patent, 1883, p. 93.

the protection of the interests of her infant children, bears the date of November 12, 1664. It binds her to pay to them their patrimonial estate of 1,000 guilders at their majority, and mortgages her land at Schenectady to secure the payment of the same.

Her second husband was killed in the French and Indian massacre, February 9, 1690, when the town of Schenectady was completely destroyed by the Indians. She was married for the third time, 1691, to Claas Janse Van Boekhoven. By their antenuptial contract, made February 27, 1691, they agreed that on the death of both, their property should go to their children.[88] Boekhoven died 1707, she in 1712.

The real estate in Schenectady belonging to her amounted to the sum of £976 12s. 6d, current money of the Province, and that of Boekhoven in Niskayuna and Albany, to the sum of £700.

Her home lot, says Pearson, was the west quarter of the block bounded by Washington, State, and Church streets, being about 200 feet square. Her grandson Capt. Arent Bratt sold in 1723 the corner parcel to Hendrick Vrooman, but it soon returned to the family, and was again sold by Arent J. Bratt, in 1769, to James Shutter. The remainder of this lot remained in the family until the beginning of last century, when it was sold to Robert Baker and Isaac De Graaf. "The ancient brick house standing on this lot, one of the few specimens of Dutch architecture remaining in the city, was probably built by Capt. Arent Bratt."

The eldest son of Arent Andriessen was Andries Arentsen. He had a brewery. He was living not far from his mother's house in 1690, when he, with one of his children, was slain in the French-Indian massacre. His wife Margarita, daughter of Jacques Cornelise Van Slyck, and his son Arent and daughter Batsheba were spared. It was this son, Arent, who became known as Capt. Arent Bratt; who was made trustee of the common lands in 1714 and continued in office until 1765, being for the last fifteen years of his life sole trustee; who in 1745 represented the county of Albany in the Provincial Assembly; and who was the father of Capt. Andries, Johannes, and Harmanus, well-to-do men. Tradition says Harmanus was the wealtiest man of the town.

The second son of Arent Andriessen was Samuel, who mar-

---

88 Ibid., p. 94.

ried Susanna, daughter of Jacques Cornelise Van Slyck. He died about 1713, leaving five sons.

The third son of Arent Andriessen, Dirk, married Maritje, daughter of Jan Baptist Van Eps. He died in 1735.

Of Arent's daughters, Aeffie married John Claas van Pelten; Ariantje married first, Helmar Otten, a baker in Beverwyck; secondly, Ryder Schermerhorn; Cornelia married Jan Putnam (Postman), supposed to be the first of the Putnam family to have emigrated to America. Putnam was born in Holland about 1645. A descendant of Jan and Cornelia Putnam married into the Van Burens ("Peckham, History of . . . Van Buren . . ." p. 297 f.)

In connection with Ariantje's first marriage the records state that it was strenuously objected to by Rev. Jacob Fabritius, a Lutheran minister from Silesia, who came to serve the Lutheran church in New York. He arrived to this country in February, 1669. In April he had a pass to go to Albany. While there he behaved ill, opposed the magistrates and imposed a fine of 1000 rix-dollars on the person of Helmar Otten (of Issens) for complying with the magistrates in the consummation of the marriage with "Adriantje Arentz, his wife according to the law of the land." On this offense, one of many similar ones committed by this over-zealous preacher, Gov. Lovlace ordered him to be suspended from his ministerial functions at Albany until his friends interceded in his behalf. (See Hazzard's Annals, p. 373.) Otten lived in Beverwyck from 1663 to 1676.

As to further details the reader may consult Jonathan Pearson, "A History of the Schenectady Patent," from which several verbatim quotations have been made in preparing this sketch.

LAURENS ANDRIESSEN.

Laurens Andriessen, often called Laurens Noorman, was a native of Norway. Nothing is known as to the time he immigrated to New Netherland. He served for some time as a soldier in the war against the Indians. He is first mentioned in the beginning of 1644.

In the Records of the Reformed Dutch Church in New Amsterdam he appears as a sponsor, February 22, 1644, at the baptism of the son of a Charles Andries.[39]   The Record calls him "Laurensz Andrieszen, Van Noordwegen" [from Norway].

Sponsorship was not taken seriously in those days.   Laurens Andriessen is a proof of that.   He and Cornelius Pietersen were prosecuted September 29, 1644, by the fiscal in New Amsterdam, for breach of peace on a Sunday and for wounding a certain Richard Pinoyer.   They were condemned to pay a fine of 150 guilders, and to ride the wooden horse during the parade, and to be conveyed thence to prison, or else to go immediately on shipboard and not return on shore, on forfeiture of their wages.[40]

Laurens seems to have been a sailor in service of the West India Company.   Prior to his sponsorship he had taken part in the war against the Indians.   He was wounded in this war.   His comrade, John Haes, taking advantage of his helpless condition, pulled off the shoes of Laurens and sold them for three guilders, in order to buy whisky.   Haes, who had also stolen a gun and shot a hog not belonging to him, was therefore tried for mischief-making.   The fiscal, however, pardoned him on February 1, 1644, in consideration of his having served as soldier "in the present company, on condition that he give security for the damage he committed, and for future good behavior; should he again be guilty of similar crimes, he shall then be 'hanged without mercy'." [41]

Laurens Andriessen was one of the signers of the petition of the Lutherans in New Amsterdam sent to the Director and Council of New Netherland, requesting that the order of the government to send the lately arrived Lutheran pastor Johannis Ernestus Goetwater back to Europe be revoked.

The petition reads as follows: [42]

To the Noble Honorable Director-General, and the Council of New
        Netherland:—

With all due respect, we, the adherents of the Unaltered Augsburg Confession, here in New Netherland, and under the jurisdiction of the Lords Principals of the West India Company, hereby show, that the Burgomasters of this City of Amsterdam in

39 Collections of the New York Genealogical and Biographical Society, II., p. 16.
40 Calendar of Historical Manuscripts. Edited by E. B. O'Callaghan, I., p. 91.
41 Ibid., I., p. 87.
42 Ecclesiastical Records of the State of New York. Published by the State under the supervision of Hugh Hastings. 1901. I., p. 405f.

New Netherland, have received an order from your Honors, first, by the City Messenger Gysbert op Dyck, and shortly after by the Honorable Fiscal, Nicasius de Sille, to the Rev. Master in Theology, Johannis Ernestus Goetwater, that he must and shall depart in the ship, the 'Waag', now ready to sail. Wherefore, in paying our respects to your Honors, we beg to say that in accordance with your Honors' orders and public announcements he has behaved as an honest man, and has never refused obedience to your orders and edicts, but has always given good heed to them; and we, too, have behaved quietly and obediently, while we expect from higher authority, the toleration of our religion — that of the Unaltered Augsburg Confession. To this result we still look forward after the receipt of another letter to us.

We humbly supplicate your Honors, that the sudden orders, the one by the City Messenger, and the other by the Fiscal, to Domine Johannis Ernestus Goetwater, may be revoked by your Honors, until we receive further orders from their High Mightinesses, our sovereigns, and from the Noble Lord Directors of the Privileged West India Company. Remaining your Honors' faithful and watchful (servants) and good Christians, all adherents of the Unaltered Augsburg Confession, and having been admitted into New Netherland, we, in the absence of the others, have signed this petition.

> Mattheus Capito,
> Christian Niesen,
> Harmen Eduwarsen,
> Hans Dreper,
> Lourens Andriesen
> Luycas Dircksen,
> xx Jan Jansen
> xx Jochem Beeckman,
> Andries Rees,
> Luycas Eldersen,
> Harmen Jansen,
> Jan Cornelisse,
> Davidt Wessels,
> Hans Sillejavck,
> Hendrick Hendricksen,
> xx Meyndert Barentsen,
> Harmen Smeeman,

Christian Barentsen,
George Hanel,
Pieter Jansen,
xx Winckelhoeck,
Claes de Witt,
xx Jacob Elders,
Hendrick Willemse.

We await your Honors' favorable decision. Amsterdam, in New Netherland, this 10th day of October, Anno 1657.

Laurens Andriessen must have been quite interested in having a Lutheran minister in New Amsterdam. In a letter of the two Dutch Reformed ministers in New Amsterdam, Johannes Megapolensis and Samuel Drisius, dated August 23, 1658 and addressed to the Director-General and the Council of New Netherland, it is stated that "Laurence Noorman" had acted sponsor at a baptism of a child of Lutheran parents, on August 18, 1656, and that this Laurence was the person believed to have been "the host who concealed John Gutwasser, the Lutheran minister last winter."

For keeping the minister, Laurens Andriessen received six guilders a week ($2.40).[48]

Rev. Goetwater, it seems, was law-abiding. No one will censure him for having ignored the unjust command of Stuyvesant, who in this matter acted as a summus episcopus of, not a state religion, but a company (West Indian) religion. The minister

---

48 Ibid., I., pp. 480. 483. September 24, 1658, the pastors in New Amsterdam wrote to the Classis of Amsterdam: ''Your letter of May 26th last (1658), came safely to hand. We observe your diligence to promote the interests of the church of Jesus Christ in this province, that confusion may be prevented, and that the delightful harmony which has hitherto existed among us here, may continue. . . . We learn that one of the English towns, through lack of a Presbyterian minister, is already engaged in seeking an Independent from (New) England. The raving Quakers have not settled down, but continue to disturb the people of the province by their wandering and outcries. For although our government has issued orders against these fanatics, nevertheless they do not fail to pour forth their venom. There is but one place in New England where they are tolerated, and that is Rhode Island, which is the caeca latrina of New England. Thence they swarm to and fro sowing their tares. The matter of the Lutherans remains still in a very obscure condition. Last year the Lutheran pastor was directed to return by ship to Holland. Instead of this he went out of the city and concealed himself with a Lutheran farmer during the whole winter, where they supported him at the rate of six guilders per week. On the 4th of August last, when we celebrated the Lord's Supper, they made a collection among themselves for him. The Fiscal was again directed to arrest him, and compel him to leave by one of the earliest ships. In the meantime the Lutherans came and represented to the Director-General that their preacher was sick at the farmer's, and besought the privilege of bringing him within the place for treatment. This was granted him. The Fiscal was at the same time empowered to watch over him, and when well again. to send him to Holland. Whether, on his recovery, he will return or conceal himself again, time must show. We fear it is a strategem to hold the matter in suspense, and gain more time. We suspect this the more, as they have said that they will make us appear in an unfavorable light before the Hon. Directors of the West India Company. . . .''

PART OF NEW YORK CITY,* 1673. Lenox Library, New York City.

THE LUTHERAN CHURCH IN NEW YORK CITY. Lenox Library, New York City.

---

* The second view is an enlargement of a part of the first. "L," in the first, shows where the templum Lutheranorum, "temple of the Lutherans," stood. It is seen in the center of the second view.

had been sent to New Amsterdam by the Lutheran Consistory in Amsterdam. He had been called by the Lutherans in New Amsterdam.

From the baptismal records we learn that Laurens had been sponsor August 18, 1656, for Hendrick, the son of Jan Hendrickszen and Grities Barents, who in 1663 are registered as being from Bushwick.[44]

It is probable that Laurens Andriessen was sponsor also at the baptism of a child of Lubbert Gerritszen, March 16, 1653, though another, Laurens Pietersen Norman, may be the person meant in the records, which simply give the name Laurence de Noorman.

As to the further doings of Laurens Andriessen, the sources give no information. The above mentioned Dutch reformed pastors claim that the signers of the Lutheran petition of 1657 "were the least respectable of the Lutheran denominations," and that "the most influential among them were unwilling to trouble themselves with it." There were, it is true, many Lutherans in New Amsterdam, who did not sign the petition. But the reason assigned by Megapolensis and Drisius may be questioned. It is a fact, however, that some of the signers were not model churchmen.[45]

BERNT BAGGE.

Bernt Bagge (Bent Bagge, Bert Bagge) was, judging from the name, a Norwegian. His surname was likely Bakke. He was in Beverwyck as early as 1664, when he with seven others signed

---

44 Compare note 42 with the New York Genealogical and Biographical Record, VI., p. 41.

45 Rev. Isaac Jogues, who was in New Netherland from August, 1642, to November, 1643. said: "No religion is publicly exercised but the Calvinist, and orders are to admit none but Calvinists, but this is not observed, for there are, besides Calvinists, in the colony Catholics, English Puritans, Lutherans, Anabaptists. W. H. Bennett. "Catholic Footsteps in Old New York," p. 33f, relates this incident of Rev. Jogues in New Amsterdam: "As he (Jogues) was leaving the fort one day, a young man, employed by a merchant of the town, ran to him, fell on his knees, seized the mutilated hands, kissed them, and with tears streaming from his eyes, cried, 'Martyr of Jesus Christ! Martyr of Jesus Christ!' The humble priest, confused and embarassed by the demonstration, embraced him affectionately, and, inquiring if he was a Calvinist, was told that he was a Polish Lutheran." (July, 1643). (See also "Relation de Nouvelle France en l'Annee 1643" in Relations des Jesuites . . Quebec, 1852.)
There were Lutherans in Brazil, as early as in the sixteenth century. Quite a number were i Curacao in 1648. They were in New Netherland as early as 1630, or a little before. In New Sweden, or Delaware, the first Lutherans (Swedes and Finns), settled as early as 1639-1640.

a petition to the Vice-Director and Commisaries of Fort Orange and the village of Beverwyck. The petition reads:

"Show respectfully the undersigned petitioners, burghers and inhabitants of the village of Beverwyck, that they are desirous of purchasing [of the Indians] a fine piece of land between Kinderhook and Neutenhook. Whereas the petitioners can no longer make a living here in the village, they are obliged to settle with their families in the country, to gain their bread with God's help, and honorably. The petitioners know well that they cannot do this without your Honors' order and consent, and therefore they request most earnestly that your Honors will give them permission to purchase the land while they promise to be governed by the usages of the country like other inhabitants. Awaiting hereupon a speedy and favorable answer they remain" etc.

Bagge signed his name with a mark.

→

Signature of Bernt Bagge.

On June 24, 1664, the Court of Beverwyck referred the petition to the Director and Council of New Netherland "to dispose thereof according to their pleasure." This body granted the petition, July 10, 1664.

In 1669, Bagge was living in Schenectady, where he had a house and lot. July 12, 1669 he let this house and lot to Jan Rinckhout, a baker, for one year. The rent was to be "nine good beavers."

In 1701 Bernt Bagge's name is found on a list of freeholders and inhabitants of the County of Albany who, as Protestants, petitioned King William III for certain rights. (See New York Colonial Documents XIII., pp. 374, 388; IV. p. 939.)

ANNETJE BARENTS.

Annetje Barents, wife of Albert Andriessen from Fredrikstad in Norway, came over to New Netherland by the ship "Rinselaers Wijck," on March 4, 1637. She was accompanied by her husband and her first three children, one of whom, Storm, was born on the ship, November 2, 1636, the voyage being a stormy one. See the article Albert Andriessen containing facsimile of the log which has the entry about the birth of Storm. Annetje settled with her husband in the colony of Rensselaerswyck and gave birth to five additional children.

There is a possibility that she was Danish, as Christian Barents from Holstein looked after the interests her husband had in New Amsterdam, in 1655, the supposition being then that she was a sister of Barents. It is probable, however, that she was Norwegian. Mr. A. J. F. Van Laer, the editor of "Bowier Manuscripts," states that she was from Rolmers. As I was not able to locate Rolmers, I communicated with Mr. Van Laer and suggested the reading Holmer instead of Rolmers. He kindly replied that he too had not been able to locate Rolmers and thinks that the reading Holmer is quite likely right.

Holmer occurs now and then in older writings as the nominative form of 'Holme,' not far from Andriessen's original home.[46]

JACOB BRUYN.

Jacob Bruyn was born in Norway, probably about 1645. He was a ship carpenter. He arrived at New Amsterdam about 1660, went later to Ulster County, settling in what is now the town of Shawangunk. About 1677 he married Gertrude Esselstein of Columbia County. She was the daughter of Jan Willemse Esselstein and Willemtje Jans. She had been baptized in New Amsterdam on May 22, 1650. Bruyn died 1684 or 1685, leaving widow and three children. The widow soon after married Severyn Ten Hout, a Hollander. Of Bruyn's children, Jan was baptized October 6, 1678, he probably died young. Jacobus was baptized November 30, 1680, died November 21, 1744. (He married, November 18, 1704, Tryntie Schoonmaker [baptized November 22, 1684, died 1763], a daughter of a German, Jochem Hendricksen Schoonmaker, and Petronella Sleght.) The third child, Esther (Hester), was baptized, February 11, 1683; she was married, March 24,

46 See O. Rygh, Norske Gaardnavne, II., Akershus Amt, 1898, p. 18. Ibid., IV., Kristians Amt, Første Halvdel. 1900, p. 218. Van Rensselaer Bowier Manuscripts.

1706, to Zachariah Hoffman, son of Martin Hoffman, a Swede, and Emmertje De Witt.

Among the descendants of Bruyn can be mentioned Jacobus Bruyn, who was born October 27, 1751, and served in the Continental army during the Revolutionary War, attaining the rank of a lieutenant-colonel; also Johannes Bruyn who served several terms in both branches of the New York state legislature and was for many years an associate judge of Ulster County.[47]

HANS CARELSEN.

Hans Carelsen, or Hans· Carelsen Noorman, was from Norway. He settled in Beverwyck and married Neeltje, a daughter of Cornelis Segersen van Vorhoudt (who had come to Beverwyck in 1644) and Brechtje Jacobs. Neeltje was, at their arrival, eight years of age, the youngest of six children.[48]

Carelsen was a fur-trader. An entry under date of August 6, 1657, shows that he sent down from Albany to New Amsterdam 2,300 beavers, and in the following month of September 1,100 beavers.[49]

In August, 1659, Geertje Hendricks sued him for a balance of 12 beavers and fl. 18 in seawan. In his defense Carelsen claimed that he had paid her more than what belonged to her, as the other half concerned Jacob Coppe, deceased. The contract was then produced in court, whereupon Carelsen admitted that he owed the sum demanded. He said, however, he could not pay it at present. But the court ordered him to pay it if he wanted release from arrest.[50]

In October, 1661, he was again engaged in litigation, this time sueing Pieter Ryverdinck, who owed him a sum of money for freighting goods to Ft. Orange.[51]

47 The New York Genealogical and Biographical Record, an article by Thomas G. Evans, XX., pp. 26, 29.
    Gustave Anjou, Records in the Office of the Surrogate, and in the County Clerk's office at Kingston, New York, Ulster County Wills, 1906. I., p. 127.
    Randolph Roswell Hoes, Baptismal and marriage Registers of the Old Dutch Church of Kingston . . . . 1891. No. 19.
    See the article "Hoffman." Part III. Also "The Hoffman Genealogy" (1899), p. 486.
48 Van Rensselaer Bowier Manuscripts, p. 833.
49 J. Munsell, Collections on the History of Albany, IV., p. 144.
50 The Records of New Amsterdam 1653-1674, III., p. 31.
51 Ibid., III., p. 387.

On April 22, 1662, he signed his name as a witness at the conveyance of a yacht.[52]

In 1662–1663 he wanted to sell his house near Beverwyck. We have an imperfect and unsigned paper stating the condition on which he proposed "to sell at a public sale to the highest bidder his house and lot lying near the village of Beverwyck by the side of the hill on the plain where he at present dwells." [53]

On June 7, 1663, his house at Wiltwyck was burnt by Indians.[54]

In January, 1664, a carpenter brought suit against Carelsen for the amount of twenty-four and a half guilders for wages earned on the boat Carelsen was sailing. Though it was shown that the plaintiff had run away from his work, the court ordered Carelsen to pay the sum sued for.[55] He had· engaged the carpenter for a year at the rate of 26 gl. per month.

In 1666 Carelsen was prosecuting a suit against Andries Andriessen, either a Swede or a Finn. The Court decided that the matter, the particular nature of which we do now know, should be adjusted by arbitrators.[56]

In 1667, his wife died.[57] There was poverty in his home. The Church records of Albany state that his wife had received aid from the deacons. Also after her death the deacons continued to aid the home of Carelsen. In December, 1667, and January, 1668, the records state that the deacons paid "17 guilders and 10 stivers for beer furnished to Hans de Noorman." In November, 1668, it is recorded that the deacons furnished "bread to Hans de Noorman."[58]

Hans Carelsen remained a widower for about four years. April 1, 1671, he married, in New Amsterdam, Geertje Teunis, widow of Cors Jansen.[59] In April, 1685, she was married to Francisco Anthony.[60] Hans Carelsen must have died some time before this.

52 Year Book of the Holland Society of New York, 1900, p. 140.
53 J. Munsell, Collections on the History of Albany, IV., p. 319.
54 New York Colonial Documents, XIII., p. 247.
55 The Records of New Amsterdam 1653-1674, V., p. 126.
56 Ibid., VI., p. 43.
57 J. Munsell, Collections on the History of Albany, IV., p. 164.
58 Ibid., I., p. 28f.
59 The Records of New Amsterdam 1653-1674, VI., p. 634. For other data see Collections on the History of Albany, IV., pp. 85, 164, 244, 319.
60 Collections of the New York Genealogical and Biographical Society, I., pp. 85, 86.

JAN CARELSZEN.

Jan Carelszen, whose name as settler in Esopus appears first 1662, came from Langesund, Norway, eighteen miles from Skien. His wife was Helena Hendricks, sometimes called Helena Rustenburg. In 1684 he was a porter or carman in New Amsterdam. March 29, in that year, he and fifteen other carmen were discharged by the common council for refusing to obey certain orders and regulations. But on April 6, he and two others were readmitted as carmen on condition of paying a fine of six shillings and conforming to the laws. Jan and Helena had several children: Carl was baptized April 25, 1677; Lucretia, in 1679; Lucretia, January 12, 1681; Henricus, March 11, 1683; Johannes, June 29, 1684; Petrus, December 11, 1687; Ibel, June 22, 1690. May 21, 1693 Carelszen and his wife were sponsors at the baptism of twins belonging to Charles Peters and Maria Thomas.[61]

CARSTEN CARSTENSEN.

Carsten Carstensen, sometimes called Christen Christensen, commonly referred to as Carsten Carstensen Noorman, arrived by the "Rensselaerswyck" at New Amsterdam, March 4, 1637.[62] He came from Flekkerö in Norway. He is first entered in the accounts of Van Rensselaer, the patroon, under the date of April 17, 1637. The patroon mentions him in a letter of May 13, 1639, to the superintendent Arent van Curler. He says: "Christen Christensen Noorman owes his mate who did not go with him fl. 20 for tools sold to him. Let him pay this to you, he will thereby pay me there what I have advanced him [his mate] here. I believe his name is Barent."[63] Before 1644 Carsten Carstensen was employed as a farm laborer, sawyer, stave splitter, mill hand and roof thatcher. He seems to have had interests in a saw mill.

61 Collections of the New York Genealogical and Biographical Society, II., pp. 127, 145, 157, 168, 183, 197, 214.
62 The New York Genealogical and Biographical Record, XIV., p. 75.
63 Van Rensselaer Bowier Manuscripts, p. 810.

Afterwards he leased a garden, which, in 1650, was granted to Gijsbert Cornelisz, from Weesp.[64]

The sources do not give much information about Carsten Carstensen. We find his name in a document in Albany, dated August 4, 1663, which he signed as a witness of a certain transaction.[65] May 7, 1667, he deeded a lot lying behind Fort Albany to Claes Teunissen: "length six rods, south breath three rods, east a low lot six rods, north the broad breadth three rods." [66]

Signature of Carsten Carstensen.

He was a poor man, as is shown in the Deacon's Account Book of the Reformed Church in Albany. This book conveys the information that the church furnished in 1668 a year's board to a child belonging to Carstensen. The board, it was computed, would amount to 32 guilders a month or 384 guilders a year.[67]

Under *"Disbursements for the poor,"* in 1665, the Deacon's Account Book shows the following entries concerning the affairs of Carstensen:

April 22.	2 schepel wheat	13.
do.	In money, and 3 lbs. soap @ 1 gl. a lb., together	7.14
April 27.	Paid for barley for Karsten Noorman	10.
May 13.	2 schepels corn from Jan Bac	10.
May 14.	2 schepels wheat	13.
July 29.	In money	3.
August	Karsten Noorman, in money	6.
" 3.	20 yards linnen [no price]	
Sept. 3.	Cash	6.
Sept. 27.	"Lenne Roberts was engaged to nurse the child of Karsten Noorman for one year for 35 guilders a month, on condition that if the child dies, she should have to pay for the whole [month] in which it might die."	

64 Ibid., p. 442.
65 J. Munsell, Collections on the History of Albany, IV., p. 329.
66 Ibid., IV., p. 423.
67 Ibid., I., p. 3.

BERGEN, NORWAY, ABOUT THE
From Braunius:

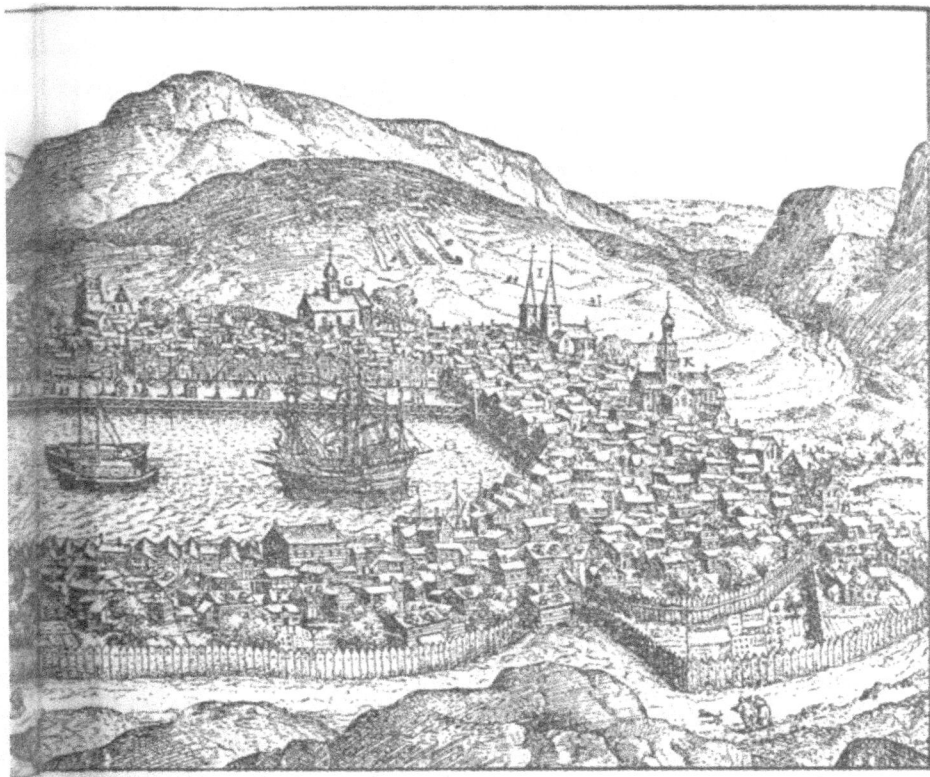

See p. 54.

BERGEN IN THE SIXTEENTH CENTURY.

From Braun's Theatrum urbium, iv.

Receipts:

Nov. 22.   4 lbs. butter from David Scuyler   7.

Disbursements:

Nov. 27.   To Lenne Roberts for one month's nursing of
            Carsten Noorman's child   ----------

Receipts:

Dec. 10.   To Karsten for Wood cutting 1 and ¼ days
            and digging post holes for the church yard
            fence   8.15

Dec. 15.   2 Linnen diapers from Karsten Noorman

Disbursements:

Dec. 15.   To small boy of Jan Toms [68] living with Car-
            sten Noorman, 1 and ¼ yards kersey, re-
            ceived of Gabriel   12.

Dec. 29.   Sold to Karsten Noorman's wife a petticoat
1666

August   Margary Deckers was paid 15 gulden for 3 and
            ¾ ells blue linnen for aprons and wrappers
            for Carsten Noorman's children.

In February, 1667, the children of Carsten Noorman are again
mentioned as recipients of charity. In September, 1668, 96 gulden
were given to Gerret Jansen Stavast and Guert Hendricksen for
the "maintenance of Karsten Norman's children, the remainder
33g. 18 should go to Hans de Norman." In November, 1671, the
deacons again gave "40 gulden for a month's board for the child
of Carsten Noorman." In April, 1672, the following entry is
made in the Deacon's Account Book: "The recipients of alms this
month were Johann Dyckman, Jacob Aertsen and Karsten de
Noorman (2 shirts, 24g.) [69]

Carsten Carstensen died in 1679 in Albany. He left two
children, Teunis, aged nineteen years, and Elizabeth, aged fourteen.
Teunis settled in Schenectady, where he married Maritie, the
daughter of Pieter Jacobse Borsbom, he died in 1691.[70]

68 Should probably be: Noorman's son living with Jan Toms.
69 Collections on the History of Albany, IV., 26, 27.
70 Jonathan Pearson, A History of The Schenectady Patent, p. 101. A lot
conveyed in Schenectady, June 23, 1671, by Ludwig Cobes to Christiaen Christianse,
does not enter into consideration here, as it is probably the Dane, Christgen Christians, who is meant, and not the Norwegian. See article Christgen Christians in
Part II. Torstein Jahr in "Symra," V., 2, p. 72, makes the statement that the
wife of Carstensen accompanied him on his voyage from Norway, 1637. I have not
been able to verify it by the revised list of immigrants.

CLAES CARSTENSEN.

Claes Carstensen was one of the early settlers in New Netherland. He was born in Norway about the year 1607. His home was Sande. In the Dutch Records in the City Clerk's Office, New York, it is stated under date of May 11, 1657, that "Claes Carstensen of Sant in Norway, fifty years old" and two others gave testimony relative to the children of a certain Jan Corn. . . of Rotterdam.[71] It would appear that Carstensen came to New Netherland about 1641, though he may have been there much earlier, as he had command of the Indian language and was employed as interpreter between the whites and the Indians on August 30, 1645, when the Dutch and the River-Indians concluded their articles of peace at the general gathering upon Schreyer's Hoek, south of the fort. La Montague was present at the occasion. Carstensen was one of those who signed the articles of treaty.[72] Thirteen years later, in 1658, he was appointed Indian interpreter to the Algonquins.[73]

On August 21, 1642, we find him making a declaration that "he was thrown out of a boat on his way to the ship yard."[74] In 1643 he was along signing the resolution adopted by the Commonality of Manhattan.[75]

On September 5, 1645, when he was doing service as a soldier, he acquired 29 morgens, about 60 acres, of land on Long Island, behind the land of John Forbus, a Swede, to whom he later sold it.[76] It was on the East River and Norman's Kill (Williamsburgh). On April 15, 1646, Carstensen married Hilletje Hendricks.[77]

On March 25, 1647, he acquired 50 morgens of land on the west side of the North River, next to Dirck Straatemakers. It had formerly belonged to Barent Jansen.[78] Carstensen sold it the same year to Jan Vinje, a Walloon. In 1667 it became the property

71 Year Book of the Holland Society of New York, 1900, p. 113.
72 New York Colonial Documents, XIII., p. 18. J. Riker, Harlem, Its Origin and Early Annals, p. 145.
73 The Register of New Netherland, 1624-1674, (compiled by E. B. O'Callaghan, Albany, 1865), p. 133.
74 Calendar of Historical Manuscripts, I., p. 19.
75 New York Colonial Documents, I., p. 193.
76 Year Book of the Holland Society of New York, 1900, p. 126. Teunis Bergen, Register . . . . of Early Settlers of King's County, 1881, p. 59.
77 New York Genealogical and Biographical Record, VI., p. 86. She is once called Hilletje Noorman. This, however, is no proof that she was a Norwegian.
78 Calendar of Historical Manuscripts, I., p. 374.

of a Dane, Laurens Andriessen.[79] The groundbrief of March 25, 1647, reads as follows: "Patent to Claes Carstensen of a piece of land in New Jersey, formerly granted to Barent Jansen deceased . . . situated on the West side of the North River next to Dirck the Streetpaver's land, stretching from a wood on the N. N.W. along a small kil to the river on the S. S.E. along the valley to the Paver's land, N.E. by E. of the Paver's kil, the wood N. N.W. all covering fifty morgens, . . ."[80]

On May 3, 1649, he acquired a lot in New Amsterdam.[81] The lot was about thirty-seven English feet wide, fronting to Hoogh Straet, or High Street, now 31–35 High Street.[82]

On July 28, 1653, he deeded to Burgher Joris, 29 morgens, 553 rods of land on Long Island, on the river side in the rear of Jan the Swede (Forbus). It was a part of Newtown.[83] On October 15, in the same year, he deeded a house and lot, on Brouwer Street in New Amsterdam, to Jan Nagel.[84]

In 1663 he served as a corporal. In October, 1655, he gave fl. 10 as a voluntary contribution and taxation to the city, following the example of many others.[85]

On April 13, 1657, he was admitted to the small burgher's rights.

Carstensen had his lawsuits, like many other citizens in New Netherland. On April 13, 1660, he was to prosecute a suit against one Goodman Bets. But both parties were in default.[86] On December 13, 1661, he was to prosecute a suit against Fredrik Aarzen (often called the Spaniard). Again the litigants were in default.[87]

Signature of Claes Carstensen.

On January 3, 1662, Carstensen appeared in court as a witness in the case of Jacobus Vis against Geertje Teunis, who in self-defense claimed that Jacobus had used very abusive language

79 New Jersey Archives. First Series, XXI., p. 2. See article Laurens Andriessen, Part II.
80 New York Colonial Documents, XIII., p. 21.
81 E. B. O'Callaghan, History of New Netherland, II., p. 586.
82 J. H. Innes, New Amsterdam and Its People, 1902, pp. 80 (map), 261.
83 Calendar of Historical Manuscripts, I., p. 378.
84 Ibid., I., p. 379.
85 The Records of New Amsterdam, 1653-1674, I., p. 370.
86 Ibid., III., p. 158.
87 Ibid., III., p. 424.

against her. Carstensen testified that he had heard words, but could not say as to whether they were abusive. or not.[88]

Under date of June 1, 1662, we note that Claes Carstensen Noorman of New Amsterdam acknowledged that he owed Nicholas De Meyer, from Hamburg, 121 guilders, 11 stivers, money advanced to the wife of a Carl Jansen.[89]

On October 1, in the same year, Carstensen sued Gerrit Hendricksen van Harderwyck, demanding that Hendricksen should be condemned to pay fifty guilders, "which he has undertaken to pay Hendrick Hendricksen Smitt for him." Gerrit Hendricksen admitted that he "had accepted the fifty guilders to pay Smitt for him," whereupon he was condemned by the Court to satisfy and pay the debt." [90]

On October 13, 1662, Claes Carstensen deeded to Albert Con-inck: "The just half of his house and lot in company with Jan Barentsen Kunst (a German), situate north of the Hoogh Straat; bounded west by brewery of Jacob Van Couwenhoven; north, by the Steegh (South William Street); east, by house and lot of Asser Levy; and south, by the Hoogh Straat, aforesaid. Broad, in front, on the street, 1 rod 9 feet 1 inch; in the rear, 1 rod 3 feet 8 inches; and on the east side, 7 rods 8 feet, with a free drop on the east side of 8 inches. (Valentine, Manual of the city of New York, 1865, p. 696.)

On January 1, 1663, Carstensen joined the Dutch Reformed Church. This Church took care of him in his old age.

On April 29, 1671, he was granted a small house lot to use during his life time, but without the right of succession. "He had seen better days," as the historian of Harlem, J. Riker, touchingly adds.[91]

On November 6, 1679, Carstensen died at the house of Johannes Vermelje. "He had been for some time in needy circumstances and was aided by the Deacons, having been a church member for many years. The deacons Arent Herman and Jan Nagel took an inventory of his effects found in his house. These were sold on November 10, 1679, at public vendue for 266 gulden 16 stivers, for the benefit of the deaconery." It would thus appear that he left no relatives.

88 Ibid., IV., p. 3.
89 Year Book of the Holland Society of New York, 1900, p. 142.
90 The Records of New Amsterdam, 1653-1674, IV., p. 155. Cf. pp. 198. 220, 221.
91 J. Riker, Harlem, Its Origin and Early Annals, p. 273.

CLAES CLAESEN.

Claes Claesen, from Flekkerö, near Christiansand, Norway, sailed by "de Eendracht" on March 21, 1630, from Texel, and arrived on May 24, 1630, at New Amsterdam. He served as farm hand on de Laets Burg with two Norwegians, Roelof Jansen of Marstrand, and Jakob Goyversen of Flekkerö.[92] After 1634 Claes Claesen's name does not appear in the records of the colony of Rensselaerswyck. Kiliaen van Rensselaer had written to Director Wouter Van Twiller, April 25, 1634, mentioning Claes Claesen as a person in whose judgment he had confidence. He says:

"Please take charge of my grain raised in my colony for which Jacob Planck has no use, and deliver it to the Company. I hope, however, that he will be able to use it all for brandy-making and beer-brewing, if he only understands his business. I have had him examined by Claes Claesen." [93]

There were several persons in New Netherland by the name of Claes Claesen; e. g., Claes Claesen Bording, a Dane. We can not state whether Claesen from Flekkerö is the one referred to in a Patent of June 29, 1664, granting to "Claes Claesen 24 morgens of upland, 3 morgens, 160 rods of valley, numbered 11, at New Utrecht, Long Island." [94] A person by his name acting as sponsor at the baptism of a child belonging to Barent Janszen, March 20, 1650, in New Netherland, is likely Claes Claesen Bording.[95] One Claes Claesen was from Ravox.

FREDERIK CLAESEN.

Frederik Claesen arrived in New Netherland in 1663 by the ship "de Rooseboom," which sailed March 15, 1663. It had seventy-five passengers on board and was commanded by Captain

92 Van Rensselaer Bowier Manuscripts, pp. 805, 222, 808. (See articles Roelof Jansen, Jakob Goyversen.)
93 Ibid., p. 282.
94 Calendar of Historical Manuscripts, I., p. 386.
95 Collections of the New York Genealogical and Biographical Society, II., p. 27.

Pieter Reyersz van Beets. In the passenger list, the words "from Norway" are appended to the name of Frederik Claesen.[96]

HARMEN DIRCKSEN.

Harmen Dircksen, from Norway, arrived at New Amsterdam in 1659 by the ship "de Bruynvis" (Brownfish). He was accompanied by his wife and his child, four years old. The ship sailed June 19, 1659, and was commanded by Captain Cornelis Maertsen.[97]

It is perhaps this Harmen Dircksen that is meant in the following data obtained from the records of Esopus.

In proceedings and sentences of the court held in Esopus April 25, 26, 27, 1667, resulting from complaints of inhabitants in Esopus against violences committed by the soldiers and illtreatment from Capt. Brodhead, it was shown that Harmen Dircksen was wounded in his leg by Richard Cugge, in so much "that he is lame unto the present day," "and that only because his goats where eaten by the soldiers." [98] His wife was taken to prison by Capt. Brodhead, who had thrown a glass of beer in her face, called her many bad names, and carried her to the Guard a prisoner. Brodhead owned this, but said that Harmen's wife had called his sister a whore, hence the quarrel.[99]

MRS. HARMEN DIRCKSEN.

Mrs. Harmen Dircksen, from Norway, arrived at New Amsterdam, June 19, 1659. She was accompanied by her husband and her four years old child. She was living at Esopus in 1666, when, as stated in the previous article, Capt. Brodhead threw a glass of beer in her face. He gave as reason for this singular demonstration of gallantry that she had called his sister names. See article "Harmen Dircksen."

96 List of passengers in Year Book of the Holland Society of New York, 1902.
97 Ibid., 1902.
98 New York Colonial Documents, XIII., p. 98.
99 Ibid., p. 99. A Harmen Dircksen is referred to as early as 1639. See Calendar of Historical Manuscripts, I., p. 67.

JACOB GOYVERSEN.

Jacob Goyversen, or Goyverttsen (Govertsen), was from Flekkerö in Norway. He left Texel, March 21, 1630, by the ship "de Eendracht" and arrived at New Amsterdam May 24, 1630. He was accompanied by two Norwegians, Roelof Jansen from Marstrand and Claes Claesen from Flekkerö, with whom he also worked on de Laets Burg, in the service of Kiliaen van Rensselaer.[100]

His name appears after his demise in the court minutes. He had given Anneke Jans, the wife of Roelof Jansen, his countryman, some dressgoods. He had bought it of Marijn Andriesen. But as he had not paid for it, Andriesen sued Anneke's second husband the Reverend Bogardus, claiming that Govertsen had no right to donate things he had not paid for and that the recipient of such unpaid gifts was obliged to pay for them. The court settled the matter by deciding that the money claimed by Andriesen should be paid from the inheritance left by Govertsen.

ARENT ELDERTSZEN GROEN.

Arent Eldertszen Groen is entered in the church records of the Dutch Reformed Church in New Amsterdam as being a widower from 'Stalange' (Stavanger), in Norway. He married, July 26, 1665, in New Amsterdam, Jannetje Willems van der Bosch (from the bush).[101]

HANS HANSEN.

Hans Hansen, from Bergen, Norway, is the common ancestor of the Bergen family of Long Island, New Jersey and their vicinity. He was a ship carpenter by trade, went from Norway to Holland, and thence, in 1633, to New Amsterdam. In the

---

100 Van Rensselaer Bowier Manuscripts, p. 222, 308, 805.
101 The New York Genealogical and Biographical Record, VI., p. 147.

records his name appears in various forms most commonly Hans Hansen Noorman, Hans Hansen Boer.

He is one of the exceptions among the Norwegian settlers in New Amsterdam in so far that he has been mentioned frequently in Norwegian-American books and papers as being a Norwegian, and that an entire book has been written about him and his descendants (Teunis G. Bergen, Descendants of Hans Hansen Bergen, one of the early settlers of New York, with notes on other Long Island families, New York, 1866; enlarged edition, 1876).

The assertion which has sometimes been made that Hans Hansen was at the head of an expedition of Dutch and Norwegians who crossed the Hudson, and settled where the present Jersey City is, is false. It has also been asserted that Bergen i New Jersey was called after Hans Hansen Bergen. But this statement is equally false. For Bergen in New Jersey was named after Bergen op Zoom (there is a Bergen in Holland and in Germany as well as in Norway). Hans Hansen had no property on the west of the Hudson where Bergen lay.[102] Bergen in New Jersey was founded after his death.

Hans Hansen married, in 1639, in New Amsterdam, Sarah, daughter of Joris Jansen Rapalje of Walloon ancestry. She was born June 9, 1625, at Albany, and was probably the first female child born of European parentage in the colony of New Netherland.

Many children were born to Hans and Sarah. The records of the Dutch Reformed church in New Amsterdam state when they were baptized and who acted as their sponsors. The children were: Anneken, baptized July 22, 1640; Brecktje, baptized July 27, 1642; Jan, baptized April 17, 1644, one of the sponsors being the Norwegian woman from Marstrand, Anneke Jans, at that time the wife of the Dutch pastor in New Amsterdam, Rev. Bogardus;[103] Michiel, baptized November 4, 1646, one of whose sponsors was Pieter Jansen Noorman, a Norwegian;[104] Joris. baptized July 18, 1649; Marretje, baptized October 8, 1651; Jacob, baptized September 21, 1653; Catalyn, a twin with Jacob, baptized November 30, 1653.[105]

102 J. O. Evjen, Nordmænd i Amerika i det 17de Aarhundrede, in "Folke-bladet" (Minneapolis), Feb. 2, 1910.
103 See article "Anneke Jans." Part I.
104 See article "Pieter Jansen." Part I.
105 Collections of the New York Genealogical and Biographical Society, II. (Baptisms). Teunis G. Bergen, Register .... of the early settlers of Kings County in Long Island .... to 1700.

Hans Hansen, we find, acted as sponsor for the child of a Norwegian, Laurens Pietersen Noorman, June 1, 1642.

In July, 1638, the following agreement for the cultivation of a tobacco plantation on Manhattan Island was made between Andries Hudde and Hans Hansen,Norman:

"Conditions and stipulations agreed to between Andries Hudde and Hans Hansen Norman, on the ninth day of July, Anno 1638, as follows:

"First, the said Andries Hudde shall by first opportunity of ships from Holland send hither to Hans Hansen aforesaid six or eight persons with implements required for the cultivation of tobacco.

"Hans Hansen shall be bound to place the said persons upon the flatland on the Island of the Manhates behind the Corlears land.

"Hudde shall bear the expense of the transportation and of engaging them and shall send the vouchers for these expenses with them.

"Hans Hansen shall also be bound to furnish as many dwellings and tobacco houses, as the time may permit; further to put to work the persons, who shall come from the Fatherland, for the profit of both of them. Hans Hansen shall also have authority over them in Hudde's absence without interference by anybody else. He shall further bear and repay one half of the expenses, incurred by said Hudde. In like manner he must provide such supply of victuals, as shall be necessary for so many persons, on condition that Andries Hudde shall likewise repay one half of the expenses incurred here by Hans Hansen.

"Mons. Hudde shall also be bound to pay Hans Hansen for his industry whatever impartial men shall deem to be just.

"Likewise Hudde shall not be allowed to demand from said Hans Hansen any rent for the land, but shall assist in every way with the means, which he has here, if he does not require them and is not prevented and all this until Hudde's return, when further arrangements shall be made. For what is above written, parties pledge their persons and property real and personal, present and future submitting to the Provincial Court of Holland and all other Courts, Judges and Justices, all in good faith without reservation or deceit.

"Thus done at Fort Amsterdam in New Netherland, the 10th of July Anno 1638.

"A. Hudde.

"This is the mark

H ꓕ

Signatures of Hans Hansen.

aforesaid." [106]

Under date of July 18, 1638, Hans Hansen gave power of attorney to Wouter van Twiller, the Director of New Netherland.

On March 13, 1647, he acquired a lot south of Fort Amsterdam "between Jan Snedeker and Joris Rapalje," that is, next to his father-in-law. On March 30, in the same year, he acquired land on Long Island "on the kill of Joris Rapalyey bounded by Lambert Huybertsen's, Jan the Swede's plantation and by Mespath Kill as far as Dirck Volkertsen." [107] This was at the head of the Kill of Mespath (Indian name for Newton), or Newton Creek, in a section called by the Dutch "t Kreuppelbosch," now corrupted Cripple Bush. The grant amounted to 400 acres.[108]

Hans Hansen was a respectable citizen, and this was stated as the cause for his being acquitted when found guilty of smuggling in 1648. The records say (May 26, 1648): "Pardon of Hans Hansen, for fourteen years a respectable resident in New Amsterdam, on a charge of having aided in smuggling, on condition that he beg pardon of God and the court." [109]

He died probably early in 1654. His widow later became the wife of Teunis Gysbert Bogert. In 1656, in a petition asking for a grant of land, she described herself as the first born Christian daughter in New Netherland.

Hans Hansen as well as his wife and her parents never learned to write, signing their names with marks, as the great majority of the inhabitants of New Amsterdam did.

106 New York Colonial Documents, XIV., p. 11.
107 See articles "Dirck Holgersen," Part I., and "Jan Forbus," Part III.
108 J. Riker, Annals of Newton, 1852.
109 Calendar of Historical Manuscripts, I., p. 17.

ANNEKEN HENDRICKS.

Anneken Hendricks, from Bergen, in Norway, was in New Amsterdam before 1650. She was the first wife of Jan Arentszen (Aertsen) Van der Bilt (Bilt = hill), the ancestor of the Vanderbilts. He married her in New Amsterdam, February 6, 1650. The church records state that Anneke was from Bergen, Norway.[110] Her husband came from the province of Utrecht, Holland.

In 1653 Anneken figured in a lawsuit. Matevis Vos, curator, brought suit against her for the payment of 24 fl. 18 stivers book debts. Jan appeared for his wife. Since he was in doubt as to whether she had not already paid, the court condemned the defendant to pay within a month or prove the debt had been paid March 10, 1653.[111]

Anneke and Jan had three children, Gerritje, Marritje, and Aert. Gerritje was baptized December 4, 1650; Marritje, December 3, 1651; Aert, April 20, 1651. Aert married. Gerritje or Gieritje was married to Jan Spiegelar, Marritje was married to Rem Remsen. Thus there is Norwegian blood both in the *Vanderbilt* and the *Remsen* family.

Marritje was quite early remembered in a will, what is seen from the account in the Records of New Amsterdam 1653—1674, VI., p. 110, under date of September 27, 1659: "Whereas Jacob Coppe has died and there has been found among his papers and property here a testament, made December 14, 1653, before Notary D. van Schelluyne and witnesses, in favor of Lysbett Cornelis, daughter of Cornelis Aarsen, and Merritje Jans, daughter of Jan van der Bilt, naming them both heiresses of his estate. Therefore the orphanmasters have resolved to appoint administrators of said estate, so that the heiresses may come to their own, and they have elected and authorized, as they hereby do, Timotheus de Gabry and Isaaq Kip, who are directed to make as soon as possible a complete inventory of all the goods and property left by Jan Coppe, his debts and credits here in the country, as well as in this place as elsewhere, and to report the same to the Orphans Court, to be then disposed of, as shall be deemed advisable."

After the death of Anneke, Jan married Dierber Cornelis.

110 The New York Genealogical and Biographical Record, VI., p. 88.
111 The Records of New Amsterdam, 1653-1674, I., p. 63.

And after the death of the latter, he married, on November 13, 1681, Maddaleentje Hanse.

Jan Aertsen van der Bilt had also a son named Jacob, who on August 13, 1687 married Maritje Van der Vliet (of the stream). I cannot say whether Jacob was born in the first or the second marriage of Jan. Jacob and Maritje had a son, also named Jacob, who was born in 1692, and married Neeltje (Cornelia) Denyson. In 1718 "the last named Jacob purchased a farm on Staten Island and moved thither from Flatbush, Long Island. From him descended the famous 'Commodore'.[112]

Signature of Aertse Vanderbilt, 1661, husband of Anneken Hendricks.

Jan Aertsen van der Bilt signed his name with marks. His mark "resembles a window sash — with four panes of glass." He died in 1705.

ROELOF JANSEN HAES.

Roelof Jansen Haes, or Roelof de Haes, was, according to the Records of the Dutch Reformed Church in New Amsterdam, a native of Norway. He married, April 19, 1643, in New Amsterdam, Gertruyd Jacobs, of Emmenes, widow of Gerrt Janszen.[118] He was then twenty years old, according to his own testimony.[114] A few days previous to this marriage, Gertruyd Jacobs arranged what portion of their father's estate should go to the children she had by Gerrt Janszen. In making this settlement she announced that she intended to marry "Roelof Jansen Haes of Norway." [115]

On July 6, 1643, Haes was granted a lot on the south end of the valley (of the West India Company), northeast of the

112 New Jersey Archives, First Series, vol. XXII., p. 563; Cornelius B. Harvey, Genealogical History of Hudson and Bergen Counties, 1900, p. 808. T. Bergen, Register . . . . of Settlers of Kings County.

118 The New York Genealogical and Biographical Record, VI., p. 85.

114 New York Colonial Documents, XII., p. 17.

115 Calendar of Historical Manuscripts, I., p. 22. "Norske Rigs-Registranter." Vo. VIII., 1641-1648, refers to a Hans Haase (Hass, Haess) as citizen of Bergen, Norway.

fort, "containing 18 rods, 9 feet." [116]   On February 19, 1647, he obtained an addition to it.[117]

On November 3, 1643, he and Pieter Kock, a Dane, made a declaration that the colony of Achter Col had been destroyed by Indians, who were swarming in that district, burning and slaying whatever they could come across.[118]

On January 28, 1644, he made a declaration as to a debt claimed by Benedict Hendricks from Burger Joris.[119]   On June 18, 1649, he made an assignment, to Commissary Keyser, of this claim against Burger Joris for 1000 guilders.[120]

On February 1, 1646, he obtained a lot northeast of Fort Amsterdam, on the road opposite the lots of Andries Hudde and Martin Crieger.[121]

He secured a lot in Water Street, at present No. 27 Pearl Street, and built a little house, the picture of which is given in a view of the "Marckveldt and't Water" (1652), which is enlarged in the illustrations facing page 58 of Innes' "New Amsterdam and Its People."   This lot was not large, as Haes's groundbrief, obtained on May 11, 1646, shows.   It is "both on the south side and the north side, one rod, seven feet, Rhineland measure, wide,"—that is about twenty English feet.   Haes's neighbor was the German physician, from Magdeburg, Hans Kierstede, son-in-law of the Norwegian woman Anneke Jans.[122]

Haes sold this lot, 1653, to Cornelis van Steenwyck, a merchant, who probably had his store on it.

On April 11, 1647, Governor Stuyvesant appointed Haes Receiver-General of excises,[123] thus showing he had confidence in him, what is also noticed in the following letter, of the directors in Holland, to Stuyvesant, dated January 27, 1649:

"Your Honor's appointment of Roeloff Jansen as Receiver-General at a yearly salary of 480 fl. without rations induces us to believe, that you must have a good knowledge of his honesty;

116 Year Book of the Holland Society of New York, 1901, p. 125.
117 Calendar of Historical Manuscripts, I., p. 367.
118 Ibid., p. 25.   New York Colonial Documents, XIII., p. 16.   See article Kock.   Part II.
119 Calendar of Historical Manuscripts, I., p. 26.
120 Ibid., I., p. 39.
121 Ibid., I., p. 370.
122 The Records of New Amsterdam, 1653-1674, VII., p. 56.
123 Calendar of Historical Manuscripts, I., p. 108.

VIEW OF THE MARCKVELDT AND 'T WATER, 1652. From "New Amsterdam and Its People," by J. H. Innes; copyright, 1902, by Charles Scribner's Sons, New York.

A. The Hoisting Crane. B. Southeast Bastion of Fort Amsterdam. C. White Horse Tavern. D. House, late of Dominie Bogardus, who married **Anneke Jans**, a **Norwegian** woman. E. Old Store-House of West India Co. F. The "Five Stone Houses" of West India Co. G. Brewery of West India Co. H. House of Cornelis Pietersen. I. House of Pieter van Couwenhoven. J. House of Jan Jansen Schepmoes. K. House of Gillis Pietersen. L. House of Eghbert von Borsum. M. House of Pieter Cornelissen van der Veen. N. House of Lambert van Valkenburgh, German. O. Schregers Hoek or Capoke. P. House of Hans Kiersted, who married **Sara Rollefsen**, a **Norwegian** woman. Q. **Roelof Jansen Haes**, a **Norwegian**. R. Pieter Cornelissen. S. Paulus Leendertsen van der Grift. T. New Store-House of West India Co. U. Augustyn Herrman, German. V. Jacob Haes, husband of **Christina Capoen Holgersen, Norwegian.** W. Old Church and Lane.

on that understanding we approve of it herewith, although in our straitened circumstances all possible retrenchments should be made for which reason we have here discharged all subaltern officers, and we believe from information received, that there are more than enough officers; all unnecessary officers should therefore be discharged, we cannot afford to keep them." [124]

In a letter of April 26, 1651, from Johan le Thor and Isaac van Beeck, in Amsterdam, to Governor Stuyvesant, it is stated that "Secretary Cornelis van Tienhoven had reported to them that Stuyvesant had appointed him receiver in the place of Haes." [125]

On August 6, 1649, Cornelis Coenrattsen, skipper, gave Power of Attorney to Claes Jansen Ruyter, to receive from Roelof Jansen de Haes the sum of 360 guilders.[126]

On March 20, 1651, Haes gave a mortgage to Hendrick van Dyck in his house and lot in New Amsterdam, situate east of William Beckman.[127] On September 9, in the same year, he gave a mortgage in his house to Jan Jansen from Göteborg, Sweden.[128] Olof Stevensen van Cortland acted as his agent.

Roelof Jansen Haes was at the time residing at Fort Naussau. For we know that on July 9, 1651, he, Andries Hudde, Jan Andries, and Pieter Harmensen, "all four free inhabitants and traders on the river, residing at Fort Naussau have been witnesses for the Director-General of a treaty between the Director-General and the Sachens Indians." [129]

On December 10, 1654, Haes secured twenty-five morgens of land.[130]

He must have died shortly afterward. For in July, 1656, his widow and Jacob Crabbe, a native of Amsterdam, gave notice that they desired to enter into matrimony. On July 27 "appears Geertruyt Jacops widow of the late Mr. Roeloff de Haes, now betrothed to Jacob Crabbe and declares her intention of proving and assigning their father's inheritance to the children, left by him, Mr. de Haes, and born in wedlock by her, Geertruy Jacops, to wit,

124 New York Colonial Documents, XIV., p. 107.
125 Ibid., XIV., p. 140.
126 Calendar of Historical Manuscripts, I., p. 47.
127 Ibid., I., p. 52.
128 Ibid., I., p. 55.
129 New York Colonial Documents, I., pp. 596, 599.
130 E. B. O'Callaghan, History of New Netherland, II., 589.

Joannes de Haes, aged about 10 years, Marrietje de Haes, aged about 9 years, Annitje about 3 years, and assigns herewith to each of the aforesaid children the sum of six carolus guilders, declaring at the same time upon her conscience, in place of an oath, that she, affiant, hereby satisfies the aforesaid children out of their father's inheritance, and this declaration is made in presence and with the consent of her affianced husband Jacobus Crabbe. . . ."[131]

By the 23d of October, 1656, the widow of Haes had become the wife of Jacob Crabbe, for on that day Crabbe appeared in court "as her husband and guardian," demanding a payment of fl. 125.11 from Teunis Tomassen, a mason. The books of Haes showed that Tomassen was indebted to Haes for this sum.[132]

Of Roelof Jansen Haes's children, Johannes became quite prominent. Gertrud was married to John Crocke [Kreek], and became a member of the Dutch Reformed Church in 1679. She lived on South William Street. A skipper contemporary with Roelof in New Amsterdam, Jan or Jacob Haes by name, was no relative of Roelof. He was probably not a Scandinavian: his name was often spelled Huys.

HERMAN HENDRICKSEN (ROSENKRANZ).

Herman Hendricksen (Rosenkranz) was from Bergen, Norway. It is not known when he came to New Amsterdam, where he, on March 3, 1657, married Magdalene Dircks (Madalena Dirx), widow of Cornelius Caper, or Cornelius Hendricksen from Dort. She had been married to her first husband on October 24, 1652.[133] At her marriage with Herman she had a minor child named Mara Cornelis, for whom she set apart 500 guilders, mortgaging her house and lot at New Amsterdam, next to Evert Duyckingh's.[134] She had become a widow in 1655, and as her deceased husband had no relations in New Netherland, and Jan Vinje was related to her, she requested, on November 9, 1655, the orphan-

---

131 New York Colonial Documents, XII., p. 149. Marritje or Maryken was baptised May 13, 1646. Her sponsors were the Director-General W. Kieft, and Anneken Loockerman. Arnoldus was baptised March 14, 1649. He probably died before 1656.

132 The Records of New Amsterdam, 1685-1674, II., p. 196.

133 The New York Genealogical and Biographical Report, VI., p. 85.

134 Year Book of the Holland Society of New York, 1900, p. 162.

masters that Jan Vinje and Hendrick Kip be appointed guardians for the child. The request was granted, but Vinje refused to serve. A week later the orphan-masters appointed as guardians of her child Abraham Verplanck and Andries de Haas.[135]

Only a few days after the wedding of Herman and Magdalena, the court records of New Amsterdam registered the following:

[March 15, 1657] "The Scout N: de Silla, pltf. v|s Madaleen Dirckx and her bridegroom, defts. The pltf. says that the defts. have presumed to insult the Firewardens of this City on the public highway, and to make a street riot, according to the complaint made to his Worship. Requesting for the maintenance of the aforesaid gentlemen's quality that the petitioners [?] be publicly punished or fined as their W. shall think proper. Deft. Madaleen Dircx appears alone in Court; admits, that she and her sister passed by the door of the Firewarden Litschoe, and as they always joked, when the Firewarden came to their house, she said:— 'there is the chimney sweep in the door, his chimney is well swept, and not another word was said about it.' And as such cannot, and ought not to be tolerated on account of its bad consequences, the Burgomasters condemn, as they do hereby, the abovenamed Madaleen Dircx in a fine of two pounds Flemish, to be applied, one half for the Church and one half for the Poor, and notify her at the same time to avoid all such and similar faults, or in default thereof other disposition shall be made. Done in Court at the City Hall at Amsterdam in N. Netherland." [136]

On August 13, 1657, "Herman Hendricksen conveyed to Joost Goderus a house and lot between Evert Duyckingh and Myndert Barents; width on the street 2 rods and 7 feet, and in the rear 1 rod, 8 feet. Depth on the east, 8 rods, and on the west 8 rods, 4 feet, being premises patented to Adrian Dircksen Coen, October, 1655." [137] This seems to have been the house Herman got by his marriage. It was situated at the present South William Street.

On November 12, 1658, Herman received the small burgher's

---

185 Ibid., p. 112. Jan Vinje was not, as has been supposed, a Scandinavian.
186 The Records of New Amsterdam, 1653-1674, VII., p. 146.
187 D. T. Valentine, Manual of the Corporation of the City of New York, 1861, p. 594.

right in New Amsterdam, for which he signed an obligation to pay to the treasurer twenty gulden in beavers within eight days.[138]

On April 12, 1659, he had his child, Alexander, baptized in the Dutch Reformed Church at New Amsterdam. The sponsors were Barent Gerritsen and Sarah Dircx, referred to above as the sister of Magdalene.[139]

After the birth of this child the parents seem to have moved to Esopus. On September 29, 1659, Herman Hendricksen escaped from the Indians at Esopus, by whom he had been kept a prisoner. On regaining his liberty he informed Ensign Dirck Smith of their strength.[140]

Other children were born to Herman and Magdalene: Annetje, who was baptized August 27, 1662, the sponsor being Lysbet Jans; Rachel, who was baptized October 21, 1663, at whose baptism Aechjen Ariaens acted sponsor; Harmanus, baptized May 2, 1666, the sponsor being Greetje Hendricks; Anna, who was baptized October 9, 1667, no name of any sponsor being given. All these children were baptized in the church at Esopus.[141] One of their children (no name given) was baptized April 28, 1674, in New Amsterdam.

It seems also that some other children were born in this marriage. For on January 17, 1726, Sarah Rosenkranz, who was perhaps the child above referred to as baptized in 1674, made a will which reads as follows:

"I, Sarah Rosenkrans, being in perfect health. I leave to my dear mother, Magdalena Rosenkrans, all my estate, real and personal, during her life, and after her decease as follows: To my brother, Alexander Rosenkrans, 6 shillings. All the rest to be divided into five parts; One part to my brother Hendrick, and after his decease to his son Hermanus; One part to my brother Dirck, and after his decease to his son Harsama; One part to my sister, Rachel Van Gorden, and after her decease to Harma Van Gorden; One part to my sister, Johana Davenport, and after her decease to her son John; One part to my sister, Christina Cortright, and after her decease to her son Hendrick Cortright. I

138 The Records of New Amsterdam, 1653-1674, VII., p. 200.
139 Collections of the New York Genealogical and Biographical Society, II., p. 52. Sara Dircks is called Sara Dircks de Noorman. Cf. Ibid., II., p. 55.
140 New York Colonial Documents, XIII., p. 115.
141 Hoes, Baptismal and Marriage Registers of the old Dutch Church of Kingston (Esopus).

PEDER JENSSØN, BAILIFF AND MEMBER OF THE COUNCIL OF BERGEN, NORWAY, 1640-1650.
From an etching by Jacob Maschius, of Bergen, about the middle of the seventeenth century.

leave to the children of Alexander Rosenkrans £30, viz.: Harma, Helena, and Johanes. I leave to Helena Davenport, 1 shilling or 12 pence, New York currency. To Sarah Cole and Christian Van Gorden, each 1 shilling. I make my brothers Hendrick and Dirck executors.

"Witness, Dirck Krans, Dirck De Witt, William Cortright. Proved in Ulster County, October 21, 1726." (See Collections New York Historical Society, for the Year 1893, p. 372.)

Under date of May 19, 1700, Magdalena Rosenkranz was sponsor at a baptism in Kingston.[142]

Herman must have had considerable property, for under date of January 19, 1681, a document, signed by five Indians, states:

"This day all the Indians have acknowledged that the land called Easineh, which Kentkamin has given to Harmen Hendricksen and Hendricus Beckman, shall belong to them and they may dispose of it at their pleasure." This and other papers were received in Court of Sessions of Sarah Rosenkranz, October 3, 1732.[143]

Herman Hendricksen died at Rochester, N. Y., about 1697. His descendants are known as the Rosenkrans family. The best known member of this family is General William Stark Rosecrans, born in Ohio, 1819. He was a graduate of West Point Academy. In the civil war he was commissioned as a Brigadier General of the Regular Army. In 1867 he resigned his commission in the army, and was afterwards Minister to Mexico. He served one term as Congressman from California, and as the first Register of the Treasury under President Cleveland. While at West Point he was converted to the Roman Catholic faith. His brother Sylvester Horton Rosecrans became a prominent bishop of the Roman Catholic Church.

In 1890, a genealogy of the Rosenkrans family was published, the author being Allen Rosenkrans. It gives the history of the family, and makes public much of the correspondence passed between the author and various archives and legations in Europe, for the purpose of ascertaining whence Herman Hendricksen originally came. "Rosenkrans" may be German, Dutch, Danish,

142 Ibid., Reference 39.
143 New York Colonial History, XIII., p. 402. Harmen Hend ↑en Rosen-krans must not be confounded with Harmen Hendricksen, mentioned i\, anes', New Amsterdam and Its People, p. 168.

Norwegian. There is a possibility that Herman was related to Henrik Rosenkrans who between 1617 and 1629 obtained permission to the fisherey of herring and whales at the coast of Greenland and Norway. This Henrik was likely an immigrated Hollander, not, however, of the nobility.

Herman Hendricksen was in all probability a plain born Norwegian, without title, and without Dutch pedigree. There were many Herman Hendricksens in New Netherland, and still more in Scandinavia. Why should Herman, in order to avoid a confusion of names, not add a new surname, taking the name of one, for whom he, perhaps, had worked in Bergen. There would be no objection to doing this in the New World. The writer knows of an instance when a Norwegian immigrant, some forty years ago took the surname of Kraft. He had worked for a Norwegian official by that name. Other Norwegians, upon coming to our country, have taken the name of the manor where they had worked or were born.

DIRCK HOLGERSEN.

Dirck Holgersen, or Dirck Volckertsen Noorman, was from Norway. We do not know when he came to New Netherland. He was, however, one of its early settlers. The claim of J. H. Innes [144] and others that Holgersen is the same person as Dirck Vockertsen, in Hoorn, who chartered a ship to carry on trade with New Netherland, is unfounded. Equally unfounded is the claim that he is the brother of a contemporary Cornelius Volckertsen, in New Amsterdam.

The fact is that there was a Dirck Volckertsen and a Cornelius Volckertsen in Hoorn, who as early as 1614 had mercantile interests in the New World, but remained in the Old. There was also a Dirck "Volckertsen" (Holgersen), and a Cornelius Volckertsen in New Amsterdam. These were not brothers: the sources do not indicate that they had any particular interests in common; that they either associated at the usual family gatherings or gave any other evidence of consanguineous relationship. Cornelius was probably Dutch, he was never called Cornelius Holgersen. Dirck

---

144 J. H. Innes, New Amsterdam and Its People.

Volckertsen can be a Dutch name. (As early as 1522 a Dirck Volkertzoon Coornhert, known in the annals of theology, saw the light of day). Dirck Holgersen was a Norwegian, as is indicated by the cognomen "Noorman," so frequently given to him in the sources, (Dirck = Hendrick or Didrik). Whenever he is called "Volckertsen," a corruption of "Holgersen" is evident.[145]

Dirck Holgersen married, before 1632, Christine Vigne, a daughter of Adrienne (Ariantje) Cuville and Guillaume Vigne, Walloons from Valenciennes in the north-eastern part of France. Adrienne and Guillaume had four children: Jan Vigne, who was probably the first white child born in New Netherland; Maria, who was married to Abraham Verplanck; Christine, the wife of Dirck Holgersen; and Rachel, the wife of Cornelius van Tienhoven. Guillaume died before 1632, when Jan Jansen Damen married his widow.[146]

Signatures of Dirck Holgersen, 1651, 1658, 1661.

Jan Jansen Damen did not like the husbands of his stepdaughters, because they would not leave him master of his house. In July, 1638, he brought suit against Abraham Verplanck and Dirck Holgersen: "On motion of the plaintiff the defendants were ordered to quit his house and to leave him master thereof." Dirck, however, charged Jan Damen with assault and furnished witnesses who testified "regarding an attempt of Jan Damen to throw his step-daughter, Christine, Dirck's wife, out of doors."[147] The published sources give no information as to how the matter was settled.

On May 1, 1638, Holgersen gave a note to Director Kieft for 720 guilders ($288, in present value $1,152).[148] On May 18, 1639, Kieft leased to him a "bouwery and stock on halves."[149]

On January 2, 1642, the Fiscal arrested Gerrit Gerritsen and

145 J. O. Evjen, Nordmænd i Amerika i det syttende Aarhundrede, in "Folkebladet" (Minneapolis), February 2, 1910. Cornelis Volckertsen was fined in 1642 for having kept a disorderly house. Simon Volckertsen was whipped, and banished from New Amsterdam in 1644. Neither of these nor a Henry Volckertsen, mentioned in a contemporary document (1635), appears to have been Scandinavian.
146 The Records of New Amsterdam, 1653-1674, II., p. 849, note.
147 Calendar of Historical Manuscripts, I., p. 163.
148 Ibid., I., p. 2.
149 Ibid., I., p. 8.

Dirck Holgersen for stealing rope from the yacht of the West India Company. Gerritsen was brought, in chains, to the guard house; Holgersen was ordered not to leave until the case had been decided. Two weeks later Holgersen declared, on oath, that he had bought the rope of Gerritsen in good faith. The court now ordered that Gerritsen and the sailors of the yacht "Reael" should appear on the next court day "in order to determine by lot which of them shall be punished, or meanwhile satisfy the Fiscal."[150]

In November, 1642, Holgersen conveyed to Govert Aertsen a house and lot on Manhattan Island.[151]

On April 3, 1645, he obtained a grant of twenty-five morgens (fifty acres) on East River and Mespath Kill.[152] He sold a portion of this, September 9, 1653, to Jacob Hay (Haes),[153] who appears to have married his daughter Christina.

On July 2, 1647, he was given power of attorney by Albert Govertsen to receive money from the West India Company.[154]

On June 2, 1649, he gave a lease of land to Jochem Calder. This lease is signed by three Norwegians. It reads as follows:

"Before me, Cornelis van Tienhoven, Secretary of New Netherland, appeared Jochem Calder of the one part, and Dirck Holgersen, of the other part, who in presence of the undernamed witnesses, acknowledged and declared that they had in all love and friendship mutually entered into and concluded a certain contract in regard to the lease of a certain tract of land on the condition hereuntowritten:

"Dirck Holgersen leases to Jochem Calder a certain lot of land, situate on Long Island, together with the land heretofore leased by him, Dirck, to Jochem Calder, for the term of twenty consecutive years, commencing Anno 1651 and ending Anno 1671. The Lessee shall have the land rent free for the first six years, and during the other fourteen following years shall pay, annually, for the use of said land, which big and little he shall cultivate and improve as he thinks proper, the sum of one hundred and fifty guilders in such pay as shall then be current. All the expenses that the Lessee shall incur in building, fencing and whatever else

---

150 Calendar of Historical Manuscripts, I., pp. 78, 79.
151 Ibid., I., p. 88.
152 E. B. O'Callaghan, History of New Netherland, I., p. 583.
153 Ibid., I., p. 278.
154 Calendar of Historical Manuscripts, I., p. 88.

is necessary shall be at the charge of the Lessee, who shall make such improvements as he will think fit; and if it happen that he, the Lessee, should die, it is stipulated that the Lessor shall not eject the wife or descendants from the land against their will. The fences and other improvements, of what nature soever they may be made by the Lessee, shall at the termination of the twenty years, belong to the Lessor, his heirs and descendants in full propriety without disbursing anything thereof.

"For further security and the performance of this contract, parties pledge their respective persons and properties, submitting to that end to all Courts and Judges.

"In testimony this is signed by the parties with Jan Nagel and Peter Jansen Noorman witnesses hereunto subscribed, this 2d of June Anno 1649, New Amsterdam.

"This is the ✕ mark of Dirck Holgersen made by himself.

"This is the + mark of Jochem Calder made by himself.

"This is the PI mark of Peter Jansen, witness, made by himself.

"Jacob Kip } Witnesses." [155]
"Jan Nagel }

On March 22, 1651, Holgersen sold to Peter Hudde and Abraham Jansen a parcel of land on "Mespachtes Kill opposite Richard Bridnels" twenty-two morgens, one hundred and thirty-six rods. We give the deed of sale below:

"Before me, Jacob Kip, in the absence of the Secretary appointed by the Honorable Director-General and Council of New Netherland, appeared Dirck Holgersen, an inhabitant here who declared that he sold and conveyed, as he does hereby, to Peter

155 New York Colonial Documents, XIV., p. 115.

Hudde and Abraham Jansen, in company, a certain parcel of land situate on Mespachtes Kill opposite Richard Bridnels, formerly the property of one Cornelis Willemsen, containing according to the groundbrief, twenty-two morgens, one hundred and thirty-six rods; which land he, the grantor, conveys to the said Peter Hudde and Abraham Jansen, in company, in one, true, free, and right ownership, therefore renouncing the right and property had thereto, with authority to enter on, cultivate and use the said land free and unmolested, on condition that the reservation mentioned in the ground brief in regard to the acknowledgement of the Lords and Patroons of this country be complied with; placing the said Peter Hudde and Abram Jansen in his stead, real and actual possession of the land aforesaid, and renouncing all pretension thereto henceforth, and for ever he promises to hold fast and inviolable this his deed and conveyance under bond as by law provided.

"In testimony I have signed this with the witnesses, this 22d of March, Anno 1651, New Amsterdam in New Netherland.

"This is the √ mark of Dirck Holgersen made by himself.

"Jacob Jansen Huys, witness.
"Gerrit Jansen, witness.
            "To my knowledge ———— Jacob Kip, Clerk.

"This day the 28th of March Anno 1651, the Hon'ble Petrus Stuyvesant and Council of New Netherland approved this foregoing proof of the purchase of the land mentioned, and accordingly the conveyance above executed by Dirck Holgersen in favor of Peter Hudde and Abraham Jansen is held valid.

"In testimony this is signed by the Hon'ble Director-General; dated as above, Manhatan in New Netherland.
            "P. Stuyvesant." [156]

On September 18, 1651, Holgersen conveyed to Roelof Teunissen, a Swedish sea captain from Göteborg, a house and lot in Smith's Valley on Manhattan Island. He had had this place since 1645, and built a house upon it. It must have stood upon

---

156 Ibid., XI., p. 187f.

the whole or a part of the site of the modern building, No. 259 Pearl Street.[157]

On September 9, 1653, Holgersen conveyed to Jacob Jansen Hey (Huys or Haes) twenty-five morgens of land, with a valley of six morgens, "beginning at the hook of Mespacht's kill, Long Island, and thence running S.S.W. along the river." [158]

On October 15, 1653, he sold a lot to Hage Bruynsen, who was from Sweden. This lot was situated on Smith's valley, "fronting on the strand or highway." [159] On February 16, 1654, he brought suit against Hage Bruynsen for payment of this lot.[160]

On October 15, 1655, he was taxed fl. 10.[161]

Under date of October 25, 1655, the court minutes contain the following entry with respect to Holgersen:

"Reyer Stoffelsen vs. Dirk Holgersen. Defendant in default. Default was granted only for the payment of fl. 9 (?), now due since three years." [162] Under date of November 8, the same year, the minutes state: "Sybout Claesen, as att'y for Reyer Stoffelsen, pltf. v|s Dirck Holgersen, deft. Defts. 2d default. Being for payment of fl. 8 belonging to Reyer Stoffelsen. Requests sequestration and satisfaction. The Court ordered, as Dirck Holgersen is in the second default, that he deposit the said fl. 8. within 8 days in the Secretary's office." [163]

The next lawsuit in which Holgersen was involved was due to his having wounded a cooper in a fight. We shall give the history of this case, following as much as possible the version of the court minutes:

[Jan. 8, 1656] "Jan de Perie pltf. vs Dirck de Noorman deft. Pltf. exhibits pursuant to the order of 18th Dec. last, two separate declarations, one of Jan Fredricksen and one of Paulus Heymans, by which it appears, that Dirck de Noorman attacked him, the pltf., and chased him from the Strand to the Clapboards, as is

157 Calendar of Historical Manuscripts, I., p. 55. J. H. Innes, New Amsterdam and Its People, p. 323.
158 Calendar of Historical Manuscripts, I., p. 378.
159 Ibid., I., p. 379.
160 The Records of New Amsterdam, 1653-1674, I., p. 161.
161 Ibid., I., p. 374.
162 Ibid., I., p. 386.
163 Ibid., I., p. 390. In this suit Dirck is called Volckertsen. In quoting the court minutes here and in other pertinent places, we have substituted "Holgersen" for the corrupted "Volckertsen".

more fully detailed in the certificates rendered before Notary de
Vos. Requesting as before that the deft. be therefore condemned
in the time lost by him and Surgeon's fees. Deft. says that he
was not the first to draw his knife, but that the pltf. had forced
him to do it, he having first struck him on his shoulder with a
knife, which he also broke having struck his truss, and afterwards
tried to kill him with a naked dagger. The court ordered the
deft. to prove his statement by the next Court day." [164]

Several months passed, and the case was still pending.
Schout d'Silla then made the demand, October 30, 1656, that "the
Court appoint Commissaries to take information in his presence
as to how Dirck Holgersen wounded Jan Perie. The request
being deemed just, Schepens Jacob Strycker and Hendrick Kip
are appointed Commissioners." [165]

On December 11 "Jan de Pree" requested "by petition, that Dirck
Holgersen be ordered to settle with him for the pain, surgeon's
bill, and loss of time which he incurred from a stab in the side received from said Dirck. Whereupon is endorsed — The petitioner
may summon his party at the next Court day, and then, if he thinks
fit, institute his action." [166]

A week later "Jan de Pree" renewed his demand in writing.
Schout d'Silla maintained, however, that "the plaintiff has no
cause of action, as he began the quarrel, and wounded the defendant by sticking a knife in his body. And whereas the defendant is in default, the plaintiff was ordered to summon him
again, and then to prove his statement."

Holgersen now summoned a Jan Peeck, his wife Mary, and
Perie's servant, Jan Fredricksen, to appear in court and testify
to the truth of what they saw and heard transpiring between himself and Jan Perie. [167]

The court minutes record the following concerning the testimony of Jan and Mary Peeck:

[Jan. 27, 1657.] "Dirck Holgersen, pltf. v|s Jan Peeck and
his wife, Mary, defts. Pltf. requests that defts., whom he has
summoned as witnesses in the case between him and Jan Perie,

164 Ibid., II., p. 256.
165 Ibid., II., p. 200.
166 Ibid., II., p. 246.
167 Ibid., II., p. 247.

cooper, would please testify to the truth. Jan Peeck therefore declared that in the morning as he lay abed, he saw Jan Perie and Dirck Holgersen playing at dice together on the floor for a . . . and heard Jan Perie, while playing, give Dirck Holgersen frequently the lie, whereupon Dirck Holgersen contradicted, and a fist fight followed: and as he, deponent, said to them that he could easily sell his wine without trouble, they went away, without his knowing anything more. Mary d' Peeck, also heard, confirms the declaration of her husband above given and declares she after-wards heard Jan Perie say, "There's Dirck the Noorman, who has a box of seawan in his sack, and he should play or the D . . . should take him"; also, that Jan Perie's man told her, he saw his master thrust his knife into Dirck Noorman's truss. Dirck Holgersen answers in writing Jan Perie's demand, concluding that the pltf. John Perie's entered demand be dismissed and he be con-demned the costs. Whereupon asked if he have further evidence, he says, Yes; Jan Perie's man, but that the others have been to him, and he is gone away. Wherefore the case is postponed."[168]

What Perie's servant testified is seen in the following:

[January 29, 1657.] "Dirck Holgersen v|s Jan Fredericksen, Jan Perie's servant, deft. Pltf. requests, that deft. shall testify to the truth before the Court as to what he saw relative to the drawing of the knife between him pltf. and Jan Perie. Therefore aforesaid deft. appeared in Court and declares he saw, on coming out of the house, Jan Perie and Dirck Holgersen standing opposite each other, each with a knife in his hand, and that Dirck Holger-sen thrust first, and stabbed Jan Perie in his belly, and that Jan Perie then thrust with the point of the knife on Dirck Holgersens truss, and saw Jan Perie afterwards chase Dirck Holgersen with a dagger. And further he cannot declare."[169]

The case was begun in December, 1655. It concluded June 29, 1658, when Holgersen, who was then city carpenter, consented to pay the fine for wounding Jan Perie.[170]

Holgersen, in the mean time, had been having other litiga-

168 Ibid., II., p. 271. Jan Peeck was an eccentric character, Indian trader, broker, speculator. His wife, Mary, was in 1664 fined 500 guilders and banished from Manhattan Island for selling liquor to the Indians (Innes, New Amsterdam and Its People,, p. 801).
169 Ibid., II., p. 278.
170 Calendar of Historical Manuscripts, I., p. 190.

tion. On February 8, 1656, he had been sued for a canoe which he had found on his land, had repaired and would not surrender before he had been paid for repairs and salvage. The court minutes state:

"Dirck Claessen Pottebacker, pltf. v|s Dirck Holgersen, deft. Pltf's wife appeared in Court, says that she has missed a canoe, which she purchased from Peter Van der Linde and after seeking for it everywhere, finally found it before deft's house and land, who refused the same to her, notwithstanding reasonable salvage was offered. Requests the Court condemn him to deliver it. Deft. says a certain canoe was brought by some Englishmen on his land, and as the same lay a long time there without a person coming after it, he found, that it was very much out of repair. He repaired it and rebuilt it. Offers to give it up to the pltf. on the condition that she will pay him for the repairs, wages, and salvage. Parties being heard, the Court referred the parties to Lambert Huybersen Mol, and Cornelis Jansen Clopper to value the labor and repair expended on the canoe, and if possible to reconcile the parties, or to report to the Board." [171]

On April 3, 1656, Holgersen was sued by Symon Joosten for a debt. The Fiscal "remained bail for the payment." Holgersen was ordered "to make an assignment when the Fiscal undertakes to pay." [172]

On March 8, 1658, Holgersen and Maria Verplanck, his sister-in-law, were sued by Claes van Elslandt, elder of the Dutch Reformed Church in New Amsterdam, for not paying for a grave. According to the court minutes, Claes van Elslandt claimed that "the defendants refused to pay the Church money for a grave of their deceased mother," Ariantje, who died 1655. (She was the mother of Maria Verplanck, and mother-in-law of Holgersen.) The defendants replied that they had not refused, "as they have once paid and counted the money to Cornelis van Tienhoven," their brother-in-law. Claes van Elslandt was then asked, why he was so slow in collecting the Church fees. He replied that Cornelis had said, "there are y o u r fees, I shall make it right with the Church wardens." The defendants claimed they paid fifty guilders

---

171 The Records of New Amsterdam, 1653-1674, II., p. 38.
172 Ibid., II., p. 83.

—thirty guilders in Holland currency and the remainder in sea-wan. After hearing this, the court ordered that the heirs in common should satisfy the Church wardens within a week.[173] Holgersen and his wife Christine were members of the Dutch Reformed Church in New Amsterdam since 1649.[174]

In April, 1657, Holgersen acquired the small burgher's rights in New Amsterdam.

In the same year he deeded to Roeloff Teunissen some property that had been conveyed to himself on August 4, 1649. It was on the present west side of Pearl Street, near the north corner of Lane.[175]

After the cessation of the Indian troubles Dirck Holgersen appears to have removed to his farm at Norman's Kill. For in a deed of October 17, 1661, "Dirck Volkers, of Bushwyck, as husband and guardian of Christina Vinge, daughter of the late Geleyn Vinge and Adriana Cuvilje," conveyed to Augustine Herman, "his certain fourth part of the inheritance and succession which belongs to him from his wife's parents, except the eighth part of the fourth part of a little field to pasture cattle, situated on the Maadge Paadje, in the rear of Lysbet Tysen" (Valentine, Manual of . . . the city of New York, 1865, p. 686f).[176]

On March 24, 1662, some landowners of Bushwick, of whom Holgersen was one, petitioned those in authority to get a road made through their land at Bushwick.

In April, 1662, they petitioned the Director-General and Council to be excused from fencing in their lands, "especially as wood is growing scarce around there and hard to obtain, and the fences would cost a great deal."

It appears that Holgersen gave some of his land to the village of Bushwick.[177] He was a magistrate of the place in 1681, and ensign of the local militia in 1689. He was assessed there in 1675. But also the city of New York taxed him fl. 5, in 1677. In 1674 his name is found on a list of owners of houses and lots of the city of New Amsterdam. His property was classed in "fourth

---

173 Ibid., II., p. 850.
174 Ibid., II., p. 849.
175 D. T. Valentine, Manual of the Corporation of the City of New York, 1861, p. 597.
176 Cf. New York Colonial Documents, XIV., p. 511.
177 Ibid., XIV., pp. 523, 524.

class" property, no value being given.[178] It was situated on the west side of the present Pearl St., between Franklin Square and Wall St., known at that time as Smith's Valley.

Dirck Holgersen had several children. On September 8, 1641, his daughter Rachel was baptized, one of the sponsors being a Norwegian, Laurens Pietersen Noorman; his son Volckert was baptized in November, 1643; his daughter Ariaentje (Adrienne), August 21, 1650; his daughter Janneken, December 7, 1653, when Pieter Jansen Noorman, a Norwegian, acted as sponsor.

According to J. H. Innes, Dirck had also a daughter called Christina Cappoens, who was first married to Jacob Jansen Huys (Hey, Heys, Hes, Haes), a skipper who had lived in the West Indies. Her second husband was David Jochemsen.

The entire tract of land which Holgersen had in Bushwick eventually "came into the hands of the Meserole family, descendants of Dirck's daughter, Christina, who held it until recent years, and may still have some portions of it."[179]

---

178 Minutes of the Common Council of the City of New York, 1675-1776, 1905, I., p. 50. Year Book of Holland Society, 1896, p. 167.

179 J. H. Innes, New Amsterdam and Its People, p. 328.

Whence the name Cappoens (Cappoen, Capoen)? In Dutch we have the name "kapoen," but this would hardly be the word from which Christina derived the name. In Norwegian "kapöen" means cape island. When I mentioned this, in a letter to Mr. J. H. Innes, as the possible meaning of "Cappoens," he replied:

"I think you have probably hit the point. The Dirck Volckertsen farm, of which the Northern half was conveyed to Jacob Hale, first husband of Christina, was really a peninsula lying at the mouth of the Mespat Kill . . . The place has always been known as the "point," . . . Green Point . . . . Bushwick Point . . . . Wood Point. Christina married again, but seems to have retained possession of the farm, which passed to her daughter Maria by Jacob Hale, and she (Maria) married Peter Praa van Landt of the old Bogardus farm, on the opposite side of the Mespat Kill, and from these the Meseroles and other late possessors of the property are derived.

"Adopting a very common custom around old New York, which I believe is also common among the Northern nations of Europe, of designating persons by their dwelling place . . . ., nothing is more likely, it seems to me, than that Christina was known among her Scandinavian neighbors as Christina Kapöen's—'at the Cape Island,' or 'at the Point'—the corrupted form no doubt came from the Dutch spelling."

In June, 1687, Christina made her will, her second husband being dead. She gave to her daughter, Maria Hays, "first my small house," "the income of my land and meadow and Bowerey lying at Maspeth Kills," and "my silver beaker, one gold vase, diamond ring, a silver cup and pepper box, and a silver cup with silver cover, and three silver spoons." To her grand-daughter, Sara Molenaer, she left her "great house," also "a saltcellar marked with the full name of Christina Roselaers and marked with her coat of arms (was she the mother of Hay?), also a silver beaker marked the same, and a silver mustard pot marked with the name of Jacob Hay. Also my Church book with silver clasps and chain, and a silver cup and six silver spoons and a silver chain, one great ear spangle with ear jewels, and my largest hoop ring, and a gold finger ring with a diamond in it, and a silver tumbler marked J. H."—To her granddaughter Catrina Praa she left a silver beaker and six silver spoons marked J. H. . . . .

The "great house and lot"' is now No. 61 Stone Street. The "small house and lot" is now the narrow alley leading from Stone Street to South William Street, and between Nos. 61 and 63 Stone Street. It is the only street in the City of New York without an official name, but was in former days popularly known as

Under date of December 14, 1643, the church record states
that Holgersen's wife acted as sponsor for a child belonging to
Roland Hackwardt. On June 5, 1650, both Holgersen and his wife
stood sponsors at the baptism of a child belonging to Jochem
Kier (Kalder) and his wife Magdalena, a Lutheran woman. Holgersen had leased some of his land to Kalder in 1649. April 28,
1651, Holgersen stood sponsor for the child of Jan Hermanszen
Schutt and Margaritje Dennis.[180]

PAULUS JANSEN.

Paulus Jansen, referred to as Paulus Jansz Noorman and
Paulus de Noorman, was from Norway. He was in New Netherland as early as November 14, 1641, when he brought a suit against
Maryn Adriaensen et al. The nature of this suit is not revealed
in the sources at our disposal, which merely state that it was referred to arbitration.[181] We glean from the records that Jansen
was wounded at three different times. First by Jacob Lambertsz
van Dortland, who in April, 1648, was prosecuted for committing
this deed; a second time, by a carpenter, Jacob Jans Flodder
(Gardenir), from Kampen.[182] He was wounded, the third time,
in the war at Esopus: June 7, 1663 "Paulus Noorman was found
wounded in the streets of Wiltwyck" (=Esopus).[183] He was
sergeant at Esopus as early as 1660.[184] Under date of May 1,
1664, Jan Martensen, at Esopus, made a written statement that

"Jews' Alley" (Mr. W. S. Pelletreau, in "Collections of the New York Historical
Society, XXV., p. 229).

The inventory of the estate of Christina Cappoens shows a very long list of
household goods, besides a considerable amount of silver ware:
  1 Silver Beaker, 12 oz., at 7s., £4.4s.
  1 Gold rose diamond ring, £5.
  1 Silver pepper box, 2½ oz., at 7s., 17s. 6d.
  1 Silver beaker, marked Christina Rasselaers, 16 oz., at 7s., £5.12s.
  1 Silver salt cellar, marked Christina Rasselaers, 14 oz., £4, 10s.
  1 Church book with silver clasps and chain, £1, 16s.
  1 Golden ear pendant, 2 oz., good, at £5 per oz., £10.
    180 Collections of the New York Genealogical and Biographical Society, II.
    181 Calendar of Historical Manuscripts, I., p. 77.
    182 Van Rensselaer Bowier Manuscripts, pp. 832, 838.
    183 New York Colonial Documents, XIII., p. 247.
    184 Ibid., XIII., p. 158.

he was indebted to "Paulus Noorman" for the sum of twenty-eight guilders.[185]

JAN JANSEN NOORMAN.

Jan Jansen Noorman was, according to Munsell's Collections on the History of Albany (IV., p. 88), a resident of Albany, from 1673 to 1696. He married Susanna Dirx, the widow of Dirck Dircksen Mayer. On April 21, 1673, Jan Jansen Noorman and his wife made their will, the witnesses being Pieter Ryverdingh, David Schuyler and Adrianvan Ilpendam. The contents of the will are not given in the printed sources.[186] One Jan de Noorman who obtained, April 28, 1667, "a lot ten rods in length and four rods in breadth" is probably Jan Jansen Noorman.[187]

JAN JANSZEN.

Jan Janszen and wife arrived at New Amsterdam in 1663. Their ship, "de Statyn," set sail from Holland, September 27, 1663. In the passenger list Norway is given as the place from which they emigrated. At least two, if not four, other passengers in their company were from Norway.[188]

MRS. JAN JANSZEN.

Mrs. Jan Janszen arrived at New Amsterdam in 1663. She came in company with her husband. Both were from Norway. See article "Jan Janszen."

---

185 J. Pearson, Early Records of . . . Albany, p. 350. The Paulus Jansen who acquired land near Wilmington (New York Colonial Documents, XII., p. 183), is a different person.

We venture here to correct a statement in O'Callaghan's History of New Netherland, II., p. 585, viz., that "Claes Jansen Noorman" was granted on March 25, 1647, twenty-five morgens of land on the West side of the North River. "Noorman" must here be a corruption of "Naerden," or perhaps what is a better explanation, Claes, is a corrupt reading for Paulus = Paulus Jansen Noorman.

186 Calendar of Wills, Compiled by B. Fernow, p. 289.

187 Munsell, Collections of the History of Albany, IV., p. 417.

188 Year Book of the Holland Society of New York, 1901, p. 26.

PIETER JANZEN.

Pieter Janzen, of Fredrikstad, was in New Netherland about 1658. All we know concerning him is contained in two entries in the court minutes of New Amsterdam:

1. (September 17, 1658) "Jan Rutgerzen, pltf. v|s Mr. Allerton, deft. Pltf. again demands from deft. payment of the sum of fl. 121.6 for two obligations executed by Pieter Janzen of Frederickstatt and Barent Eversen of Stockholm, for which the deft. has signed bail to pay him. Deft. says, he will prove, that the abovenamed Pieter Janzen of Frederickstatt and Barent Evertsen of Stockholm, had determined to run away from the ship; maintaining therefore he is not bound to pay. The Court orders the deft. to give security for the monies, and to prove within three weeks that the abovenamed Pieter Janzen of Frederickstatt and Barent Eversen of Stockholm were willing to run away from the ship." [189]

2. (May 8, 1663) "Pieter Janzen Noorman, pltf. v|s Joris Dopzen, deft. Deft. in default. Pltf. says he is a foreigner and is about to depart; as he cannot come to any settlement with the deft. he requests an order to settle together. Burgomasters and Schepens order Joris Dopzen to settle with Pieter Janzen Noorman without delay, as he is about to depart and is a foreigner." [190]

PIETER JANSEN.

Pieter Jansen, or Pieter Jansen Noorman, sometimes called Pieter Jansen Trynenburgh (Trimbol, Tribolt) was, according to the records of the Dutch Reformed Church in New Amsterdam, a native of Norway.[191] These records also show that he was

---

189 The Records of New Amsterdam, 1658-1674, III., p. 11.
190 Ibid., IV., p. 286. He must not be taken for Pieter Jansen Noorman, who died in 1662. See the following article.
191 Collections of the New York Genealogical and Biographical Society, I., p. 14. Perhaps he was from Trelleborg, which has belonged to Sweden since 1658.

sponsor at the baptism of Norwegian children, e. g.: On July 5, 1646, he was sponsor for Engel, a child belonging to Laurens Pietersen; November 4, 1646, for Michel, a son of Han Hansen from Bergen; December 7, 1653, for Janneken, a daughter of Dirck Holgersen.[192]

He married on July 7, 1647, Lysbeth Jansen of Amsterdam.[193]

On March 9, 1644, he testified that he had been present at the burning of Jochem Pietersen Kuyter's house by the Indians, and that the government soldiers did not come out from the place they were sleeping, until the house was entirely burned down. Jansen was at the time twenty years of age.[194] He had been in the employ of the brave Dane Jochem Pietersen Kuyter. At the fearful night of the burning of the property of Kuyter, the savages had their own way, as the defense was in minority, consisting only of dairymaids four soldiers and five laborers, of whom Jansen was one.[195]

On March 11, 1647, Jansen in company with Huyck Aertsen received a groundbrief of land, 74 morgens, 106 rods between Montagishay valley and Tobias Teunissen's bowery "extending to the end of the kill [196] coming out of the North River and thence N.E. and S. by N. along the high hill on Manhattan Island."[197] The next year Aertsen died, and Jansen was left in sole care of the bowery.

On April 27, 1649, Pieter Jansen mortgaged to Jan Forbus, a Swede, a tract of land on the East River "formerly occupied by the Norwegian Claes Carstensen, David Andriesen and George Baxter.[198] It appears that Forbus had sold this tract of land to him.

Pieter Jansen was involved in much litigation on account of his land, some of which he leased to Herman Barensen and finally sold to Jan Cornelisen Zealander.

The Court minutes throw some light upon this litigation.

Under date of August 8, 1658, Wilhelm Beeckman brought suit against Pieter Jansen Noorman: The plaintiff demanded of

192 Ibid., II.
193 Ibid., I., p. 14.
194 New York Colonial Documents, XIV., p. 53.
195 J. Riker, Harlem, Its Origin and Early Annals, 1904, p. 148.
196 Sherman's Creek.
197 Calendar of Historical Manuscripts, I., p. 372.
198 Ibid., I., p. 46.

the defendant "a balance of about the sum of 230 gl., which he deft. agreed to pay for Jan Forbis, and says he agreed with deft. for firewood to be delivered to him, of which he has remained in default and afterwards offered him, pltf., pease, demanding pay-- ment with damages and cost. Deft. says he bought a piece of land from Jan Forbis of three times 25 morgens and he has not conveyed it to him, maintaining that so long as it is not delivered he is not bound to pay Heer Beeckman and that he has nothing to do with the Heer Beekman. Pltf. exhibits to the Court the deed of sale, in which it is mentioned that the land must first be paid for before it shall be conveyed. The Court having heard parties, condemn the deft. to pay the pltf. the sum demanded with costs thereon in the space of one month."[199]

Under date of September 3, 1658, Pieter Jansen brought suit against Herman Barensen, who appears to have been in litigation quite often and was finally banished from New Netherland.

"Pieter Jansen Noorman, pltf. v|s Hermen Barensen, deft. Pltf. says, he hired his land to the deft. for the time of six years for which the deft. shall pay rent for the first year fl. 250 and every year after fl. 300 to the end of the lease according to contract exhibited in Court, but that the deft. has not fulfilled the contract. Deft. answers he leased the land from the pltf., when the grain was standing and he could not examine it; and afterwards found, that the land was nothing else than rocks and stone and [he] could not make that money of it, and aided the pltf. 15 days: also that he the pltf. leased the land again for fl. 600 for four years, being willing to prove it. Pieter Jansen is asked if he has hired the land again? Answers, he has partly agreed with Lauwerens Grootschoe, but has not concluded, as he wants fl. 200 (?) a year and Lauwerens will not give more than fl. 200." The Court ordered the defendant Herman Barensen to prove on next court day, that the pltf. Pieter Jansen has re-leased the land.[200]

On the next court day Barensen was in default.

Pieter Jansen also had some difficulties with Jan Cornelisen, to whom he had sold some land.

---

199 The Records of New Amsterdam, 1658-1674, II., p. 371.

200 Ibid., II., p. 2. Grootschoe (Big Shoe) was a nickname for Laurens Duyts, a Dane.

He brought suit against Cornelisen on January 27, 1660, claiming that Cornelisen had "refused [to allow him] to ride over his land, over which a wagon-road passes and has been [refusing this] for some years, and that he permits freely the deft. to ride over his valley." To quote from the Court Records, he "requests the Magistrates will be pleased to aid him therein. Deft. appeals to the ground brief, saying, if this be exibited, it could be seen where the fault lies and the Magistrates could find more light. The Court orders Pieter the Noorman to produce the ground brief on the next court day." [201]

PI

Signature of Pieter Jansen.

A few days later Cornelisen appeared in court. But he was ordered to have Pieter Jansen notified by the Court Messenger.

On February 10, 1660, the two litigants again appeared.

Cornelisen's demand was, that the defendant should exhibit the ground brief, so as to see the error in question. "Deft. exhibits the ground brief. Pltf. says, he bought 25 morgens of land from deft., showing a declaration dated 7th February, 1660, of Lauwerens Pieters and Barent Joosten, who testify that Pieter the Noorman sold the 25 morgens to Jan Cornelissen. Deft. says, he sold pltf. no more, than Claas van Elslant measured, and the land was pointed out in the pltf's presence. Jan Cornelisen, the Zealander, is asked why he summoned Pieter the Noorman? Answers on a|c of the cart road and declares, that the witnesses heard from Pieter the Noorman, that he sold to Jan Cornelisen the Zealander 25 morgens of land and says, no one but they and their wives were by at the sale. The Court orders pltf. to bring in proper form a notarial declaration, that deft. sold him twenty-five morgens of land." [202]

Cornelisen next appeared in Court on March 2, and produced the notarial declaration of Lauwerens Pieters and Barent Joosten, dated February 25, 1660. They stated they heard Jansen say that he sold Cornelisen twenty-five morgens of land. Jansen now requested copy of the declaration, but Cornelisen demanded "to proceed for costs and damages." This demand was granted.

---

201 Ibid., III., p. 115.
202 Ibid., III., p. 185.

On March 16, Jansen answered the declaration of the persons produced by Jan Cornelisen, and the Court ordered a copy to be furnished to Cornelisen. The latter did not seem to mind, and on April 27, 1660, Pieter Jansen requested that Cornelisen give a reply:

"Pieter Jansen Trynenburgh, alias Noorman, requests by petition, that Jan Cornelisen the Zealander shall be again ordered to render his reply on the next Court day, on pain of nonsuit with costs, inasmuch as he has remained in default to reply according to the order of the 16th March last. Jan Cornelisen the Zealander is hereby for the second time ordered by the court of this city to prosecute his suit, that he has against Pieter Jansen Noorman, and to reply to the aforesaid Pieter Jansen's answer on the next Court day."[203]

It seems as if Cornelisen finally dropped the case. We hear nothing more of it.

Jansen's litigation with Cornelisen caused him to sue Forbus, who had sold him the land but failed to give him the deed. The matter was treated in court, resulting in a letter sent to Forbus by the secretary of the Council of New Amsterdam. It was dated February 7, 1660:

"Jan Forbus— Whereas you have as yet failed to convey in due form to Pieter Jansen Trynburgh, commonly called Pieter the Noorman, the land you sold to aforesaid Pieter Jansen and for which you received payment; and Pieter Jansen has sold the land again to Jan Cornelisen the Zealander, and Jan Cornelisen demands the deeds of said lands from him; and whereas Pieter Jansen has received as yet no deed from you, therefore cannot give any conveyance: you are in consequence hereby ordered and charged by the Presiding Burgomaster to come immediately hither and to convey the aforesaid land to the above named Pieter Jansen and in default thereof to bear all costs that may accrue thereto. Whereby you have to regulate yourself.

---

203 Ibid., III., p. 157.

"Done Amsterdam in N: Netherland 7th Febr. 1660.

"By the Order of the presiding Burgomaster of the City above-named.

"Joannes Nevius, Secy." [204]

Jansen's difficulties with Cornelisen may have been due partly to the former's arbitrating a case in which Cornelisen was concerned. This took place seven years before as is shown in the Court minutes. Borger Joris had brought suit against Jan Cornelisen to obtain payment for a building which Cornelissen had erected on the land he had hired from Burger Joris, also to settle a matter concerning some cows let on calves. The Burgomasters and Schepens referred the dispute of the parties to two arbitrators, Peter Noorman and Jochem Calder, who were to inspect the premises and examine the matter and finally decide the question according to their ability. Perhaps Jansen decided in favor of Joris. [205]

On June 29, 1660, Pieter Jansen was again involved in litigation, this time being the plaintiff in a case against Frederick Hermzen, of whom he demanded "fl. 85. balance of fl. 90. purchase of a small house" Hermzen did not deny that he owed Jansen this sum. He offered "the interest due and to give security for payment" and he requested time, saying, he would find means. The Court, however, ordered Hermzen to pay the debt. [206]

On January 20, 1661, the Council ordered Burgher Joris and Pieter Jansen Noorman to move their houses and barns, from the boweries, to the village [207] of Bushwick. It would appear that the order was obeyed.

In 1662, probably in the early part of the year, Jansen petitioned the Council that he might move away from Bushwick. The Year-Book of the Holland Society of New York, 1900, p. 141, contains the following extract of the petition.

"1662. [No date.] Petition by Pieter Jansen Trimbol, alias De Noorman, whose land is situated on this side of Noorman's

204 Ibid., VII., p. 246.
205 Ibid., I., p. 142.
206 Ibid., III., p. 183.
207 Calendar of Historical Manuscripts, I., p. 220.

Kill, Long Island, requesting Director-General and Council to be permitted, on account of the distance, to move away from Boswyck, and also for the purpose of assisting people, etc., who are obliged to travel by night and in inclement weather. Four or five families are ready also to erect houses and form a hamlet there. He has already partitioned off two lots on his property, one for Isaack De Forest, and one for Harmen Steppe (or Stegge). . . . Pieter Jansen was charged 3 guilders 15 stivers by Notary La Chair for writing above petition."

Under date of May 25, 1662, a notice states that the Council permitted Jansen "to make a concentration of four families on his land, on the south side of Noorman's Kill, near Bushwick." [208]

He seems to have had a boat of considerable size, as he was sued in March, 1661, by Arien Symonson who demanded of him 40 guilders for a "mizzen mast." [209] Possibly the fragmentary notice "Peter Noorman's negro belonged to the Pilot" (August 1656, New York Colonial Documents, II., p. 31), refers to this.

Jansen must have been a man of some ability. Riker calls him a "hardy Norwegian." We have noted that he served as arbitrator in the Cornelissen—Joris dispute. He also served as guardian for Magdalena Walen's five children, after the death of her husband Jochem Kalder. She was Lutheran, as the Reformed preachers in New Amsterdam, Johannes Megapolensis and Samuel Drisius, stated in a letter to the Council.[210]

Also Pieter Jansen Noorman was a Lutheran; and the pastors Megapolensis and Drisius made mention of that too. He was one of the signers of the petition of the Lutherans requesting that the order to deport the Lutheran pastor Johannis Ernestus Goetwater might be revoked (Reference 42). He was, no doubt, the person whom Megapolensis and Drisius, in their letter of August 23, 1658, to the Director-General and Council of New Netherland, were pleased to call a "stupid northerner who was neither a Lutheran nor of the Reformed Religion and who had not intelligence enough to understand the difference between them," a man who "about two years ago" "nibbled at" certain questions concerning baptism,

208 Ibid., I., p. 287.
209 The Records of New Amsterdam, 1658-1674, III., p. 287.
210 Ecclesiastical Records of the State of New York, I., p. 430.

"but could not give any reasons against them, or receive or try to understand a reason in their favor."[211]

These pastors were not any too well disposed to the Lutherans, as the following extract from their letter, just referred to, indicates. After giving their opinion about the "stupid northerner," they continue:

"Nevertheless they [the Lutherans] have sought, for five or six years, to call a Lutheran preacher, as Paulus Schrick once said to Heyer Stoffels, whom he took to be a Lutheran, because he sang German songs on shipboard on the way to Holland. When Schrick returned from Holland in 1655 he became a chief promoter of this work. Separate meetings began to be held, until the year 1656, when your decree forbidding them was issued. We believe that, as the Pharisees were offended at the words of Christ, Matt. 15: 12, 13, so also has it been in this case; that not only a few words in the Form for the administration of baptism but also the preaching of the divine Word itself was objectionable to them; for blind men easily run against any obstacle. We say blind men, for to our knowledge, there is hardly one among them here who has any proper acquaintance with the teachings of Dr. Luther. They praise Luther only because they call themselves by his name. They are Lutherans, and will remain such, because their parents and ancestors were Lutherans, as Paulus Schrick their leader in his wisdom once declared."[212]

Of Lysbeth Jansen, the wife of Pieter Jansen, we know but little. Once in August, 1659, when she was present in "respectable company," the wife of Hendrick Jansen Sluyter started to fight with her and committed such indecencies and damage that the matter was brought before the court. Lysbeth Jansen was spared. But Sluyter had to promise to send his wife away to Holland or to pay the fine and the "damage done by fighting."[213] Sluyter himself had no good record. He had been dismissed from his position as watchman on Rattle watch.[214] He took sod from

211 Ibid., p. 428. There were probably two Pieter Jansens who signed the petition of 1657. The other was Pieter Jansen of Winckelhock.

212 Schrick was from Nuernberg, Germany, one of the leading men in New Amsterdam.

213 The Records of New Amsterdam, 1653-1674, III., p. 23.

214 Ibid., VII., p. 208.

Christina Capoen's land and was reprimanded.[215] He "wanted to tap, but was denied for good reasons." [216]

Pieter Jansen died before October 6, 1662, when his widow married Joost Janszen Cocquyt, from Brugge, who was at the time an inhabitant of Bushwick.[217]

ROELOF JANSEN.

Roelof Jansen arrived at New Amsterdam by "de Eendracht," May 24, 1630.[218] The ship sailed from the Texel, March 21, 1630. He was to work in the colony of Rensselaerswyck for $72 a year.[219] He was accompanied by his wife Anneke (Anetje) Jans, his daughters Sarah, (Katrina) and Fytje.[220] Until quite recently it has been believed that Roelof Jansen and his family were Dutch. In the "Van Rensselaer Bowier Manuscripts," (p. 56f. note) it is shown by A. T. F. van Laer, Archivist of New York State, that they were not from "Maasterland," but from "Masterland" or "Maesterland," meaning Marstrand, which is on a small island off the coast of Sweden, near Göteborg (Gothenburg). The editor and translator of "Bowier Manuscripts" concludes therefore that Jansen's family probably were Swedes. But why not Norwegians? Marstrand belonged to Norway prior to 1658, and it is significant that Claes Claesen and Jacob Goyversen, both from Flekkerö, Norway, sailed with Roelof and worked with him on "de Laets Burg." There were on July 20, 1632, only three men on this farm: Jansen, Claesen, Goyversen, three Norwegians.[221]

On July 1, 1632, Roelof Jansen was appointed schepens. The oath of the schepens, administered by the Schout to Jansen, and

215 Ibid., III., p. 341.
216 Ibid., I., p. 288. Christina was a daughter of Dirck Holgersen.
217 Collections of the New York Genealogical and Biographical Society, II., p. 28.
218 Van Rensselaer Bowier Manuscripts, p. 218.
219 Year Book of the Holland Society of New York, 1896, p. 131.
220 Van Rensselaer Bowier Manuscripts, p. 308.
221 Ibid., pp. 305, 222. Masterlandt is explained as Marstrand in a letter of the year 1644, in "Bijdragen en Mededeelingen van het Historisch Genootschap (Gevestigd te Utrecht). Negen en twintigste deel," Amsterdam, 1908, p. 279. The first writer who made the claim that the family of Roelof Jansen was Norwegian, was Mr. Torstein Jahr, in "Symra" (Decorah, Iowa), Vol. IX., Part 1, p. 8f: "Nordmenn i Ny Nederland. Anneke Jans fra Marstrand, hennes farm og hennes slekt". See "Preface" to the present volume.

other schepens, among whom was Laurens Laurensen, another Norwegian, was as follows:

"This you swear, that you will be good schepens, that you will be loyal and feal to my gracious lord and support and strengthen him in his affairs as much as is in your power; that you will pass honest judgment between the lord and the farmer, the farmer and the lord, and in the proceedings between two farmers, and that you will not fail to do this on any consideration whatsoever.

"So help you God."

As schepen, Roelof Jansen got a "black hat, with silver bands.[222]

As to Roelof's farming, but little can be said. Van Rensselaer, always exacting in his demands, complained in a letter written July 20, 1632, to Wolfert Gerritz, that it showed "bad management that Roeloff Jansen could not get any winter seed. I hope that he has sown the more summer seed." [223]

Likewise in a letter of April 23, 1634, to Director Wouter van Twiller, the Patroon said: "I see that Roeloff Janssen has grossly run up my account in drawing the provisions, yes, practically the full allowance [even] when there was [enough in] stock. I think that his wife, mother, and sister and others must have given things away, which can not be allowed. He complains that your honor has dismissed him from the farm, and your honor writes me that he wanted to leave it." [224] It would thus appear that Jansen left the colony of Rensselaerswyck in 1634.

Roelof Jansen moved with his family to New Amsterdam about 1634 or a little later. In 1636 he received a groundbrief of thirty-one morgens of land lying along East River.[225] "It formed a sort of peninsula between the river and the swamps which then covered the sites of Canal Street and West Broadway." Here Jansen "probably erected a small farmhouse upon a low hill near the river shore at about the present Jay Street; but he had hardly made a beginning in the work of getting his bouwery under culti-

---

222 Van Rensselaer Bowier Manuscripts, p. 208.
223 Ibid., p. 219.
224 Ibid., p. 281. His mother-in-law, Tryn Jonas, and his sister-in-law, Marritje, are meant. See articles "Tryn Jonas" and "Marritje Jans."
225 E. B. O'Callaghan, History of New Netherland, II., p. 581.

SIEGE OF MARST
From an engr

RAND, 1677.
B. Stopendael.

vation when he died, leaving his widow the arduous task of caring for a family of five children in a colony hardly settled as yet."[226] Of Jansen's children, Sarah, Katrina and Sofia married in New Netherland (See the articles following). Annetje died as a child. Jan (Roelofsen) settled in Schenectady and was killed by the Indians in the massacre of 1690.

Jansen's widow married again. The Dutch Reformed preacher in New Amsterdam Everardus Bogardus took her for his wife in 1638. See the article "Anneke Jans." Of all Scandinavian immigrants in early New York she is probably the best known.

ANNEKE JANS.

Anneke Jans arrived with her husband and three children at New Amsterdam May 24, 1630. As we have seen in the foregoing sketch, she came from Marstrand, Norway. She was with her husband at Fort Orange until 1634 or 1635 when the family moved down to New Amsterdam and settled on sixty-two acres of land, which Jansen received in 1636. He died shortly afterward.

Anneke was left with five children, though she, no doubt received some aid from her mother, Tryn Jonas, midwife, and from her sister, Marritje, both of whom were in New Amsterdam. Kiliaen van Rensselaer released her from what she owed him. In a letter of September 21, 1637, to Director van Twiller he said: "I only have from you the recommendation of the widow of Roeloef Jansen, written to me hastily and with few words and your oral greetings by Jacob Wolphertsen. I released the said widow from her debt long ago. My reason for so doing I will tell you orally, when we meet, God willing, in good health.'[227]

In March, 1638, Anneke was married to the Dutch Reformed pastor in New Amsterdam, Everardus Bogardus, who in 1633 had come to New Amsterdam to succeed the ministry of Jonas Michaelis. He had at the time a little church on the East River

---

226 J. H. Innes, New Amsterdam and Its People, p. 18. ''The present boundaries of the land Jansen obtained in 1636 are the North River, Christopher Street, Bedford Street, West Houston Street, Sullivan Street, Canal Street, West Broadway, Barclay Street, Broadway, and Fulton Street, around to the river again'' (Appleton's Cyclopaedia of American Biography, I., p. 301).

227 Van Rensselaer Bowier Manuscripts, p. 352. Anne is the Norwegian spelling of Annetje or Anneke.

shore, or upon the present Pearl Street, between Whitehall and Broad Streets, and adjoining it was the parsonage. In addition to his clerical duties he assumed the cares of a landed proprietor. In the marriage settlement, still extant, Anneke had provided for the securing to her first husband's children the sum of 200 guilders each.[228]

The sixty-two acres of land which she inherited from her first husband now got the name of the "Domine's Bouwerie." "United in early English days to the Company's Bouwerie, it formed part of the famous tract, which, bestowed in the time of Queen Anne upon Trinity Church, in the eighteenth and nineteenth centuries was the subject of repeated and hotly contested action at law in which Annetje's name conspicuously figured."[229]

On August 12, 1638, Everardus Bogardus, as the "husband of the widow of Roelof Jansen of Masterlandt" gave Power of Attorney to Director van Twiller "to collect money due said Jansen.[230]

Anneke, no doubt, was now a lady of leisure compared to what she had been when she was farming with Roelof on de Laets Burg. But her position as the wife of a parson was severely tested immediately after her second marriage. Anthony Jansen from Salee and his wife, Grietje Reiners, were none too well disposed to Domine Bogardus and Anneke. Grietje found an opportunity of circulating the report that Anneke had given public offense. Anthony Jansen, whose tongue vied with that of his wife, helped to spread the report. The matter came before the Court.[231]

Mrs. Lamb's version of this case is as follows:

"Mrs. Bogardus went to pay a friendly visit to a neighbor; but on getting into the 'entry', discovered that Greitje Reinirs, a woman of questionable reputation, was in the house, and thereupon turned about and went home. Grietje was greatly offended at this 'snubbing' from the Dominie's lady, and followed her, making disagreeable remarks. While passing a blacksmith's shop, where the road was muddy, Mrs. Bogardus raised her dress a little, and Grietje was very invidious in her criticisms. The Dominie

---

228 J. H. Innes, New Amsterdam and Its People, p. 16.
229 Ibid., p. 14. It must not be confounded with Dominies Höck, some other land belonging to Bogardus.
230 Calendar of Historical Manuscripts, I., p. 3.
231 Ibid., I., pp. 4, 65.

thought fit to make an example of her; hence the suit. Grietje's husband being in arrears for church dues, Bogardus sent for him and ordered payment, and not getting it, finally sued for the amount." (See Lamb, History of the City of New York, I. p. 86).

Anneke's second husband was a fearless and outspoken person. He was at variance with Governor Van Twiller as well as with his successor Governor Kieft. He accused Van Twiller of maladministration and in consequence was himself charged with unbecoming conduct, and was about to depart for Holland to defend himself, but was detained by Governor Kieft. He opposed Kieft's policy in regard to the Indians, and in 1645 denounced him for drunkenness and rapacity. He was therefore brought to trial, but compromised with Kieft. But the old difficulties appeared again. In 1646 the Director and Council of New Amsterdam summoned Bogardus to appear and answer charges against him. The "summons" is as long as it is violent, likely the work of Kieft. We shall give a few extracts from it:

". . . We have letters in your own hand, among others, one dated June 17, 1634, wherein you do not appear to be moved by the Spirit of the Lord, but on the contrary by a feeling becoming heathen, let alone Christians, much less a preacher of the Gospel. You there berate your magistrate, placed over you by God, as a child of the Devil, an incarnate villain, whose buck goats are better than he, and promise him that you would so pitch into him from the pulpit on the following Sunday, that both you and his bulwarks would tremble. . . .

"You have indulged no less in scattering abuse during our administration. Scarcely a person in the entire land have you spared; not even your own wife, or her sister, particularly when you were in good company and jolly. Still, mixing up your human passions with the chain of truth which has continued from time to time, you associated with the greatest criminals in the country, taking their part and defending them. . . .

"On the 25th of September, 1639, having celebrated the Lord's Supper, observing afterwards in the evening a bright fire in the Director's house, whilst you were at Jacob van Curler's, being thoroughly drunk, you grossly abused the Director and Jochim Pietersen, with whom you were angry. . . .

"Since that time many acts have been committed by you, which no clergyman would think of doing. . . .

"Maryn Adriaensen came into the Director's room with predetermined purpose to murder him. He, notwithstanding, was sent to Holland in chains against your will. Whereupon you fulminated terribly for about fourteen days and desecrated your pulpit by your passion. . . . Finally, you made up friends with the Director, and things became quiet. . . .

"In the summer of . . . (1644) when minister Douthey administered the Lord's Supper in the morning, you came drunk into the pulpit in the afternoon; also on Friday before Christmas of the same year, when you preached the sermon calling to repentance. . . .

"On the 21st March, 1645, being at a wedding feast at Adam Brouwer's and pretty drunk, you commenced scolding the Fiscal and Secretary then present, censuring also the Director not a little, giving as your reason that he had called your wife a ———, though he said there that it was not true and that he never entertained such a thought, and it never could be proved. . . .

"You administered the Lord's Supper . . . without partaking of it yourself, setting yourself as a partisan. . ." [282]

Such was the husband of Anneke Jans in the opinion of the highest official in the land who himself was so hateful to the people that he was obliged to resign.

Signature of Everhard Boghardus, second husband of Anneke Jans.

When Kieft returned to Holland, after the arrival of Governor Stuyvesant in 1647, Bogardus sailed in the same vessel to answer the charges brought against him, before the classis in Amsterdam. The vessel entered Bristol Channel by mistake, and struck upon a rock, going down with eighty persons, among them Bogardus and Kieft. This happened on September 27, 1647.

---

282 Ecclesiastical Records of the State of New York, I., p. 196ff.

Anneke was thus widow for the second time of her days.
No doubt she had borne her share of the discomfort caused by the
enmity between Kieft and Bogardus. The following extract of
a letter of Rev. Megapolensis in Albany, written August 25, 1648,
to the Classis of Amsterdam shows what she still had to contend
against, and what was his opinion of the Kieft-Bogardus feud.

"After the Lord God was pleased to cut short the thread of
life of Domine Bogardus by shipwreck . . ., his widow came here
to Fort Orange . . . to reside and make her living. She has nine
children living, some by a former husband and some by Domine
Bogardus, and is also deeply in debt. She has, however, no way
to liquidate her debts, nor means for her own subsistence, unless
the West India Company pay her the arrears of salary due her
husband. Domine Bogardus repeatedly asserted that a higher
salary was promised him, before leaving Holland, than he ever
received here. . .

"It is now about two years since I was called upon by Director-
General William Kieft, to settle the difficulties between said Kieft
and Domine Bogardus. I attempted several times to smooth the
differences which had arisen here, but all in vain. Domine Bogardus asserted that it could not be done here, but that the matter
ought to be laid before the Hon. Directors; or even if it could be
determined here, he would, nevertheless, be obliged to go home,
in order to demand, before his death, the salary promisd him,
for the maintenance and support of his family. . . .

"He had been paid for a considerable time only 46 guilders
per month, with 150 guilders extra per year for board money. . .

"Annetje Bogardus . . . has requested me to write to the
Rev. Classis, in her name and in her behalf, in order that the
Rev. Classis, or the Deputies thereof, might, for the sake of a
preacher's widow, petition the Company for the money due her,
to be paid to her or her attorney, to enable her to pay her debts
and support her family. . . ." [288]

The letter of Megapolensis, it would appear, does not ex-
aggerate her distress. She had several little children to support,
though three of her grown-up daughters were married. Her house
in New York was situate on what is now No. 23 Whitehall Street.

---

[288] Ibid., I., p. 287.

In 1652 she was enabled to buy a lot in Albany on the corner of James and State Streets. Here she built a house and resided the remainder of her life. It would appear that her son-in-law Pieter Hartgers secured this property for her. It was "bounded east by land of Jonas and Peter Bogardus, and west by Evert Janse Wendell. Being 2 rods 8½ feet wide, and 5 rods 9 feet long." On June 21, 1663, after the death of Anneke, it was sold by the heirs to Dirck Wessells. The price was "1,000 guilders in good merchantable beaver skins, at 8 guilders a piece." (Collections of the New York Historical Society, IV., p. 488).

In 1654 she obtained from Governor Stuyvesant a patent in her own name on the land she had inherited from her first husband.

This Patent reads as follows:

"Petrus Stuyvesant, Director-General of New Netherland, Curacao and the Islands thereof, on the behalf of their Noble High Mightinesses the Lords States-General of the United Netherlands and the Honorable Directors of the Incorporated West India Company, together with the Honorable Councillors, declare that We on this day, date underwritten, have given and granted to Annetje Jans, widow of the late Everardus Bogardus, a piece of land situate on the Island of Manhattan on the North River, beginning at the palisades near the house on the Strand it goes north by east up to the partition line of old Jan's land is long 210 rods; from thence along the partition line of said Old Jan's land it extends E. by S. up to the Cripple bush (swamp) it runs S. W. long 160 rods from the Cripple bush, to the Strand it runs westerly in breadth 50 rods; the land that lies to the south of the house to the partition line of the Company's land begins on the east side, from the palisades southward to the posts and rails of the Company's land, without obstruction to the path, it is broad 60 rods; long on the south side along the posts and rails 160 rods; at the east side to the corner of Kalchhook is broad 30 rods; to the division line of the aforesaid piece of land it goes westerly in length 100 rods; it makes alltogether 31 morgens." (Historic New York. Ed. by Goodwin, Royce and Putnam I., p. 84 f.)

Her will, dated January 29, 1663, and on record in the original Dutch in book of Notarial Papers, in the County Clerk's office, Albany, reads as follows:

"Will of Anneke Jans Bogardus. — In the name of the Lord, Amen. Know all men by these presents, That this day, the 29th of January, 1663, in the afternoon, about four o'clock, appeared before me, Derrick Van Schelluyne, notary public, in the presence of the witnesses hereafter mentioned, Anneke Janse, widow of Roeloff Janse, of Master Land, and now lastly widow of the Reverend Everhardus Bogardus, residing in the village of Beverwyck, and well known to us, notary and witnesses; the said Anneke Janse lying on her bed in a state of sickness, but perfectly sensible and in the full possession of her mental powers, and capable to testate, to which sound state of mind we can fully testify. The said Anneke Janse considering the shortness of life and certainty of death and the uncertainty of the hour or time, she, the said Anneke Janse, declared after due consideration, without any persuasion, compulsion, or retraction, this present document to be her last will and testament, in manner following: First of all recommending her immortal soul to the Almighty God, her Creator and Redeemer, and consigning her body to Christian burial, and herewith revoking and annulling all prior testamentary dispositions of any kind whatsoever, and now proceeding anew, she declared to nominate and institute as her sole and universal heirs her children, Sarah Roellofson, wife of Hans Kierstede; Catrina Roeloffsen, wife of Johannes Van Brugh; also Jannetje and Rachel Hartgers, the children of her deceased daughter, Fytie Roeloffsen, during her life the wife of Peter Hartgers, representing together their mother's place; also her son Jan Roeloffsen, and finally, William, Cornelius, Jonas, and Peter Bogardus, and to them to bequeath all her real estate, chattels, money, gold and silver, coined and uncoined, jewels, clothes, linen, woolen, household furniture, and all property what soever, without reserve or restriction of any kind, to be disposed of after her decease and divided by them in equal shares, to do with the same at their own will and pleasure without any hindrance whatsoever; provided never the less with this express condition and restriction that her four first born children shall divide between them out of their father's property the sum of one thousand guilders, to be paid to them out of the proceeds of a certain farm, situate on Manhattan Island, bounded on the North river, and that before any other dividend takes place; and as three of these children at the time of their marriage received certain donations, and as Jan Roeloffsen is yet unmarried, he is to receive a bed and milch cow; and to Jonas and Peter Bogardus she gives a house and lot situated to the westward of the house of the testatrix in the village of Beverwyck, going in length until the end of a bleaching spot, and in breadth up to the room of her, the testatrix, house, besides a bed for both of them and a milch cow to each of them, the above to be an equivalent of what the married children have received. Finally, she, the testatrix, gives to Roeloff Kierstede, the child of her daughter Sara, a silver mug; to Annetje Van Brugh, the child of her daughter Catrina, also a silver mug; and to Jannetje and Rachel Hartgers, the children of her daughter Fytie, a silver mug each; and to the child of William Bogardus named Fytie also a silver mug; all the above donations to be provided for out of the first moneys received, and afterwards the remainder of the property to be divided and shared aforesaid. The testatrix declares this document to be her only true last will and testament, and desiring that after her decease it may supersede all other testaments, codicils, donations, or any other instruments whatsoever; and in case any formalities may have been omitted, it is her will and desire the same benefits may occur as if they actually had been observed; and she requested me, notary public, to make one or more lawful instruments in the usual form of this, her, testatrix, last will and desire. Signed, sealed, and delivered at the house of the testatrix in the village of Beverwyck, in New Netherland, in the presence of Ruth Jacobse Van Schoonderweert and Evert Wendell, witnesses.

"This is the + mark of Anneke Janse with her own hand.

"Rutger Jacobus,
"Evert Jacobus Wendell.
"D. V. Schelluyne, Notary Public, 1663."

(For this and other translations I am indebted to Collections of the New York Historical Society, IV., p.487 ff.)

Anneke died March 19, 1663, and lies buried in the Middle Dutch Church Yard, on Beaver Street.

She was the first Norwegian "predikantsvrouw" (pastor's wife), in New York. And of all the pastors' wives in New York she has become the most famous. But this fame is due to chance and circumstance rather than to Anneke herself. Mrs. Lamb says: "Although she (Anneke) may not have seemed rich in the days when great landed estates were to be bought for a few strings of beads, yet she is reverenced by her numerous descendants as among the very goddesses of wealth. She was a small well-formed woman with delicate features, transparent complexion, and bright, beautiful dark eyes. She had a well-balanced mind, a sunny disposition, winning manners, and a kind heart. . . "

Anneke Jans' fame rests on property and progeny. Her descendants are numerous. Many of them are wealthy, some of them have been conspicuous in the litigation regarding Anneke Jans' farm. John Fiske speaks of this litigation as "one of the most pertinacious cases of litigation known to modern history." (The Dutch and Quaker Colonies in America, II., p. 32).

We have mentioned that Director Stuyvesant gave the heirs of Anneke a patent, on the land in question, in 1654. This patent was confirmed in 1664 by Governor Nicolls, after the English had conquered New Netherland. In 1671 five of the heirs conveyd the whole farm to Col. Francis Lovlace, then governor of the province of New York. In 1674 the Duke of York confiscated it, so that it was the "Duke's Farm" until 1685, when with James' accession to the throne it became the "King's Farm." In 1705 it was leased or granted by the colonial authorities under Queen Anne to Trinity Church. One of Anneke's sons, Cornelius, had not joined in the conveyance of 1671; the heirs of this son have claimed that his failure to join invalidated the sale and that they therefore had a right to their share of the property. Between 1750 and 1847 not less than sixteen or seventeen suits in ejectment were brought against Trinity Church by heirs who coveted the property. They were brought "with such a persistency which seemed to learn no lesson from defeat. In 1847 Vice-Chancellor Sanford decided that, after waving all other points, the church had acquired a valid title by prescription, and all the adverse claims were vitiated by lapse of time" (Fiske, Dutch and Quaker Colonies, II., p. 258).

Let us also quote from the article "Annetje Jans' Farm," in "Historic New York" (I., p. 95):

"Sixty-eight years after the sale to Lovlace, and thirty-one years after Queen Anne's grant, the descendants of Cornelius Bogardus began to protest against the occupancy of Trinity Church. There was a confused notion then as to what they could claim, and this confusion has increased in the minds of the "heirs" during two hundred years. The history of the repeated suits is long and involved. No court has sustained the claims of the· "heirs" for a minute, and yet, with every generation, new claimants appear, though every possible right has long since been outlawed. Mr. Schuyler says in his Colonial New York: 'In view of the repeated decisions of the highest judicial tribunals and of their publicity, any lawyer who can now advise or encourage the descendants of Annetje Jans to waste their money in any proceedings to recover this property must be considered as playing on the ignorance of simple people, and as guilty of conscious fraud, and of an attempt to obtain money under false pretenses.' Mr. Schuyler made a close study of the subject, and is himself a distinguished descendant of Roelof and Annetje Jans."

As late as 1891 Trinity Corporation found it necessary to publish the following:

"To all whom it may concern:

"As letters are being constantly received from various places in the United States making inquiries about suits pending against this corporation in respect to its property, or about negotiations assumed to be on foot in respect to the alleged claims of the descendants of Anneke Jans or of other persons, notice is hereby given that no such suits are pending, and no such negotiations are going on, and all persons who suppose themselves to be descendants of Anneke Jans, or otherwise interested in claims hostile to this corporation, are cautioned against paying out money to any person alleging the pendency of such suits or negotiations."

Societies have been formed like the Anneke Jans Association, founded in Astor House Library in New York, 1867, The Anneke Jans International Union, etc. But no organized endeavor has as yet succeeded in invalidating the claim of the Trinity Corporation. It has continued to enjoy all the benefits and revenues of the vast property to this day. No wonder that Trinity Church can contribute more than four hundred thousand dollars a year to charity!

Trinity Church is Episcopal. It is the wealthiest church organization in America and it is continually reminded of it, even in the twentieth century.

For as late as 1909 Trinity Corporation was sued again by an heir of Anneke Jans. Mary Fonda wanted, as heir, one per cent of valuable Trinity property.

Regarding the descendants of Anneke Jans, see: I. Munsell, Collections on the History of Albany II.; and The New York Genealogical and Biographical Record.

See also S. P. Nash, Anneke Jans Bogardus, her farm, and how it became the Property of Trinity Church, New York, 1896.

Of the many prominent families which by ties of marriage have augmented the genealogy of Anneke Jans, Mr. Torstein Jahr's article in "Symra" mentions Bayard, De Lancey, De Peyster, Jouverneur, Jay, Knickerbocker, Morris, Schuyler, Stuyvesant, Van Cortland and Van Rensselaer.

FYNTIE ROELOFS (JANSE).

Fyntie Roelofs (Janse) accompanied her parents, Roelof Jansen and Anneke Jans, to New Netherland, in 1630. She was from Marstrand, then belonging to Norway. She lived from 1630 to about 1634 with her parents on de Laets Burg, and since 1635 in New Amsterdam. She married Pieter Hartgers, who came to New Amsterdam in 1643 in the service of the West India Company, and first settled at Fort Orange. He was engaged much of his time in trading with the Indians. He made long expeditions into the forest to get their trade. From November 1, 1644, to February 1, 1648, he received in the colony of Rensselaerswyck a salary of fl. 14 a month. During this period he seems to have assisted de Hooges in the management of the colony of Rensselaerswyck. As early as 1646 he appears to have had a brewery. On May 4, 1649, he and de Hooges leased, for three years, a garden between Fort Orange and the patroon's hoof, where formerly the patroon's trading house stood. About the same time he agreed to pay an annual rent, beginning in 1653, of four beavers for a lot for his mother-in-law, Anneke Jans, on which lot he built a house for her. From May 1, 1653 to May 1, 1658 Pieter Hartgers, Volckert Janszz (a Dane), and Jan Thomasz were joint lessees of a farm on Papscanee Island.

Signature of Pieter Hartgers, husband of Fyntie Roelofs.

He was one of the magistrates in Albany in 1658. He acquired the reputation of a great expert as to the value of Indian money (shell money), and was appointed in 1659 a commissioner at Albany to estimate Indian wampum.

In 1652 he bought a parcel of ground, in New Amsterdam, from Van Couwenhoven. (About his house and lot in New Amsterdam, see Valentine's Manual of the City of New York 1865, pp. 659, 663.)

In 1664 his property was confiscated, perhaps on account of a refusal to take the oath of allegiance to the English government.

By Fyntie Roelofs, Hartgers had two children, Jannetys and Rachel. Fyntie died before 1663, when her mother Anneke Jans made her will. The portion of inheritance which Fyntie was entitled to was therefore willed to her daughters Jannetys and Rachel. (See Van Rensselaer Bowie Manuscripts, p. 834; J. H. Innes, New Amsterdam and Its People, p. 80.) Jannetys (Janneke) was baptized September 5, 1649.

KATRINA ROELOFS (JANSE).

Katrina Roelofs (Janse), a daughter of Roelof Jansen and Anneke Jans, from Marstrand, Norway, came with her parents to New Netherland in 1630. She lived with them on de Laets Burg till 1634—1635, when the entire family moved to New Amsterdam. She was married first to Lukas Rodenburgh, who was Vice Director of Curacao (1644 to 1655), then, on April 24, 1658, to Johannes Pietersen van Brugh, who was a merchant and later member of the first board of aldermen in New Amsterdam, captain in the New York militia, burgomaster of New Orange. (New Amsterdam or New York was called New Orange from February, 1673 to November 1674.) In 1674 Katrina and her husband lived in their house, rated as first class and valued at $15,000, in New Amsterdam, on the present west side of Pearl St. between Wall and William St. (Year Book of the Holland Society of New York, 1896, p. 167.) They were members of the Dutch Reformed Church.

Signature of Johannes Van Brugh, 1659, second husband of Katrina Roelofs.

Katrina and one of her daughters whom she had by Roden-burgh are mentioned several times in the Journal of Jasper Danck-aerts, 1679—1680 (edited by Rev. B. B. James, in "Original Narratives of Early American History," 1913). Danckaerts and his companion, Sluyter, were Labadists who had come over to this country in order to find a location for the establishment of a colony of Labadists. Aided by Ephraim Herrman, who was the eldest son of Augustine Herrman and had married Elizabeth Rodenburgh, September, 1679, they received a tract of 3,750 acres upon Bohemia Manor, in Maryland, a part of the 24,000 acres of land belonging to Augustine Herrman of Prague. The elder Herrman was at first favorably impressed with Danckaerts and Sluyter, and, as he was ambitious of colonizing and developing his estates, he consented to deed them a large tract of land. The two Labadists soon set sail for Europe. But when they returned in 1683, Augustine Herrman had repented of his bargain. By recourse of law the Labadists compelled him to live up to its terms, and in consequence received the tract of 3,750 acres.

We shall quote the following, from Jasper Danckaert's Journal (September, 1679):

"Ephraim had for a long time sought in marriage at New

York a daughter of the late governor of Carsou . . . Johan van Rodenburgh. She lived with her mother on the Manhatan, who, after the death of her husband, Rodenburgh, married one Johannes van Burgh, by whom she had several children. Her daughter, Elizabeth van Rodenburgh, being of a quiet turn of mind, and quite sickly, had great inclination to remain single. Ephraim, how · ever, finally succeeded in his suit, and married her at New York. He brought her with him to Newcastle on the South River, and we accompanied them on the journey . . . Elizabeth van Rodenburg has the quietest disposition we have observed in America. She is politely educated. She had through her entire youth a sleeping sickness of which she seems now to be free. She has withdrawn herself much from the idle company of youth, seeking God in quiet and solitude. She professes the Reformed religion, is a member of that Church, and searches for the truth which she has found nowhere except in the word and preaching, which she therefore much attended upon and loved, but which never satisfied her, as she felt a want and yearning after something more. She was so pleased at our being near her, and lodged at her house, she could not abstain from frequently declaring so, receiving all that we said to her with gratitude, desiring always to be near us; and following the example of her husband, she corrected many things, with the hope and promise of persevering if the Lord would be pleased so to give her grace. We were indeed much comforted with these two persons, who have done much for us out of sincere love."

Under date of January 2, 1680, Danckaerts relates that he and his companion, on a journey northward, had letters along from Ephraim and his wife which they gave "to her mother and father (step-father Van Brugh), who welcomed us. We told them of the good health of their children, and the comfort and hope which they gave us, which pleased them." February 6, the same year, Danckaerts writes: "I . . translated the Verheffinge des Geestes tot God [The Lifting up of the Soul to God. Labadie's publication, 1667] to Dutch [evidently he had the original French text in hand], for Elizabeth Rodenburgh . . . in order to send her a token of gratitude for the acts of kindness enjoyed at her house, as she had evinced a great inclination for it, and relished it much, when sometimes we read portions of it to her while we were there."

It was not Elizabeth, but her husband that the Labadists succeeded in converting. Ephraim, after living with his wife for nine years, abandoned wife and family to join the Labadists. He soon repented of his step, returned home, became insane and "died cursed by his father for having associated with those religious visionaries."

On March 24, 1692, Elizabeth, then a widow, was married to John Donaldson, from 'Galleway'. Catharina, whom Katrina Roelofs had by her second husband, married, March 19, 1689 (?), Hendrick van Rensselaer, grandson of Kiliaen Van Rensselaer. She had nine children.

An extract of the will of Katrina Roelof's third husband is found in "Collections of the New York Hist. Society," XXV., pp. 89 f., 93 f.

SARA ROELOFS (JANSE).

Sara Roelofs (Janse) was the first daughter of Roelof and Anneke Jans, with whom she arrived in New Netherland in 1630. She was with them on "de Laets Burg" till 1634—1635, when the family removed to New Amsterdam and settled on their farm of 62 acres, on which Roelof had obtained a patent in 1636.

Sara was married three times. Her first husband, to whom she was married June 29, 1642, was Hans Kierstede, a German, from Magdeburg. He was a physician in New Amsterdam. Sara and Hans lived in the house next to that of a Norwegian, Roelof Jansen Haes. It was at their wedding, that Governor Kieft, taking advantage of the condition of the guests after the fourth or fifth drink, induced them to subscribe very liberally toward building a new church in the Fort. "The disposition to be generous was not wanting at such a time. Each guest emulated his neighbor, and a handsome list was made out. When the morning came, a few were found desirous of reconsidering the transaction of the wedding feast. But Director Kieft would allow no such second thought. They must all pay without exception." By Hans Kierstede Sara had ten children. Both Hans and Sara were members of the Dutch Reformed Church.

Mrs. Van Rensselaer, in "History of the City of New York,"

I., p. 190, says, Kierstede and La Montagne "were the chief physicians of New Amsterdam, although one named Van der Bogaert practised before their arrival, and by 1638 there were three others, probably ships' surgeons whose stay was brief. Kierstede's descendants followed in his steps: it is believed that always since his time New York has had a physician or an apothecary of his blood and name."

Sara was styled one of the "good women" of New Amsterdam, at least in 1662, as is seen from the following:

On September 19, 1662, a Jan Gelder sued Grietje Pieters for three guilders, sixteen stivers, wages she owed him. Grietje admitted the debt, but said that she had given to Gelder's wife some linen to make caps, and she spoiled the caps. The Court referred "the matter in question to Sara Roeloftzen, wife of Mr. Hans Kierstede, and to Metje Greveraats to take up the matter in question, to inspect the linen caps, to settle parties' case, and if possible to reconcile them; if not to report their decision to the Court." On October 3, the case was again before the court. The defendant was in default. "Pltf. says that the deft. is not willing to appear before the "good women" (female arbitrators), and that Sara Roelofs, appointed by the W. Court will not have anything to do with the matter, as she will not be opposed to either one party or the other." The Court insited that Janneke van Gelder must either appear before the "good women" or make good the damage estimated by them.[284]

Sara was more than the ordinary arbitrating "good woman." She was well acquainted with the Indian language, and acted on divers occasions as interpreter for Peter Stuyvesant and the Indians. In return for her service, Oratany, sachem of Hackingkesacky, made her a present of a large neck or tract of land on the west side of the Hudson.

Her second husband, to whom she was married September 1, 1669, was Cornelius of Borsum, owner of the Long Island ferry. Her third husband was Elbert Elbertsen Stouthoff. She was married to him in 1683.

---

284 The Records of New Amsterdam, 1653-1674, IV., pp. 136, 143.

Sara had several slaves as appears from her will which reads as follows:

"Sara Roeloffse." In the name of God, Amen. Be it known to all whom it may concern, that I, Sara Roeloffse, late widow of Elbert Elbertse Stouthoff, considering the frailty and shortness of Human life, Do make my last will in manner folowing. 1st. I commit my immortal Soul into the merciful hands of God Almighty, and my body to a decent burial. 2nd. I revoke all other wills. Now I will before anything else to my daughter Blandina, of this city, a negro boy, Hans. To my son Luycas Kierstede, my Indian, named Ande. To my daughter Catharine Kierstede, a negress, named Susannah. To my son-in-law, Johannes Kip, husband of my said daughter Catharine, my negro, Sarah, in consideration of great trouble in settling the accounts of my late husband, Cornelius Van Borsum, in Esopus and elsewhere. To my son Jochem Kierstede, a little negro, called Maria, during his life, and then to Sarah, the eldest daughter of my son Roeloff Kierstede by Ytie Kierstede. To my son Johannes Kierstede, a negro boy Peter. I leave to my daughter Anna Van Borsum, by my former husband, Cornelius Van Borsum, on account of her simplicity, my small house and kitchen, and lot situate in this city, between the land of Jacob Mauritz and my bake house, with this express condition, that she shall not be permitted to dispose of the same by will or otherwise, but to be hers for life and then to the heirs mentioned in this will.

"It is my will that my son Luycas Kierstede shall have the privilege of buying the house where he now lives and the bake house and lot belonging to the same and to pay the money for the same to the other heirs, he to retain his share. I have fully satisfied my sons Hans Kierstede and Roeloff Kierstede for their share in thier father's estate, being 40 Beavers, as by account for the same, the rest of my estate I leave to the seven children of me and my deceased husband, Hans Kierstede, viz, Roeloff, Blandina, Jochem, Luycas, Catrine, Jacobus, Rachel, and the children of my deceased son Hans Kierstede by his wife Jannike equally. Only Hans Kierstede the eldest son of my deceased son Hans Kierstede shall have £1 for his birthright. I appoint as guardians of my daughter Anna Van Borsum, and managers of her house and lot my son-in-law Johannes Kip, and my son Luycas Kierstede, and my son-in-law Wm Teller, giving them full power as executors.

"Dated July 29, 1693. Witnesses Wm. Bogardus, Jacobus Maurits, — Hoaglandt.

"Codicil, August 7, 1693, confirms the above will and leaves all her clothing to her daughters Blandina, Catharine and Rachel, and to each of the wives of my 5 sons a silver spoon."

"Witness Brandt Schuyler, Justice of the Peace. Proved, October 21, 1693."

(Collections of the New York Historical Society, XXV., pp. 225. The will is corrected according to ibid. XL., p. 24.)

TRYN JONAS.

Tryn Jonas, or Kathrine Jonas, was from Marstrand, Norway.[235] She was the mother of Anneke Jans, wife of Roelof Jansen, who with his family immigrated to New Netherland in 1630. For a long time she occupied a position under the West India Company as its official midwife, an incident showing how the Company made provision for the welfare of its colonists. "She was," says J. H. Innes, "duly sensible of the dignity and importance of her office, which she exercised with great independence, even to the extent of refusing upon various occasions to attend certain of her patients with whose antecedents she was not satisfied."[236] Under date of August 31, 1642, Catalina Trico and her daughter Sarah Rapalji made a declaration "respecting the conduct of Tryn Jonas, midwife, when sent for to attend said Trico."[237] We do not know the nature of this declaration, nor of another declaration of the midwife herself, on July 7, 1644, "respecting a confession of Helligond Joris as to the paternity of her child"[238] — very likely some of the manuscript material in Albany will reveal it — but it seems that Tryn Jones was an exacting midwife.

It would appear that she stayed sometime with her daughter

235 Van Rensselaer Bowier Manuscripts, 57, note.
236 J. H. Innes, New Amsterdam and Its People, p. 15.
237 Calendar of Historical Manuscripts, I., p. 20.
238 Ibid., I., p. 28.

in the colony of Rensselaerswyck. For Kiliaen van Rensselaer complained in a letter of April 23, 1634, that Roelof Jansen was drawing too heavily on his accounts. He was inclined to believe that Roelof's wife, sister-in-law, and mother-in-law had given things away.[289]

After Jansen had moved down to New Amsterdam, Tryn Jonas had no reason to be lonesome. Her daughter Anneke had several daughters who married and got children. Anneke herself had children by her second husband Domine Bogardus, whom she married in 1638. We find Tryn Jonas as sponsor at the baptism of Anneke's and Bogardus's child, Cornelis, who was baptized on September 9, 1640; likewise at the baptism of their child, Jan, January 4, 1643. On September 21, 1644, she was sponsor at the baptism of Jan, son of her granddaughter Sara and Dr. Kierstede.[240] Tryn Jonas could also visit her other daughter, Marritje, whenever she desired; for she, too, lived in New Amsterdam and had a family.

On February 4, 1644, Tryn Jonas obtained a grant of land from the West India Company, a lot upon Pearl Street where she built a house.[241]

On September 15, 1644, her son-in-law, Bogardus brought, in her behalf, action against Jacob Ray (Kay, Hay?) "for a small piece of ground." It was ordered "that the Director and Council examine the ground in dispute." [242]

She died before 1647. The West India Company was owing her money at the time. Her daughters claimed it, and her son-in-law, Rev. Bogardus, was to collect it. Dirck Cornelissen, the second husband of her daughter Marritje (he had married her September 9, 1646), gave, in 1647, power of attorney to Bogardus "to receive money due said midwife by the West India Company." [243] After the death of Rev. Bogardus, his widow Anneke gave power of attorney to Cornelis Willemsen Bogaert, a brother of the pastor and a resident of Leyden, "to receive moneys due

289 Van Rensselaer Bowier Manuscripts, p. 281. It is possible that Tryn Jonas was in New Amsterdam before 1680.
240 Collections of the New York Genealogical and Biographical Society, II., pp. 11, 14, 16, 18.
241 Calendar of Historical Manuscripts, I., p. 868. Year Book of the Holland Society of New York, 1901, p. 125.
242 Calendar of Historical Manuscripts, I., p. 91.
243 Ibid., I., p. 41.

Tryn Jansen, her mother, late midwife, by the West India Company at Amsterdam." [244]

MARRITJE JANSE.

Marritje Janse was the sister of Anneke Jans from Marstrand and the daughter of Tryn Jonas. Kiliaen van Rensselaer mentions her in a letter of April, 1634, as being, in his opinion, partly to blame for Roelof Jansen's "grossly" running up his accounts in drawing provisions: "I think that his wife, mother and sister and others must have given things away, which can not be allowed."

Marritje married three times. Her first husband was Tymen Jansen (born in 1603) who for several years, from 1633 or perhaps earlier, was the leading shipwright in New Amsterdam, where he constructed many vessels. At the request of the Director he made in 1639 a list of the ships that had been built or repaired in New Amsterdam during Van Twiller's administration (1633—1638). He, too, may have been from Marstrand. [245]

We shall give the following data concerning Tymen. On May 30, 1639, he gave a note for 100 guilders to the deacons of the church in New Amsterdam. [246] On September 29, in the same year, he gave power of attorney to Laurens Laurensen, to collect money due him in Holland. [247] On February 17, 1640, he and Domine Bogardus furnished bond as guardians of the children of the "late Cornelis van Vorst." [248] On August 2, 1640, he sued Laurens Haen for slander. On August 23, he won his case, and

---

244 Ibid., I., p. 49.
245 New York Colonial Documents, XIV., p. 17. Mrs. Van Rensselaer, in "History of the City of New York," I., p. 108, says that Director Minuit subsidized in 1631 certain Swedish shipwrights, who, bringing the timber from far up the North River, built at Manhattan a great Ship called the "New Netherland," one of the largest merchantmen then afloat, everywhere exciting wonder by its size and by the excellence and variety of the timber used in its construction. Is the assertion that they were Swedish an inference? I have found no documentary evidence in support of it. Would the supposition be unfounded that Tymen, as one of these shipwrights, originally was from Marstrand, or from some other part of Norway, or from Denmark? He appears to have lived for some time at "Munikendamm".
Marritje probably came to New York in 1630.
246 Calendar of Historical Manuscripts, I., p. 8.
247 Ibid., p. 11.
248 Ibid., p. 12.

Laurens Haen was fined.[249]   On September 9, Tymen was sponsor at the baptism of Cornelis, son of Bogardus.

In 1642 he received land on the east side of Mespachtes kill, behind Domine's Hook (Newton, Long Island).[250]

On April 31, 1642, he gave power of attorney to Dirck Corsen Stam to receive a certain procuration from Dr. Thomas Sees. In August he was in litigation with Dirck Corsen Stam concerning a collection of 550 guilders.[251]

On December 6, he gave power of attorney to George Grace to receive certain tobacco for him in Virginia.[252]

On July 3, 1643, he obtained a patent of 640 rods, 10 feet, 5 inches of land on the Island of Manhattan.   On July 13, in the same year, he received a groundbrief of 22 morgens, 324 rods of land with valley on Long Island (Newton).[253]

Tymen must have resided upon the land which he received, July 3, 1643, for ten or twelve years before he obtained the patent of it.   "It seems to have stretched along the river road, about from the present No. 125 Pearl Street to what is now the rear of the Seaman's Savings Bank building at the northwest corner of Pearl and Wall streets, — a distance of about four hundred and fifty feet.   In depth this plot of ground averaged almost two hundred and twenty-five feet, so that its area amounted to more than two acres." [254]   In 1644 it became the property of Jan Jansen Damen, the step-father of Dirk Holgersen's wife.

The land which Tymen received in 1642 and July 3, 1643, covers "the site of the present court house of Queen's County and its vicinity, in Long Island City." [255]

In 1644 the Director and Council complained against "Andries Rouloffsen, the Company's boatswain, and Tymen Jansen" for neglecting to repair the yachts "Amsterdam" and "Prins Willem." Tymen replied "that he has done his best, and cannot know when a vessel is leaky unless those in charge inform him of the fact; furthermore that nothing can be done without means." [256]   He was independent.

---

249 Ibid., pp. 72f.
250 Ibid., p. 366.
251 Ibid., p. 81.
252 Ibid., p. 367.
253 Ibid., p. 368.
254 J. H. Innes, New Amsterdam and Its People, p. 271.
255 Ibid., p. 276.
256 Calendar of Historical Manuscripts, I., p. 26.

After 1644 we hear nothing more of Tymen Jansen. He died before 1646. For in that year (September 9) his widow married Dirck Cornelisen, of Wensveen.[257]

Marritje had by Tymen a daughter, Elsie, who was born about 1633—1634. Marritje was member of the Dutch Reformed Church.

Marritje's second husband was a carpenter, probably the son of Cornelis Leendertsen. His house appears to have stood on the western end of the present Coffee Exchange. He died about two years after the marriage. By him Marritje had a son, Cornelis, who was baptized February 17, 1647,[258] the sponsors being Hans Kierstede, Willem Kay, Anneke Bogardus. This son died in 1678.

Marritje now married, July 20, 1649, her third husband, Govert Loockermans, a widower. Loockermans brought her his two little daughters, from a former marriage, Marritje and Jannetje, respectively eight and six years old. His original home was Turnhout, a town about twenty-five miles from Antwerp. He had come to New Amsterdam in 1633 as assistant cook on a yacht. He had served as clerk in the office of the West India Company, had become a fur trader, had made a visit to Netherlands in 1640, returning in 1641 with a wife. He was, as Mr. Innes says, a bold and enterprising trader "careless of whose corns he trod upon . . . in his pursuit of gain: ready, apparently, at any time to furnish the Indians with firearms, powder, and balls, in exchange for their furs; and declining to permit any interference in his business by persons of adverse interest." [259]

Govert Loockermans became one of the richest men in the province of New York. He died intestate 1671. In 1674 widow Loockermans (Marritje) lived in a house valued at $4000, situated on the present west side side of Pearl Street, between Wall and

---

257 Collections of the New York Genealogical and Biographical Society, I., p. 14.

258 Ibid., II., p. 22.

259 J. H. Innes, New Amsterdam and Its People, p. 241. E. B. O'Callaghan says: "Loockerman had by Marritje" Elsje, Cornelis, Jacob, Johanna, and Marritje. Elsje married, 1st, Cornelis P. Van der Veen, by whom she had Cornelis, Timothy, and Margaret. She next married Jacob Leysler . . . . Marritje Loockermans married Barthasar Bayard, step-son to Governor Stuyvesant, and a respectable brewer in New York. Joanna, or Jannitje Loockermans, was the second wife of Surgeon Hans Kierstede, and her children were Areantje, Cornelis, Jacobus, and Maria. Govert Loockermans, after filling some of the highest offices in the Colony, died, worth 520,000 gl. or $208,000; an immense sum, when the period in which he lived is considered. His widow was buried 20th November, 1677." (History of New Netherland, II., 38 note.)

William Street, near a part of the street called the Waer Side
(Year-Book of the Holland Society, 1896, p. 167 f.)

By Loockermans, Marritje had one child, Jacob, born in 1652.
After his father's death Jacob continued to reside for some years
with his mother. After his mother died, he went to Maryland,
where he pursued the study of medicine. He appears later as a
magistrate of Dorchester County. Jacob seems to have been much
more under the influence of Elsie, his half-sister upon his mother's
side, than under that of his half-sisters upon the father's side.
In 1679, two years after his mother's death, he conveyed to Elsie's
husband Jacob Leisler all his right to the estate, in the Province of
New York, of his father as well as his right to all which had come
to him through his mother and his half-brother Cornelius. "Nearly
the whole estate of Govert Loockermans and of his wife had thus
come into the hands of his step-daughter Elsie." [260]

Signature of Govert Loockermans, 1659, husband of Marritje Jans.

Elsie — the granddaughter of the midwife Tryn Jonas; the
niece of the pastor's wife Anneke; the daughter of one of the
wealthiest woman in the province: was destined to be the most
unfortunate of the Norwegians in early New York.

January 7, 1652, she married an eminent trader, Cornelius
Pietersen Van der Veen. In 1658, being then described as "an old
and suitable person," he was made a great burgher of New Amsterdam. He was Schepen of the city and held other offices of
trust in the church and in the community. He died in the summer of 1661.[261]

After his death Elsie married, on April 11, 1663, Jacob Leisler, a German, from Frankfurt.[262] In 1674 he had property in
New Amsterdam on the west side of the present Whitehall St.,
there also a part of the Water Side. It was valued at $30,000.

---

260 Ibid., p. 245.
261 D. T. Valentine, History of the City of New York, p. 150.
262 Whether from the Oder or the Main, is not stated.

He was executed for treason May 16, 1691. When England experienced her last revolution, in 1689, the question was raised in the colonies: Should they remain as simple dependencies on the crown of England, or should they by the people manage their own affairs. Leisler became a leader in the democratic movement. But he lacked discretion and treated his opponents as rebels, making a technically illegal seizure of power. For this he was executed, but with such undue regard for fair trial that his execution amounted to judicial murder. His son-in-law Jacob Milborne shared the same fate. Their property was confiscated. But four years later the English parliament reversed the attainder for treason of Leisler and Milborne, and restored the confiscated property to the heirs.

Unhappy indeed was she on that rainy morning of May, 16, 1691, when her husband and her son-in-law were led to the scaffold, from which the words of her husband could be heard, "I hope my eyes shall see our Lord Jesus Christ in Heaven; I am ready! I am ready!" or the words of her son-in-law: "We are thoroughly wet with rain, but in a little time we shall be washed with Holy Spirit.[268]

It was a crushing blow to Elsie Leisler. Her troubles endeared her to her children and many sympathetic neighbors. But she was a brave woman "of reserved and humble deportment, mixing but little with the world and confining herself to her own domestic sphere."

Marritje Janse did not live to see the misfortunes of her daughter. She died in 1677. In her will, executed the same year, she mentions her own children and grandchildren, not, however, her two step-daughters.

To use the words of Collections of the New York Historical Society, XXV., pp. 60ff., Marritje "leaves to Cornelius, Timothy and Margaretta Van der Veen, children of her daughter, Elsie Leisler, by Peter Cornelis Van der Veen, each 100 guilders, in Beavers, at 8 guilders a piece. To Anna Bogardus, daughter of Wm. Bogardus, 50 guilders. Leaves the rest of the property to

---

268 For interesting accounts of the acts and the trial of Jacob Leisler, see John Fiske's, The Dutch and Quaker Colonies in America, II.; Mrs. Van Rensselaer's History of the City of New York, II. Leisler's Speech at the Gallows is recorded in Ecclesiastical Records of the State of New York, II. p. 1016f.
Also see Appendix D: Jacob Leisler.

DUTCH HOUSE IN NEW YORK CITY, 1679.

her children, Elsie Tymans, married to Jacob Leisler. Cornelis Dirchsen, married with Gelise Hendricks, and Jacob Lockermans, not married yet. Makes her cousin (?), Mr. Johanes Van Brugh, and Mr. Francis Rumbout, alderman of this city, her executors.

"Dated May 7, 1677. Witnesses, John Dervall, Cornelis Cregier.

"Codicil, November 1, 1677. Leaves to son, Cornelis Dircksen, a negro boy. To daughter, Elsie Leisler, a golden ear ring, made of gold, which was partly given to her by her grandmother. To son, Jacob Lockermans, her diamond rose ring. To son Cornelis, the Great Bible, and to his wife 3 silver spoons. To Mary, daughter of Johanes Van Brugh, a silver bodkin. To her granddaughter, Margaret Van der Veen, a silver chain with keys. To grand-daughter, Susanah Leisler, a silver chain with a case and a cushion.

"Witnesses, her neighbors, Mr. Carsten Learsen and Mr. John Cavilleer."

BARTEL LARSEN.

Bartel Larsen, from Norway, was in New Amsterdam as early as the beginning of 1647. Under date of January 10, 1647, a document, making him a party in a transaction to the amount of forty-four guilders—the other party was one Hendrick Jansen—states that he was from Norway.[264] It calls him "privateer."[265]

ANDRIES LAURENSEN.

Andries Laurensen, or Andries Noorman, Adriaen Laurens de Noorman, was in New Netherland as early as 1639. Under date of September 8, 1639, it is stated in the Council Records, that the Fiscal of New Amsterdam confiscated wine from Andries Noorman, "as it was not properly entered.[266]

264 Calendar of Historical Manuscripts, I., p. 43.
265 Was he the commander of a privateer?
266 Calendar of Historical Manuscripts, I., p. 69.

On July 15, 1646, Andries acted as sponsor at the baptism of Engel, a child belonging to Laurents Pietersen, a Norwegian. The records of the Reformed Dutch Church in New Amsterdam enter his name as Adriaen Laurens de Noorman.[267] On October 5, 1656, he was examined in regard to a soldier's selling a gun. Whether Laurensen was the soldier that was guilty of this offense, is not clear. E. B. O'Callaghan makes this statement: "Examination of Andries Laurensen, a soldier, sent prisoner from Ft. Casimir on charge of having sold a gun."[268] Possibly the words "in regard to" should immediately follow "Laurensen." As the statement reads now, Laurensen must have been the prisoner. If this was the fact, his offense must have been regarded as a light matter, or the accusation against him was unfounded. For he afterwards was holding positions of trust in the army. On August 5, 1658, he sent a communication to Director Stuyvesant in regard to the continued insolence of the Indians, and requested a supply of ammunition.[269] On October 31, 1659, he wrote to the Director that he was a prisoner among the Esopus Indians (Albany).[270] On March 1, 1660, instructions were given him as sergeant to go to "South River to engage some Swedes and Finns to enlist in the Company's (West India) service."[271]

He seems to have owned a house in New Amsterdam, in 1657, and it would appear that the name of his wife was Anna Claas. We infer this from two entries in the Minutes of the orphan Masters of New Amsterdam, 1655-1658, pp. 38-39, 41-42.

Under date of November 28, 1657, the first entry reads: "Whereas, Roelof Jansen, mason, has died at the house of Arent Lauwerensen, on the 16th of this month of November, 1657; and whereas said Arent Lauwerensen by a petition to the Burgomasters and Schepens of this City has requested that they would please to direct and authorize one or two persons to sell at public auction to the highest bidder, according to inventory, the property left by said Roelof Jansen, that thus might be paid the expenses of his funeral, his house rent and other known and unknown debts. Therefore their said Worships order the Orphanmasters to enter

---

267 Collections of the New York Genealogical and Biographical Society, II., p. 21.

268 Calendar of Historical Manuscripts, I., p. 175.

269 Ibid., p. 285.

270 Ibid., p. 288.

271 Ibid., p. 208. Swedes and Finns had settled there ca. 1639-1640.

upon said estate and to do therewith what ought to be done, and they herewith authorize and direct Siur Mattheus de Vos, Notary Public, and Arent Lauwerensen to have the estate sold at auction by the Secretary of the Burgomasters and Schepens, as well as of the Orphanmasters, whereby the debts, as above stated, shall be paid, and the surplus handed to them to dispose of as they shall find best."

The second entry , dated December 12, of the same year, reads:

"Anna Claas, with Sieur Mattheus de Vos, Notary Public, and with Arent Lauwerensen, administrator of the estate of Roelof Jansen, mason, dec'd, appeared and proved by the affidavits of two credible persons that said Roelof Jansen, dec'd, had given her in his lifetime his everyday clothing, his gun, powderhorn, and what belonged to it; she also produces an account for house rent, for caretaking and money advanced, amounting to 99fl. 18st., wherein are included 7 beavers, the balance being in wampum. She requests that the affidavits and the account may be approved. The orphanmasters approve the affidavits and account, ordering their Secretary to pay the account, after deducting what the husband of said Anna Claas has bought from the estate."[272]

On December 12, 1657, a Jan Gillesen Kock was authorized "to collect bills of . . . Arent Lauwerenzen, Tielman Van Vleeck, Gerrit Pietersen,"[273]

On May 10, 1662, "Arent Louwersen" secured a new lot in New Amsterdam.[274]

In 1664 he took the oath of allegiance, when the English conquered New Netherland.

JAN LAURENSEN.

Jan Laurensen (Jan Laurensen Noorman) and wife arrived at New Amsterdam, in 1659, by the ship "De Trouw," which sailed from Holland on February 12, 1659, and was commanded by Jan Jansen Bestevaer.[275]

272 Year Book of the Holland Society of New York, 1900, pp. 114, 115.
273 Ibid., p. 119.
274 E. B. O'Callaghan, History of New Netherland, II., p. 592.
275 Year Book of the Holland Society of New York, 1902.

LAURENS LAURENSEN.

Laurens Laurensen, or Laurens Laurensen Noorman, sometimes called Laurens Laurensz van Copenhagen or Laurens Laurensen van Vleckersen (Flekkerö, Norway) came to New Netherland in 1631. He was a Norwegian, as is evident from his being frequently called Noorman and, at least twice, in 1646 and 1663, "van Vleckeren" or "van Vleckersen." In an agreement he made with Van Rensselaer, July 2, 1631, he is called Laurens Laurensz van Copenhagen. We cannot give the reason for this. It has been supposed that "Noorman," in the records of New Netherland is a general term for Scandinavian. But this supposition has no warrant whatever in the documents in question, where "Noorman" always means Norwegian.

In the agreement which is given in extenso at the close of this sketch, as well as in a notarial copy from minutes of the Chambers of Amsterdam of the West India Company, July 7, 1631, it will be seen that besides Laurensz there were two other Norwegians, Andries Christensen from Flekkerö and Barent Thonissen from Hellesund, near Christiansand, who were to emigrate to the colony of Rensselaerswyck. All three were to work together and run a saw-mill and a grist-mill.

Laurensen and Thonissen arrived in New Netherland by "de Eendracht," which sailed from the Texel shortly after July 7, 1631.[276] They were seafaring men. But Christensen, who was not a seafaring man, failed to go; he "ran away," as Van Rensselaer puts it. Laurensen was thirty-six years of age, and seems to have been married when he came to New Netherland, for in a letter of April 23, 1634, the patroon says to Director van Twiller: "I have paid f. 50 to the wife of Laurens Laurensz, but I do not know how much is still owing him. He bargained for no wages. All I have to do is to provide his board, or in place of board pay him f. 100 yearly—while I have half of all that he earns. He is also responsible for the other two for the advance money that I gave to Andries Christensen."[277] The name of his wife was Tytie Lippes. . . [278]

---

276 Van Rensselaer Bowier Manuscripts, pp. 186ff., p. 807.
277 Ibid., p. 285.
278 The New York Genealogical and Biographical Record, VI., p. 147.

The agreement, of July 7, 1631, between Van Rensselaer, Laurensen, et al, reads:

Notarial Copy of Extract from Minutes of Amsterdam of the West India Company, July 7, 1631.

The translation by Mr. J. F. van Laer reads as follows:

Extract from the resolution book of the honorable directors of the Chartered West India Company.   Chamber of Amsterdam.

Monday, the 7th of July 1631, in Amsterdam.

Appeared before the meeting Mr. *Kilian van Rensselaer*, who requested that he be permitted to send over by the ship *d'eentracht* some colonists and eight or ten calves, namely:

> *Cornelis Gerritssz van flecker* [Flekkerø in Norway]
>
> *Lourens Lourenssz van Coppenhagen*
>
> *Barent thonissz van Heiligesondt* [Hellesund in Norway]
>
> *Claes Brunsteyn van Straelsondt*
>
> *Andries Christenssz van flecker* [Flekkerø].

In regard to which it was decided first to hear the skipper, who declares that he will do all he can, whereupon his honor's request is granted, on condition that the skipper in case he should be inconvenienced thereby, may throw them [the calves] overboard or allow them to be eaten, without thereby obliging the Company to give any compensation.   Underneath was written: Agrees with the aforesaid resolution book.   And was signed: *Jacob Hamel.*

Agrees with its original

quod attestor infrascriptus

[signed]   *J: vande Ven*

Nots Pub^{cus}: ss^{tt}.

Ao :   21.
———— 1634.
4.

In 1632 Laurensen was appointed schepen on de Laets Kil, which is the present Mill Creek in the city of Rensselaer. On June 3, 1638, he was appointed "servant" of the West India Company.[279]

On September 29, 1639, Tymen Jansen gave him power of attorney to collect money due him in Holland.

On October 8, 1646, a declaration was made by Isaac Allerton and Edward Ager, showing that Isaac Abrahams and Laurens Laurensen had made a contract, and that "Isaac Abraham had fulfilled his contract with Laurens Laurensen." In Calendar of Historical Manuscripts, I., p. 34, from which this notice is taken, nothing is said as to the nature of the contract.

Laurensen obtained grant of a lot in Beverwyck on October 25, 1653, where he owned a house in 1657.[280] He also owned property in New Amsterdam; for in 1655 he paid a voluntary contribution and taxation of twelve florins to this city; and in 1665 his widow was assessed as one of its inhabitants—in the Smith's Valley.[281] He may have had a parcel of land there for storing lumber; for he was running a saw mill as late as 1663. He seems to have freighted his own lumber, as he had several yachts. But he also built ships and sold them. For some time his partner was Reyner Pietersen, shipmaster.[282] He and Pietersen were sued, December 2, 1659, by Walewyn van der Veen for a "statement of the account conveyed" to Walewyn by one Jan Ariaansen. Laurensen contended that he did not owe Ariaansen anything, and that Ariaansen had been overpaid.[283]

Later Laurensen had a new partner: Dirck Jansen, a woodsawyer from Oldenburg. On January 13, 1660, Laurensen and Jansen sued Ritzer Raymont, demanding from him the payment of the sum of fl. 1400, "for purchase of a yacht named Swarten Arent (the Black Eagle), sold to him, or security of payment." Raymont admitted that he was indebted to the plaintiffs. There were found some errors in the contract of sale and date, but the Court condemned the defendant to pay and satisfy the plaintiffs.[284]

279 Van Rensselaer Bowier Manuscripts, p. 203. Calendar of Historical Manuscripts, I., p. 62.
280 Munsell. Collections on the History of Albany, III., p. 13.
281 The Records of New Amsterdam, 1653-1674, I., p. 375; IV., p. 225.
282 Year Book of the Holland Society of New York, 1900, p. 282.
283 The Records of New Amsterdam, 1653-1674, III., p. 84.
284 Ibid., III., p. 101. Dirck Jansen sold, October 26, 1662, a sloop named "The Hope", for 2000 guilders.

Laurensen lost one of his yachts, as is seen from evidence offered in a suit which Jacob Jansen Moesman brought against Laurensen, September 25, 1663. The plaintiff claimed that the defendant owed him money. Laurensen replied that he had paid some of it, but "his books and proofs are lost with his yacht." The Court postponed the case until the next Court day or "till the arrival of Abraham, the carpenter."[285]

We have referred to documents of 1646 and 1663, which speak of Laurensen as being from Flekkerö. Under date of September 21, 1646, an order was issued, at New Amsterdam, directing Everardus Bogardus, the minister, to deliver to the Council a bill of exchange, 2,500 guilders, given by the Swedish governor to Jacob Sandelyn for goods sold to the governor. The goods had been sold contrary to law. The bill of exchange had been delivered by "Laurens Vleckeren" to Bogardus. Laurensen was examined "respecting the sending of above [mentioned] bill by Jacob Sandelyn to Reverend Mr. Bogardus." He admitted that he had delivered a package of letters to Bogardus to be sent to Holland, amongst which were some from the Swedish government."[286]

It would seem that Laurensen had received the package of letters when visiting the Swedish colony in Delaware, with his sloop.

Seventeen years later the name Laurensen van Vleckeren, or Vleckersen, appears in the court minutes of New Amsterdam: "August 21, 1663, Lambert Huyberzen Mol, pltf., v|s Lauwerens Lauwerensen van Vleckersen, deft. Pltf. demands from deft. ninety-five @ six Fort Orange inch plank, sixteen feet long. Deft. admits debt, but says he cannot deliver them, as they are not sawed and durst not saw through fear of the Indians. The W. Court order the deft. to satisfy and pay the pltf. within three weeks' time."[287]

Laurensen died before 1665; for on August 23, 1665, his widow, Tytie Lippes, was married to John Roelofsen, also from Flekkerö, and a resident in New Netherland since 1663.[288]   Her

285 Ibid., IV., p. 307.
286 New York Colonial Documents, XII., p. 27, Calendar of Historical Manuscripts, I., p. 105.
287 The Records of New Amsterdam, 1653-1674, IV., p. 288.
288 The New York Genealogical and Biographical Record, VI., p. 147.

name appears in April, 1665, in a list of burghers and inhabitants assessed in New Amsterdam.

For the agreement between the Patroon Kiliaen Von Rens-selaer and Laurens Laurensen and others, see the following:[289]

"July 2, 1631.

"At the request of *Andries Christenssen van Vlecken*, 40 years of age, *Laurens Laurensz van Coppenhagen*, 36 years of age, and *Barent Thonissen van Heijligesont*, 22 years of age, *Kiliaen van Rensselaer*, in his capacity as patroon of his colony situated above and below Fort Orange on the North River of New Nether-land, has agreed and contracted with the aforesaid persons for the term of three years, commencing on their arrival in that country, with the condition that the contract is binding on them for the said term of three years, but that the said *Rensselaer* may terminate it whenever it pleases him. First regarding the transportation of the said persons, *Rensselaer,* having obtained from the Chartered West India Company, Chamber of Amsterdam, the privilege of transporting seafaring men for their board without wages on the condition that they do proper ship duty, *Laurensz Laurensz, Barent Theunisz* and all seafaring men accept the same, but *Andries Chris-tensz,* not being a seafaring man, must pay out of his wages six stivers a day for board. As to the return voyage, the said Rens-selaer promises to exert himself likewise, without being further responsible in the matter, to have them come hither at the least expense, whether their term of service has expired or whether he chooses to order them to come home. Arriving there with God's help, they shall betake themselves at the first opportunity and at their own expense to Fort Orange, to settle either on the mill creek or opposite the fort on the east side of the North River, where there is also a good waterfall, and build their houses in the lightest fashion on the one or the other of said places, and on no other without consent; further to erect a suitable sawmill, which can saw.wood 40 feet, or at least 33 feet long, towards which he, *Rensselaer,* shall pay one-half of the hardware, and the tools which they need therefor, and must take with them from here, and they the other half, for which he, *Rensselaer,* shall furnish

289 This interesting document is taken from the "Van Rensselaer Bowier Manuscripts," being the letters of Kiliaen Van Rensselaer, 1630-1643, and other documents relating to the colony of Rensselaerswyck, translated and edited by A. J. F. van Laer, Archivist. Albany, 1908.

them the money in advance. They promise, all four of them, to erect the said mill within the space of three months and when it is finished, they may hew the largest, finest and best oak trees standing in the entire colony of the said *Rensselaer,* and for seven leagues next adjoining, and bring the same to the place where the saw-mill stands in order to saw therefrom suitable ship planking, gunwale timber or such other timber as he, *Rensselaer,* shall direct or they in the absence of directions shall deem fit. The mill being made, the logs cut, brought to the mill and sawed, one-half thereof shall belong to the said *Rensselaer* and the other half to the four of them, the same to be shipped hither with the most convenient speed at the joint expense of both parties, provided that *Rensselaer* shall not charge the men more for freight and the other expenses than he will have to pay himself; and of the proceeds of the said timber here in this country over and above expenses, one-half shall go to him, *Rensselaer,* and the other half shall be paid to the aforesaid persons or those having their right and title, but first and above all, deduction must be made of the sums advanced by him, promised or paid for them personally, in return for which he, *Rensselaer,* promises to provide such board for the said four persons as is customary in that country or else, in lieu thereof, to pay 100 guilders a year for each of the four persons, amounting together to 400 guilders a year, so that Rensselaer shall provide their board as above and they shall faithfully and diligently do their work to the satisfaction of the said *Rensselaer* or his agents and each side receive one-half of the profits after deduction of all expenses as above.

"*Rensselaer* also agrees to pay in hand to each of them the sum of 20 guilders to be deducted from the board, or 100 guilders a year, which he must pay to each of them and to *Andries Kristensen* the sum of 40 guilders, besides the advance for hardware, millstone and what is further required for the building of the said saw and grist-mill, on condition that the amount be hereafter again deducted and retained as above.

"And inasmuch as they are also to make a grist-mill in connection with the said sawmill, they shall also be entitled to one-half of what is earned therewith (deducting the expense of grinding).

"In case the said *Rensselaer,* as patroon, or his agents, need the aforesaid four persons or any of them in his private service, they must let themselves be employed for all sorts of work, whether farming, house carpentering, felling of logs, burning of pitch and tar, or whatever it may be, nothing excepted, at 15 stivers a day besides board, which they have in addition as above, provided that *Rensselaer* shall enjoy one-half of the aforesaid wages of 15 stivers.

"If *Rensselaer* or his agents, after the mill is built, should have any wood brought to be sawed, they must do this at 20 stivers for 100 feet in length by one foot in breadth, and for wider, shorter or longer boards accordingly, on condition that *Rensselaer* shall receive one-half thereof as above.

"Regarding the boards, beams or planks which they may have in stock and which Rensselaer may need for his other work, he shall be allowed to take these by paying them one-half of the price ordinarily paid by the skippers in Norway.

"If these people sow, mow or plant any land, or catch any game or fish, one-half (of the product) shall go to them and the other half go to *Rensselaer,* or be deducted from the 100 guilders for board.

"During the period of this agreement, each one shall be responsible for the other, as *Rensselaer* is dealing with them jointly, but not willing to deal or to keep accounts with each in particular.

"In case any one of them should happen to find or to discover any mines, minerals, pearl fisheries or anything of the kind, he shall disclose the same to no one but the patroon or his agent, who shall make them a handsome present for the same according to the importance of the matter. They shall further under the sovereignty of the High Mighty Lords the States General, all submit themselves to the authority of the directors of the Chartered West India Company in general and of the aforesaid *Rensselaer* as their patroon in particular, and observe all the ordinances and regulations to be passed there by them respectively in matters of police and justice, and be obliged to take oath of obedience and fidelity, especially to refrain from trading, negotiating or carrying on business there against the order and intention of the Company and their aforesaid patroon, whether in skins, seawan or other goods found there, and not to accept the same by way of present or otherwise, nor to take merchandise from here with them for themselves or for others directly or indirectly, in any manner whatsoever, on pain of confiscation and penalties fixed by the Company or still to be fixed, and furthermore of banishment from the colony as perjurers and refractory characters, for which they all together in common and each one in particular for himself and the others bind themselves to answer and stand responsible.

"They shall further not be allowed to contract with any one else or to enter any one else's service, on forfeiture of this entire agreement to the benefit of the said patroon, each one's share in the mill, in the hewn and sawed timber and what may in any way belong to them, to be forfeited and left to be disposed of as above, and in case one or more of the aforewritten persons should leave or drop out, the remaining ones must fill the places as quickly as possible with other suitable persons and by every ship and yacht sailing hither send proper reports and accurate accounts of every thing, in all sincerity without concealment. In testimony of the truth of the above agreement, this is signed by the patroon and the persons aforesaid with their own hands, in Amsterdam, this second of July of the year sixteen hundred and thirty-one, and signed with the several hands and X marks of *Andries kristensen*, the X mark of *Laurens Laurensz*, X *Berent Thonisz, kiliaen van Rensselaer*. Underneath was written: *Kiliaen van Rensselaer* charged with board of *Andries kristenssen*, due to him for transportation nine guilders."

ANDRIES PIETERSEN.

Andries Pietersen, or Andries Pietersen Noorman, came to New Netherland in 1660 by the ship "de Moesman," which sailed on March 9, 1660.[290] In the ship's passenger list his name is given as "Andries Noorman from Sleewyck" (Sleviken (?) in Norway), and he is called a soldier.[291] In 1661 he was a member of the garrison at Esopus.[292] July 2, 1666, it is stated in the Church Records of Albany, that he "used the large pall"—perhaps for

---

290 Year Book of the Holland Society of New York, 1902, p. 13. He was not from Schleswig, Denmark, as some would maintain. He was a "Noorman". He may have been from "Sletvik," a name we have seen in Rygh's "Norske Gaardnavne".

291. He was not from Schleswig, Denmark, as some would maintain. It is plainly stated that he was a "Noorman" (Norwegian). He may have been from Sleviken, or Sletvik, Norway.

292 New York Colonial Documents, XIII., p. 202.

some relative of his.[293] It is not unlikely that Marcus Pietersen (also from Sleviken [?]), who sailed with Andries, was his brother. Shortly afterward, Andries came near using the pall himself, as we immediately shall see.

In proceedings and sentences of the court held at Esopus, April 25-27, 1667, "resulting from complaints of the inhabitants of Esopus against violences committed by the soldiers and illtreatment from Capt. Brodhead, it was shown that Andries Pietersen, being at the said time in the house of (Cornelis Barentsen) Sleght, was beaten by Christoffer Berresfort with his halberd, that the said Andries fell down in a sounding and was in great danger of his life."[294]

A document of April 28, 1667, signed by Andries Pietersen and other burghers of Wiltwyck, shows that they were in arms during the Brodhead mutiny,[295] as Brodhead had threatened to burn their village.

Other traces of Pietersen are found in the "Marriage and Baptismal Registers of the old Dutch church of Kingston" (Wiltwyck, Esopus). He and Heyltjen Jacobs were witnesses on December 12, 1666, at the baptism of Marretjen, a child belonging to Hendrick Aertsen.[296]

According to the same Record, "Andries" and Maertie Davidson had their children, Christoffel, Andries, Johannes, Cornelia baptized on October 6, 1678, April 24, 1681, January 27, 1684, October 18, 1685, respectively.[297] It is probably Andries Pietersen from Sleviken that is meant here.

ANDRIES PIETERSEN.

Andries Pietersen, from Bergen, arrived at New Amsterdam by the ship "de Rooseboom," which sailed in March, 1663. In the list of passengers the words "from Bergen" are appended to

293 Munsell, Collections on the History of Albany, I., p. 26.
294 New York Colonial Documents, XIII., p. 407.
295 Ibid., p. 414.
296 R. R. Hoes, Baptismal and Marriage Registers of the Old Dutch Church of Kingston, N. Y.
297 Ibid., pp. 10, 14, 21, 24.

his name.[298]   It is presumably Bergen in Norway, that is meant, not Bergen op Zoom or Bergen in Germany; for Andries Pietersen is a Scandinavian name. A Norwegian, Frederick Claesen, sailed with Pietersen on the same ship.

HANS PIETERSEN.

Hans Pietersen was in New Amsterdam as early as 1655. That he was from Norway, is stated in the court minutes which relate about a suit between "Hans Pietersen of Norway" and "Paulus van der Beecq," whose servant he was.[299] He had left his master, who consequently brought suit against him for breach of contract.   The first notice of this is found in an entry under date of January 28, 1655, showing that the case had been tried in Breuckelen and that the verdict rendered was not in accord with the desires of Van Beecq.

The minutes record under date of January 28: "Writ of inhibition.   In the case of Paulus van der Beecq, appellant vs. Hans Petersen, from a judgment of the court of Breuckelen, and summons to the respondent to appear before the Council."[300]   On February 9, 1655, the minutes read: "Judgment in case of appeal Paulus van der Beecq vs. Hans Petersen; decision of the court of Breuckelen reversed and respondent ordered to serve out his term according to contract, to pay costs and to be committed until he pay the fine fixed by law."[301]

It seems that Hans preferred to go to prison, or that he took quarter at the prison later and for some other unknown cause. For on December 23, 1655, he was discharged from prison, "on his own personal security."[302]   Perhaps he took advantage of the liberty given him and fled.   On November 7, 1658, an order was issued to the magistrates of Flushing and Eastdorp to arrest him.[303]

In June, 1662, he was at Esopus (Albany).   He petitioned the magistrates that he might keep a tavern there.   The petition

298 Year Book of the Holland Society of New York, 1902, p. 13.
299 Calendar of Historical Manuscripts, I., pp. 58, 127.
300 Ibid., I., p. 145.
301 Ibid., I., pp. 293, 58.
302 Ibid., p. 157.
303 Ibid., p. 202.

was not granted. For the keeping of a tavern there "would tend to debauch soldiers and other inhabitants, and it was feared that strong liquor might be sold to savages."[304]

In 1674 he asked for permission to purchase land in Katskil, Albany.[305]

On April 13, 1676, he obtained a patent of land in Delaware.[306] In the same year he had a lawsuit with the Swedish pastor in Delaware, Laurentius Carolus (Lars Lock), regarding the "recovery of a mare." The pastor was the injured party.[307] It would seem that Hans Pietersen must have been, by this time, quite an expert in defending himself before a court. We take leave of him where we found him: in court.

LAURENS PIETERSEN.

Laurens Pietersen, or Laurens Pietersen Noorman. from Tönsberg, in Norway, was in New Amsterdam as early as 1639. On June 16, of that year, he was declared sole heir to the real and personal property of a Roellof Roeloffsen, the witnesses being Pieter Jansen, likely the Norwegian by that name, and Hans Stein.[308] In the Calendar of Wills, where this declaration is contained, Laurens is called "Laurens Pietersen van Tonsback" (Tönsberg). In the Church Records of New Amsterdam, containing the entry of his marriage with Anetie Pieters from "Brutsteen," Germany—August 18, 1641—, it is stated that he is from Tönsberg.[309]

His name appears quite often in the church records as sponsor —August 8, 1641, for Rachel, daughter of Dirk Holgersen, the Norwegian; December 8, in the same year, for Rommetje, the child of Hans Hansen van Nordstrand in Holstein; May 21, 1646, for Nicholas, a son of Barent Janszen; April 14, 1647, for Aert, a child of Caesar Albertsz[310]; March 20, 1650, for Nicholas, a son

304 New York Colonial Documents, XIII., p. 389.
305 Ibid., XIII., p. 481.
306 Ibid., p. 548.
307 Calendar of Historical Manuscripts, I., p. 353f.; New York Colonial Documents, XII., p. 622.
308 Calendar of Wills. Compiled by B. Fernow, 1896, p. 334.
309 The New York Genealogical and Biographical Record, VI., p. 88.
310 Ibid., V., pp. 30, 87, 89.

of Barent Jansen; January 28, 1663, for Joost, the son of Barent Joosten and his own daughter Sytie.[311]

Laurens had his own child Sytie baptized June 1, 1642, one of the sponsors being Hans Hansen from Bergen. His child Engel was baptized July 15, 1646, three Norwegians being sponsors: Pieter Jansen Noorman, Andries Laurensen Noorman, and Maryken Tymens (sister of Anneke Jans and wife of Tymen Jansen.[312]

On March 12, 1647, Laurens obtained a lot on Manhattan, between the lots of Peter Hilyaender and Evert Duyckingh's.[313] Mr. J. H. Innes says: "He owned a house and lot on the south side of Prinse Straet, about fifty feet from Broad Street. The house is mentioned as standing there as early as 1647. It was the first house built on Prinse Straet, the second being built about the year 1652—on the south side of the street—by Albert Pietersen from Hamburg," whose wife was Danish.[314]

Under date of March 22, 1651, we have a declaration of Laurens Pietersen to the effect that Dirck Holgersen (Norwegian) had purchased of Cornelis Willemsen a plantation on the west side of Mespath Kill, Long Island, opposite to Richard Brudenel.[315]

On March 10, 1660, Laurens petitioned "for the appointment of guardians and curators over his minor child," which petition was granted.[316] It is probable that his request included also his other child. For under date of January 20, 1661, we have a petition from "the guardians of Laurens Petersen's children for instructions in regard to the division of the estate."[317]

$$ G \; P $$

Signatures of Laurens Pietersen.

On March 10, 1661, he gave his consent "to the payment of her portion of the estate to his daughter Engeltje, shortly after her

311 Year Book of the Holland Society of New York, 1897, p. 147.
312 The New York Genealogical and Biographical Record, V., pp. 31. 88.
313 Year Book of the Holland Society of New York, 1901, p. 129.
314 J. H. Innes, New Amsterdam and Its People, p. 150f.
315 Calendar of Historical Manuscripts, I., p. 52.
316 Ibid., I., p. 208.
317 Ibid., I., p. 220.

marriage to Jan van Cleef."[318]   Engeltje was at the time only fifteen years old, her husband was thirty-three.

Laurens' other daughter, Sytie (Fytie, Eytie?), was married
on December 12, 1658, to Barent Joosten from "Witmont in Embderlandt." They had a child baptized in 1659. Their other
child, Joost, was baptized on January 28, 1663, in the Dutch Reformed church of Brooklyn. Laurens Pietersen himself was one
of the sponsors. The other sponsors were Symon Hansen and
Magdalentje Walingx.[319]

Pietersen is mentioned as selling land between the years 1654
and 1658.

On February 18, 1656, he sold to Harck Syboutsen his "lot on
the east side of the Graft, between the lots of Evert Dyckingh and
Abraham Rycken, as broad and long, large and small as it belongs
to said Lauren Pietersen Noorman by patent to him of 12 March,
1647." D. T. Valentine describes it as being on the east side
of Broad Street, south of Beaver Street.[320]

In 1664, Laurens signed the resolution adopted by the commonalty of the Manhattans.[321]

MARCUS PIETERSEN.

Marcus Pietersen is enrolled among the soldiers who were
to sail in the ship "de Moesman" for New Netherland on March
9, 1660. He was from Sleewyk (Sleviken, or Sletvik, in Norway), and is presumably the brother of Andries Pietersen Noorman, who was from the same place and sailed in the same ship.[322]

He seems to have received employment from Jochim Beeckman, a shoemaker, immediately upon his arrival in New Netherland. For on November 8, 1661, Beeckman brought suit against
Pieter Pietersen Smitt, complaining that he had been slandered
about a year before by the defendant, "according to declaration of

318 Ibid., I., p. 222.
319 See note 311.
320 Year Book of the Holland Society of New York, 1902, p. 129. D. T.
Valentine, Manual of the Corporation of the City of New York, 1861, p. 583.
321 New York Colonial Documents, I., p. 193.
322 Year Book of the Holland Society of New York, 1902, p. 13.

Marcus Pietersen and 'Gerrit Lebes,' who were working at the time with the plaintiff." Smitt denied the slander and requested that Marcus Pietersen and the other witness be heard before the court. On November 8, they were examined by the court. Marcus declared that he had not seen, but heard that Pieter Smitt had pushed open the door of Beeckman's chamber, and saw it was open. Gerrit declared, however, that Pieter Smitt pushed open the door and that he abused Beeckman "as a thief and worse than a thief."

The relation between the plaintiff and the defendant must have been verging on the comical, for Beeckman appeared again in court and complained "that he cannot walk the streets in peace in consequence of the deft. calling him black-pudding and insulting him." The defendant, however, denied it and said, "he does not speak a word."[323]

OULE POUWELSEN.

Oule Pouwelsen was in New Amsterdam about 1643. All we know of him is contained in an entry in the Calendar of Historical Manuscripts, I., p. 85, under date of June 11, 1643: The fiscal brought a charge against him "for insolence in his master's house. The defendant was committed to prison at his master's expense, until evidence be heard." Oule Pouwelsen, judging from the name, was probably a Norwegian. There was an Olaf Pålsson in New Sweden in 1641. (See Pennsylvania Magazine of History and Biography, III., p. 462f.)

JAN ROELOFFSEN.

Jan Roeloffsen, from Norway, arrived at New Amsterdam by the ship "de Statyn," which sailed September 27, 1663. Among the forty-six passengers aboard were also other Norwegians: Cornelius Teunissen, Jan Jansen and wife.[324] Jan Roeloffsen

---

323 The Records of New Amsterdam, 1653-1674, pp. 401, 407f.
324 Year Book of the Holland Society of New York, 1902.

married on August 23, 1665, in New Amsterdam, Tytie Lippes, the widow of Laurens Laurensen, who was from Flekkerö, Norway. In the register of marriages of the Dutch Reformed church in New Amsterdam, it is stated that Roeloffsen was from Flekkerö.[325] This Jan Roelloffsen must not be taken for Jan Roeloffsen, son of Roelof Jansen and Anneke Jans.

ROELOFF ROELOFFSEN.

Roeloff Roeloffsen was in New Amsterdam about or prior to 1639. Under date of July 16, 1639, his will makes Laurens Pietersen in New Amsterdam, a Norwegian from Tönsberg, the sole heir of his real and personal property. The witnesses were Pieter Jansen and Hans Stein. Laurens Pietersen was probably a relative of Roelloffsen, who, in that case, it would seem, was a Norwegian—an inference which receives support in his Norwegian sounding name.[326]

CORNELIUS TEUNISSEN.

Cornelius Teunissen, from Norway, arrived at New Amsterdam by the ship "de Statyn," which sailed September 27, 1663. Among the forty-six passengers aboard were three other Norwegians: Jan Roeloffsen from Flekkerö, Jan Jansen and wife.[327]

DIRCK TEUNISSEN.

Dirck Teunissen, or Dirck Teunissen Noorman, was in New Amsterdam as early as 1650, or before. The first notice we have of him is contained in the church record of the Dutch Reformed

---

825 Collections of the New York Genealogical and Biographical Society, I., p. 81.

826 Calendar of Wills. Compiled by B. Fernow, 1896, p. 834.

827 Year Book of the Holland Society of New York, 1902, p. 26.

church in New Amsterdam, which states that he married, on October 22, 1650, Adriantje Walich, a widow, from North Holland.[328]

Our knowledge of him is derived, in the main, from court records.

It appears that he had leased land of Abraham Verplanck. But he began to burn lime upon it. Verplanck therefore brought suit against him, on April 15, 1652, claiming that Teunissen by burning lime upon his land "spoiled it, impoverished the soil." The court, after hearing the parties, decided that Verplanck should in compensation receive one-fourth of all the lime burnt.[329]

Signature of Dirck Teunissen.

Teunissen did not abide by the decision of the court. The wife of Verplanck, therefore, appeared in court on February 10, 1653, and complained of Teunissen's negligence. But the court would do nothing before Verplanck appeared in own person.[330]

A week later Verplanck made his appearance in court and claimed that he had received only one-seventh part of the products of the land he had leased to Teunissen, and that he had not received "one-fourth part of the lime under sentence of the court." Teunissen admitted that he had leased the land, but claimed that he had given Verplanck exactly one-fourth of the crops. He demanded proof to the contrary. He also claimed that he had measured off a fourth of the lime. The Court refused to decide the case before the litigants proved their statements.[331]

On February 4, 1653, the court authorized two men, Thomas Hall and Egbert Woutersen to decide, as arbitrators, the difference between Abraham Verplanck and Dirck Teunissen concerning "the product of the land and the lime."[332]

On March 31, the court was informed that Teunissen would not submit to arbitrators. As no settlement was reached, the court again referred the litigants to arbitrators. It also stated that if

---

328 Collections of the New York Genealogical and Biographical Society, I., p. 16.

329 New York Colonial Documents, XIV., p. 177. Calendar of Historical Manuscripts, I., p. 126.

330 The Records of New Amsterdam, 1653-1674, I., p. 50.

331 Ibid., I., p. 52.

332 Ibid., I., p. 54.

the arbitrators could affect no settlement, court action was to follow.[333]

It would seem that the matter was settled out of court, as the minutes record nothing further about it.

Teunissen had a second law suit on December 1, 1653, when Jan Hendricksen demanded to get his boat, which was in the hands of Teunissen. The boat had been lost by Hendricksen. Teunissen had found it. He had not used it, but would not give it to the owner before he had paid one rix dollar in salvage. The court decided that Hendricksen should pay the rix dollar.[334]

Teunissen's third suit was begun September 6, 1655. It was against Jacob Clomp. We shall quote from the court minutes.

"Pltf. says, the deft. removed 3 of his canoes from the wharf, and used the same on board (his vessel) and has allowed them to drift away; requesting restitution of the canoes, one of which was laden with lime belonging to Willem Bentin. Deft. denies having removed any canoes from the wharf, but that one canoe, with lime, and two, without lime, drifted by his vessel, which he saw and brought to his ship; they had drifted away from him by night, in bad weather, breaking the ropes. Claims damages because pltf. has arrested him with his laden bark here, offers to declare on oath and to prove, that the canoes drifted, that he saw them coming right athwart his vessel and that they were carried away at night from his ship. Asks, that pltf. shall prove his assertion. Parties were referred by the Court, inasmuch as there is no proof of their statements, to Thomas Hall and Laurens Cor(neliu)s van Wel, who is hereby authorized to reconcile the parties touching their case; otherwise to communicate their opinions in writing to the Board."[335]

The fourth suit of Teunissen was against Gabriel de Haes. Teunissen demanded a payment of fl. 6. But de Haes claimed that the plaintiff owed him stable rent. He had had his cattle for about one month in his stable. Teunissen denied that he had hired the stable, though his cattle had stood in it five days. The

333 Ibid., I., p. 77.
334 Ibid., I., p. 188.
335 Ibid., I., p. 352.

Court referred the matter to Egbert Woutersen and Geurt Coerton for arbitration.[336]

We now come to the last suit, the most serious of them all When Teunissen married Adriantje Walich (Walings), he became a step-father, Adriantje having a daughter, Tryntie Cornelis by name.   In the beginning of 1657 there was a report current that the relations between the step-father and the step-daughter were criminal.   The mother, therefore, presented a petition to the court, requesting that the matter be investigated by competent persons, "as her daughter was falsely accused of having committed adultery with her step-father."   The petition was granted, providing "Teunissen and the girl appear personally before the Council."[337]
On April 17, 1657, it was petitioned that Tryntie Cornelis, the accused girl, be confronted with her accusers.   The petition was granted.   On April 24, she and her mother were examined.[338]
The sources at our disposal give no detail about the trial, but a petition of June 12, 1657, shows that Teunissen and Tryntie had fared ill.   For they requested that they be admitted to bail.   Another petition, of May 16, confirms this: Jan Evert Bout requested that he be permitted to rent his farm at Midwout to another person "in case Dirck Teunissen, the Noorman's wife, is not able to hire it."   The petition was granted.[339]   Midwout was the place where Teunissen was farming, when he was arrested: he was called Dirck Teunissen of Midwout.[340]
Under date of March 19, 1658, we find an order of the court directing Dirck Teunissen to pay jailer's fees.[341]   This may have reference to the lawsuit of 1657, though it would not, even if this be the case, necessarily imply that Teunissen had been found guilty. In fact, there is some evidence that the charge against him was unfounded.   First, the mother's implicit belief in the daughter's innocence.   Secondly, that Teunissen was not severely punished, if at all; for on December 22, he acted as sponsor at the baptism of Christian Pieterszen and Tryntie Pieters.[342]   Thirdly, that this Tryntie Pieters was no other than his own accused step-daughter,

336 Ibid., II., p. 20.
337 Calendar of Historical Manuscripts, I., p. 181.
338 Ibid., I., p. 183f.
339 Ibid., I., p. 186.
340 Ibid., I., p. 181.
341 Ibid., I., p. 192.
342 Collections of the New York Genealogical and Biographical Society, II., p. 59.

Tryntie Cornelis.[348] She had been married, October 28, 1657, to Christian Pieters (see the article "Christian Pieters," Part II ot this volume).

Teunissen had stood sponsor before this: On June 22, 1653, and on October 8, 1656, at the baptism of Jan and Frans, children af Joost Goderus.[344] On April 25, both Teunissen and his wife were sponsors at the baptism of Gerrit, son of Lubbert Gerritsen.

The will of Teunissen, 1662, mentions one of these children, and incidentally reveals the name of Adriantje Waling's former husband. It reads as follows:

"In the name of God, Amen. On the 9th day of October, 1662, appeared Dirck Theunissen and his lawful wife Ariantie Walens, of the Town of Bergen, on the west side of the North river, being in good health, going and standing. If the testator dies first, the widow is to have all for life. If necessary she may spend one-half, and the other half is to go to the children of the widow lawfully begotten by her deceased husband, Frans Pieters Sloo and Cornelis Janse Shubber. Legacies to Jan, son of Joost Goderus, and 50 guilders to the poor (not recorded)."[345]

Mrs. Goderus was the sister of Adriantje Walings.

Adriantje died before March, 1669, when Teunissen married Catalyntie Frans, a widow. In 1686 both he and Catalyntie were members of the Dutch Reformed Church in New Amsterdam. They lived on Pearl Street (Valentine's History of the City of New York, p. 333). Even as early as 1662, Dirck Teunissen's name appeared on a list, which was to show that he and several others were willing to contribute money—no specified sum is given—to a clergyman, for whom the magistrates of Bergen (New Jersey) had petitioned the government.

On January 16, 1691, inventory of the estate of Teunissen and Catalyntie, deceased, was taken. The house and ground was on Broadway, and valued at 4000 guilders, and other property at 2,125 guilders (Collections of the New York Historical Society, XXV., pp. 165, 467).

348 The New York Genealogical and Biographical Report, VI., p. 86.
344 Collections of the New York Genealogical and Biographical Society, II., pp. 34, 43.
345 New York Colonial Documents, XIII., p. 232.

BARENT THONISSEN.

Barent Thonissen was from Hellesund, Norway. With Laurens Laurensen and Andries Christensen he was engaged by Kiliaen van Rensselaer to erect and run a saw mill in the colony of Rensselaerswyck. He arrived at New Amsterdam in 1631 by the ship "de Eendracht," which sailed from the Texel shortly after July 7, in the same year. His name does not appear in the account books of the colony of Rensselaerswyck.[846] It is probable that he had relatives in New Netherland, for on July 27, 1666, a young man, Theunis Willemse, declared "that Barent Theunisse was his deceased uncle."[847]

BERNT OSWAL NOORMAN.

Bernt Oswal Noorman was a seaman in the service of New Netherland. All that is known about him, is limited to an entry in 1662: that he received his wages, the sum of fl. 2.13.[848]

GOVERT NOORMAN.

Govert Noorman, a private, is mentioned by Riker as having taken part in the raid on the Indians, 1663. He was enrolled in the company of soldiers at Esopus.[849]

JACOB DE NOORMAN.

Jacob de Noorman was in Esopus in 1663. He was a private soldier who took part in the raid on the Indians.[850] In 1674 he petitioned for a building lot in Esopus.[851]

846 Van Rensselaer Bowier Manuscripts, p. 807. See also article "Laurens Laurensen."
847 J. Pearson, Early Records . . . of Albany, p. 402.
848 New York Colonial Documents, II., p. 181.
849 J. Riker, Harlem, Its Origin and Early Annals, 1904.
850 Ibid., p. 201.
851 Year Book of the Holland Society of New York, 1897, p. 122.

ROELOFF NOORMAN.

Roeloff Noorman was enrolled as a private in the company of soldiers at Esopus, where he, in 1663, took part in the raid on the Indians.[352]

JOHN WISKHOUSEN.

John Wiskhousen was enrolled as a soldier who was to sail to New Amsterdam, April 15, 1660, by the ship "de Bonte Koe." In the passenger list it is stated that he was from Bergen in Norway.[353]

352 J. Riker, Harlem, Its Origin and Early Annals, p. 203.
353 Year Book of the Holland Society of New York, 1902.

Excursus.

I.

JOCHEM KALDER AND MAGDALENE WAELE.

Jochem Kalder and his wife Magdalene Waele, both of whom belonged to the earlier settlers in New Amsterdam, were probably Scandinavians,—either Norwegian or Danish.

Mr. J. H. Innes says, very little information can be gathered from the records respecting Kalder. He relates that one of the houses occupying, in the year 1655, the site of the present large building known as Nos. 31 to 35 Stone Street, was the cottage of Jochem Kalder, who had obtained a groundbrief for the land in 1645, and who seems to have built within a short time thereafter upon the westerly side of his plot about thirty-seven English feet in frontage.

On June 2, 1649, Dirk Holgersen leased to "Jochem Calder" for twenty years, 1651-1671, a tract of land on Long Island "together with the land heretofore leased by him, Dirck, to Jochem Calder." Kalder was to have the land "rent free" for the first six years; during the other following years he was to pay 150 guilders in annual rent. For the wording of the instrument, see article "Dirck Holgersen." Part I.

One of the earliest notices of Kalder dates from 1643, in which year he signed a note (August 8). He had children: Jacob was baptized in New Amsterdam March 9, 1642 (the father's name is given as Kayker)*; Jeurgie, March 13, 1644; Annetje, March 11, 1646, (father's name: Jochem Carels); Michel and Dorothe, twins, June 5, 1650, (father's name, Jochem Kier. This

---

* At this baptism, Teuntje Bronck, the wife of Jonas Bronck, was sponsor. Bronck and his wife were Danes.

cannot refer to one Jochem Kiersted, who died in 1647) ; Jacobus, February 9, 1653 (father's name Callaer).

As is seen above, there is no uniformity in the spelling of Kalder's name. The same lack of uniformity appears in the records, when they mention Kalder as a sponsor. On May 17, and July 8, 1654, his name is entered in the column of sponsors as Calder; July 4, 1655, as Calser; September 26, 1655, April 9, 1656, July 16, 1656, as Caljer. The church records under date of August 18, 1658, give the spelling Caljer; of March 1, 1659, when Kalder's widow married again, as Calker.

Why this variety? It is likely due to a pronunciation of Kalder's name, which sounded strange to the Dutch. And whence this difficult pronunciation?

We would not seek it in France or in Germany, e. g. in Cleves, where there is a "Calcar." We may conjecture: Kolkjär in Denmark; this would perhaps explain the spelling Kier, Calker, Kayker. The Norwegian "tykke l" (thick "l") is likely the cause of the confusion. Hence we look to Norway for an explanation.

O. Rygh, in "Norske Gaardnavne," IV., Kristians Amt |1|, p. 163, finds the island of Kaldhol pronounced as Kaldor (1520); Kalder (1578; 1604); Kaldor (1594); Kallul, Kaldor (1668). He says, the form of Kaldor is due to misunderstanding the thick "l" sound. This "l" sounds somewhat like "r" and "l" combined.

Signature of Jochem Kalder.

In "Norske Gaardnavne," XIV., Söndre Trondhjems Amt, p. 384 f. (Selbu), the name Kallar is spelled Kallir (1590), Kaller (1626, 1668), Kalder (1723). Kalder is a name quite familiar. also among the present Norwegians.

It is thus probable, though not certain, that Jochem Kalder was from Norway.

It is significant that the lease he received in 1649 was signed by Dirck Holgersen and Pieter Jansen, both of whom were Norwegians; and that Pieter Jansen and Jochem Kalder were arbitrators in 1653; moreover, that Pieter Jansen was appointed guardian of Jochem's children at the demise of the latter (Year Book of the Holland Society of New York, 1900, p. 116).

This appointment was made at the request of Magdalene Waele, widow, February 12, 1659, when she announced her intention of marrying Gysbert Teunissen, who had four children by a former marriage. Magdalene had then five children living. Perhaps she was related by the ties of blood or nationality to Pieter Jansen Noorman.

In the church records her name is entered as Margaret or Magdalene Wale (July 8, 1654), Waels (April 9, 1656), or as "Magdalene, the wife of Caljer." If she was a relative of Pieter Jansen, we would seek her original home in Norway: in Vaage (Walde, Walle. See O. Rygh, Norske Gaardnavne, IV., Kristiansamt (I), p. 77); or in Ringebue (Vaalen, Vale, Volle, Waalen (1668); Ibid., p. 142); or in Tune (Valle, Volde, Walle, 1667. Ibid. I., p. 300); or in Onsö (Valde, Walle, 1635, l. c. 311).

Signature of Gysbert Teunissen, 1659, second husband of Magdalene Waele.

She was, what in those times could be expected of a Scandinavian,—a Lutheran. The Dutch pastors Megapolensis and Drisius, addressed, August 23, 1658, a letter to the Director and Council of New Netherland, in which letter they state the following:

"Indeed, it happened only last Sabbath, Aug. 18th, while we were yet ignorant of the complaint of the Lutherans against us, that a child was baptized, neither of whose parents was present; but only two Lutherans, who presented the child, and stood god parents, viz., Laurence Noorman, who, they say, was the host who concealed John Gutwasser, the Lutheran minister, last winter, and Magdalen Kallier, a Lutheran woman (Ecclesiastical Records of the State of New York, I., p. 430).

The Church Records mention only "the wife of Jochem Caljer" as sponsor at the baptism (August 8, 1658) of Hendrick, a child of Jan Hendrickszen and Gritie Barents, who, in January, 1663, were living in Bushwick.

Magdalene married, March 1, 1659, Gysbert Toemszen (Teunissen) from Barnevelt, the widower of Aeltje Wouters. Her daughter Dorothea was married to Wouter Gysbertsen. In 1678 she became a member of the Dutch Reformed church.

On April 15, 1660, Magdalene sold the lot of her first husband's on South William Street to Ariaen Van Lear, "a lot north of the Hoogh Straat; bounded on the west by the house and lot of him the appearer [Gysbert Teunissen, Magdalena's second husband]; north by the Slyck Steegh; east by the house and lot of Mr. Oloff Stevensen; west, by the lot of Abraham De la Noy; north, by the house and lot of Gerrit Jansen Roos; east, by the Graght aforesaid. On the east side, 23 feet 3 inches; west side, 23 feet 6 inches; north side, 52 feet 6 inches; south side, 4 rods. (Valentine, Manual of the City of New York, 1865, p. 668.)

On July 9, 1663, "Gysbert Teunissen deeded to Jochim Baker, of Fort Orange "a lot north of the Hoogh Straat; bounded west by the house and lot of Albert Coninck; north, the Slyck Steegh; east, the house and lot of said Jochim, baker; and south, the Hoogh Straat. Broad, front and rear, 21 feet 3 inches; long, on the east side, 6 rods 2 feet 7 inches; on the west side, 6 rods 7 inches." (Ibid., 1865, p. 702.)

———

II.

UNCLASSIFIED NAMES.*

We wish to state that there are several persons with Scandinavian names in the early history of New York, who are not treated in the present volume. As conclusive evidence is lacking to establish their nationality, we do not count them among our Scandinavian immigrants.

---

* In our "Preface" we stated that there were no Norwegians and Danes who immigrated to New Sweden. The "Pennsylvania Magazine of History and Biography," VIII., mentions two persons who may be exceptions. Both have Swedish names. The one, Ole Hakeson Buur, came to "New Sweden" in 1649. He was born in Mandal. (There is a Mandal in Norway, and in Denmark.) The other, a boy, Hendrick Benckson Buller, arriving in the same year, was born in Danish "Hysing" (island of Hisingen, near Göteborg).

To illustrate, we may here briefly consider the following names:

MARTIN BIERKAKER.

Martin Bierkaker should be classified as a Norwegian, if Bierkaker means Birkaaker (Bjerkaker), near Trondhjem in Norway. I have not counted him among the fifty-seven Norwegian immigrants, because Bierkaker may denote something else than a geographical name. In Van Rensselaers Bowier Manuscripts, a Marten Hendricksz from Hamelwörden, near Freiburg on the Elbe, Hanover, is referred to (in 1657) as Marten de bier Craaker and Marten de bierkracker. This Marten came on den Härinck in 1639, and was engaged for almost seven years in the colony of Rensselaerswyck. In 1651 he appears to have had an interest in a brewery, with Evert Pels.

We meet Martin Bierkaker in the courts of New Amsterdam in 1657, where he is called Bierkaker. Our knowledge of him is, however, quite limited.

On May 1, 1657, he appeared as a witness in a law suit against Steven Jansen, who was charged with drawing his knife and wounding Seger Cornelissen.

On August 15, 1657, an affidavit was presented in New Amsterdam, signed by Johannes La Montagne, Philip Pietersen Schuyler, Jan Thomassen, who were magistrates, and Hendrick Jochemsen, a lieutenant of the burgher company, stating that Bierkaker, on the south side of the town limits, had sold brandy to a Mohawk Indian.

On the same day Bierkaker and his wife Susanna Jansen were interrogated respecting these charges.

Under date of August 20, Susanna pleaded "in her extenuation her extreme poverty and that her husband is incapable of working, due to a hernia on both sides." The proceedings were accordingly dropped.

(See "Calendar of Historical Manuscripts." Ed. by E. B. O'Callaghan, I., pp. 314, 316. Rygh's "Norske Gaardnavne,"

XIV., p. 170, gives these forms as variations of Birkaaker: Bierk-ager, Birckagir (1559, 1590), Berckager (1624) . . . Bierckagger (1631), Birchagger (1664), Bierchager (1723).

OLOFF (OR OLAV) STEVENSEN.

Oloff (or Olav) Stevensen, an early settler in New York, who added Van Cortlandt to his name, was probably a Scandinavian, perhaps a Norwegian. Olav is a Norwegian name. It is neither Dutch nor German, nor English (a school in England, called St. Olave, shows Norwegian influence). Stevensen came out in 1637 as a private soldier in the employ of the West India Company. He became one of the most influential men in the colony. It is supposed that he was born in Wijk, near Utrecht, Holland, in 1600; that he had his name Van Cortlandt from having resided in the Duchy of Courland, opposite the Swedish island of Gothland. If he was born in Wijk (there are many places in Norway called "Vik"), this would not necessarily argue against his Scandinavian ancestry (Mrs. Van Rensselaer in History of the City of New York says that he "possibly was a Scandinavian, as Oloff is not a Dutch name"). "Cortlandt" may have a local meaning, too. Translated into Scandinavian it means "short land."

Olav's descendants were extensive landholders, and, as J. H. Innes, says, "either directly or by marriage . . . controlled at one time all the land along the east side of the Hudson River, from the highlands above the modern Peekskill to the Spuynten Duyvil Creek, a distance of about thirty miles, and extending several miles back into the country. Their name is perpetuated in that of the town of Cortlandt in Westchester County, and in Courtlandt Street and the Van Courtlandt Park of the City of New York" (about 800 acres). See article "Van Cortlandt", in Appleton's "Cyclopedia of American Biography," VI.

SKIPPER SYVERT VAN BERGEN.

Skipper Syvert van Bergen was likely a Norwegian. In 1665 he is mentioned in the Records of New Amsterdam as being involved in litigation with Schepen Jacques Cousseau and Abraham van Tright. Syvert was to freight some tobacco to Holland on the ship "Broken Heart," at first owned by Tright, later by Cousseau. Syvert refused to freight the tobacco, amounting to several dozen "tubs," as his ship was loaded. The verdict of the court was, that Syvert should take aboard a quantity of thirty hogsheads, "and that each shall have to bear his own costs."

CASPER HUGLA.

Casper Hugla, mentioned in the Records of New Amsterdam, as involved, in 1671, in a suit with Albert Bosch, plaintiff, was probably from the island of Hugla, Helgeland, Norway. Nothing is stated as to the nature of the suit, which was amicably settled by the litigants.

ANDRIES HOPPEN.

Andries Hoppen (or Hoppe), often mentioned in the Records of New Amsterdam, may have been from Norway. Rygh's "Norske Gaardnavne" (XIV, 44, 66), mentions a bowery in Agdenes Herred, Söndre Trondhjems Amt, called Hopen (spelled Hoppen, 1618); also Hopen in Hitteren Herred, in the same "amt" (spelled Hoppen, 1630). Hopen, from 'Hopr', means, in Norwegian, a closed in bay or gulf of small dimension. The name Hoppe may also be German. Cfr. David Heinrich Hoppe, born 1760 in Vilsen, Germany, who was a noted physician. The name may also be Dutch.

Andries Hoppen came with his wife, Geertje Hendricks, and daughter Catrina to New Amsterdam about 1653. He died in 1658, leaving her with five children. The widow Hoppe married, 1660, Dirck Gerritesen van Tright and acquired Broncks Land, now Morrisania. See article "Jonas Bronck." Part II.

*   *   *

Names like *Aris Otten, Edward Randall,* and many others in the Records of New Amsterdam, may be Norwegian, but may also represent persons of other nationalities. Without more or less definite information pointing to Norwegian antecedents, we can not register them here, though it would be tempting to do so.

The Norwegians, we may say Scandinavians, formed a respectable percentage of the population of New Netherland, but it would be gross exaggeration to say that they formed "one-half or a fourth of it," though the percentage was larger in the earlier days than in 1674.

PART II
DANISH IMMIGRANTS
IN NEW YORK
1630-1674

WILLEM ADRIAENSZ.

Willem Adriaensz, mentioned in the "Van Rensselaer Bowier Manuscripts" (p. 418) as being *"van els seneur,"* was from Helsingör, in Denmark. Our knowledge of him is confined to a letter of Kiliaen van Rensselaer to Jacob Planck, officer and *commis* in the colony of Rensselaerswyck. The letter is written May 12, 1639, and shows that Adriaensz was a cooper, and had an "account against the lords directors of Groningen signed by Tyaert Brongers, supercargo." Planck was instructed to find out whether Adriaensz had received any payment on the account, as the patroon had received nothing from the directors on this account.

HELSINGÖR, ABOUT THE CLOSE OF THE SIXTEENTH CENTURY.
From Braunius: Theatrum urbium.

Some time prior to 1638 Adriaensz must have been in Holland. According to the letter to Planck he was somewhere near Albany in 1638. In what year he left Holland or Denmark for the new world, is not stated.

CLAES ANDRIESSEN.

Claes Andriessen, from Holstein, came over to New Netherland by the ship "de Eendracht," which sailed April 17, 1664.[354] Perhaps he was a fisherman. For on August 7, 1665, a Claes Andriessen in New Amsterdam was granted license for fishing.[355] On August 22 he was accused by the sheriff of having been out racing with a boat on Sunday, August 13, which was contrary to "the Placard of June 20." The sheriff demanded of him a fine of twenty-five guilders and the costs. Andriessen claimed in self-defense, however, that he went with his boat to "Waele Bogt," and thence to the church at "Vlacke Bos" (Flatbush). The court demanded that he should prove these statements. As we hear nothing further about this matter, the case was likely settled out of court.[356]

LAURENS ANDRIESSEN.

Laurens Andriessen, or Laurens Andriessen van Boskerk (Buskirk), was from Holstein.[357] Tradition says he was Dutch and had emigrated from Holland, by way of Denmark, to New Netherland in 1655. But he was a Dane, and had gone from Denmark to Holland, and thence to New Amsterdam. It seems that he was in Amsterdam in 1654. On July 15, 1656, he brought suit in New Amsterdam against Frerick Adryaensen, "his man" who "ran away from him last Sunday morning without either words

---

354 The New York Genealogical and Biographical Record, XIV., p. 182.
355 Ibid., XIII., p. 185.
356 The Records of New Amsterdam, 1653-1674, V., p. 290.
357 See under date December 12, 1658, in Collections of the New York Genealogical and Biographical Society, I.

or reason, and he hired him in Amsterdam for three years and he is bound yet for more than one year."

Andriessen was a turner by trade. In the records he is often called Laurens Turner or de Drayer. In the suit of 1656 he is called van Boskerk. He got this name from living on premises by a church near the woods. He seems to have obtained these premises in 1656, and to have added to them in 1659, when he was granted land by certain church wardens; and in 1660, when he again purchased land from the church wardens, on the west side of Broadway, north of what was then the church yard, between Morris and Rector Streets.[358] It was west to the river, 43 feet wide, 195 feet long. He built on this lot, for which he paid 200 guilders.[359]

In June, 1656, he bought and sold lots on the present east side of Broad Street and south of Beaver Street. The persons with whom he was dealing in these transactions, were Lucas Dirksen Van Berg, Jochem Beeckman, and Jacobus Backer.[360]

On December 12, 1658, Andriessen married Jannetje Jans, widow of Christian Barentsen. Barentsen was probably a Dane, from Holstein (See Excursus, Part II), and Jannetje, it would appear, was Norwegian. For in "The Records of New Amsterdam," April 11, 1658, a Christian [Barentsen] is spoken of as the husband of the "Noorman's daughter".

By her first husband she had three, if not four, children: Barent, Cornelis, Johannes. In her second marriage she had four children: Andries, Lourens, Pieter, and Thomas.

Andries was baptized, according to the records, on March 3, 1659. Some genealogies have changed this into March 3, 1660. The change may have been done in the interest of a perfected chronology, but the original date is according to the New Style, thus needing no change. If Andries was born on March 3, 1659, he was likely the son of Christian Barentsen. Andries died in Bergen, New Jersey, 1683.

Laurens married Hendrickje Van der Linden. His will is proved in Bergen County, June 4, 1724.

358 D. T. Valentine, Manual of the Corporation of the City of New York, 1861 and 1865. Cfr. Year Book of the Holland Society of New York, 1901, p. 158. The Danish word for turner is "dreier", pronounced as Drayer.
859 The Records of New Amsterdam, 1653-1674, III., p. 290.
360 D. T. Valentine, Manual . . . of the City of New York, 1861, 586f.

Peter was born January 1, 1666, died 1738. He married Trintje Harmense, by whom he had three children.

Thomas married Margaret Hendrickje Van der Linden, died 1745. They had ten children.

Laurens Andriessen acquired much land in Bergen County, New Jersey, and became influential in political life. He held several offices of trust. He had a good handwriting, his signature is given in the New Jersey Archives, First Series I., p. 97. He often served on juries. He was a member of the Bergen Court, 1677 to 1680, president of it, 1681, president of the County Court, 1682. He was also for several years member of the Governor's Council.

Signature of Laurens Andriessen.

On April 10, 1682, he obtained a patent of 1076 acres of land at Hackensack, New Jersey.[361] On May 23, in the same year, he obtained a deed for "half a parcel" of land, adjoining Cornelis Christians, likewise at New Hackensack, and "a half a meadow lot." [362]

On March 24, 1683, he was appointed Justice of Peace of the Quorum, for the counties of Essex, Middelsex, Monmouth, and Bergen.[363]

The will of Laurens Andriessen and his wife is dated August 29, 1679. It was proved March 19, 1693.[364]

Of Laurens Andriessen's children, Laurens (born 1663), represented Bergen in the Fifth Provincial Assembly, 1709. He died 1724. He had seven children.

Laurens Andriessen is the common ancestor of the Van Buskirks, well known in the annals of New Jersey and New York.

---

361 New Jersey Archives, First Series, XXI., p. 48.
362 Ibid., XXI., p. 185.
363 Ibid., XIII., p. 89.
364 Ibid., XXI., p. 193. Jannetje died July 13, 1694.

His great-grandson Jacob Van Buskirk * born at Hackensack, in 1739, probably was the first American-born Lutheran minister in the United States. A descendant of his is Dr. J. Singmaster, President of the Theological Seminary at Gettysburg, Penn.

The Buskirks have intermarried with many of the leading families in the Eastern Section of the United States. A brief Genealogy of this family is given in Wm. E. Chute's "A Genealogy and History of the Chute Family" (1895). See also C. S. William's "Christian Barentsen Van Horn and his Descendants" (1911).

---

* The Library of the "Phrena" Society, Pennsylvania College, Gettysburg, Pa., possesses an interesting copy of Luther's Small Catechism in Dutch. The title reads:

"Die kleine |Catechismus| van Do Martinus Lutherus |mit getuigenissen des Geestes Gods uit de Heilige Schriftuur Kort, — delyk en grondelyk tot behoef van de Eenvoudige, De onveranderde Augsburgse Confessie toegedaan synde. | Verklaard en bewezen | Tit. 1. 9. Houd vast over het Woord dat gewis is, en leeren kan Te Amsterdam. By Hendrik Bosch, Boekverkooper, over't Meisjes Wees-huis, 1727."

This work has once been the property of Rev. Johan Christian Leps, whose note-book from the University of Halle, where he studied in 1764, is in the same library. Leps was ordained in Philadelphia in 1774. He was not a Dane, as is claimed by Rev. Rasmus Andersen in "Danske i Amerika" (pp. 396ff), but a German, as Prof. Fr. Loofs, of the University of Halle, informs me. According to Loofs, Leps was from Freuenbritsen in the Province of Brandenburg. He registered as studiosus juris at the University of Halle in 1763.

This catechism—in two small volumes, in hog's leather,—of 79 pages and 410 questions, also contains sixty closely written leaves, though not in the hand-writing of Leps, but in that which we find in several other books, which he had in his library. The writer seems to have been a conscientious catechist, probably pastor of the Dutch church at Loonenburg, now Athens, Green County, N. Y. The book gives us an idea of the size of the confirmation class to which Jacob von Buskirk belonged, as it, like many other old books, contains more than what its printed characters convey to us. The catechist has supplied the last pages with a hand-written list of the names of twenty-nine boys and twenty-one (twenty-three?) girls, under the rubric "Naamen der Catechisanten." Among the names are Jacob van Boschkerk; Gertrud van Bjoskerk; Mathys Bronk, a descendant of Jonas Bronk (see article, Jonas Bronck, Part II).

The names are:

(Boys)	(Girls)
Henrich Evertson.	Aynetje Halenbek
Martin Haalenbeck.	Marya Halenbek.
Nicolai von Loon.	Marya van Loon.
Joachim Halenbek.	Catharina Ehman.
Ysaak Halenbek.	Gertrud von Bjoschkerk.
Valentin Schram.	Ebgeltje Schram.
Jacob Van Boschkirk.	Maria Hardeck.
Johannes Schram.	Janeke van Hoesen.
Johannes Landman.	Marya van Loon.
Jan v. Hoesen Jas C. . .	Catharina van Horen.
Petrus Ganson.	Gertye van Hoeren.
Nicolaus van Hoesen.	Jannetje van Hoes.
Wilhelm van Hoesen.	Rebecca van Loon.
Justus van Hoesen.	Lisabeth van Hoesen.
Nicolaus Landmand.	Maria van Hoesen.
Joh Landmand sen	Elaje van Hoesen.
Rulof Ganson.	Paley Hardeck.
Cornelius Halenbeck.	Marytye van Hoesen.
Lisabeth Landman.	Annet van Hoesen.
Jan Janson van Hoesen.	Jantje van Hoesen.
Dirk van Hoesen.	Marytye van Hoesen.
Evert van Loon.	(Maria de Grot.)
Math v Long.	(Hell v. Dyk.)
Jurry Gertsen Klaus.	
Frans Klan.	
Mathys Bronk.	
Jurgen Schram.	
Jan Jacobsen van Hoesen.	
Jan van Hoesen.	

PIETER ANDRIESSEN.

Pieter Andriessen, a Dane, from Bordesholm in Holstein, came over to New Amsterdam in 1639, in the ship "de Brant van Trogen." Among his fellow passengers were other Danes: Captain Jochim Pietersen Kuyter, Jonas Bronck (?) and Laurens Duyts.[365] Duyts and Andriessen were to work for Jonas Bronck in Morrisania, the present Borough of the Bronx. Bronck had advanced the two men about 121 florins to pay their board on the ship.[366]

On October 19, 1645, Pieter Andriessen got the patent of a lot behind the public tavern on Manhattan, that is on Hoogh Straet. On the same date he obtained a patent of "74 morgens, 327 rods of land on the East River, opposite Hog Island, east of Domine's Hook."[367] The house which was erected upon this farm was nearly opposite the foot of the present Fifty-fifth Street on Manhattan Island.[368]

Andriessen owned, it would appear, some cattle before he became an independent landowner. When working in Morrisania, he bought live stock. Under date of October 15, 1641, we find a receipt of his "for a milk cow from Philip de Truy on shores."[369] His farm must have frequently been visited by men who passed his house on the river, for he had a tavern there as early as 1648.[370] Besides being a farmer and a tavernkeeper, he also was a chimney-sweep. He was called Pieter de Schoorstenveger (the chimney-sweep). We do not know much about his movements. When he was in the city, he likely left his farm in care of his negro slaves.

He had not been long in this country before he had, like many other early settlers, his hands in a lawsuit, and that against a woman. We have a notice of this under date of August 9, 1642, when he sued Aeltje Douwes for slander. The result of the proceedings was, that Aeltje "begs pardon of the plaintiff in court

---

365 See articles on these men. Part II.
366 Calendar of Historical Manuscripts, I., p. 9.
367 Ibid., I., p. 370.
368 J. H. Innes, New Amsterdam and Its People, p. 164.
369 Calendar of Historical Manuscripts, I., p. 17.
370 The Records of New Amsterdam, I., p. 8.

VIEW ON THE EAST RIVER, 1679.
From "Historic New York," edited by M. W. Goodwin.
By Permission of G. P. Putnam's Sons, New York.

and acknowledges that he [Andriessen] is an honest and upright man."[371]

On August 5, 1653, he was sued by Guliaem Wys, who demanded "payment of fl. 499:4 according to note dated 5 August, 1652." Andriessen "confessed the debt" and requested delay. But the court condemned him "to pay according to obligation within one month from date."[372]

A notice dated September 11, 1655, gives us the key to the nationality of Pieter Andriessen. It states that "Pieter Andrisz Van Bordolholm [Bordesholm]" is indebted to Cornelis Steenwyck, as attorney for Jacobus Schelle, the sum of 415 guilders for merchandise received in 1652. It also states that he resided on Long Island.[373]

It is erroneous to identify [374] Pieter Andriessen with a Pieter Andriessen from "Thresoni, in Brabant," who married, in 1661, Geertruyd Samson, widow of Jan Theunissen van Wesp, and died in 1664.[375]

On June 5, 1650, Pieter Andriessen, the subject of our sketch, was sponsor at the baptism of Michel and Dorothe, twins belonging to a Norwegian, Jochem Kier (Kalder).

There was a Pieter Andriessen who bought a lot in New Amsterdam on March 14, 1661. Whether this person be Pieter from Brabant or Pieter from Bordesholm can not be decided with the aid of the material at our disposal.

Pieter Andriessen, the chimney sweeper, received his small burgher right on April 13, 1657.

Before we take leave of him we shall relate these two incidents connected with him and his house on the farm.

In 1655 the Indians made one of their raids. Andriessen was one of those who suffered by it: he lost his cattle. In order to recover some of his live stock, he and a few others sailed up

---

371 Calendar of Historical Manuscripts, I., p. 72.
372 The Records of New Amsterdam, 1653-1674, I., p. 118.
373 Year Book of the Holland Society of New York, 1900, p. 159.
374 Collections of the New York Genealogical and Biographical Society, I.,
p. 27.   J. H. Innes, New Amsterdam and Its People, p. 165.
375 The Records of New Amsterdam, 1653-1674, V., p. 66.

the East River, to his farm, which he had left when the raid took place. But the Indians caught them and kept four of them, including Andriessen, prisoners. First after the city authorities ` had paid a ransom for their release, were they liberated.

In regard to the capture of Andriessen and the ransom which the Indians demanded before they would liberate the captives, the following documents are of value. The Indians received a ransom; not, however, the extravagant one they had demanded according to the documents.

Director Stuyvesant wrote to Captain Brian Nuton [Newton], October 12, 1655:

"This is to inform you, that three or four canoes with savages have been seen near the Hellegat on Long Island, who have taken Pieter, the chimney-sweep, prisoner; therefore you will have to be on your guard and keep your men close together; and whereas I have been informed, that the free people, contrary to my order, do not remain together, but that every one runs here and there to his own plantation, you must once more, and this the last time, warn them, that they take care and keep together according to my order, or that I shall be obliged to take other measures herein. You are hereby especially directed to keep your soldiers together and keep a good watch. Farewell . . ."

From the minutes in regard to the appearance, before the Council, of Stephen Necker, one of the prisoners, who had been sent by the Indians to demand the ransom, we quote the following:

[October 13] "Stephen Necker appeared before the Council and reported that Peter, the chimney-sweep, with five others, of whom he was one, had sailed to the aforesaid chimney-sweep's plantation to fetch some animals from there; after they had been there about half an hour, they were attacked by about thirty savages, he does not know of what nation, who took them all prisoners; four of them had been wounded, and he with Cornelis Mourissen (afterwards shot in the back with an arrow, "which has been cut out by the barber") has been sent here by the savages, to ask for their ransom the following articles, which the savages had marked with notches on a stick:

20 coats of cloth.	40 knives.
20 handfuls of powder.	10 pairs of shoes.
10 bars of lead.	10 pairs of socks.
10 kettles.	10 addices.
2 muskets.	10 hatchets.
3 swords.	20 tobacco-pipes.
20 strings of wampum.[376]	

Almost at the same time and during Andriessen's absence from his house, a white settler and two negroes, one of whom was a servant of Andriessen, took possession of his house, in order to enjoy a repast of stolen chickens. They had been in the neighborhood for their prey, and had frightened the few people there by feigning Indians. They had shouted and yelled, battered the doors and on the whole played their role of savages so well, that those who were not initiated, were scared away. Finally one of the latter, Harmen the cooper, made his way to Andriessen's house, where he saw a light. He heard, to his surprise, Dutch spoken, entered the house boldly and caught the miscreants red-handed. The new visitor found a large fire in Pieter's house, and "Claes de Ruyter preparing to spit the (stolen) fowls." The visitor censured them, but the miscreants answered "that they were forced to do it by hunger"—a fabricated defense, as the city was not far distant. The city authorities got knowledge of the matter, and the visitor related before the court what had transpired in the "chimney-sweep's house." He even told that De Ruyter requested him to remain silent about the matter, and that he, on arriving at the Manhattans, would pay for the fowls."[377]

The city government, now knowing that others besides the Indians were playing the role of plunderers, issued an "Order against isolated plantations." It commanded the subjects to settle close to one another in villages and hamlets. It imposed a penalty on those who refused to comply with the command and gave notice that they must not expect any aid from the government in case of trouble with the Indians.

---

376 New York Colonial Documents, XIII., p. 43f.
377 The Records of New Amsterdam, 1653-1674, IV., p. 394f.

CLAES CLAESEN BORDING.

Claes Claesen Bording was from Denmark (possibly from Bording). He was in New Amsterdam as early as 1648 or before. There is no Danish name in the Records of New Amsterdam that appears so often as that of Claes Claesen Bording. He was a respectable mariner and a politician of some influence. He was several times nominated for offices, e. g., the office of schepen, but he "is not found to have been appointed to any crown station."[378] He received the small burgher's right in 1657, and his nomination for the office of schepen would indicate that he also had the great burgher's right. He was often in court as curator or as arbitrator in disputes.

He had a good house on Pearl Street, between Whitehall Street and the Battery.

His wife was Susanna Lues (Lees, Lies, Marsuryn). Susanna and Claes had many children, who were baptized between 1650 and 1673.

The dates of the baptism of their children are as follows: Marritje, September 11, 1650; Tryntje, November 5, 1651; Marritje, May 3, 1654; Lysbeth, October 25, 1656; Claes, May 11, 1658; Simon, February 5, 1662; Jannetje, November 2, 1663; Hester, December 7, 1667; Lysbeth, September 10, 1670; Claes, October 26, 1673.[379]

Bording and his wife were often present as sponsors at baptisms.

He was sponsor at the baptism of Grietie, a child of Cors Pietersen, May 25, 1648; at the baptism of Daniel and Anneken, children of Pieter Laurentszen, February 4, 1654; at the baptism of Sytie, child of Pieter Pieterszen, January 23, 1656; at the baptism of Jacobus, child of Jacob Theunissen de Key and Hillegond Theunis, November 27, 1672; at the baptism of Lysbeth, child of Cornelis Kregier and Annetje Bordings, August 2, 1676; at the baptism of Samuel, child of Thomas Lourenszen, July 9, 1679.[380]

---

878 D. T. Valentine. History of the Corporation of the City of New York, 1853. p. 91. Tradition says, he was from Dansig. Jens Worm's Lexicon mentions several persons having the name of Bording, born in Ribe or Aarhus or Antwerp.
879 Collections of the New York Genealogical and Biographical Society, II., pp. 27, 30, 37, 43, 53, 64, 75, 89, 99, 112.
880 Ibid., II., pp. 24, 36, 41, 107, 124, 140.

Susanna, his wife, was sponsor at the baptism of Gritie, child of Hendrick Hendrickszen Obee, August 17, 1659; at the baptism of Thomas, son of Thomas Laurenszen and Marritje Jans, March 13, 1673; at the baptism of another child of Thomas Laurenszen and Marretje Jans, July 15, 1674.[381]

Bording and his wife joined the Dutch Reformed Church between 1649 and 1660.

On November 6, 1648, Bording dissolved partnership with Aryn Jansen, which fact would seem to indicate that he must have been in New Amsterdam for some time, perhaps many years, prior to the fall of 1648.[382]

On March 24, 1651, Claes Bording and Pieter Jacobsen Marius gave power of attorney to Pieter Cornelissen to collect money due them at the South River.[383]

On August 18, 1653, Bording sued Willem Albertsen for a balance of seven beavers "by virtue of a note for sixteen and one-third beavers." The result of the suit was that Albertsen was condemned to pay what he owed the plaintiff.[384]

On December 8, 1653, Cornelis van Tienhoven appeared in court and declared that Bording had been examined before the Director and Council on a charge of smuggling gunpowder and lead, and that they had provisionally confined him in the council chamber. He requested the Burgomaster and the Schepen to examine into the matter.[385] Nothing is recorded as to how the matter was concluded.

On March 16, 1654, Bording was authorized and appointed by the court as curator of the property left by a Gillis Jansen deceased.[386]

On April 13, he appeared before the court prosecuting a certain attachment levied on a sum of 100 gl. in the hands of Jacob Strycker on account of Jan Snediger, whom he (Bording) had cited and who refused to appear. The court declared the attachment valid. In the following month the case was tried, and

381 Ibid., II., pp. 53, 109, 115.
382 Calendar of Historical Manuscripts, I., p. 45.
383 Ibid., p. 52.
384 The Records of New Amsterdam, 1653-1674, I., p. 99.
385 Ibid., I., p. 138.
386 Ibid., I., p. 174.

Snediger was ordered by the court to pay what he owed Bording.[387]

In May, 1655, Bording and six other inhabitants of New Amsterdam signed a petition: that the court order Jacob Stevensen and Mary Joosten, his wife, to leave the city or be punished on account of their "wicked, enormous, beastly, dreadful and immoral lives."

It appears that Bording and Pieter Jacobsen Marius were partners in business. We have noted that they had transactions in common in 1651. They had such transactions also in 1656, 1658, and 1670.

On October 2, 1656, they appeared in court complaining that they could not obtain payment from Jacob van Couwenhoven, a brewer, according to the judgment passed some time before by the court. They requested that execution might be proceeded with. The court declared the request just and ordered Couwenhoven to give immediate satisfactory security.[388] Couwenhoven was at this time greatly hampered by his debts.

A week later, Couwenhoven got extension of time from the court. But Bording again appeared and renewed his former request. At the same time he prosecuted the arrest of "the horse and all that Wolfert Gerritssen has on his bouwerie, which is mortgaged to him." The court declared the mortgage valid, but would not alter the recent ruling with respect to Couwenhoven.[389] On November 1, Bording made his third appearance in court, again requesting that execution might be legally issued against van Couwenhoven. But the court persisted in the previously issued order.[390] At the end of the year the case was again considered. The court found that the request of Bording and Marius was just, but it also desired to be accommodating to van Couwenhoven.[391]

On September 23, 1658, Bording and Marius appeared in court against Lauwerens Jansz, widower of Anna Cornelis, deceased. Jansz was about to depart for Holland, and the plaintiffs

387 Ibid., I., pp. 188, 190.
388 Ibid., II., p. 177.
389 Ibid., II., p. 188.
390 Ibid., II., p. 214.
391 Ibid., II., p. 242.

requested that he should render account for the estate of Jacob Jacobs, son of Anna Cornelis.[392]

In the early part of 1670 Bording and Marius brought suit against Andrew Messenger, who was indebted to them for goods and merchandise to the sum of fl. 331,12 in seawan. They won their case. Andrew had also to pay the costs of the suit. But as late as November, Andrew had not paid them, and they again complained. The court ordered the sheriff to collect the money or pay it himself. The sheriff was Allard Anthony. As he took no steps to collect the sum, even after getting the orders of the court, the court ordered, on December 16, that the marshall should serve the execution upon the estate of Allard Anthony without any further delay. In March, 1672, the court renewed this order.[393]

Bording seems to have been persistent in his suits, and he generally won. We shall mention two: one in 1655, which he lost, and one in 1662, which makes it evident that he frequently had his own way in court matters.

On October 18, 1655, he sued Pieter Wolfertsen for some spoiled tobacco which he had received from him. He said he had received in all six hogsheads of tobacco, but 418 pounds were spoiled. The court, upon hearing the evidence, which showed that "the tobacco had been shipped in good condition in tubs properly inspected," dismissed the case.[394]

On January 10, 1662, Paulus van de Beeck, collector of excises demanded in court twenty-six gl. of Bording for "excise of a beast and two hogs, entered by him, with costs." Bording faced the officer and court with the question "if men must give twice as much heavy money." The court answered him that he could satisfy the excise by "paying with such pay as the beast is bought in." The question seems to have been one about the medium of exchange, whether seawan was on par with metal.[395]

We have stated that Bording was a mariner. Mention is often made of his yacht, in the New York Colonial Documents.[396]

392 Year Book of the Holland Society of New York, 1900, p. 114.
393 The Records of New Amsterdam, 1653-1674, VI., 280, 344, 347.
394 Ibid., I., p. 379.
395 Ibid., IV., pp. 6, 8.
396 New York Colonial Documents, XIII., pp. 250, 264, 365.

We do not know when Bording died. In 1686 Susanna Marsuryn is mentioned as the widow of Bording. She was then living at Pearl Street. (In 1674 his property on this street was valued at $3000.) But as late as 1691 we have a will signed by him. The records state:

"In den namen des Herren (In the name of the Lord,) Amen. On October 31, 1691, appeared before me, William Bogardus, Public Notary, Claas Burden (or Bordinge) and his wife Susanah. The survivor of the two is to have all the estate for life, and then to their children, Tryntie, Catharine, wife of Lucas Van Thienhoven, Maria, Annettie, wife of Cornelis Gregoe, Symon and Hester."

"Signed 'Claas Bordinge.'

"Witnesses, Peter Jacobs Marius, John Vandeventer.
"Proved, Tuesday, May 5, 1691." [397]

JAN BROERSEN.

Jan Broersen was from Husum, in Denmark. As early as 1644, he, as a young man, served Jacob Hay (Huys) in the West Indies. He later came to New Netherland. We find him at Esopus in May, 1658, when he and other settlers of this place made an agreement to remove their dwellings and form a village.[398]

About the same time he and six others sent a letter to the Council of New Netherland, complaining of the Indians, and asking for assistance. The letter states that there were 990 schepels of seed-grain in the ground, that the country was fine, that between sixty and seventy Christian people were living there and were in the habit of attending divine services "on all proper days," and that they maintained their [church-] reader at their own expense. To protect them against the ravages of the Indians, the subscribers ask "for help and succor of about forty to fifty men." [399]

---

397 Collections of the New York Historical Society for 1893, p. 403.
398 New York Colonial Documents, XIII., p. 81.
399 Ibid., XIII., p. 79.

On August 17, 1659, he, with a number of others, signed a petition requesting that the Rev. Bloem be appointed their minister.[400]   In 1661 he subscribed, at one occasion, fifteen florins for the support of the Rev. Bloem, who in response to the petition had been appointed preacher at Esopus.[401]

In March, 1660, Broersen served as a soldier at Esopus.[402] On account of the Indian raids it was necessary that all who could carry arms should belong to the local militia.   In September, 1659, a letter signed by the settlers at Esopus, including Broersen, was sent to Stuyvesant relating that they were besieged in the fort by Indians.[408]

Signature of Jan Broersen.

Broersen visited New Amsterdam as occasion required.   He was there in 1659.   Not long afterward Aeltje Bickers, wife of Nicholas Velthuysen, sued him for a debt of fl. 44.   She claimed that "Reinert Jansen Hoorn had promised to pay her in four days for Jan Broersen, and that she thereupon allowed Jan Broerson to depart and that Hoorn will not pay the sum, but gave her ill words."   Hoorn admitted that he had promised to pay for Broersen, but as Aeltje Bickers and her husband were quarreling, he claimed that he had reasons for not paying her.[404]

Broersen was again in New Amsterdam in November, 1661, when he sued a Norwegian woman, the daughter of Dirck Holgersen and widow of Jacob Huys for labor he had done for her husband in the West Indies.   We shall let the court minutes relate the details of the case.

[November 15, 1661.]

"Jan Broerzen, pltf. v|s Christyntie Capoens, deft.   Pltf. demand from deft. sixty guilders Holland currency for wages earned

400 Ibid., XIII., p. 103.
401 Ibid., XIII., p. 214.
402 Ibid., XIII., p. 154.
408 Ibid., XIII., p. 119.
404 The Records of New Amsterdam, 1658-1674, III., p. 63.

in the West Indies from deft's. late husband. Deft. says she does
not know the pltf., and full fifteen years is passed, and if pltf.
can bring proof that she owes it, she will pay. Pltf. was asked,
if he had never spoken to deft's. late husband about the matter?
Answers, Yes and was to him at Breukelen with Albert Cornelissen's wife, when he gave for answer, that he did not owe him
and must bring proof. The W: Court order pltf. to bring proof,
that something is due him by the deft." [405]

[November 20, 1661.] "Jan Broerzen, pltf. v|s Christyntje
Capoen, deft. Deft in default. In pursuance to the order of the
last court day, pltf. produces a declaration of Adrian Huybersen
Sterrevelt, who states, it is within his knowledge that Jan Broersen served Jacob Hay as a boy about seventeen years ago in the
West Indies, both at Santa Cruz and Curacao, without having
received, to his knowledge, any pay therfor: Also a declaration of
Tryn Herders declaring that she had been with him to Jacob Hay,
and speaking about money was refused any by him. Burgomasters
and Schepens order the pltf. to summon Christyntje Capoens and
Tryn Herders by the next Court day." [406]

[November 29.] "Jan Broerzen, pltf. v|s Christyntje
Capoens and Tryn Herders as witnesses, defts. Whereas Tryn
Herders is not present, the matter is postponed to the next Court
day and she is ordered to be summoned again." [407]

Evidently the case was dropped or adjusted out of court.

Jan Broersen married Heltje Jacobs. They had children:
Gaerleff, baptized at Kingston (Esopus), February 26, 1662;
Grietje, August 31, 1664; Maddelen, June 27, 1666; Fitie, June
18, 1671.

His wife was deceased December 24, 1679, when Broersen
married Willemtje Jacobs, who had been married to Albert Gerit-
sen and to Jan Cornelissen, a Swede from Göteborg.[408]

In 1673, Jan Broersen was nominated magistrate by the inhabitants of Horly and Marble. The Governor accordingly appointed him a magistrate and notified the inhabitants of it in

405 Ibid., III., p. 407.
406 Ibid., III., p. 411.
407 Ibid., III., p. 415.
408 R. R. Hoes, Baptismal and Marriage Registers . . . of Kingston, pp. 2,
4, 5, 8. Gustave Anjou, Ulster County Wills, I., p. 30.

a letter of October 6, 1673. Besides being magistrate Broersen was also lieutenant of the militia.[409]

JONAS BRONCK.

Jonas Bronck, who arrived at New Amsterdam in 1639, and whose name is perpetuated in Bronx Borough, Bronx Park, Bronxville — in New York — was a Scandinavian, in all probability a Dane, and originally, as it seems, from Thorshavn, Faroe Islands, where his father was a pastor in the Lutheran Church. Faroe then belonged to Denmark-Norway and had been settled by Norwegians. The official language of the island in Bronck's days was Danish.

For a long time, writers were diligently searching for the antecedents of Jonas Bronck.

Bronck may have been a Swede if we judge by the name alone, for the name of Brunke is well known in Sweden. This possibility receives some support in the fact that a relative of Bronck, likely his son, Pieter Jonassen Bronck, made mention of a Swedish woman in his will, Engeltje Mans. He gave her husband, Burger Joris, power of attorney to collect some debts. There thus appears to have been ties of relationship or friendship between Engeltje Mans and the Bronck family. (See articles Pieter Bronck, Part II., and Engeltje Mans, Part III.) Of course, the fact that Engeltje Mans resided in Sweden does not necessarily make her Swedish, though we have classified her as such. As to the first Brunke in Sweden — he died in 1319 — Swedish annals regard him as a foreigner. Brunkeberg, north of Stockholm, has been named after him.

Jonas Bronck, again judging by the name, may have been a Norwegian. According to O. Rygh, "Norske Gaardnavne," I., p. 48, documents of 1612 and 1616 mention Brunckeslett, a place in Smaalenenes Amt in Norway. Norway has also a river called Bronka, entering Elverum (98 miles from Christiania). A document of 1557 mentions Brunckefos, a fall in the Bronka river. This fall was the property of the Norwegian Crown. There is

---

409 New York Colonial Documents, II., p. 626.

also in Norway a Bunckestadt which is mentioned in 1578, a corrupt form, Rygh conjectures, of Brunckestadt (Rygh, "Norske Gaardnavne," III., Hedemarkens Amt, p. 305). From "Bronka" Rygh explains the name of Brunkeberg in Telemarken, Norway. It refers to a parish and several boweries. A creek called Bronka may have given rise to the name in Telemarken. Rygh also registers Norwegian names like Bronkebakken, Bronketorpet, Bronken sea (pronounced Bronka). "Bronke" may be derived from "bruun", in earlier times meaning "bright," "glossy"; or from "brun" meaning "edge."

Meanwhile, the Norwegian records do not, to our knowledge, speak of persons having the name of Bronk, Bronken, or Brunck. But the Danish records do.

Rev. R. Anderson, of Brooklyn, N. Y., who has contributed to "Danske i Amerika," and who more than any other has taken an interest in the Danish genealogy of early New York speaks of a number of Brunkes in Danish history. He makes the conjecture that Rev. Morten Brunck who was in Aaker, on Bornholm, 1604—1624, may be a relative of Jonas Bronck.

Confining myself to my own investigation of original sources, I find a Jens Brunck, who in 1503 was in Yding,[410] in Denmark; likewise a Rev. Torchillus Brwnck (Torkil Brunck), who in 1532 was stationed in Lund [411]; and, again, a Lavrits Michelsen Brunch, pastor in Stubbekjöbing, in 1564. [412]

Just recently, however, a claim has been put forth which seems to offer a satisfactory solution as to the antecedents of Jonas Bronck. Baron Joost Dahlerup, of New Rochelle, N. Y., in writing on the influence of the Danish element in early New York (Politikens Kronik, Jan. 4, 1914), became instrumental in calling forth an article on Bronck by the historian N. Andersen, of Denmark, who for many years was an official in Faroe Islands, and, perhaps second to none, is acquainted with Faroese history.

Mr. N. Andersen, in reading Mr. Dahlerup's article (which the author has kindly loaned me) recollected having seen the name of Brunck in Faroese history. He set to work, and published the result in "Personalhistorisk Tidsskrift," VI R., 5. B., pp. 73—75. (Copenhagen).

---

410 J. P. Trap, Kongeriget Danmark, V., p. 243.
411 Holger Rördam, Historiske Kildeskrifter, 2 R. II., p. 392.
412 H. F. Rördam, Ny Kirkehistoriske Samlinger, V., p. 425.

According to Mr. N. Andersen, Morten Jespersen Brunck was Lutheran parish minister in South Strömö, residing in Thorshavn, the capital of Faroe Islands. In 1583 he received an assistant pastor in Christian Pedersen Morsing, thus appearing to have been feeble in health. In 1590 he died. His wife's name was Bille, and his son was, no doubt, the person who had attended the Latin School in Roskilde, Denmark, and in 1619, registered in the University of Copenhagen as Johannes Martini Farinsulanus (John Mortenson Faroese Islander).

The possible objection that Jonas, because his father died in 1590, must have been at least thirty years of age when he entered the university, Mr. Andersen meets by giving instances where students registered in the university at the age of thirty-five or more.

The education which Jonas could have got in Thorshavn, was more or less elementary: reading, writing, and some branches common to a Latin school for such pupils as desired to continue their studies in a classical gymnasium, which Faroe Islands did not possess. If Jonas attended the school at Thorshavn, say between 1625 and 1631, he was one of six or seven pupils, and probably the only one preparing for the Latin school.

Several students from Faroe had, in the course of time, attended the University. They added to their names designations, showing whence they came: Ferronensis, Feroensis, Färö.

These Faroese students, as a rule, returned to their native land, becoming assistants of their fathers, who were pastors. Jonas Bronck, however, did not return to get a charge, for his father was dead.

Mr. N. Andersen leaves it an open question as to what regions Jonas Bronck visited between the time he left the university and the time he came to New Netherland. He says, he may have lived during this period in Holland, he may have served either the Danish or the Dutch East India Company.

Mr. Andersen also makes the conjecture that Bronck's sister was the wife of Jochem Pietersen Kuyter (See article "Kuyter." Part II.) Her name was Martens = daughter of Marten or Morten; that is, daughter of Rev. Morten Jespersen Brunck, of Faroe.

This new explanation, of Mr. Andersen, is plausible. All

the evidence we have, tends to show that Bronck was a man of university training. His library was mainly Danish, those with whom he mostly associated were Danish, his first workmen in the new world were Danes.

It would appear that Jonas Bronck had spent considerable of his time on the seas. Harry T. Cook in "The Borough of the Bronx 1639—1913" makes the following statement, which, with the aid of my present material, I am not able to verify, but which appears to be based on quite legendary data.

" 'The Magazine of American History,' January, 1908, tells us that Jonas Bronck was one of the worthy but unfortunate Mennonites who were driven from the homes in Holland to Denmark by religious persecution. He gained rapid promotion in the army of the King of Denmark, who was very tolerant toward the sect known as Mennonites. He served as commander in the East Indies until 1638, when with others of the prosecuted he set sail for America."

In discussing the antecedents of Bronck, attention must be called to the fact that a Jan Peeck prosecuted, in 1653, Jan Gerritsen in New Amsterdam for the payment of victuals consumed at the funeral of one Jems Bronck, a soldier, who had been shot dead, "for which Gerritsen had given security." Peeck demanded 48 fl. 18 stivers. The court records state in regard to the defense:

"Deft. says, it is true, he has been at the party consuming the victuals, but as he is no heir nor has received any benefits from deceased, he is not bound to pay. Having heard both, Burgomasters and Schepens decide that deft. is not bound to pay, but that pltf. must look for the payment of his claim or his pay from the Company." (West India).

Under date of July 21, 1653, the Records again refer to the case: "As he (Peeck) can not obtain payment out of his (Bronck's) estate or pay from the Company, except 12 fl. through the Officer, pltf. demands that deft. as surety shall pay the balance as per note. Deft. refers to his former answer and the decision of the Court, dated the 17th of February, requesting that pltf's. demand be dismissed. The Court refers pltf. to the Company to receive his due out of the pay of deceased agreeably to the promise of the Fiscal."

Who was this Jems Bronck? Our sources fail to tell us anything more about him.

Returning to the subject of our article, the wife of Jonas Bronck, Teuntje Jeurians, seems to have been a relative of Marritje Pieters of Copenhagen, who appointed, on August 15, 1639, "Teuntje Jeurians of [New] Amsterdam or Jacob Bronck, her present husband, as heirs . . . " (See article "Marritje Pieters." Part II.)

Writers generally agree that the year of Jonas Bronck's arrival at New Amsterdam was 1639, though E. B. O'Callaghan in "History of New Netherland," II, 531, states that Bronck leased land in New Netherland as early as 1637. This may be purely conjectural on the part of O'Callaghan. Evidently the year he gives should have been 1639.

Some writers also state that Bronck and James Pietersen Kuyter (See Article "Kuyter") arrived at the same time by the ship De Brant van Trogen, sailing from Horn, that Bronck owned the ship, and Kuyter commanded it. I am not in a position to verify this. But this much can be said: Kuyter and Bronck were the best of friends, and two of Bronck's workmen, Laurens Duyts and Pieter Andriessen, came with Kuyter on De Brant von Trogen. The ship also carried implements and cattle for commencing a plantation on a large scale.

Bronck either now, or, if O'Callaghan is correct, in 1637 got a list of patent from the Dutch government — the Ranague tract. To-day it is known as Morrisania. It lay between the Great Kill (Harlem River) and the Aquahaug (Bronx River).

Bronck not only paid for the property, but he advanced money to pay the passage of his workmen. And yet he had money to loan to Andries Hudde, who on July 18, 1639, gave him a note for 200 carolus guilder "received from him at [New] Amsterdam."

That Bronck was well pleased with the purchase of his property, is shown by a letter he penned to Pieter Van Alst, in the old world.

Harry T. Cook, in "The Borough of Bronx," says that Van Alst was a relative of Bronck. In the letter Bronck wrote:

"The invisible hand of the Almighty Father surely guided me to this beautiful country, a land covered with virgin forest and unlimited opportunities. It is a veritable paradise and needs but the industrious hand of man to make it the finest and most beautiful region in all the world."

Bronck called his home Emmaus. It was situated near the present Harlem River station of the N. Y. New Haven and Hartford Railroad, at 132 Street.

He erected on his newly acquired land a stone dwelling, which he, evidently to the surprise of other immigrants, covered with tiles; a barn; several tobacco houses; and barracks for his servants. The inventory of his property taken at his death is our authority for this statement. It also shows that the luxury of extension tables and table cloths, alabaster plates and napkins, silver spoons and silver dishes was not foreign to the new home of Jonas Bronck. Mention is also made in the inventory of gloves, a satin suit, and a gold signet ring. Above all, his library, a list of whose contents is given below, shows that Bronck was a man of education and refinement.

Some of the books and pictures he owned, may still be preserved in libraries in this country — or even in Europe. A silver cup that belonged to Bronck is now owned by Mr. R. Bronck Fish, an attorney in Fultonville, N. Y. Mr. Frank C. Bronck of Amsterdam, N. Y., has in his possession a copy of the inventory of Bronck's personal effects.

On July 21, 1639, Bronck engaged two Danish workmen, who had come over with him, to undertake the clearing of a tract of 500 acres of his property. It was Indian property before Bronck got it. To-day it covers what is known as Morrisania. The men with whom he contracted were Pieter Andriessen from Bordesholm, and Laurents Duyts. (See articles on these men. Part II.)

We shall give the wording of this interesting lease in full. It is a document in which three Danes are interested, and thus a parallel to the document given in Part I, where three Norwegians are the signers. (See Article "Dirck Holgersen", Part I.)

"[Lease of Land in Westchester County.]

"Before me, Cornelis van Tienhoven, Secretary in New Netherland and the undersigned witnesses, appeared Sr. Jonas Bronck, of the one part and Pieter Andriessen and Laurens Duyts of the other part, who amicably agreed and contracted as follows:

"First: Sr. Bronck shall show to the said parties a certain

piece of land, belonging to him, situate on the mainland opposite to the flats of the Manhates; on which said piece of land they shall have permission to plant tobacco and maize, on the condition, that they shall be obliged to break new land every two years for the planting of tobacco and maize and changing the place, the land, upon which they have planted to remain at the disposal of said Sr. Bronck. They shall also be bound to surrender the land, every time they change, made ready for planting corn and plough-ing. They shall have the use of the said land for three consecutive years, during which time the said Sr. Bronck shall make no other claim upon them, than for the land, which Pieter Andriessen and Laurens Duyts by their labor shall have cleared, who on their side shall be obliged to fulfill the above [mentioned] conditions. If Pieter Andriessen and Laurens Duyts demand within a year from said Sr. Bronck 2 horses and 2 cows on the conditions, on which at present the Company gives them to freemen, the said Bronck shall deliver the animals to them, if he can spare them.

"Pieter Andriessen and Laurens Duyts further pledge their persons and property, movable and immovable, present and future, nothing excepted, for the payment of what Sr. Bronck has ad-vanced to them for board on ship 'de Brant van Trogen', amount-ing to 121 fl. 16 st., of which Pieter Andriessen is to pay fl. 81.4 and Laurens Duyts fl. 40.12. They promise to pay the aforesaid sums by the first ready means, either in tobacco or otherwise and in acknowledgment and token of truth they have signed this re-spectively.

"Done at Fort Amster dam the 21st July 1639.

"This is the mark ⚹ of Laurens Duyts.

"Pieter Andriessen.
"Maurits Janse, witness." [418]

On August 15, 1639, Bronck leased also some of his land, for a period of six years, to the brothers Cornelius Jacobsen and

---

418 New York Colonial Documents, XIII., p. 5. Calendar of Historical Manuscripts. I., p. 9.

Jan Jacobsen, both surnamed Stille or Stol. Jan was married to Marritje Pieters of Copenhagen.

Bronck was as we have said a well-to-do man. Exceedingly interesting is the list of inventory taken at his house at his death, in 1643. It shows that he must have been a man of means, who had read much and traveled much.

DANISH CALENDAR, COPENHAGEN, 1642.

But nothing perhaps is so interesting as his library. It was a little library, but merits the words of Mrs. Van Rensselaer (History of the City of New York, I., p. 186):

"This polyglot little library is the earliest of which any record survives in the annals of New York." It contained books on theology, medicine, and law; books in Danish, Dutch, Latin, and German. It had pictures and manuscripts. But in language it was more Danish than anything else, in theology it was more Lutheran than Reformed, what we should expect of a Dane in those times.

What did this library contain?

1 Bible, in folio.
Calvin's Institutes, folio.
Bullingeri. (Henry B., reformed theologian, Zürich).
Schultetus dominicalia (a celebrated surgeon at Ulm).
Moleneri praxis, quarto.
1 German Bible, quarto.
Mirror of the Sea (Seespiegd), folio.
1 Luther's Psalter.
Sledani, folio (A Lutheran theologian).
Danish Chronicle, quarto.
Danish Law-book, idem.
Luther's whole Catechism.
The praise of Christ, quarto ('t Lof Christi).
The four ends of Death (de vier Uyterste van ae doot) Two
    Treasuries, small folio.
Petri Apiani. (A geographer and astronomer.)
Danish Child's book.
A book called Forty Pictures of Death, by Symon Golaert.
Biblical Stories.
Danish Calendar.
Survey of the Great Navigation ('t Gesichte der grooten Seevaerts).
A parcel of 18 old printed pamphlets by divers authors, both Dutch
    and Danish.
17 manuscript books, which are old.
11 pictures, big and little.

The contents of this library, and the fact that Bronck called his house Emmaus, would indicate that he was of a religious turn of mind, interested in the study of theology. But we venture to say something more: Does it not reflect the piety, which Lucas

Dend liden (eller mindre)

CATECHISMUS
D. Mart. Luth.

For Børn.

Med Børnelærdoms vi-
sitatz I Aldmindelighed/ oc omb een-
foldig Skriftemaal/ med nogle nyt-
tige Spørsmaal/ effter D. M. L.
rette Meening/&c.

Cum Privilegio &c.

Effter dend ædition som er tryckt I Kiøbenhafn,
Aff Salomone Sartorio/ 1628.

(Luther's small (or lesser) Catechism for children, 1628.)

The above given facsimile of the Catechism, somewhat reduced, is taken from a Norwegian "Explanation" of Luther's small catechism. This "Explanation" consists of eight ponderous volumes, each of about 1000 pages, the entire work, without binding, weighing fourteen pounds! The author of this formidable work is the Rev. Christen Stephansen Bang, † 1678, from Aalborg, Denmark. About 1614 he became chaplain in Solum, in 1621 pastor in Romedal, Norway. The first five volumes treat of the "Five Parts" of the catechism; the last three deal with special ethics. The entire eight tomes are known as "Postilla catechetica". They were published in Christiania, 1650-1665, but ruined the author financially.

To get this and other works published, Bang caused the art of printing to be

Debes describes in his treatise, 1675, of the Faroese people, among which Bronck had lived? *

But — to come back to the inventory, which no doubt will prove a surprise to those who have not learnt to appreciate the "kultur" of the pioneers of New York:

3 guns.

1 musket.

1 do. with silver mounting.

1 Japanese cutlass.

1 dagger with silver mounting.

1 black satin suit.

1 old quilted satin doublet.

2 old grogram suits.

1 blue damask woolen shirt.

2 hats.

1 black cloth mantle, and 1 gold signet ring.

1 old mantle of colored cloth.

6 old shirts.

19 pewter plates.

---

introduced into Norway. He induced a Danish printer, Tyge Nielsen, to come to Christiania. In 1643 Nielsen issued the first three books printed on Norwegian soil. He did not, however, live up to the contract with Bang, who in 1644 took possession of his printing establishment, and tried to dispose of it. New printing firms were established in Norway, and, with the help of these, Bang was enabled to finish his "Postilla catechetica" in 1665. Norway was the last country in Europe but one (Turkey) to introduce the art of printing, it being up to the middle of the seventeenth century almost entirely dependent on Denmark for typographical work. It is interesting that an explanation of Luther's catechism proved instrumental in securing for Norway, with all its rich literature from the time of the sagas to the present, its first printing shop.

Exactly 250 years have passed since Bang's Explanation of Luther's catechism was completed. A competent Norwegian authority on printing says: "Det . . . er et af de største trykverker, som er udført i Norge."

A copy of the first volume is found in the Heggtveit Collection at Augsburg Seminary, Minneapolis.

* Says Debes: "Efter at Gud hafver antændt et større Lius for disse Indbyggere ved Evangeliets rette Forklaring, da hafve de saaledis tiltaget udi den sande Guds oc deris Saligheds Kundskab, at det kand i Sandhed skrifvis, at deris lige iblandt den Gemene-Mand udi Religionens Kundskab findis icke udi Danmarck. Thi efter at de faa sjælden Guds Ord at høre lydeligen aff deris Lærere, da øfve Tilhørerne sig selff udi Læsning, hafve deris Danske Postiller, hvoraf de for deris Folck udi Præstens Fraværelse Evangelii Forklaring gifve, hafve derhos andre aandelige Skrifter, saavelsom den hellige Skriftis Böger, hvilcke de flitteligen læse: Hvorudofver de saaledis ere grundede udi Guds Ord, at de vide med god Fynd at conferere med deris Lærere udi deres Forsamlinger om Religionens adskillige Artickler saa oc andet merckeligt, der kand falde udi Guds Ord. Oc eftersom alt Huus-Folcket sidde den største Tid hjemme udi deris Huuse om Vinteren, øfve de sig idelig udi Psalmer at sjunge. . . . Oc effterat Tilhørerne de gamle er saaledis forfremmede, lære de deris Ungdom ocsaa flitteligen, hvortil de ocsaa troligen tilholdis aff deris Præster saa oc Prousten udi Visitatsen. Hvorudofver de unge mange, som icke ere ofver deris ti eller tolf Aar gamle, kunne uden ad paa deris Fingre icke alleniste Luthers Catechismum med sin enfoldige Forklaring, men endoc S. Doctor Jesper Brochmands Sententser aff den H. Skrift sammendragne ofver Religionens Artickler. Hvorfor dette fattige Folck er rigeligen opfyldt med allehaande Viisdom oc Forstand udi Gud."

12 ditto large and small.
7 silver spoons.
1 silver cup.
1 silver saltcellar.
1 do. little bowl.
4 tankards with silver chains.
2 mirrors, 1 with an ebony, and the other a gilt frame.
6 little alabaster plates.
3 iron pots.
2 carpenter's axes.
3 adzes and some other carpenter's tools.
3 beds and 6 pairs of sheets.
4 pairs pillows.
4 table cloths.
16 or 17 napkins.
1 small brewing kettle.
3 half barrels.
1 half vat.
3 tubs.
1 hogshead.
1 churn.
3 milk pails old and new.
4 muds (vessel containing four bushels).
5 old empty corn casks.
1 suit, of black cloth.
1 pair of gloves.
3 copper kettles.
1 ditto skimmer.
1 extension table.
1 chest containing sundry parcels.
A few panes of window glass.
A lot of old iron.
1 stone house covered with tiles.
1 barn.
1 tobacco house.
2 barricks (Bergen), [sheds consisting of movable roof set on
    posts — to shelter hay and grain against rain and snow].
2 five year old mares.
1 six year old stallion.
1 two year old ditto.

1 yearling stallion.
2 mares of one year.
5 milch cows.
1 two year old cow.
2 yoke of oxen.
1 bull.
3 yearling heifers.
Hogs, number unknown, running in the woods.
6 schepels of wheat.
66   "   "   rye.   } sown on the bowery
3   "   "   winter barley. } on the cleared land.
7   "   "   peas.   }
1 ox plough.   } with appurtenances.
1 foot plough. }
1 iron harrow.
1 block wagon.
2 sickles.
2 new scythes.
1 old ditto.
23 new axes.
4 old ditto.
2 hoes.

There is otherwise very little on record about Jonas Bronck. Under date of July 21, 1639, is a notice that he sued Clara Mathys for a breach of contract and that he obtained judgment against her. The nature of the contract is not stated.[414] The early dating would indicate that Bronck had come to New Netherland before July, 1639.

He was an advocate of peace. "Ne cede malis" was engraved on the family coat of arms, which is the same as on the windows of the Old Dutch Church in Albany where his son, Pieter, worshipped. This coat of arms was found on some of Bronck's belongings. It is engraved on a silver cup of his, still preserved.

The motto is in harmony with the name of his house "Emmaus." At this house, on March 28, 1642, the signing of a treaty of peace with the Winquaesgeckers, an Indian tribe, took place. Present were Cornelius van Tienhoven, secretary; Hendrick van

---

414 Calendar of Historical Manuscripts, I., p. 68.

Dyck, officer; Everhardus Bogardus, pastor; Jonas Bronck; and several Indians, two of whom had sold land to Bronck.[415]

Jonas died in 1643 — it has been said at the hands of Indians. The latter is improbable, for his house and property were intact at the inventory of his effects. At this inventory, which we have reproduced in detail, his son, his wife, his friend Jochem Pietersen Kuyter and Rev. Bogardus were present. Kuyter and Bogardus were appointed guardians. Prior to the fire in the Albany Capitol (1911), the original inventory was on file at the Secretary of State's office.

Bronck had married in Europe, probably in Denmark, Teuntje Jeurians (Teuntje = Antonia, or Sofia). She may have been a relative of Marritje Pieters, of Copenhagen, who in her marriage contract appointed Teuntje one of her heirs. Some writers designate her as Antonia Slaghboom.

After the death of Bronck she married Arent Van Curler, one of the most prominent men in Rensselaerswyck. She survived him also. She died at Schenectady Dec. 19, 1676.

Van Curler sold, July 10, 1651, Bronck's estate to Jacob Jans Stoll, evidently a relative of Jan Jacobsen, the husband of Marritje Pieters from Copenhagen, to whom Bronck had leased some of his land in 1639.

Stoll transferred it to a Mr. Hopper.* When he died, and as he had not paid Stoll in full, the latter started suit against Hopper's widow. She had to pay the remainder of the debt, and was now given a satisfactory deed in December, 1662. We learn from this law-suit that no less than 1300 tiles had been taken away from Bronck's house when the Hoppers received it.

Mrs. Hopper transferred the property to Harman Smeeman, a Dane. But the latter did not keep it long. He conveyed it to Samuel Edsall, who in 1674 (1670) deeded it to a Mr. Morris, whence the new name of Bronck's five hundred acres: Morrisania.

As to the history of the property once owned by Bronck, see, besides the work of Harry C. Cook, Randall Comfort, "History of Bronx Borough" (1906); Stephen Jenkins, "The Story of Bronx 1639—1912" (1912). Harriett Van Buren Peckham's

415 New York Colonial Documents, I., pp. 199, 410.
    * Hopper or Hoppen may have been a Norwegian. See Excursus II., in Part I.

"History of Cornelis Maessen Van Buren" (1913) contains a brief genealogy of the Bronck family. See also New York Genealogical and Biographical Magazine, Vol. 39, p. 274.

PIETER BRONCK.

Pieter Bronck was in New Amsterdam as early as 1643 or before. He was present in 1643 at the inventory of the goods and effects in the house of Jonas Bronck. He must have been a relative of Jonas, in all probability his son. In a document of 1646 he is called Pieter Jonassen Bronck. This would go to prove that he was the son of Jonas Bronck. The same document — Pieter's will — makes mention of "Engeltje Mans, father, mother and other kindred." Engeltje Mans was from Sweden, she was the wife of Burgher Joris.[416]

Pieter Bronck came to Beverwyck in 1645. He became the owner of several house-lots and a brewery at this place, where he also built a tavern, then the third tavern of Beverwyck. He sold it in 1662, and bought 126 morgens of land at Coxsackie, where he settled. In 1665 his farm consisted of 176 morgens (352 acres), besides a calf pasture of six morgens.[417]

When he removed to Beverwyck he gave, on October 9, 1646, Burgher Joris of New Amsterdam, the husband of the above-mentioned Engeltje Mans from Sweden, power of attorney to collect debts due him.[418]

In the colony of Rensselaerswyck he is charged with an annual rent of four beavers for a lot, in the village, on which he received permission to build. He paid this rent 1650—1652 and perhaps longer.[419]

On May 29, 1657, judgment was obtained against him in a court proceeding for his having with a knife assaulted a person. He was fined 100 guilders.[420]

On January 22, 1658, Lewis Cobus, Secretary of Albany, sued

416 See article "Jonas Bronck". B. Fernow, Calendar of (N. Y.) Wills, p. 55.
417 E. B. O'Callaghan, History of New Netherland, I., pp. 441, 591.
418 Calendar of Historical Manuscripts, I., p. 85.
419 Van Rensselaer Bowier Manuscripts, p. 840.
420 Calendar of Historical Manuscripts, I., p. 814.

Pieter Bronck and Dirck Bensingh, a Swede, for his fees in taking an inventory of Hans Vosche's property at Katskil. The Court ordered the defendants to pay the fee.[421]

Pieter Bronck married Hilletje Tyssinck. He died 1669, in Coxsackie, leaving two children: Jan who was born in Beverwyck, or Albany, 1650; and Pieter.[422]

Jan was a member of the Reformed church at New Albany.[423] He married Commertje Leendertse Conyn. He became the heir of his father. A part of the inheritance was the old Bronck House, still standing, though the brick parts were added in the eighteenth century.

Jan had nine children. Agnietje married Jan Witbeck, son of Andries and Engeltje Vokertse (Douw) Witbeck. Antje married, 1733, Rev. George Michael Weiss. Pieter married Antje Bogardus, daughter of Pieter and Wyntie Cornelise (Bosch) Bogardus. Jonas married, in 1689. Philip, baptized in 1691, died young. Philip, baptized 1692, married. Hilletje married, 1712, Thomas Wiliams. Caspar married, 1739, Catharine, daughter of Gerit van Bergen and Annatje Meyer. Leendert married, 1717, Anna, daughter of Johannes de Wandelaer and Sarah Shepnoss.

The Bronck family has a military record.

Jan, the grandson of Jonas Bronck, pioneer at Bronx, became a lieutenant in 1709, and a Justice of the Peace in Albany in 1728.

Jan Leendertsen, the great-grandson of Jonas Bronck, married Elsie Van Buren, and "established the rights of his descendants to all societies with early military claims by becoming Captain of Militia in 1740, and in 1770 was commissioned to that rank by Lieutenant-Governor Cadwalder Colden; later he was promoted to the rank of Major of the 11th Regiment."

The sole male heir of Jan Leendertsen, Leonard, born 1751, was First Lieutenant in 1778, Major in 1793, Lieutenant-Colonel in 1796. He was a member of the New York State Assembly 1786—1798, State Senator, 1800. He was first Judge of the Court of Appeals of Green County.

---

421 Calendar of Historical Manuscripts, I., p. 817.
422 Munsell's Collections on the History of Albany, IV., p. 104.
423 Year Book of the Holland Society of New York, 1904, p. 4.

Many of the members of the Bronck family took part in the French and Indian wars.

The Bronck genealogy of the eighteenth and nineteenth centuries would cover several pages in this work. The reader may be referred for further details to Miss Van Buren Peckham's "History of C. M. Van Buren."

PETER BRUYN.

Peter Bruyn, from Rensborg, Schleswig, was a member of the company of soldiers at Esopus, in March, 1660. He lived in the village of Wiltwyck (Esopus) in 1661, where he was listed as paying excise on beer and wine.[424]

JOHAN CARSTENZ.

Johan Carstenz, from Barlt, in Holstein, came to New Amsterdam by the ship "den Houttuyn", August 4, 1642. He was employed by Van Rensselaer in his colony, drew wages from August 4, 1642. In July, 1644, he appears as servant of Michael Jansz.[425]

In November, 1655, Coenraet Ten Eyck sued "Jan Carstensen from Husum" for fl. 204.8. He had sold him goods to this amount, and requested the court to condemn him to pay the amount in beavers. Carstensen acknowledged the debt — he had given a note for it — and said he would pay in seawan, as he had no beavers for the time being. The court, however, condemned Carstensen "to pay plaintiff the aforesaid sum of fl. 204.8 according to a signed note, in beavers." [426]

In 1660 a Jan Carstensen, from Husum, Denmark, served in a regiment in Albany. Johan Carstensen from Barlt and Jan Carstensen from Husum likely are the same person.[427]

424 New York Colonial Documents, XIII., pp. 154, 212.
425 Van Rensselaer Bowier Manuscripts, pp. 609, 827.
426 Records of New Amsterdam, 1653-1674, I., p. 399f.
427 New York Colonial Documents, XIII., p. 154.

PIETER CARSTENSEN.

Pieter Carstensen, from Holstein, arrived at New Amsterdam in 1663. He came over, accompanied by his son, who was sixteen years of age, on the ship "de Statyn," which sailed September 27, 1663.[428]

PIETERSEN (CARSTENSEN).

Pietersen (Carstensen), son of the abovementioned Pieter Carstensen, came over from Holstein in 1663. He was then sixteen years old.

CRIETGEN CHRISTIANS.

Crietgen Christians arrived at New Amsterdam in 1659. He was from Tönning [now belonging to Germany], Denmark. He came over on the ship "de Bever," which sailed April 25, 1659.[429]

He had a house lot in Schenectady with a front of 100 feet on Union Street, one half being now included in the lot of the First Reformed church. He sold this lot in 1694 to Neetje Claes. We owe this information to Jonathan Pearson's "Early Records of . . . Albany," p. 485. In that work is also found the following deed, which refers to the property of Crietgen Christians:

"Appeared before me, Ludovicus Cobes, secretary of Albany, in the presence of the honorable Herren commisaries, etc., Philip Pieterse Schuyler and Jan Hendricxe Van Bael, Paulus Janse, who declares that in true rights, free ownership, he grants, conveys and makes over by these presents to and for the behoof of Christiaen Christiaense, dwelling at Schaenhechtede, in his plantation lying there, consisting of one and a half morgens and bounded according to the patent thereof from the right honorable general of New York, Francis Lovlace, dated the 24th of May, 1669, to which

428 Year Book of the Holland Society of New York, 1902.
429 Ibid.

reference is herein made; free and unincumbered, with no claims standing or issuing against the same, excepting the lord's right, without the grantor's making the least claim thereto any more, acknowledging that he is fully paid and satisfied therefor, the first penny with the last and therefore giving *plenam actionem cessam*, and full power to the aforesaid Christiaen Christiaense, his heirs and successors or assigns, to do with and dispose of said plantation, as he might do with his patrimonial estate and effects; promising to protect and free the same from all such troubles, claims and liens of every person as are lawful, and further, never more to do nor suffer anything to be done, with or without law, in any manner, on pledge according to law therefor provided.

"Done in Albany, the 23d of June, 1671.

"Philip Pieterse.

"Jan Hend: Van Bael.

"Poulys Jansen.

"In my presence,   Ludovicus Cobes, Secretary."

HANS CHRISTIAENSEN.

Hans Christiaensen, or Hans Kettel, was from Holstein. He was in New Amsterdam as early as 1658 or before. On August 10, 1659, he married, in New Amsterdam, Marritje Cornelis, from Flensborg in Holstein. His first wife was Engeltje Jans.[430]

Hans and Marritje had a child, Neeltje, who was baptized on November 12, 1660.[431]

Hans was dead when Marritje, on May 31, 1665, married Cornelis Beckman, of "Stift" Bremen.[432]

What we otherwise know of Christiaensen is found in an entry in the court minutes, the substance of which is as follows:

[September 10, 1658.]   Hans Christiaensen was sued by Mathys Boon who complained that Christiaensen's dog has bit his [Boon's] hogs, one of which lies sick, several of which are missed. Christiaensen declared, he did not know whether this

---

430 Collections of the New York Genealogical and Biographical Society, I., p. 81.

431 Ibid., II., p. 59.

432 Ibid., I., p. 81.

occurred or not, as he locks up his dog by day, and lets him loose at night. Boon's farm was enclosed, but the hogs could get through the enclosure. After getting this testimony the court appointed Pieter Jansen Noorman and Teunis Gysbersen Middag to inspect the fence.[433]

The case was to be tried at the next court session. But both litigants were sick when the session was announced. Perhaps the matter was settled out of court.

PIETER HENDRICKSEN CHRISTIANS.

Pieter Hendricksen Christians was in New Netherland as early as 1659. On January 17, of that year, he married, in New Amsterdam, Christina Bleyers from "Stoltenon," in Lüneburg. The marriage record [434] states that Christians was from "Voorburg" (Varberg in Sconia), which belonged to Denmark until 1658, but since then is part of Sweden.

HENDRICK CORNELISSEN.

Hendrick Cornelissen, from Holstein, was at Esopus as early as 1658 or before, witnessing, in May, 1658, the massacre committed by the Indians.[435]

Signature of Hendrick Cornelissen.

On August 17, 1659, he signed a petition requesting the government to appoint the Rev. Bloem as pastor at Esopus. He signed the document with his mark: [436] In the same year he signed

433 The Records of New Amsterdam, 1658-1674, III., pp. 7, 12.
434 Collections of the New York Genealogical and Biographical Society, I., p. 28.
435 New York Colonial Manuscripts, XIII., p. 78.
436 Ibid., XIII., 108f.

a declaration sent by the inhabitants of Esopus, stating that no blame could be attached to Ensign Smith in certain military troubles which they were involved in when fighting the savages.[437] In June, 1661, Cornelissen did military duty at the local garrison.[438]

On April 25, 1663, he was given a grant of land at Esopus, "a piece of land, situate at the Esopus, in the village of Wiltwyck, bounded on the East by the Kill, on the West and South by the meadow lying under the village, containing in these bounds between the Kill and the meadows two morgens and five hundred sixty rods." On November 7, in the same year, he received an additional grant of six morgens (twelve acres).[439]

In 1667 there were some riots in Esopus between the soldiers of Captain Brodhead and the inhabitants which terminated in the death of Cornelissen. In the proceedings and sentences of the local court, April 25—27, 1668, resulting from complaints of the inhabitants against the violence of the soldiers and illtreatment from Captain Brodhead, it was shown that Hendrick Cornelissen Lindrayer was "by William Fisher, without any the least reason, wounded in his belly'" and that he died of the wound (this part of the document is missing, but the title shows that Cornelissen died of the wound).[440]

JAN CORNELISEN.

Jan Cornelisen, from Flensburg, Denmark, received the small burgher's right in New Amsterdam, April 14, 1657. In 1659 he was a carrier of beer with wages of a trifle more than six guilders a week.[441] On December 31, 1660, he and some other beer carriers appeared in court to defend themselves against a complaint, made by the Farmer of Beer and Wine. The complaint was, that they had taken beer from the breweries and brought it to the burghers' houses without having a permit from the Farmer. They

---

437 Ibid., XIII., p. 118f.
438 Ibid., XIII., p. 202.
439 Ibid., XIII., pp. 240, 241.
440 Ibid., XIII., p. 407; III., p. 150.
441 The Records of New Amsterdam, 1653-1674, VII., p. 286.

were also represented as having brought an anker of strong beer to Johannes de Decker's house without a permit. The reply made by the accused was that the Farmer was mistaken: there was a permit for it, and Mr. Decker knew it. The court recommended the "comparants not to remove any beer without having a permit for so doing." [442]

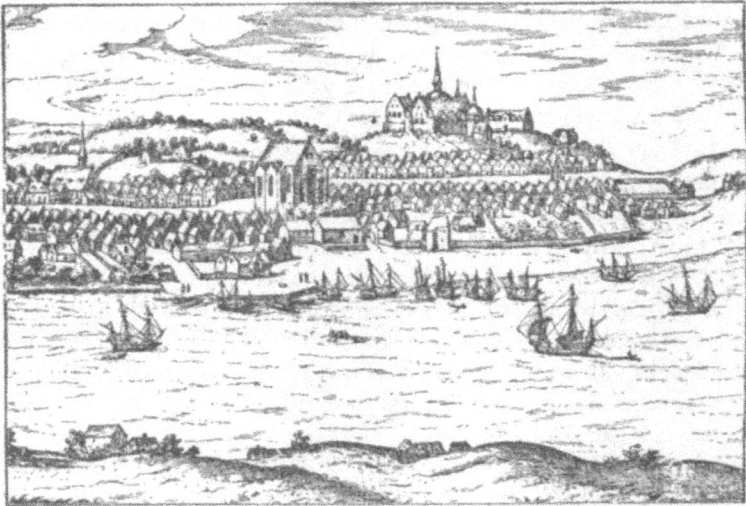

THE NORTHERN PART OF FLENSBURG, ABOUT THE CLOSE OF THE SIXTEENTH CENTURY.
From Braunius: Theatrum urbium, iv.

On January 10, 1661, Jan Cornelisen and seven others appeared in the city hall offering their services as watchmen. They were accepted by the burgomasters as Watch. The wages for each watchman was eighteen guilders a month. Cornelisen took the usual oath of fidelity to the "Instructions for Watchmen." [443]

Under date of March 13, 1659, it is stated in an instrument of conveyance that Cornelisen bought of Reinhout Reinhoutsen a lot in New Amsterdam, situated on the Schape Weitie, west of the Prince Graft. His lot was bounded on the south by a lot, for some time owned by Reinout Reinoutsen but transferred by

---

442 Ibid., VII., pp. 152, 262.
443 Ibid., VII., p. 265.

him, March 13, 1659, to Thomas Verdon.* On the north it was bounded by a lot belonging to Pieter Rudolphus; on the west by the tannery of Reinhoutsen; on the east by Prince Graft. Its dimensions were on the east side 24 feet; on the west side, 17; north and south side, 119.

On July 15, 1661, Cornelisen deeded to Willem Jansen Van Borckloo this lot, and a house that he had built upon it.†

LAURENS CORNELISSZEN (COECK).

Laurens Corneliszen (Coeck), from Denmark, was in New Amsterdam as early as 1676, or before. The marriage records of the Dutch Reformed church in New Amsterdam states that he was from Denmark. He married Margriet Barents, March 5, 1676.[444] He is not to be taken for another resident of New Amsterdam, known as Captain Laurens Cornelissen.

On March 21, 1677, Laurens Corneliszen and Margariet Barents had a child baptized, Cornelis, the sponsors were Barendt Arentszen and Marritie Cornelis, perhaps a sister of Laurens. Their child, Grietie, was baptized, December 21, 1678; their daughter, Marritje, June 22, 1687.

On March 1, 1691, their son Barent was baptized. The father's name in the baptismal records is, in this instance, entered as Laurens Corneliszen Coeck.[445]

MARRITJE CORNELIS.

Marritje Cornelis, from Flensburg, was in New Amsterdam as early as 1659, when she was married to Hans Christiaensen, from Holstein. After his death, she married, May 31, 1665, Cor-

* D. T. Valentine, Manual of the Corporation of the City of New York, 1865, pp. 657-8.
† Ibid., 1865, p. 681.
444 Collections of the New York Genealogical and Biographical Society, I., p. 41.
445 Ibid., pp. 127, 185, 180, 202.

nelis Beckman, of "Stift Bremen." By Christiaensen she had a daughter, Neeltje, who was baptized November 12, 1660.

PAULUS CORNELISSEN.

Paulus Cornelissen was in New Netherland as early as 1654. He was from Flensburg, in Denmark. Under date of September 1, 1654, a note was given, at Fort Orange, of the following content: "I, the undersigned Claes Cornelissen, acknowledge and confess that I am well and truly indebted to Paulus Cornelise (Van Flensburgh), now ready to depart for Patria, in the sum and number of six beavers."[446] Whether he be the Paulus Cornelissen who, in New Amsterdam, in January, 1668, sued Thomas Lourens, and who worked for the Dane Laurens Duyts, I can not determine.

Paul Cornelissen is also mentioned as late as 1671.[447]

PIETER CORNELIS.

Pieter Cornelis, or Pieter Cornelis Low, a laborer from Holstein, came to New Amsterdam in 1659, in the ship "de Trouw," which sailed on February 21, 1659.[448]

He married Elisabeth, a daughter of Mattys Blanchan, and had issue, i. e., Cornelis, who was born 1670 in Esopus, and married in New York, July 5, 1695, Margaret Borsum. Pieter had other children also.

Under date of November 1, 1676, is a testamentary document of Pieter and his wife, which reads as follows:

". . . The survivor shall possess the entire estate; at remarriage one-half thereof shall go to the children. If both parties should die without having remarried, the children are to inherit the property, the minors first being brought up. If either party

---

446 Munsell, Collections on the History of . . Albany, III., p. 199.

447 The Records of New Amsterdam, 1653-1674, VI., p. 108. Ibid., IV., p. 86.

448 Year Book of the Holland Society of New York, 1902.

should survive and not marry, such survivor shall have the use of the estate until death."[449]

There is a later will, dated December 20, 1690, in which Pieter designates himself as "Pieter Cornelissen Low," yeoman of Kingston.[450]

His progeny have been numerous and widespread.

PIETER CORNELISSEN.

Pieter Cornelissen was from "Warbeer" (Varberg in Sconia), in Denmark. Varberg has been a Swedish town since 1658, and hence Cornelissen may have received the surname "the Swede": in a document of 1666 he is spoken of as Pieter Cornelissen, alias the Swede. Or he may have been called Swede, because his wife was Swedish. He had married on August 5, 1656, in New Amsterdam, Brieta Ollofs, from Göteborg, Sweden. By her he had a daughter, Margariet, who was baptized on April 15, 1657.

In December, 1666, Brieta, having become a widow, married Jan Jacobsen from Friesland. The Orphanmasters appointed, in the same month, Focke Jans and Cornelis Aerts as guardians for her daughter.[451]

Whatever else is recorded of Pieter Cornelissen, is limited to a notice in the court records, viz., that he on November 1, 1664, sued Bastian the Wheelwright for an ox he had sold to him, for which he demanded 230 guilders. The matter was likely settled out of court, as arbitrators were appointed to reconcile the parties.[452]

SYBRANT CORNELISSEN.

Sybrant Cornelissen, a soldier in the service of the West India Company, was in New Amsterdam about 1664. On Jan-

449 G. Anjou, Ulster County (N. Y.) Wills, 1906, I., p. 85.
450 Ibid., I., p. 78.
451 Year Book of the Holland Society of New York, 1900, p. 128.
452 The Records of New Amsterdam, 1653-1673, V., p. 149.

VARBERG, ABOUT THE CLOSE OF THE SEVENTEENTH CENTURY.

uary 31, in that year, he made a declaration, at the request of one
Paul Pietersen, in regard to a quarrel between Maritie Tomas and
Tryntie Martens, the wife of Paul.[453]

Sybrant Cornelissen was from Flensburg in Denmark, as we
learn from a notice of July 17, 1664, stating that he, on that date,
was appointed assistant surgeon, and that he was to be employed
in shaving, bleeding, and administering medicine to the soldiers.[454]
In other words, Sybrant appears to have been an old-time barber-
surgeon. In E. B. O'Callaghan's "Register of New Netherland,"
p. 124, Sybrant is listed as "Physician and surgeon at Esopus."

URSEL DIRCKS.

Ursel Dircks, from Holstein, came in 1658 to New Amsterdam with his two children, aged two and ten, by the ship "de Moesman," which sailed May 1, 1658, for New Netherland.[455]

LAURENS DUYTS.

Laurens Duyts came over to New Netherland in 1639 in the
ship "de Brant van Trogen." Among his fellow passengers were
the Danes Captain Jochem Pietersen Kuyter, Jonas Bronck (?),
and Pieter Andriesen. Duyts and Andriesen were to work for
Jonas Bronck: to clear a tract of five hundred acres, which Bronck
had purchased from the Indians. Duyts thus became one of the
pioneers of the present Borough of Bronx. He was commonly
known as Laurens Grootschoe (Big Shoe). He was born in Holstein in 1610.

He married Ytie Jansen. By her he had three children: a
daughter, Margariet, who was baptized on December 23, 1639, the
sponsors being Gerrit Jansen of Oldenburg (perhaps he was Ytie's
brother), Teuntje Joris and Tyntje Martens; a son, Jan, who was

453 Year Book of the Holland Society of New York, 1900, p. 157.
454 Calendar of Historical Manuscripts, I., p. 278.
455 Year Book of the Holland Society of New York. 1902.

baptized on March 23, 1641; another son, Hans, who was baptized in 1644. Jochem Pietersen Kuyter was sponsor at the baptism of the boys.[456]

Duyts appears to have been farming in different places, leasing the lands he tilled.

In March, 1654, he had a land dispute with Francoys Fyn. Fyn had a certain parcel of land lying on Long Island over against Hog Island (now Blackwell's Island). Duyts had sold this without Fyn's knowing it, claiming it was his own land.[457]

Duyts leased for some time the bowery of the Norwegian woman ·from Marstrand, Anneke Jans. He was to pay her two hogs in rent. As he had paid only one, he was sued, in May, 1658, by Anneke's son-in-law, Johannes Pietersen Verbrugge, later mayor of New York, and was condemned to deliver the hog to the plaintiff.[458]

Duyts's moral life does not deserve mention. But in order to show hos Laurens "Big Shoe" trampled upon the laws of decency and how such a lawbreaker was punished, we relate that Laurens Duyts of Holstein received a most severe sentence from Stuyvesant on November 25, 1658. For selling his wife, Ytie Jansen, and forcing her to live in adultery with another man and for living himself also in adultery, he was to have a "rope tied around his neck, and then to be severely flogged, to have his right ear cut off, and to be banished for fifty years."[459]

Signature of Laurents Duyts.

Laurens died at Bergen, New Jersey, about 1668. His son, Hans, lived at Harlem in 1667. Also the other son, Jan, lived there. "He bore a good name at Harlem, and did not deserve the

---

456 See articles "Bronck," "Kuyter," "Pieter Andriessen." J. Riker, Harlem, Its Origin and Early Annals, p. 256.

457 The Records of New Amsterdam, 1653-1674, I., p. 188f. Tradition says that Francois Fyn was an Englishman. Could he have been a Dane—from Fyn, Denmark? See Excursus. Part II.

458 Ibid., II., p. 380.

459 Calendar of Historical Manuscripts, I., p. 208.

taunt uttered one day by Jeanne de Ruine, in presence of Mons Pietersen, a Swede or Finn: You villain, run to your father Dane." Pietersen claimed that Jan had said nothing to provoke it. Jan married in 1667, again in 1673.

Hans had a daughter, Cathrine, who at the age of fourteen (1688) was married to Joost Paulding from Holland. Paulding went to Westchester. He was the ancestor of John Paulding, one of Major Andre's captors.[460]

CARSTEN JANSEN EGGERT.

Carsten Jansen Eggert, from Dithmarschen, in Schleswig-Holstein, was in New Amsterdam in 1655, or before. On January 3, 1656, Luycas Eldersen sued him for rent. Eggert claimed that he did not owe Eldersen. The Court, however, referred the matter to arbitrators, who were to try to reconcile the contending parties. (Records of New Amsterdam, 1653-1674, II., p. 5.)

On October 26, 1656, Eggert appeared as attorney for a Dane, Herman Smeeman, in a suit started by Jan Barentsen. (See article "Herman Smeeman." Part II.)

On January 8, 1657, Pieter van Couwenhoven sued Eggert for 101 lbs. tobacco, which had been delivered to Eggert "in excess by Thomas Hall." Eggert did not deny that he had received the tobacco, but said he "must have from Hall fl. 19 for freight and 3.10 for labor," and consequently could offset that. His papers were in Virginia, but he would furnish the court with proof upon the arrival of Hall. The court decided to postpone decision until the arrival of Hall. (Ibid., p. 257.)

On March 16, 1660, David Jochimzen sued Eggert, demanding to know why he had given up his agreement, entered into with Jacob Hay and Pieter Claesen. He had leased from them some land, once owned by Dirk Holgersen, a Norwegian, but later transferred to Hay. The land lay in the present Greenpoint, Brooklyn. Eggert said, in his defense, that he could not remain dwelling on the bowery, as the government had ordered those who were dwelling on the boweries in that region to move away and form a

---

460 J. Riker, Harlem, Its Origin and Early Annals, p. 256.

village. He also said that he could not make use of the land, as he had to transport his grain over three and a half thousand paces through the rough forest. The court decreed that Jochimzen must first deliver the house standing on the farm at the village at his own cost, and then the lessee shall fulfill the conditions of the lease. (Ibid. III., p. 144.)

On July 12, 1661, Christina Capoens, wife of Jacob Hay, later wife of David Jochimsen, sued Carsten Jansen Eggert and Hendrick Janzen Sluyter because they had taken sods from her meadow. She wanted them to indemnify the loss she had suffered, "and, moreover, to pay something for the poor." The defendants replied that they did not know that the land belonged to the plaintiff. The Court dropped the matter by reprimanding the defendants, charging them not to repeat the offense. (Ibid., II., p. 342.)

On November 28, 1673, Eggert sued Dirck Claessen Pottebacker, claiming that he had lent Pottebacker's wife three beavers, of which he had only received one back. Pottebacker was condemned to return the other two also. (Ibid., VII., p. 27.)

Carsten Jansen Eggert was listed in 1674 as possessing in New Amsterdam property on the present South William Street, then known as The Mill Street Lane. It was rated as "fourth class" property, no value being given. (Year Book of the Holland Society of New York, 1896.)

Eggert had several relatives in New Amsterdam, as is seen by his will, in which his sister Anneke Jans, who was from Holstein, is mentioned; also his sister, Grietje Jans, who is mentioned in the marriage records as being from Dithmarschen; and finally Dirck Jansen.

Under date of May 9, 1678, we find in "Collections of the New York Historical Society," I., p. 48, this interesting entry:

"Whereas, Carsten Jans Eggert, of this city, did in his last will bequeath his estate part by way of legacy, and the rest to be disposed of by way of gifts to his next relations, that is to say the sum of 500 guilders, wampum, to the Lutheran Church, as a legacy, and to his sister, Greetje Jans, wife of Jacob Pietersen, 150 guilders, wampum, the rest to be divided equally between his brother, Dirck Jansen De Groot, his sister, Greetye Jansen, and

Bruyn Ages, the son of his other sister, Annatje Jans and Bruyn Ages, both deceased, making Hendrick Williams and David Westells executors, as in said will, and additions the 7th and 19 of April last. The same was confirmed May 9, 1678."

So far as we know, Eggert was one of the few Lutherans in the new world, who at such an early period bequeathed a legacy to the Lutheran church of the City of New York.

JACOB ELDERSEN.

Jacob Eldersen, sometimes called Jacob Eldersen Brower (the brewer), was in New Amsterdam as early as 1656, when Gerrit Fullewever conveyed a lot to him. In the instrument of conveyance it is said that Jacob was from Lübeck, where the Danes are numerous. He was probably a Dane.[461] After having lived in New Amsterdam, he went to Harlem, of which he was one of the founders (1661).[462] He was at Esopus in 1667. In a document of 1670 his name is written Eldessen; in a document of 1674, Elbertsen.[463]

When he was in New Amsterdam he signed the petition of the Lutherans (1657), requesting that the Lutheran preacher Goetwater might stay in the city instead of being deported.[464]

Jacob Eldersen's record in New Amsterdam, however, does not give much evidence of his being a model churchman.

From the court minutes we glean the following:

In February, 1656, Andries Van der Sluys brought action against him for rent.[465]

On September 18, Marritje Pietersen sued him for shooting her dog. She requested indemnification for it to the amount of

461 D. T. Valentine, Manual of the Corporation of the City of New York, 1861, p. 582.
462 J. Riker, Harlem, Its Origin and Early Annals, p. 190. Riker says he was a Dane.
463 Year Book of the Holland Society of New York, 1897, p. 122.
464 See note 42.
465 The Records of New Amsterdam, 1653-1674, II., p. 47.

fl. 16. Eldersen acknowledged that he had shot the dog in self-defense. In catching a stone to drive him away, Jacob was bit in the finger, so that he was obliged to have it dressed by a surgeon. The plaintiff replied that he "shot the dog when she called him and he was by her person," and she denied that the dog bit him. On the next court day, the surgeon, Hans Kierstede's, declaration relative to the wound was exhibited by Eldersen, in court. But the plaintiff was absent.

On January 14, 1658, Eldersen again appeared in court, summoned by the Schout, and charged with striking Bruin Barensen, a cooper at Brooklyn. Eldersen now claimed he had struck Barensen with a broom stick, warding off Barensen, who drew a knife. He averred he had not used a club. Barensen was severely beaten and lay a long time abed. Eldersen was put in prison.

A few days later, intercession was made for his release from imprisonment, but the Court took no action.

On January 23, Eldersen escaped, and the Schout requested that "his goods and effects, which he has in this country, may be provisionally seized and he be summoned by bell ringing to appear in person within eight days and to hear such demand and conclusion as the Schout shall have to make." The request was approved by the court.

On January 28, an order was given that no one should harbor or hide the fugitive. He was summoned, February 15 and 22, was found February 25, but would not appear. Hence he was arrested. He secured the aid of an attorney, and through him he obtained release, promising to reply within 48 hours to the answer "in reconvention of the Fiscal entered before the Director-General."[466]

On February 12, 1658, Bruin Barentsen, whom Eldersen struck, died.

On March 11, the Court therefore passed the following sentence:

"Whereas, Jacob Eldersen, brewer's servant, a good while ago seriously beat and wounded one Bruyn Barensen with a sledge hammer with which wood is cleft, according to declaration thereof, and with a broom handle according to his own confession, whereby the above-named Bruyn Barensen lay a long time bed ridden, and

[466] Ibid., II., pp. 166f., 298, 301, 309, 318, 339, 340.

he, Jacob Eldersen, was placed provisionally in confinement by the Schout at the request and with the consent of the Court, and again released on bail; nevertheless, as the longer it was with the wounded, the worse, and the bail importuned the Schout to have the bail bond discharged, the above-named Jacob Eldersen was again placed in close confinement to await the issue of the patient, to be then proceeded against according to the circumstances of the case; therefore, he, the above-named Jacob, having remained a few days, violated the public prison, broke out of the same and fled away. Whereupon the Schout, demanding citation of the absconder from the Director-Gen(era)l and Council, obtained it from their Honors, and thereupon (he) was three several times summoned by sound of the bell to hear all such demand and conclusion as the Schout should have to make against him: finally, three days after the third citation he again made his appearance, whereupon the Schout placed him for the third time in his former prison after communication with the Court of this City, and whereas Dirck van Schelluine being allowed and authorized by the aforesaid Jacob Eldersen to act for the above-named Jacob, requested release of the prisoner, and having obtained it from the Court, has proceeded in virtue of authority and consent for the above-named Jacob Eldersen against the Schout in his case, which he, the Schout, had against him, Jacob Eldersen; which papers, documents and proofs, used in the suit on both sides, being seen and maturely weighed by the Court as before, they cannot find, that they avail anything in behalf of the aforesaid Jacob Eldersen by sufficiently proving that he acted on the defensive; moreover, the breaking jail perpetuated by him was a sign, that he was convinced in his mind of his guilt: They, therefore, hereby condemn Jacob Eldersen above-named, to pay as a fine for having inflicted a wound on Bruin Barentsen above-named, the sum of three hundred guilders; as he has broken the public jail, which justly deserves corporal punishment, yet in consideration, that he willingly surrendered himself he was therefore condemned in the sum of one hundred guilders, all to be applied as is proper; and further in the costs of suit. Thus done and sentenced in the Court of Burgomasters and Schepens of the City of Amsterdam in N. Netherland. Datum ut supra [March 11, 1658].

"By order of the Burgomasters and Schepens of the City above named, "Joannes Nevius, Secret(ar)y.[467]

---

467 Ibid., II., p. 852f.

Five years later Jacob Eldersen was severely beaten in Harlem by some workmen, who perhaps were trying to pay off Eldersen for the death of their countryman. (See the article Pieter Jansen Slot. Part II.)

Eldersen had other litigation in New Amsterdam. On September 3, 1658, Mighiel Jansen sued him for a debt, and a week later Christian Pieters, a Dane, did the same.

In June, 1662, Eldersen himself brought action against William Britton, George Jewel, James Clerk, and John Too, of Newton, for "alleging that he had stolen said Britton's tobacco."[468]

The material at our disposal does not permit of forming any judgment as to Eldersen's character. His weakness was perhaps his temper coupled with a demeanor or disposition which caused people to tease him or indulge in merriment at his expense. He has nevertheless the honor of being one of the founders of Harlem.[469]

THOMAS FREDERICKSEN.

Thomas Fredericksen, from Oldenburg, Holstein, was in New Amsterdam as early as 1650. He was a cooper, and was known as Thomas Fredericksen de Kuyper. On July 11, 1651, he signed a document as witness in a transaction, the particulars of which need not be stated here.[470]

His wife was Marretie Claes Adriaens, by whom he had children: Adrian, baptized September 18, 1650; Tryntie, baptized February 23, 1653; Francyntie, April 4, 1655; Tryntie, January 16, 1658; Cornelis, January 15, 1659; Tryntie, September 3, 1662; Thomas, February 4, 1672.[471]

As early as 1655, Fredericksen was engaged in distilling brandy. In February, 1656, he petitioned for permission to keep a tavern, which was granted him by the Court of New Amsterdam.[472]

On June 22, 1656, he secured a lot in Sheep Pasture, the pres-

468 Ibid., III., pp. 3, 7.
469 Riker, Harlem, Its Origin and Early Annals.
470 New York Colonial Documents, XIV., p. 142.
471 Collections of the New York Genealogical and Biographical Society, II., pp. 27, 33, 39, 47, 51, 66, 104.
472 The Records of New Amsterdam, 1653-1674, I., p. 403; II., p. 33.

ent William Street, west side, near Exchange Place.   In August
he conveyed it to Coenrat Ten Eyck.[473]

Signature of Tomas Fredericksen, 1659.

His wife was no exception to many of the early New York
women in finding her way to the court of justice.   She had a
quick tongue.

In October, 1654, she complained against Hendrick Egberts
that he had railed at her and said that "General Stuyvesant had
caused her to be dragged from the ship and that he would have a
post fixed for her, and other such expressions.   Egbert denied that
he had used such injurious words, but acknowledged that he called
her a whore, because she first called him a banished knave and
rogue, and such like names."   Marritje denied this.   The parties
were ordered to prove their mutual statements.[474]

On September 18, 1656, she was again before the Court, this
time as defendant.   The entry in the court minutes referring to
this case is as follows:

"Schout N. de Silla, pltf. vs Marretie Claes, and Jochem
Beeckman's wife, for quareling and slander perpetrated on
Highway (Broadway).   Marretie Claesen appears in court, complaining that Jochem Schoester's wife scandalously slandered her,
while she stood at the door, with many dishonorable speeches and
proposals, and requesting that she be ordered to let her in peace.
Jochem Beeckman and his wife appeared both in court complaining that they were slandered by Martie, and flew at each other
in court with hard words, without having proof on the one side
or other. — Therefore the Court imposed silence on parties and
ordered them to live henceforth quiet and in peace and order, as
good neighbors ought to; or failing therein, that on first complaint
and proof, other disposition shall be made in the matter; condemning Jochem Beeckman or his wife in the penalty of fl. 10, and

<hr>

473 D. T. Valentine, Manual . . of the City of New York, 1861, p. 588.
474 The Records of New Amsterdam, 1653-1674, I., p. 258.

Thomas Fredericksen or his wife in the penalty of fl. 6 for the benefit of the deaconry of this City."[475]

Thomas Fredericksen seems to have been of a more peaceable disposition than his wife. In March, 1657, he was appointed weigh house laborer at the warehouse of the West India Company, having, with others, joint supervision of the scales and the carriage of beer and wine. In September, 1659, he resigned his office, "thanking the magistrates for the favor; who accept it, thanking him for the service."[476]

In the fall of 1660 he had a dispute with Abraham Lubbersen in regard to a small boat. Lubbersen demanded of him sixty florins for this boat. Fredericksen was at the time at Fort Orange. When he returned, the court authorized two citizens to decide the question and if possible reconcile the litigants.[477]

Fredericksen had considerable property in New Amsterdam. On June 29, 1656, he conveyed to A. Lubberszen a lot "situated west of the Prince Graft boundary to the South on the house and lot of Nicholaas Dela Plaine and to the North the tannery of Coenrat Ten Eyck. Wide in front on the street or West side twenty-six feet, in the rear twenty-seven feet, length on the South as well as the North side fifty-nine feet."[*]

On July 15, 1659, he deeded another lot to Abraham Lubberszen, "A lot west of the Prince Graght; bounded east by Prince Graft; south, by house and lot of said Tomas Frericksen; west, by lot of Touseyn Briel; and north, by lot of said Frericksen. Broad, in front on the street, the east side, 26 feet; in the rear, the like; deep, 35 running feet."[†]

On July 10, 1660, he, in company with Dirck Jansen, deeded to Boel Roeloffsen a lot east of the Prince Graght. See article Dirck Jansen, under date of July 10, 1660.

On February 12, 1664, Fredricksen conveyed to Cornelis Barensen Van der Kuyl: "a house and lot north of the Bever's Graft; bounding west the lot of Touseyn Briel; east, the Prince Graft. Front and rear, 34½ feet; east and west sides, 51 feet 7

475 Ibid., II., p. 166.
476 Ibid., VII., p. 146; III., p. 43.
477 Ibid., III., pp. 203, 222.
* Collections of the New York Historical Society, XLVI., p. 77f.
† Valentine, Manual of the . . City of New York, 1865, p. 661.

inches." Under same date he conveyed to Abraham Lubbersen: "a lot west of the Prince Graft; bounding south, the house and lot of Nicolaas De la Pleine; and north, the tannery of Coenraat Ten Eyck. In front, 26 feet; rear, 27 feet; south and north sides, 59 feet."‡ He had once before sold this lot.

TRYNTIE HARDERS.

Tryntie Harders, from Tönning, which formerly belonged to Denmark, was in New Amsterdam before 1643, when she as widow of Hendrick Holst, was married—June 14—to Hugh Aertsen, widower of Annetje Theunis.

After the death of Aertsen, Tryntie married, December 23, 1648, Albert Corneliszen Wantenar, from "Vechten."[478]

JAN PIETERSEN HARING.

Jan Pietersen Haring was in New Amsterdam as early as 1669, when, on February 31, his child Cozyn was baptized. Haring's wife was Grietje Cozyns, who had been married to Herman Theunissen Van Zell, April 19, 1654. Haring's second child, Marytie, was baptized October 11, 1679. Haring was, as the name indicates, a Dane: Haring is in Denmark. He was deceased before 1685, when his widow married Daniel de Clerq.

LAURENS HARMENS.

Laurens Harmens came over to New Netherland in 1660. He was a farmer from Holstein. He arrived, accompanied by his wife, on the ship "de Leide," which sailed March 4, 1660.[479]

‡ Ibid., 1865, p. 706.
478 Collections of the New York Genealogical and Biographical Society, I., pp. 13, 14.
479 Year Book of the Holland Society of New York, 1902, p. 12.

MRS. LAURENS HARMENS.

Mrs. Laurens Harmens arrived, with her husband, in New Netherland in 1660. Laurens Harmens was a farmer from Holstein. It is probable that both he and his wife were Danes, and not Germans.

MARTEN HARMENSEN.

Marten Harmensen, from Krem (Krempe), in Holstein, about four miles N. N.-E. of Glückstadt, was in Esopus 1660-1663. He was a mason. His name was on the muster roll of the soldier's company at Esopus, March 28, 1660.[480] In 1661 he subscribed fl. 25 towards supporting the preacher Hermanus Bloem, who had been called as pastor by the inhabitants of Esopus.[481]

On January 29, 1662, he married Claesje Teunis, widow of Cornelis Teunissen.[482]

He owned a bowery in Wiltwyck (=Esopus). On June 7, 1663, after the massacre in this new village, he was found killed and stripped naked behind a wagon. From his bowery one woman and four children were taken prisoners.[483]

BERNARDUS HASSING.

Bernardus Hassing, from Hassing, in Denmark, was in New Amsterdam before November 13, 1666, when he acted as sponsor at a baptism. On July 7, 1669, he married Aeltje [Neeltje] Couwenhoven. They had children. Warnardus was born 1670; Jacob, 1672; Hester, 1674; Heyltje, 1677; Johannes, 1678; Pieter, 1679, and Lysbeth, 1685. Hassing and his wife were members of the Dutch Reformed church in 1686, and lived "Longs de Wall" (Wall St.).

---

480 New York Colonial Documents, XIII., p. 158.
481 Ibid., XIII., p. 214.
482 R. R. Hoes, Baptismal and Marriage Register of the . . . Dutch Church, Kingston, p. 499.
483 New York Colonial Documents, XIII., p. 245.

HEYLTJE HASSING.

Heyltje Hassing acted as sponsor at a baptism in New Amsterdam, November 13, 1666.   She was possibly   a   relative of Bernardus, and a Dane.

JOHANNES HASSING.

Johannes Hassing stood sponsor Nov. 13, 1666, at a baptism in New Amsterdam.   He was probably a relative of Bernardus Hassing, and a Dane.   An Anna Hassing became a member of the Dutch Reformed church in New Amsterdam, 1668.   Was she his wife?

JAN HELMSZ(EN).

Jan Helmsz(en) (Jan de Bock), from Barlt in Holstein, arrived at New Amsterdam by" den Houttuyn" on August 4, 1642, and drew wages from August 13, 1642, in the colony of Rensselaerswyck.   From about 1650 to 1658 he is charged with an annual rent of fl. 445 for a farm at Bethlehem, which he appears to have taken over from Jan Dirksz from Bremen.   In 1651 he had on this farm six horses and seven cattle.[484]

On October 9, 1650, he acted as sponsor in New Amsterdam at the baptism of Arent, son of Barent Jacobsen.[485]

A letter of May 5, 1660, from Stuyvesant to Ensign Smith of Esopus, seems to refer to Jan Helms: "At the request of I. . . . Helms, made to us, we have given him permission to bring twenty or twenty-five schepels of bread from the Esopus."[486]

---

484 Van Rensselaer Bowier Manuscripts, p. 827.
485 Collections of the New York Genealogical and Biographical Society, II., p. 28.
486 New York Colonial Documents, XIII., p. 165.

FREDRICK HENDRICKSEN.

Fredrick Hendricksen (Kuyper=Cooper) was a Dane from Oldenburg. He was in New Amsterdam as early as 1659. On June 1, in that year, he married Annetje Christoffels, of Amsterdam.[487] He must not be taken for Frederick Hendricksen, a skipper, who was his contemporary in New Amsterdam.

Frederik the cooper had his share of litigation. His wife also had hers.

In 1661, his wife was litigating with Jan Hendricksen from Bommel, whom she accused of having said that she stole pork and sausage from him. The parties appeared several times before the court. But "inasmuch as no sufficient proof was produced on both sides in their suit" the court ordered that they "shall remain at peace towards each other, nor further trouble one another regarding previous disputes, and each bear his own costs."[488]

On November 8, 1664, Frederick Hendricksen was sued by Balthazar de Haart, who demanded of him thirty-seven and a half guilders for a half year's rent due. He also demanded that Hendricksen's wife should vacate the house. Hendricksen replied that he had rented it from people who had gone to Holland, and that he had paid them. De Haart rejoined that Hendricksen had promised to pay him the rent. Hendricksen denied this, but was ordered by the court "to satisfy and pay the plaintiff."

On December 6, De Haart demanded execution of the judgment, which he obtained against Hendricksen, with costs. The court granted this and ordered the marshal to put "these in execution with the costs accrued thereon."[489]

Hendricksen appeared as plaintiff in the court of New Amsterdam on November 8, 1664. He sued Huge Barentzen and Annetje Jacobs, saying that "the defendants accused him and no one else, of having robbed Annetje Jacobs to the amount of the sum of forty guilders." Annetje said, in defense, that no other person than Hendricksen and his wife could come into the house.

487 Collections of the New York Genealogical and Biographical Society, I., p. 24.

488 The Records of New Amsterdam, 1653-1674, III., pp. 268, 289, 299, 314, 331.

489 Ibid., V., pp. 153, 169.

Barentzen now demanded a copy of the declaration to give an answer thereunto, and the court granted this request, ordering Hendricksen to prove on the next court day that the defendants had accused him of theft. The case, it would seem, was dropped, as the records contain nothing more about it.[490]

From a list of the inhabitants of New Amsterdam who were assessed in 1665, we learn that Hendricksen lived in High Street.[491]

He was employed by the West India Company as a cooper. In January, 1662, he petitioned the Council for an increase of wages. The Council granted it.[492]

On August 22, 1665, Hendricksen was sued by Jan Bos, who demanded of him the sum of fl. 10 in seawan. Hendricksen admitted the debt and was ordered by the court to pay it and the costs of the suit.[493]

In March, 1667, Jan Otten sued Hendricksen for fl. 18 in seawan to pay a debt. Hendricksen's wife "admitted the debt," whereupon the court ordered that it should be paid.[494]

In 1670, Mary Mattheus sued Hendricksen for fl. 45.16 to cover a debt contracted by him. He was ordered to pay the debt with costs of the suit.[495]

ENGELTJE JACOBS.

Engeltje Jacobs "van Hoogharsteen in Holsteyn" was married, February 15, 1658, in New Amsterdam, to Christiaen Toemszen "van Strabroeck in Brabant."[496]

---

490 Ibid., V., p. 154.
491 Ibid., V., p. 222.
492 Calendar of Manuscripts, I., p. 233.
493 The Records of New Amsterdam, 1653-1674, V., p. 289.
494 Ibid., VI., p. 61.
495 Ibid., VI., p. 259.
496 Collections of the New York Genealogical and Biographical Society, I., p. 22.

PIETER JACOBSEN.

Pieter Jacobsen came to New Netherland by the ship "de Trouw" which sailed on February 12, 1659. He was, as is stated in the list of passengers, from Holstein.[497] He was a miller, and settled in Esopus or Wiltwyck. The Baptismal Register of the old Dutch church in Kingston (=Esopus) giving the date of the baptism of Pieter's son, Pieter, — October 1, 1662, states that the father is "miller here." [498] In September, 1663, the court induced him "to give his mill for forty or fifty soldiers to lodge them." [499]

In 1664 he is mentioned as being in partnership with Pieter Cornelissen.[500]

On January 15, 1663, he and others, belonging to the local militia of Wiltwyck, wrote a letter to Director Stuyvesant, complaining that the civil magistrates of Wiltwyck had pulled down an ordinance published by them (the militia).

In the same year he signed an ordinance "to be observed in time of need," made by the officers of the "train band." [501]

The wife of Pieter Jacobsen was Grietjen Hendricks Westercamp.[502] Pieter died at or before the beginning of 1665.[503]

ANNEKE JANS.

Anneke Jans, from Dithmarschen in Holstein, was married March 29, 1653, in New Amsterdam, to Hage Bruynsen, from Vexiö, in Smaaland, Sweden.[504] She was a sister of Dirck Jansen, Carsten Jansen Eggert, and Greetje Jansen.[505] Hage Bruynsen bought a house in New Amsterdam, in 1653, apparently upon the

---

497 Year Book of the Holland Society of New York, 1902, p. 8.

498 R. R. Hoes, Baptismal and Marriage Registers of the old Dutch Church .. in Kingston, p. 2.

499 New York Colonial Documents, XIII., p. 841.

500 Year Book of the Holland Society of New York, 1897, p. 124.

501 New York Documentary History, XIII., pp. 236f.

502 See reference 498.

503 See reference 500.

504 Collections of the New York Genealogical and Biographical Society, I., p. 18. There were many having the name Anneke Jans in New Netherland.

505 Collections of New York Historical Society, I., p. 48.

site of No. 255 Pearl Street. This house is one of interest, as the lodging place, in 1679, of the Labbadist missionaries Danker and Sluyter.[506]

In October, 1653, Bruynsen bought a house lot in Beverwyck, with the intention, it would seem, of moving to that place. His wife was to accompany him. But, for a time at least, she was obliged to postpone the journey. This postponement was due to a suit which she had brought against Mrs. Abraham Genes.

On July 14, 1653, she made the complaint before the court, that "on Tuesday last, when four napkins, bought by her of her master Croon from Holland were lying out to bleach," Mrs. Gennes "picked them up and carried them away." The minutes proceed: "Deft. says she had been robbed, and pltf. demands proof that they [the napkins] had been stolen from deft. or else return of the napkins and suitable satisfaction. Deft. admits having taken up and away from the bleaching ground 4 napkins in the presence of Martin Loockermans and Engeltje Mans, because they belonged to her, and she says, that she misses other napkins and linen, which she had not yet seen or found; also that neighbors have compared the said napkins with others, daily used by her, and have found them to be of the same pattern and linen, while upon one of them there is the same mark as shown by affidavit; she has left it with Anneke Loockermans and Tryntie Kips for safekeeping. The latter, called into Court with it, state, that it is the same napkin, as left at their house, but is not like the one, shown by pltf. Having been examined by pltf., she says, that two of the napkins, taken by deft. are changed and that the one with the mark may have been mixed with hers by Engeltie Mans at her wedding. The Court examines and compares the four napkins with those of the deft. and find them to be alike."

Under date of September 8, 1653, the court minutes, again referring to this case, state:

"Madame Genes being summoned into court by the Schout . . . is asked (since Madame Genes intends to remove to Fatherland, and Annetiie aforesaid intends to go to Fort Orange) whether she can produce any further proof. She gives for answer: No other proof than before: that they are found in all respects like her napkins, and she is willing, if she can retain her napkins and

506 Calendar of Historical Manuscripts, I., p. 379. J. H. Innes, New Amsterdam and Its People.

will remain unmolested on that account, to forgive the said Annetie her fault, and, never to trouble her on that account."

Under date of September 9 the minutes state the following: "Annetie . . . , wife of Age Bruynsen, appeared in Court; requests a pass to go to Fort Orange. Wheras she instituted the suit about the four napkins of Mme. Genes, and the case has not been prosecuted by her, therfore Burgomasters and Schepens notify her, the petitioner, first to settle with Mme. Genes, or else prosecute her suit, and remain bound over to the Court, so that their Worships of the Court may remain exempt from any complaint of refusing justice, etc.[507]

The records say nothing as to how the case was settled.

Anneke and Hage had a son, who was born in 1654, and married Gessi Schuman of New York, in 1681.[508] Anneke was dead when Hage, April 7, 1661, married Egbertie Hendricks, of Meppel.

CILETJE JANS.

Ciletje Jans, from Christianstad, which before 1658 belonged to Denmark, now to Sweden, was married on April 7, 1661, in New Amsterdam, to Hendrick van der Wallen.[509] Her husband was from Harlem in Holland and had been sent over as an experienced clerk to assist Claes van Ruyven.[510]

A daughter, Elizabeth, was born to Ciletje and Hendrick. She was baptized July 2, 1662. Ciletje's husband and two other men had united their efforts in liberating a slave belonging to Nicholas George, for ten pounds sterling. The money was not paid. On March 25, 1664, suit was therefore brought against Ciletje, who was then a widow, to obtain the amount. The Court decreed, however, that Ciletje should not pay more than one third of it.[511]

Her husband was dead before November 23, 1663, when she

---

507 The Records of New Amsterdam, 1653-1674, I., pp. 87, 113f., 118.
508 See article "Hage Bruynsen." Part III.
509 New York Genealogical and Biographical Record, VI., p. 143.
510 New York Colonial History, XIV., p. 418.
511 The Records of New Amsterdam, 1653-1674, V., p. 40.

declared in court that she knew "nothing about her deceased husband's business in Holland." [512]

On February 9, 1664, she married Paulus Richard "Van Rochel" in France. Johannes Schivelberg was appointed guardian of her child.[513]

She seems to have married a third husband, Jan Hoppen, who may have been a Norwegian. They joined the Dutch Reformed church.

On January 11, 1665, she petitioned the Court that she be released from a house in which she was residing, and which had been rented by her deceased husband: "She finds it difficult to make up the rent, and says that Jacques Cousseau stated to her," that the curators of the estate of the owner of the house "told him, she should be released from the last year's lease;" she also understood that they "have offered to rent the house to Juffw. Wessels." The curators had made an attachment on her goods for rent. On January 31, she produced an extract from the Register of the Resolution of the Orphan chamber, wherein it was proved, according to the order of the Burgomasters and Schepens, that Jacques Causseau told her that the curators should have to release her from the last year's rent. The court looked over the extract and decreed that she should be released from the last year's rent. — "If she was to have paid anything on it, they ought to have notified her thereof." It declared that the attachment made on the goods was valid.[514]

DOROTHEA JANS.

Dorothea Jans, from "Breestede" (Bredstedt) came in companv with her brother, Jan Jansen and Engeltje Jans, to New Amsterdam, in 1636. She was married to Volckert Jansen from Fredrickstad, and had several children. She also had two sisters and one brother in New Amsterdam. See the articles "Engeltje Jans," "Tryntie Jans," "Jan Jansen van Brestede," "Volckert Jansen." (Part II).

512 Year Book of the Holland Society of New York, 1900, p. 125.
513 The Records of New Amsterdam, 1658-1674, V., p. 53.
514 Ibid., V., pp. 176, 181.

ELSJE JANS.

Elsje Jans, from "Breestede" (Bredstedt), a daughter of Jans Jansen and Engeltje Jan van Breestede, came with her parents to New Netherland in 1636. She was married, on May 17, 1643, to Adriaen Pietersen van Alcmar, widower of Grietje Pietersen.

The Council minutes of that period tell us how Adriaen wooed and won her as his wife. It appears that Elsje was in the service of Cornelis Melyn of Staten Island. She left the service before her term had expired, in order to marry Adriaen. Melyn was much displeased at this, and brought suit against Egbert Woutersen, her stepfather, "husband and guardian of Engel Jan, her mother," for damages on account of Elsje's marriage engagement.

Elsje appeared in court on September 11, 1642, and testified that "her mother and another woman had brought a young man to Staten Island." She claimed she had never seen him before. They desired that she should marry him. She declined at first, but finally consented. "She concluded her testimony by returning in court the pocket-handkerchief she had received as a marriage present."

Five days later she made the declaration that she sent for Adriaen Pietersen, and that on his coming to Staten Island she accompanied him on board his yawl.

A week later, Melyn and the Fiscal had Pietersen before the court, charged with Elsje's abduction. Pietersen was ordered to bring her into court, deliver her to Melyn, and receive her again from him "on giving security for the payment of the damage Melyn may have suffered."[515]

After the death of Adriaen Pietersen, Elsje married Hendricksen Jochemsen, of Esopus. After his death she married Cornelis Barentsen Slecht (Sleght), who was in New Amsterdam in 1662, and at Wiltwyck (Esopus) in 1664.[516]

Elsje had three sisters and one brother in New Netherland.

See articles "Dorothea Jans," "Engeltje Jans," "Tryntie Jans," and "Jan Jansen van Breestede."

---

515 New York Genealogical and Biographical Record, VII., p. 117.
516 The Records of New Amsterdam, 1653 1674, IV., p. 170. T. F. Chamber, The Early Germans in New Jersey, 1895, p. 497.

ENGELTJE JANS.

Engeltje Jans, from "'Breestede" (Bredstedt, in Schleswig), came with her husband, Jan Jansen, to New Amsterdam about 1636. By him she had the following children: 1) Tryntie, who was married to Rutger Jacobsen Schoonderworth or Van Woert, and whose descendants assumed the name of Rutgers; 2) Jan Jansen van Breestede, who in 1647 married Marritje Lucas (Andries); 3) Dorothea Jans van Breestede, who in 1650 was married to Volckert Janszen from Frederickstadt, and whose descendants comprise the Dow family of New York; 4) Elsie Jans van Brestede, who was married three times.[517] See articles "Dorothea Jans," "Elsje Jans," "Tryntie Jans," "Jan Jansen van Breestede."

After the death of Jan Jansen, Engeltje Jans was married, on September 1, 1641, to Egbert Woutersen, of Isselsteyn. He is often mentioned in the Court Record of New Amsterdam 1653–1674 as arbitrating in disputes. He and his wife were frequently invited to stand sponsors at baptisms.

They made their will on June 20, 1652.[518]

Woutersen took the lease of a bowery on December 1, 1646, on Manhattan; and on May 10, 1647, he obtained a patent for a tract of land, called in Indian Apocalyck, lying across the North River, west of the Manhattan.

Woutersen died 1680, without issue.

GRIETJE JANS.

Grietje Jans was from Dithmarschen, in Schleswig-Holstein. She was a sister of Dirck Jansen, Anneke Jans (Holstein), and Carsten Jansen Eggert, in whose will she is mentioned. See article Carsten Jansen Eggert. On October 6, 1652 she was married, in New Amsterdam, to Jacob Pietersen Van Leyden.[519] They had a son, Pieter, who was baptized on August 31, 1653.

517 New York Genealogical and Biographical Record, VIII., p. 117.
518 Calendar of (N. Y.) Wills, Compiled by B. Fernow, p. 480.
Engeltje Jans stood sponsor several times. In 1642, she stood sponsor at the baptism of a child of Hans Nicholaessen, who was possibly a Dane. All the sponsors at this baptism seem to have been Scandinavians.
519 The New York Genealogical and Biographical Record, VI., p. 81.

MAGDALENTJE JANS.

Magdalentje Jans, from Dithmarchsen, was married January 22, 1650, in New Amsterdam, to Jan Peers.[520]

TRYNTIE JANS.

Tryntie Jans from "Breestede" (Bredstedt) came to New Netherland with her parents, Jan Jansen and Engeltje Jans, in 1636.[521] She had two sisters and one brother in New Netherland. See the articles "Dorothea Jans," "Elsje Jans," "Jan Jansen van Breestede."

On June 3, 1646, she was married, in New Amsterdam, to Rutger Jacobsen, a resident of Rensselaerswyck (Albany).

Rutger Jacobsen came from Schoonderwoert, a village some twelve miles south of Utrecht, Holland. He served as a farm hand on the farm of Teunisz from Breuckelen, for the term of six years, beginning in April 1637, at fl. 100 a year.

In 1643 he was engaged as foreman on the great Flats in Rensselaerswyck at fl. 220 a year and some clothes.

From 1648 to 1654 he is charged with an annual rent of fl. 125 for a saw mill on the fifth creek, and for the same period he is charged, jointly with Barent Pietersz, with an annual rent of fl. 550 for a saw mill and grist mill, also on fifth creek. From about 1648 he owned a sloop plying upon the Hudson between Rensselaerswyck and New Amsterdam.

Signature of Rutger Jacobs, husband of Tryntie Jans.

On April 4, 1649, he agreed to pay fl. 32 a year, for three years, for rent of his house-lot and the right to fur trade. In October 1860, he and Goossen Gerritsz were authorized to brew

---

520 Ibid., VI., p. 38.
521 Munsell, Collections on the History of . . . Albany, IV., pp. 89, 158f.

beer, on condition of paying a duty of one guilder for every barrel of beer and of brewing, free of charge, the beer needed for the households of Van Slichtenhorst and de Hooges.[522]

Jacobsen seems to have lived most of the time in Rensselaerswyck, though he and his family occasionally resided in New Amsterdam, where he, in 1649, bought a lot on High Street, on which he built a house. In 1656, at Fort Orange, he mortgaged this house and lot for the amount of 1528 guilders.[523] His wife gave another mortgage in this house and lot in 1658, when she also mortgaged her house and lot at Fort Orange. This was done to meet what the officer Cornelis Steenwyck was trying to collect from the Jacobsens: a sum of 5,482 guilders.[524] Jacobsen retained the house in New Amsterdam till the fall of 1660, when it was sold at public auction to one Johannes Withart, his own attorney. Jacobsen contested the sale in Court, and requested an advance on the price, claiming that the house and lot were not "held up" before they were sold. The Court considered the complaint. After having several hearings, it decided that Jacobsen had no reason to start suit. But as Jacobsen started litigation anew, arbitrators were appointed to decide the matter.[525]

Tryntie's husband was a prominent man in Beverwyck.[526] On April 23, 1652, he secured a lot in this town. He was engaged in public life, being a councilor, from 1649 to 1651, in Rensselaerswyck, for which he received fifty florins a year.[527] In 1656 he was a magistrate of Rensselaerswyck, and laid the corner-stone of the new Dutch Church, situated at the intersection of the present State Street and Broadway in the city of Albany.

We know very little about Tryntie. Her daughter Engel was baptized April 10, 1650; and her daughter Margrietje was married, in 1667, to Jan Jansen Bleecker, from Meppel in the province of Overyssel, ancestor of the Bleecker family, well known in the annals of New York.[528]

Rutger Jacobsen died before December 9, 1665.

522 Van Rensselaer Powier Manuscripts, p. 812.
523 Year Book of the Holland Society of New York, 1900, p. 161.
524 Ibid., 1900, p. 165.
525 The Records of New Amsterdam, 1653-1674, III., pp. 224, 229, 236, 238, 254, 261, 297.
526 E. B. O'Callaghan, History of New Netherland, II., p. 587.
527 Van Rensselaer Bowier Manuscripts, p. 812.
528 J. H. Innes, New Amsterdam and Its People, p. 173, note. ,

BARENT JANSEN.

Barent Jansen (Van Ditmars) married, in 1664, in New Netherland, Catalyntie De Vos. She was the widow of Arent Andriessen (p. 34), a Norwegian, and the daughter of Andries De Vos, deputy director of Rensselaerswyck. He was killed in the French and Indian massacre in 1690, when the town of Schenectady, where he lived, was destroyed by Indians.

DIRCK JANSEN.

Dirck Jansen (de Groot), from Dithmarschen, was a cooper in New York. He was brother of Carsten Jansen Eggert, Greetje Jansen (wife of Jacob Pietersen), and Anneke Jans (wife of Hage Bruynsen).*

At the death of his sister, Anneke Jans, in 1661, Dirck was appointed guardian of her son Bruyn Hage. In 1668, Bruyn's father died, whereupon Dirck Jansen and two others requested the court that they might proceed to administer the estate of Bruynsen.

Under date of September 4, 1674, the Records of New Amsterdam state this:

"Dirck Jansen, cooper, appearing in Court as guardian of Bruyn Haagen, late servant of Hendrick Bosch; exhibits in Court an award of the arbitrators appointed, respecting the binding out of said Bruyn Haagen, requesting that this W. Court may be pleased to approve it and to order the abovenamed Bosch to observe and fulfill it. The W. Court having seen and examined the said award, together with the indenture of said Bruyn Haagen made by the Notary Math. de Vos, approve said award of the arbitrators, and order said Hendrick Bosch to observe and fulfill the same punctually, and to pay the costs herein incurred. Costs together, fl. 12."†

On July 22, 1677, Dirck Jansen married Rachel Detru (du

---

* Collections of the New York Historical Society, I., p. 48.
† Records of New Amsterdam, 1653-1674, VI., p. 147; VII., pp. 120, 130f. Hendrick Bosch was a chimney sweep.

Trieux), widow of Hendrick Van Bommel. His first wife was Wybrug Jans. By his second wife he had a son, Jan, who was baptized March 27, 1678; a daughter Grietie, who was baptized February 8, 1679; again a son, Abraham, baptized April 26, 1682. His second wife is sometimes called Rachel Rosella du Trieux, also Rachel Philips. She was a member of the Dutch Reformed Church in New York, 1686.

Dirck and his wife lived on Marckvelt Straat (Market-field St.).

Dirck Jansen of Dithmarschen, must not be taken for Dirck Jansen of Oldenburg, a contemporary in New York who was woodsawyer, ship builder, and real estate dealer. See article "Anneke Jans," "Carsten Jansen Eggert," "Greetje Jans," Part II; "Hage Bruynsen," Part III.

HANS JANSEN.

Hans Jansen, or Hans Hansen, van Nordstrand, in Holstein, came to New Netherland in 1639. We do not know, who was his wife. He married early, as he had a child, Rommetje, who was baptized on December 8, 1641, in New Amsterdam. The sponsors at this baptism were Laurens Pieters, a Norwegian, Janneke Melyn and Styntie Jans.

On November 29, 1652, he married Janneke Gerrits van Loon op't Sandt.

He was a farmer and owned Bruyenburg or Buyennesburg. His will is dated August 20, 1679.*

JAN JANSEN.

Jan Jansen, the progenitor of the Ditmars family in this country, was from Dithmarschen in Holstein. He was known as Jan Jansen platneus (flatnose). He had land in New Amster-

* Teunis G. Bergen, Register . . of the Early Settlers of Kings County, . . . N. Y., p. 849. Collections of the New York Genealogical and Biographical Society, I., p. 17; II., p. 12.

dam, in 1643 or earlier. [529]   On March 23, 1647, he obtained a patent for fifty-eight acres of land. Sometime before 1650 he sold this land to Joris Stevensen.[530]

He died before 1650. His widow, Neeltie Douwes, married January 9, 1650, Lovis (Teunis?) Joriszen, "Van der Veer in Zealandt." [531]   Jan Jansen had two children: John and Douwe or Dow.

John settled at Flatbush, and married.[532]

JAN JANSEN.

Jan Jansen, from "Breestede," (Bredstedt), came over to New Netherland with his parents, Jan Jansen and Engeltje Jans, and his three sisters, Elsje, Dorothea and Tryntie Jans, in 1636.[533]

Jan Jansen married, November 1, 1647, in New Amsterdam, Marritje Lucas (Andries), by whom he had six children, who were born and baptized in New Amsterdam.

Jannetje was baptized July 19, 1648; Wouter, December 25, 1650; Johannes, October 27, 1652; Engel, November 29, 1654; Pieter, June 15, 1656; Simon, February 10, 1658.[534]

Jansen and his wife joined the Reformed Church in New Amsterdam before 1660.

Jan Jansen was a cooper. In 1658 he was appointed marker of beer barrels, or gauger. On April 25, 1659, he appeared in court "requesting, as he is gauger, that the magistrates would be pleased to fix a time, when he shall stamp the barrels and what he may demand for stamping, and marking a small number of barrels. Whereupon Burgomasters resolved that the marking of barrels shall take place in the month of May, and for each barrel under the number of ten, marked at one time to take two stivers,

529 New York Colonial Documents, XIV., p. 49.
530 Ibid., XIV., p. 141.
531 Collections of the New York Genealogical and Biographical Society, I., p. 15. New York Colonial Documents, XIV., p. 142.
532 J. Riker, Annals of Newtown, p. 390.
533 New York Genealogical and Biographical Record, VI., p. 87. Regarding his parents, see article Engeltje Jans. Part II.
534 Ibid., V., pp. 91, 95, 118, 158, 176, 182.

and above ten one stiver each, but to communicate it to the whole Board of Burgomasters and Schepens."[535]

In 1668 he was appointed inspector of pipe staves and the packing of meat. The city record says:

(Jan. 28, 1668). "Jan Jansen van Breestede and Jurian Jansen van Aweryck being sent for to Court, the W. Court proposes to them the necessity, that some persons may be appointed within this City for the inspection and counting of pipe staves, packing of meat and pork and they being asked to perform the said service. The same was accepted by them, and they have taken the oath in this regard at the hands of the W. Court." [536]

On January 5, 1674, Jan Jansen van Breestede and several others were appointed firewardens and chimney inspectors in the city of New Orange [new name for New Amsterdam] "for the term of the current year." [537]

We append the report of these men, and the resolution of the Council acting upon it.

"Pursuant to the commission of the Worship Magistrates, the Schout, Burgomasters and Schepens of this city N. Orange, we the undersigned have, as Firewardens, visited on the 12th January, 1674, the houses of all the inhabitants of this city aforesaid, and found divers fire places very much exposed to cause a conflagration, wherefore we warned and notified them to remedy and improve the same, thus to prevent mischief; we have also caused the City Crier to publish and make known, that if any of the inhabitants of this City had by them any City fire buckets they are to deliver them up without delay at the City Hall or to hand them to us Firewardens: we however have not as yet been able to collect more than 57 Buckets, three of which are at Abel Hardenbroecks to be repaired: we have also found two old fire hooks with one old fire-ladder at the City Hall, but they are unfit for use in case of fire or other misfortune; we therefore request your Worships to be pleased to provide therein, that so many fire ladders and fire hooks may be made as your Honors shall think necessary.

535 The Records of New Amsterdam, 1653-1674, VII., p. 221. On Nov. 10, 1676, an Andrew Brested Cooper was assessed 12s, 6d. in the City of New York; Jan van Bresteed Witt was assessed 6s, 8d.
536 Ibid., VI., p. 113.
537 Ibid., VII., p. 85. New Orange was the name given the City of New York by the Dutch in 1673.

"Herewith we remain Your Worship's humble and faithful Subjects and obedient servants

"(was signed)   Jan van Bresteede
                            ."Reynier Willemsen
                            "Jonas Bartelsen.

"The annexed petition of the Firewardens of this city being considered, read and taken into serious deliberation in Court, as well as their representation of the necessity of making some provision of fire hooks and ladders &c to be used occasionally and in time of fire — It is apostilled —

"The petitioners are fully authorized by the W. Court to have made such supply of ladders, hooks and such like materials at the expense of the City as they shall consider to be necessary (Feb. 26, 1674)." [538]

Two of Jansen's sons followed the earlier calling of the father: gauging barrels.

Jansen died, it is supposed, about the year 1675.

His descendants in later years have been known as Breestede.

JAN JANSEN.

Jan Jansen, from Flensborg, married on April 11, 1680, in New Amsterdam, Willemyntie Huygens de Kleyn, a daughter of Hugh Barents Kleyn (Clein), resident of New Amsterdam.[539] Willemyntie was the widow of Barthemeus Schaet.[540] Jan Jansen had several children by her . The twins, Maria and Catharina, who were baptized December 10, 1680; Maria, baptized January 20, 1682; Johannes, February 15, 1684. After her death, he married, April 14, 1687, Margaret Martens (from Boston, 1678), widow of Claes Roelofsen. By her he had a daughter, Catharina, who was baptized July 24, 1689.[541] He joined the Dutch Reformed Church in New Amsterdam on December 4, 1679. It would seem that he was a baker.*

538 Ibid., VII., p. 66f.
539 Ibid., VII., p. 2.
540 New York Genealogical and Biographical Record, VII., p. 33.
541 Ibid., VIII., p. 38.
* Minutes of the Common Council of the City of New York, 1675-1776.
I., p. 176.

JEURIAN JANSEN.

Jeurian Jansen arrived at New Amsterdam in 1662. He came on the ship "de Vos," which sailed August 31, 1662. In the list of passengers, it is stated that Jansen was from Holstein.[542] He must not be taken for Jeurian Jansen from East Friesland, a cooper who married, June 1, 1658, in New Amsterdam. If Jansen from Holstein was a soldier, it is probable that he was the Jansen who died on September 25, 1663, by falling out of a canoe and drowning.[543]

LAURENS JANSEN.

Laurens Jansen, from Denmark, was in New Amsterdam as early as in March, 1647, when he secured a lot which he conveyed to Pieter Jacobsen Marius, ten years later, October 4, 1657. It was in Pearl Street, between the lot of Paulus Schrick (A German from Nürnberg), on the east, and the house of Thomas Lamb on the west; or — as we would say: the lot was on the south side of Pearl Street, between State Street and Whitehall Street.[544]

Laurens married Lysbeth Hendricks. But he was dead before July 19, 1659, when she married Jan Gervan . . . , a soldier. In the marriage record she is called the "widow of Laurens Jansen of Denmark."

Laurens Jansen of Denmark must not be confounded with the Laurens Jansen who is frequently mentioned in the "Records of New Amsterdam," as inhabitant of Gravesend.

VOLCKERT JANSEN.

Volckert Jansen, sometimes referred to as Volckert Hans, or Volckert Jans Douw, was in New Netherland as early as 1638.

---

542 Year Book of the Holland Society of New York, 1900.
543 New York Colonial Documents, XII., p. 842.
544 D. T. Valentine, Manual of . . the City of New York, 1861, p. 593.

In the marriage record of the Dutch church in New York, it is said that he was from "Frederickstadt." Whether this means Fredrikstad in Norway or Friedrichstadt in Schleswig-Holstein, founded in 1621 for Dutch Arminians, is difficult to decide.[545]

One writer claims that Volckert descended from Jan Douw of Leuwarden, a province of Friesland in Holland; that he was a captain in the Dutch army when driven from his home by the persecution waged against the Mennonites; that he fled to Friedcrichstadt, taking his family along. The same writer says that Volckert Jansen married Dorothea Jans van Breestede while in Holland.[546]

This claim is in part contradicted by the sources. For Volckert Jansen married Dorothea Jans van Breestede on April 19, 1650, in New Amsterdam, not in Holland. In 1673 he appears as a Lutheran: in that year he and some others signed, in Albany, a petition requesting that their "congregation of the Augsburg Confession at Willemstadt (Albany)" be given "free exercise of their religious worship, without let or hindrance, to the end that they may live in peace with their fellow burghers."[547]

If he was from Holland, he may have been a Mennonite. The change in confession might then have been due to his wife, who likely was a Lutheran. But if he was not from Holland, he must have been a Dane or a Norwegian, judging from the entry in the church record. Fredrikstad, founded, 1570, in Norway, was better known than the younger Danish city, the present Friedrichstadt, founded a half century later. Naturally the person who wrote "Frederickstadt" in the church record would not add a geographical explanation to it if he had the Norwegian town in mind. He probably would have done so if he thought of the twenty-nine years old Danish town. On the other hand, the latter was well known among the Dutch.

Volckert Jansen is mentioned in Albany under date of April 27, 1642. In 1647 he was employed at the Vlackte. From 1647 to 1649 he and John Thomas (Witbeck) are jointly charged 32 florins a year for ground rent and the right to trade. From 1649

---

545 New York Genealogical and Biographical Record, III., p. 82. Ibid., VI., p. 89.
546 Cuyler Reynold, Hudson Mohawk Genealogical Family Memoirs, New York, 1910, p. 384f.
547 Ecclesiastical Records of the State of New York, I., p. 686.

to 1652 Jansen is charged with 32 florins a year for his place "on the hill," on which he built a house.[548]

In 1650 he accompanied Arent van Curler, manager of the colony of Rensselaerswyck, on an embassy to the Maquas. In 1654 he was sponsor for Engel, his niece, a daughter of Jan Jansen van Bresteede.

Volckert Jansen was a trader, brewer, and dealer in real estate.

On April 23, 1652, he acquired a lot in Beverwyck.[549]

From May 1, 1653, to May 1, 1658, he, Pieter Hartgers and Jan Thomas are jointly charged with an annual rent of fl. 560 for a farm on Papscanee Island, formerly occupied by Jurian Bestval. Volckert Jansen and Jan Thomas bought this farm in 1658 for 950 beavers or 7,600 florins. On March 31, 1659, Volckert Jansen secured a plantation at Fort Orange [550] and later one of 33 morgens at Esopus.[551]

In company with Jan Thomas he conducted a brewery. This brewery situated on the east half of the Exchange block (in Albany) and extending to the river was sold in 1675 to Harmen Rutgers, son of Rutger Jacobsen, who was Volckert's brother-in-law.

In 1663 Volckert and his partner bought, of the Indians, Schotack and Apjens Island and the main land lying east of it.[552] On January 24, 1664, the Council of Rensselaerswyck passed a resolution annulling the purchase of land from the Indians, at Schodac," without the consent of the colony. When notice of this resolution was served on Volckert and his partner, they produced a patent from Director Stuyvesant, dated November 3, 1663.

Volckert Jansen also owned Constaples Island, lying opposite Bethlehem, half of which he sold, in 1677, to Pieter Winne.

In 1672 he owned Schutter's Island, below Barent Island, which he sold to Barent Pietersen Coeyman.

548 Van Rensselaer Bowier Manuscripts.
549 E. B. O'Callaghan, History of New Netherland, II., p. 587.
550 Ibid., II., p. 591.
551 Ibid., II., p. 592.
552 New York Genealogical and Biographical Record. III., p. 82f.

Volckert Jansen died in 1686, his wife Dorothea in 1701. The descendants comprise the Dow family in New York.[553]

There were eleven children born to Volckert and Dorothea, four boys and seven girls: Jonas, Andries, Volckertje, Dorothe, Catrina, Engeltje, Hendrick, Elsje, Rebecca, Volckert, Grietje.[554]

Jonas married first Magdalena, daughter of Pieter Quackenbos, on November 14, 1683, and secondly, Catrina, daughter of Jan Thomas Witbeck (the partner of his father) and widow of Jacob Sanders Glen on April 24, 1691. He had four children. He died 1736.

SIEGE OF KREMPE AND GLUECKSTADT, 1628.

Andries was, in 1684, master of the open boat "John," plying between Albany and New York. He married three times and had five children.

Hendrick married Neeltje, daughter of Meyndert Fredricksen from Jeveren, October 3, 1697. He died 1754, leaving six children.

Volckert married Margaret, daughter of Abraham van Fricht, November 16, 1701. He died 1753, leaving five children.[555]

---

553 Munsell, Annals of . . . . Albany, IV., p. 118.
554 See reference 546.
555 See reference 552.

PIETER JANSEN.

Pieter Jansen was from Glückstad (now a part of Germany), Denmark. All that we know about this person is contained in a notice in the Court Record of New Amsterdam. It appears that he died about 1663. On November 29, 1663, Jan van Gelder and Claas Gangelofzen Visser (or Claas Jansen Visser) were appointed curators of Jansen's estate. As Visser went to Curacao, Gelder requested, on November 2, 1664, that another might be appointed in his stead. The court then appointed Pieter Wolferzen van Couwenhouven as curator.[556]

JACOB JANSZ.

Jacob Jansz, from Nordstrand, Schleswig, was in the colony of Rensselaerswyck as early as 1642, when supplies furnished to him are charged to Cornelis Hendricks Nes. He took the oath of fealty, November 28, 1651. (Van Rensselaer Bowier Manuscripts p. 830.)

THOMAS JANSEN.

Thomas Jansen was in New York in 1677. In the marriage records it is stated that he was from Denmark, and married, on June 11, 1677, in Brooklyn, Jannetje Brouwers. He must not be taken for his namesake, also called Thomas Franszen, mentioned in Teunes G. Bergen's "Register of the early Settlers of King's County," p. 117, and in "Dr. Valentine's Manual of . . . the City of New York," 1865, pp. 664, 684.

TEUNTJE JEURIANS.

Teuntje Jeurians (Sofia, Antonia), who came to New Netherland in 1639 or before, was the wife of the Dane, Jonas Bronck, who died in 1643. Bronck married her in Europe, perhaps in Denmark. She was probably Danish, as Marritje Pieters of Copenhagen mentions Teuntje in her marriage contract, as an heir. The fact that she mentions Teuntje first and Bronck second, would indicate that the relationship existed between the women.

She had at least one son by Bronck, Pieter Bronck. Could Jems Bronck, who died in 1653, and whom we have mentioned in the article "Jonas Bronck," have been her other son?

After the death of Bronck, she married Arent Van Curler, sheriff in Rensselaerswyck. In a letter, addressed to Kiliaen van Rensselaer and dated at the Manhattans, June 16, 1643, Van Curler writes: "I am at present betrothed to the widow of the late M. Jonas Bronck. May the good God vouchsafe to bless me in my undertaking, and please grant that it might conduce to His honor, to our mutual salvation."

Anthonia Jeurians is also called Anthonia Slachboom, or Slaghboom. "Slag" and "bom" appear as first syllables in Danish proper names. "Slagbom" is Danish-Norwegian = turnpike, barricade, bar. In German the equivalent is "Schlagbaum," in Dutch "Slagboom." From the name alone we can form no conclusion as to the nationality of Anthonia, or Teuntje.

She was an aunt of Catalina De Boog, who married Wilhelmus Beekman in New Amsterdam, in 1649. Catalina De Boog was a daughter of Hendrick de Boog, of Albany, the surname of whose wife was Slagboom. Anthonia stood sponsor, June 26, 1650, at the baptism of Maria, daughter of Beekman and Catalina de Boogh, whose name also occurs as De Bough and De Hoogh. Hendrick de Boog or Hendricks De Hoogh was captain of a Hudson trading-vessel.

Teuntje married Van Curler, probably in 1643 (1646, according to Appleton's Cyclopedia of American Biography). He was a gifted person, and only eighteen years when he sailed from Holland to New Netherland, at the end of December, 1637. He was a cousin of Kiliaen van Rensselaer, became secretary and bookkeeper of the colony of Rensselaerswyck. In 1644 he sailed for Holland, but returned to New Netherland, probably in 1647. He was now appointed a *Gecommitteerde*. For a while he was trustee of voluntary contributions for the erection of a school. He early mastered the tongue of the Iroquois Indians. In 1650 he was chosen to go on an embassy to the Maquas.

Van Curler and his wife, after returning from Netherlands, lived on their farm near West Troy, N. Y. Here he worked for peace with the Indians and for checking the sale of "fire water." He may be considered as the "real founder of that Dutch policy of peace with the Indians that was afterward followed by the English, which by making an invincible obstacle to French ambition, aided so powerfully to secure this continent to Germanic instead of Latin civilization."

In 1661, being tired of the semi-feudal ideas of the patroon system, he became one of the leaders of a company of free settlers from Holland to Schenectady, where he founded an agricultural settlement, in which all purchasers could hold land in fee simple.

In 1667, while on a visit to Canada, he was drowned in Lake Champlain.

Signature of Arent van Curler, second husband of Teuntje Jeurians.

He left about 2000 letters and papers, which are preserved chiefly in Albany, New York.

His uncle, Kiliaen van Rensselaer, sent him many a word of admonition and censure, and asked him to follow the advice of older people. In 1643 he wanted to know to what extent Van Curler was intemperate, as he had heard rumors about his drinking and participating in attendant evils. In the same year he was displeased at his having contributed to the erection of a church:

"I also hear that he [Arent] has contributed some muddles of wheat toward the erection of the church at the Manhatans.

What orders has he to give away my goods in this fashion? I could use them very well for the erection of my own church. I hope that it is not true. These young people, like Arent and Van der Donck do not think at all of my interests, each one thinks of his own advancement . . . " [1643].

Teuntje survived also her second husband. She died in Schenectady, Dec. 19, 1676. Three years before this, she had petitioned as "widow of Arent van Curler for leave to trade with the Indians at Schenectady." *

We give below a fac-simile of a part of Kiliaen van Rensselaer's letter, Dec. 29, 1637, to Peter Minuit, Director of New Netherland. It begins "The bearer of this letter, my cousin Arent van Corler, sailing to my colony as assistant, is recommended to you to accomodate him as much as your honor's situation will allow. I should also be much pleased, inasmuch as he is still young and inexperienced, if you had a little instruction given to him in the process of ship's bookkeeping as well as in the keeping of land accounts, as his master Jacob Planck, with whom he will be, is not too expert in these matters himself." The conclusion, of which the fac-simile is given, reads, as translated in "Bowier Manuscripts":

"With him go the following young men engaged for my colony to wit:
"*Arent van Corler,* assistant, 18 years old.
"*Elbert albertsen,* 18 years old
"*Claes Jansen,* 17 years old
"*Gerrit hend,* 15 years old
"*Gijsb Arentsen,* 22 years old

> "Loaded also
> one barrel
> of pitch, well hooped
> f18
> 2 barrels of tar, together
> f 5

"On Saturday, with the goods went:
    Jacob Arentsen, 25 years old

LAST PART OF LETTER OF KILIAN VAN RENSSELAER TO PETER MINUIT, DECEMBER 29, 1687.
From Van Rensselaer Bowier Manuscripts.

"Together six persons, who are recommended to your honor and whom, with my goods, you will please cause to reach the *manatans* at the earliest opportunity that circumstances will allow. From there I hope they will get further. I wish your honor good luck on the voyage."

MARRITJE JEURIANS.

Marritje Jeurians was from Copenhagen, Denmark. She was married on June 2, 1657, in New Amsterdam, to Pieter Janszen Romeyn (Van de Lange straet), a widower. Jansen's first wife was Dirckie Jansz Van Meffelen, daughter of Jan Ruthers. By her, Jansen had a son who was born about 1651, and who at his father's second marriage received Jan Ruthers and Jan de Jongh as guardians.[557]

By Marritje, Jansen had several children: Jeurian, who was baptized November 15, 1662; Dirck, baptized July 25, 1666; Belitje, baptized July 25, 1666; twins who were baptized on October 26, 1668.

Jansen was a tavern keeper. His partner was a Dane, Severyn Laurenszen, from Roskilde. (See article "Severyn Laurenszen," Part II.)

Marritje and the Rev. Jacob Fabritius, who in 1669 was sent by the Lutheran consistory of Amsterdam to New Amsterdam and who managed to get into various kinds of trouble in New Amsterdam, being frequently in court, had a dispute in which the pastor was worsted. The Fiscal charged him with having "used force and violence against Marritje Jeurians in her own house." He demanded a fine of five beavers with payment of costs. Fabritius admitted the charge, but said that Marritje "did provoke him with harsh language." After the court had heard the witnesses, it fined Fabritius "two Beavers with costs." [558]

---

557 Year Book of the Holland Society of New York, 1900, p. 118.
558 New York Colonial Documents, II., pp. 692, 693.

PETER KLAESEN.

Peter Klaesen [Claessen] arrived, with his wife and his two children, — the one ¾ years old, the other six — at New Amsterdam in the year 1658. He was from Holstein, and a farmer by occupation. He came over in the ship "de Vergulde Bever," which sailed May 17, 1658.[559]

On December 7, 1664, Pieter Claessen van Dietmarssen was by Governor Richard Nicoll granted a request, he had made, to pass on the ship "Unity" to any port or harbor in Holland. It is probable that this is the Klaesen who came over in 1658. His wife and children may have died in the mean time.[560]

MRS. PETER KLAESEN.

Mrs. Peter Klaesen arrived at New Amsterdam in 1658, accompanied by her husband and two children. Klaesen and his wife were from Holstein, and probably were Danes.

PIETER LAURENSZEN KOCK.

Pieter Laurenszen Kock was from "Alberrch," Denmark. Alberrch is not to be identified with Albjerg, but with Aalborg, which on the map of Denmark in Theatri Europäi, Part V, (Anno M. DC. XLCII) is spelled Alborch. He was in New Netherland as early as 1643, or perhaps before. In 1643 he commanded, as sergeant, an expedition against the Indians. He and one Baxter then had sixty-five men, who marched to Wetquescheck, which consisted of three Indian "castles." These castles "were empty, though thirty Indians could have stood against 200 soldiers, in as much as the castles were constructed of plank five inches thick, nine feet high, and braced around with thick plank studded

559 Year Book of the Holland Society of New York, 1902.
560 New York State Library Bulletin on History, No. 2, 1899.

with port holes." Kock's party burned two of the "castles", reserving the third for a retreat. "Marching eight or nine leagues further, they discovered nothing but a few huts, which they could not surprise, as they [themselves] were discovered [by the enemy]. They returned, having "killed only one or two Indians, taken some women and children and burnt some corn." [561]

In the same year Kock and Roelof Jansen Haes, a Norwegian, made a report to the Secretary of the Colony that "the colony behind the Col" had been destroyed by the Indians:

"Before me Cornelis van Tienhoven, Secretary of New-Netherland appeared Pieter Cock, 30 years old and Roeloff Jansen, 20 years old, well known to me, the Secretary, who at the request of Cornelis Jansen Coelen, declare and testify, promising to confirm their attestation by solemn oath, if so required, that after the Colony behind the Col had been burnt by the savages, it was impossible to go there by land or by water to examine the place and its condition, because of the great number of savages who burn and slay whatever they can lay hold of in the woods, on the Kill or elsewhere. This the deponents declare to be correct and true, etc.

"Done the 3d of November 1643 at Fort Amsterdam.

$$P X$$

Signature of Pieter Laurenssen Kock.

"Roeloff Jansen Haes."[562]

On March 28, 1647, Kock bought a lot on Manhattan Island, opposite H. Kip.[563]

In 1653 he was considered to be one of the "principal burghers and inhabitants" of New Amsterdam, and was as such consulted in regard to measures intended by the city government to increase the treasury.[564]

In February, 1653, if not before, Kock brought action before the court against Annetie Cornelissen Van Vorst, whose step-

---

561 New York Colonial Documents, I., p. 186f.
562 Ibid., XIII., p. 16.
563 Year Book of the Holland Society, 1901, p. 130.
564 Records of New Amsterdam, 1653-1674, I., p. 126.

NEW AMSTERDAM AS IT APPEARED ABOUT 1640.

A. The Fort. B. Church of St. Nicholas. C. The Jail. D. Governor's House. E. The Gallows. F. The Pillory. G. West India Company's Stores. H. The Tavern. From "Historic New York." Edited by M. W. Goodwin. By Permission of G. P. Putnam's Sons, New York.

father was Jacob Stoffelzen. They had been engaged and she had broken the engagement. This brought on the suit. We shall not give the history of it, but content ourselves to state the findings of the court, given on May 18, 1654.

"The Commissioners to examine the papers in the suit between Pieter Kock and Anna van Vorst made their report to the Board and their opinion, which is the following judgment, and the same being examined, Burgomasters and Schepens decide, that said judgment shall for reasons not yet be pronounced but remain in abeyance until future occasion and request of parties.

"A suit has been instituted before the Court of the City of New Amsterdam by Pieter Kock, bachelor, a burgher and inhabitant of said City, pltf. against Anna van Vorst, spinster, living at Ahasimus [in New Jersey] deft., respecting a marriage contract, or an oral promise of marriage, mutually entered into between said Pieter Kock and Anna van Vorst, and in confirmation thereof, certain gifts and presents were made by the pltf. to the aforesaid deft.; however, it appears by the documents exhibited by parties, that the deft. the fiancee of pltf., in consequence of certain misbehavior, is in no wise disposed to marry said Pieter Kock, and also proves by two witnesses (see affidavit dated the 24 December 1653) that Pieter Cock had released her, with promise to give her a written acquittal to that effect, therefore Burgomasters and Schepens of this City having attentively perused and examined all the documents by parties, adjudge, as they do hereby, that the promise of marriage having been made and given before the Eyes of God, shall remain in force, so that neither pltf. nor deft. shall be at liberty without the knowledge and approbation of the Worsh. Magistrates and the other one of the interested parties to enter into matrimony with any person, whether single man or single woman. Also that all the presents made in confirmation of marriage shall remain in possesion of deft, until parties with the pleasure, good will, contentment and inclination of both shall marry together, or with the knowledge of the Magistracy shall release and set each other free. Furthermore, both pltf. and deft. are condemned equally in this cost of the suit. Thus done and adjudged in the Court aforesaid this 18th of May, 1654."[565]

565 Ibid., I., p. 199f.

Pieter Laurensen Kock married another, however, June 13, 1657. This was Marries Anneken Dircks. A child was born to them and baptized "Gallas" on September 21, 1659. Not long afterward Kock died, for on November 26, 1660, Marries requested as "the widow of Pieter Kock" that Daniel Litschoe and Jacob Hendricks Varrevanger should be appointed guardians of her child.[566]

Meantime Kock's name had appeared quite often in the court minutes of New Amsterdam.

On December 1, 1653, Kock petitioned the Court that he might be indemnified for theft committed at his house by Jan Gerritsen, a smith. The Court directed him to apply to the officer[567]

On January 18, 1655, Cornelis Jacobsen Steenwyck instituted action against Kock, demanding repayment of fl. 200 in wampum, which he had loaned him. Kock acknowledged the receipt and debt, but "requested that the money be paid to him which had been realized from the sale of the property of John the Smith, who absconded for robbery committed in his house, in consequence of which he had been obliged to contract this debt, in order to restore the Wampum to the Deaconry; in order therewith to meet this obligation." The Court decided that Kock should pay Steenwyck. But it also decreed the following:

"Whereas Jan Gerritsen, Smith, being accused of stealing about 5 to 600 guilders in wampum from the house of Pieter Kock, Burger and inhabitant of this city, has absconded, and to this date has not returned to answer; therefore the Burgomasters and Schepens of this City, have, at the request of the aforesaid Pieter Kock, and for the restoration of the stolen wampum, consented, that, he shall appropriate the monies, accrued from the old iron work sold to Burger Jorissen, according to obligation of fl. 111.7½. together with 6 beavers sequestered by the Secretary and should he know of anything else belonging to the aforesaid Jan Gerritsen, he shall report the same, so as to obtain something back towards his loss. Therefore Secretary Kip is ordered to hand over to him the aforesaid obligation with assignment, in the name of the Burgomasters and Schepens, together with the sequestered Beavers."[568]

Under date of April 19, 1655, the court minutes state in

566 New York Genealogical and Biographical Record, VI., p. 85. Year Book of the Holland Society of New York, 1900, p. 120.
567 The Records of New Amsterdam, 1653-1674, I., p. 184.
568 Ibid., I., p. 277.

regard to this matter: "On the obligation, order and insinuation against Borger Jorissen, relative to the payment of fl. 111.7½. for purchased ironwork from the shop of Jan the Smith, according to a note drawn in favor of Peter Kock, is endorsed — Whereas aforesaid obligation concerns only Peter Kock, and ironwork was sold for his behoof, Borger Jorissen is again condemned to pay the same, on pain of execution, whereunto the Constable is authorized.[569]

Kock's next case of litigation, in December, 1656, was started in consequence of one of his sheep having been bit and killed by a dog. He brought suit against the owners, who after much argueing, were condemned to pay him for the loss of the sheep, each (Pieter van Couwenhoven and Jan Gillesen Verbrugge) "one half of three merchantable beavers, besides the costs incurred herein."[570]

In September, 1659, he was ordered by the court to produce by next court day his papers, made use of in a suit between him and Solomon La Chair, Farmer of the Burger Excise of beer and wine. La Chair accused him of smuggling: Kock had eleven ankers of liquor, he disposed of one, consumed one himself, presented three ankers for tapper's and Burgher's excise. The remaining six ankers were seized by the Fiscal. The court dismissed La Chair's suit, but both he and Kock were condemned to pay the costs. Notwithstanding as Kock had been intended to tap, and had not taken out any license, as the Law required, he was fined twelve guilders in another suit instituted against him by the Schout. He was also condemned to pay the costs of this suit, January 20, 1660.[571]

Aside from what the court records tell us, we know but little of Kock's doings. In July, 1659, he and a Willem Pietersen were examined "regarding expressions by Jacop Coppe concerning a will."

The court minutes relate several matters concerning his widow, who continued keeping the tavern which Kock had built on

---

569 Ibid., I., p. 808, cfr. p. 824.
570 Ibid., II., pp. 248, 257, 270.
571 Ibid., III., p. 105.

the opposite side of the Marckveldt in New Amsterdam, near the place where the country people landed their country boats. We shall mention a few of the lawsuits in which she was the defendant.

A suit instituted against her on May 24, 1661, by Robert Rollantsen and Abraham Janzen, carpenters, shows the patriarchal character of the Court of New Amsterdam. They claimed that they had contracted to build a house for her deceased husband; but she had "agreed for it with another." She replied that with the death of her husband, the contract is also dead. The Court, however, ordered the "defendant to allow the plaintiffs to build the house or satisfy them." [572] The house, which Anneke Kock occupied in her widowhood was "large and fine," situated on the corner of Battery place (Valentine's History of the City of New York, 98). Her neighbor was one of the notable citizens of that period, Martin Cregier.[573]

Four other suits against her show her as the tavern keeper.

On February 18, 1662, she was asked by the court why she charged a certain Abraham Pieters so much for pins. To this she replied he had charged her a very high price for hogs. She had also charged him nine guilders expenses: "three given to the officer, three to the Notary, and three spent on drink." The court decided that she had to pay those expenses herself.[574]

But on September 12, 1662, Geertruyd de Witt brought a suit against Anneke Kocks, which was of a more serious nature. In the words of the court minutes:

"Pltf. says, that deft. besides other insulting expressions has abused her husband as a cuckold, struck and kicked her in the side and bit her in the ear. Deft. denies having struck her first and says, that her husband threatened to beat her maid, that they mumbled at each other and that she, the pltf., first seized her by the cap, tearing the same from her head; can prove the same by Martin Cregier's daughter; whereupon she [Anneke] gave her a slap or two. The officer concludes, that the deft. shall be amerced in a fine of two hundred guilders, for that the deft. struck and kicked the pltf. on her body, being a pregnant woman, going on close of her term. Jan de Witt, husband and guardian of the

---

572 Ibid., III., pp. 310, 364.
573 D. T. Valentine, History of the City of New York, p. 98.
574 The Records of New Amsterdam, IV., p. 84.

pltf., concludes in writing, that deft. shall repair the injuries inflicted on him and his wife, honorably and profitably at the estimation and taxation of this W. Court; and pay, in addition on the taxation as above, for the suffered pain, smart, loss and surgeon's fee. . . ." On October 10, the Court condemned Anneke Kock "for having dared to beat Jan de Witt's wife, being pregnant, to pull the hair from her head and treat her rudely, in the fine of fifty guilders payable to the Deaconry of this City; all with costs of suit.[575]

On October 29, 1667, she was condemned to pay a fine of eighty guilders wampum and charges of a suit brought against her for having sold liquor to Indians on a Sunday.

On August 4, 1668, she was again fined five pounds sterling with costs of suit for having sold "Rom (rum) to the Indians, contrary to the Law."

Very likely, Anna Cornelisen, who was deceased in September, 1658, and whom Kock had sued for breach of marriage contract would have been the better wife of the tavern keeper from ancient Aalborg.

JOCHEM PIETERSEN KUYTER.

Jochem Pietersen Kuyter, one of the most influential colonists in New Netherland, arrived at New Amsterdam, in July, 1639. He was a native of Dithmarschen (not Darmstad, as some have said). He came in a private ship "De Brant von Trogen" (The Fire of Troy). Captain David Pietersz De Vries, who was not far from New Amsterdam at the time, and who has left us accounts of several of his voyages, has also given us some information about Kuyter:

". . . We found two ships had arrived from our Patria, one of which was a ship of the company, the *Herring,* the other was a private ship, *The Fire of Troy,* from Hoorn, laden with cattle on account of Jochem Pietersz, who had formerly been a commander

---

575 Ibid., IV., pp. 180, 184, 140, 146.

in the East Indies, for the King of Denmark. It was to be wished that one hundred to three hundred such families with laborers, had come, as this would very soon become a good country."

Where Kuyter got his name, often spelled Cuyter, has not been ascertained. Sometimes it occurs as Kayser. Could the original have been Keyser or Reyser or Knyter? For twelve years, he had been, according to tradition, in the service of the Danish East India Colonies. Mr. N. Andersen, of Denmark, who has written about Bronck (Personalhistorisk Tidsskrift VI R. Vol. V, Part I) leaves it an open question as to what the position which Kuyter held, actually was. Kuyter may, he says, have been in the service of the fleet, or in the service of the East India Company as "capitaine d' armes" or as skipper, "capitaine de vaisseau."

Kuyter was a man of good education, what is evident by his dealings with Governor Kieft, whom he gave many a thrust in his well-written documents.

It has been said by historians that Kuyter's friend, Jonas Bronck, another Dane, came over in the same vessel with Kuyter: 1639. I will not dispute this. But I have seen no direct proof of the statement. If E. B. O'Callaghan's list is correct in "History of New Netherland" II, 531, Bronck got land in New Netherland as early as 1637. This early date, however, seems to be a mere conjecture.

Kuyter associated much with Bronck, whose sister he seems to have married. But his name is more intimately connected with that of Cornelis Melyn. Both he and Melyn were pleading for justice to the Indians, when the government of New Netherland was flagrantly disregarding the rights of the Red Man.

A Mandamus of April 28, 1648, shows that the government had received a communication from Kuyter and Melyn, stating with what difficulty they had to wrestle in coming over to New Netherland and in their endeavor to colonize parts of it. It says:

"The States General of the United Netherlands, To the first Marshal or Messenger having power to serve when requested, Greeting: Make Known, that we, having received the humble supplication presented to us by and in behalf of Jochem Pietersz Cuyter and Cornelis Melyn, containing that they, petitioners, with permission and leave of the Assembly of the XIX of the General West India Company, with wife and children and with private means, besides a large herd of cattle, in the year one thousand six hundred and thirty nine, transported themselves from these countries to New Netherland, so that they, petitioners, after enormous expenses, difficulties and inexpressible labor, got into condition, in the year sixteen hundred forty three, their lands, houses and other undertakings which in the aforesaid year on account of the war (waged by Director Kieft unjustly and contrary to all international law, with the savages or natives of New Netherland) they have been obliged to abandon and as a consequence lost all their property."*

What is set forth in this Mandamus is correct except as to the year of Melyn's arrival. He came with his family to New Netherland in 1641, not 1639, but he had made an inspection of it earlier.

Cornelis Melyn, formerly a leather dresser at Amsterdam, sailed for New Netherland in May 1638, by the ship " het Wapen van Noorwegen" (The Arms of Norway), arriving at Amsterdam about August 4. Melyn was supercargo. The colony of Rensselaerswyck had a half interest in the ship which on its trip, May—August, 1638, was so heavily laden that the sailors protested that they would not risk their lives on it. It carried over a number of colonists and a large quantity of goods, including eighteen young mares, thousands of bricks, ironwork, clothing material, spices, cheese, soap, oil and a box filled with earth in which were planted young grape vines.[576]

After arriving in New Netherland and after inspecting the new country, Melyn conceived the plan of founding a colony on Staten Island. He returned to Holland, and in July, 1640, got a deed for all of Staten Island save that which David Pietersz De Vries had occupied. In August, in the same year, he set sail for New Netherland with his people, cattle, goods and all other implements necessary for agriculture, but he was taken by a Dunkirk frigate. He got assistance, however, and arrived, 1641, with the ship "Den Eyckenboom" (The Oaktree) in New Netherland on Staten Island with 41 persons. He began to build houses, to

---

* Collections of the New York Historical Society, Second Series, Vol. III., p. 88.
576 Bowier Manuscripts.
About this ship, see Education Department Bulletin, No. 462. Not all the ships were so aptly named as The Arms of Norway. One entering the port of New York was called "King David," another "King Solomon," a third "Adam and Eve," etc.

plough land, and to do everything conducive to establishing a good colony.

The Indians were restless. One of them, of the Weckqua-skeek tribe, murdered a white man. The government promptly demanded of the tribe that it surrender the murderer. Governor Kieft was looking for an opportunity to exterminate the Indians. A savage massacre of them was the result of his plotting with a few citizens, for the vast majority of the white population would have no war with the Indians. The Indians retaliated. Within a short time they reduced some thirty farmhouses on Manhattan Island to four or five. Melyns colony was saved for a time, but late in 1643 it was attacked. This attack left everything in ruin. Kuyter's plantation was devastated by the Indians in the following year.

Melyn and Kuyter, having sustained enormous loses, knew that the government, with Kieft at the head, was to blame. Its shortsighted policy in dealing with the Indians had brought on the disaster to the whites. They therefore made their influence felt against Kieft, and worked for getting a better government.

But — to come back to the beginnings of Kuyter's plantation. Kuyter settled with his farmers and herdsmen upon a tract of four hundred acres of fine farming land, of which he had obtained a grant from the West India Company. This tract stretched along the Harlem River from about the present One Hundred and Twenty-seventh to One Hundred and Fortieth streets, and was commonly known, long after his memory had faded away among men, as 'Jochem Pieter's Flats'. Kuyter himself called it Zegen-daal, or 'Vale of Blessing'."*

Kuyter spent much of his time at the other end of Manhattan. But he was interested in the growth of the village. In 1642, he was chosen 'kerkemester,' to oversee the erection of the new church in the fort. His insight into architecture and command of people and building material was, no doubt, better than his command of Reformed theology. He had evidently been a Lutheran when in Dithmarschen, and the assertion of the pastor in New Amsterdam, that Kuyter was a "good Calvinist" was possibly made to ward off

---

* Cfr. J. H. Innes, New Amsterdam and Its People, p. 108f.

current ideas to the contrary. Kuyter was also Elder of the
church.

None of the other Danes in New Amsterdam obtained the
social prestige of Kuyter. He was a member of the Board of
Twelve Men from August 29, 1641, to February 18, 1642; of the
Board of Eight Men which board existed from September, 1643,
to September, 1647. After a journey to Holland he was made a
member of the Board of Nine Men, which existed from September
25, 1647, until the city was incorporated, in 1653, when he was
made Schout or Sheriff.

Kuyter's plantations were yielding good returns of tobacco.
But they were exposed and unprotected, and could be ruined by
the Indians speedily and without opposition. Like most of the
Twelve Men, Kuyter was opposed to using violent measures
against the Indians. He foretold Director Kieft the quick retribu-
tion which would ensue for their massacre.

His own bowery house was well palisaded. It therefore
escaped the first devastation of the Indians, but on March 5, 1644,
his buildings were set on fire in the night and destroyed by the
savages. Kuyter himself was absent. The house was guarded,
but little resistance was offered. Among the guards was Pieter
Jansen, a Norwegian. (See article Pieter Jansen. Part I.)

One of Kuyter's concerns was, as has been indicated, to get
a better government, and a better Director.

Director Kieft, in order to increase the finances of the West
India Company, imposed an excise upon the wines and spirits at
the rate of four stivers per quart, likewise upon every beaver skin
one guilder. In proclaiming this excise, Kieft acted in opposition
to the Board of Eight Men. They claimed that imposing taxes
was an act af sovereignty which the West India Company did not
possess, and that the hiring and keeping of soldiers was the business of the company and not of the settlers. Kieft showed himself
rude in dealing with the Board of Eight Men. Once he snubbed
the board by summoning three of its members—Kuyter, Melyn
and Hall—to come a certain day at eight o'clock in the morning.
They came and waited till past noon. Kieft had gone off somewhere on other business, and the three finally went off "as wise as
they came."

Another error of Kieft's was that once when the brewers refused to pay the taxes, he caused sundry casks of liquor to be con fiscated and handed over to thirsty soldiers!

After six months of wrangling, the Eight Men sent their eloquent "Memorial" to the States General, in which they described the condition of the country and registered their gravamina. The petition asked for a new governor and for some limitation of his power by representatives of the people.

Meantime Kuyter had been forced, on account of the burning of his bowery house, to move to New Amsterdam. He purchased a small house at the corner of Pearl and Broad Streets. His former neighbor, Cornelis Melyn, proved a faithful ally to him. But like Kuyter he was a thorn in the flesh of Director Kieft.

Kieft was now replaced by Peter Stuyvesant, who had been governor of the island of Curacao. Stuyvesant had lost a leg in a fight with the Portuguese at San Marin, had returned to Holland in 1644, and was appointed as Director General of New Netherland in May, 1645, but did not arrive before in May, 1647.

When Kieft surrendered the government, he asked the people to give his administration their formal endorsement. They refused. Kuyter and Melyn declared they had nothing to thank him for. Within a few days after Kieft had delivered up his office, Melyn and Kuyter, as representatives of the old Board of Eight Men, brought a formal complaint against Kieft and asked for an inquiry in the abuses of his late government and respecting his treatment of the Indians.

Stuyvesant was averse to entertain the complaint. He saw that it would form a precedent in case his own administration proved inefficient. His dignity was ruffled: the sacredness of the Directorship must be sustained.

Kieft was enraged and accused Kuyter and Melyn of being the real authors of a "Memorial of the Eight Men" sent to the States General. He said the memorial was a false libel, which Kuyter and Melyn had sent to Holland without the knowledge of their colleagues.

They were accordingly summoned to show cause why they should not be banished as "pestilent and seditious persons." They appeared and answered so well for their acts that Kieft had to take up a new line of proceeding. They offered to bring forward the four survivors of the Eight Men to testify that these had signed the charges against Kieft of their own will and not through the influence of the persons accused.

John Fisk says: "Indictments were brought against Kuyter and Melyn, on sundry trumped-up charges, chiefly alleging treacherous dealings with the Indians, and attempts to stir up rebellion. With shameless disregard of evidence, a prearranged verdict of guilty was rendered." Melyn was sentenced to seven years' banishment and a fine of 300 guilders. Kuyter to three years' banishment and a fine of 150 guilders. They were sentenced on July 25, 1647.

On August 17, in the same year, Kieft set sail for Holland. He took with him Melyn and Kuyter as prisoners. In the same ship was Domine Bogardus, who had his share of trouble with Kieft and was to answer charges in Holland. By some error of reckoning, the ship struck on the rocks near Swansea. Eighty-one persons, including Ex-Governor Kieft and Reverend Bogardus, were drowned. Twenty reached the shore in safety. Among these were Kuyter and Melyn. Kuyter told how he had lashed himself to a portion of the after deck of the vessel and how when the first dim light broke after the night of horror, he had discovered himself to be alone upon the floating fragment, except for what he took to be another person likewise lashed fast. Speaking and receiving no answer, he concluded that the man was dead; it turned out to be a cannon, which with the wreck and Kuyter was thrown by the violent storm upon the beach.*

Kuyter and Melyn had the shallow waters dragged, for three days, until they brought up a chest containing their most important papers.

Kuyter and Melyn reached Netherlands at the end of the year 1647 and laid their case before the States General. This body was favorably disposed to them. An appeal was granted from the verdict pronounced upon them by Governor Stuyvesant and his Council. Stuyvesant was summoned to appear before them to justify his acts.

It was arranged that Melyn should go back to New Nether-

---

* J. H. Innes, New Amsterdam and Its People, p. 114f.

land and have the papers served on Stuyvesant. Kuyter should, however, remain in the Netherlands, to be in readiness if Stuyvesant acted treacherously or arbitrarily.

Melyn arrived in New Netherland in March, 1649, Kuyter followed later.

There is on record a letter from the Prince of Orange to Director Stuyvesant, informing him that Melyn and Kuyter had received permission to return to New Netherland, and ordering the Director not to molest them. It reads thus:

"The Prince of Orange

"Honorable, Prudent, Discreet, Dear Sir:
"You will receive by the bearers here of Jochem Pietersen Cuyter and Cornelis Melyn, the commands, which their High: Might: the States General have concluded to issue to you, directing you to allow these men to enjoy their property there free and unmolested by virtue of the provisional appeal, granted to them by their High: Might: with the clause suspending the sentence passed over them by you on the 25th of July 1647.

"Although I do not doubt, that you will obey and respect these orders, yet I desire hereby to admonish you earnestly and advise you expressly, that you allow these men to enjoy quietly and without contradiction the result of the resolution passed by their High: Might:

"Herewith, etc.,
"At the Gravens' Hague,
"May 19th, 1648.   Your very good friend
                                     "W. d'Orange.

"To the Honorable
Prudent, Discreet, Our
Dear and Special Friend
Petrus Stuyvesant
"Director of Netherland."[577]

Kuyter made his peace with Stuyvesant, whom with two others he admitted in 1651 into joint ownership with himself in his plantation on the Harlem flats, where he was now actively en-

---

[577] New York Colonial Documents, XIV., p. 87.

THE EAST RIVER SHORE NEAR THE "GRAFT," 1652.

From "New Amsterdam and Its People," by J. H. Innes; copyright, 1902, by Charles Scribner's Sons, New York.

AA. Houses on the Marckveldt. BB. Houses on Marckveldt Steegh and Bever Graft. C. Rear of the "Five Houses." D. Brewery of West India Co. E. Old Church. F. Old Parsonage, where Anneke Jans, from Norway, lived. G. Hend. Hendricksen Kip. H. Anthony Jansen van Vees. I. Hendr. Jansen Smit. J. Hendr. Willemsen, baker. K. Houses of Teunis Craie. L. Jacob Wolphertsen van Couwenhoven. M. Cornelis Melyn (later occupied by Jacob Loper, a Swede). N. Capt. Jochem Pietersen Kuyter, a Dane. O. Sibout Claessen. P. Cornelis van Tienhoven. Q. Adriaen Vincent.

gaged in restoring his impaired fortunes.   But in 1654 he was
murdered by the Indians at Harlem.

Kuyter was married to Lentie Martens, who possibly was a
sister of his friend, Jonas Bronck.   As Bronck's full name appears
to have been Johannes or Jonas Martensen Bronck, his father's
name was Marten or Morten; hence the daughter's surname would
be Martens.

On April 24, 1654, "Leyntie Martens, widow of Jochem Pr.
Kuyter, late elder and schepen of New Amsterdam, confers powers
of attorney upon Govert Loockermans, merchant, and Dirck Van
Schelluyne, notary public, especially for the purpose of representing her in settling affairs regarding lands named Segendael with
. . . . Stuyvesant . . . ., Roodenborch, Cornelis Potter, as per contract dated Sept. 23, 1651.   Witness Arent Van Hattem, Burgomaster, and Paulus Leendersz Van die Grift, schepen."*

Lentie Martens did not long remain a widow.   On December
18, 1654, she was married to Willem Jansen, from Gelderland, the
superintendent of the Harlem plantation.   But during the outbreak
in the fall of 1655, she too was killed by the Indians.   She was a
member of the Dutch Reformed Church.

Kuyter left no children.

J. Riker, the historian of Harlem, says about Kuyter:

"By his bold defense of popular rights he conferred invalu-
able benefits upon his fellow colonists and those succeeding him,
and which entitles him to a place on the roll of public benefactors.
Kuyter should have a memorial in Central Park" in New York
City.

JOHN LARASON (LARSEN).

John Larason (Larsen), was a "Danish nobleman, compelled
to flee and lose his estates by confiscation on account of a conspiracy, in 1660, because of taxes.   He fled to Scotland, and, hearing that a price was set on his head, came to America, and purchased a large tract, about 1,700 acres, near Brooklyn, L. I."

* Year Book of the Holland Society of New York, 1900, p. 178.

John Larason is on the rate list of Newton, L. I., 1683. He probably married, (1) May 22, 1683, Jemima Halsey; (2) December 22, 1686, the widow Mary Howell. He died at Chester (?), N. J., at an advanced age. He probably had a son.

"Larason" may be a corruption of "Lauridsen," or an assumed name. "Larasen" often occurs in older Norwegian records.

Catharine Larason, who was married in 1779; Anne Larason, married in 1768; David Larason, married in September, 1780; James Larason, married in 1783 (see New Jersey Archives, First Series, XXII., pp. 236, 247), may be descendants of John Larason.

RIBE, ABOUT THE CLOSE OF THE SIXTEENTH CENTURY.
From Braunius: Theatrum urbium.

I must add that this information is given mainly on the authority of Theodore Freylinghuysen Chambers. The flight of Larason, as well as the price on his head, would perhaps throw some interesting light on the so-called Revolution in Denmark in 1660, when the nobility lost their power and the king was made an absolute monarch. The flight, if at all historic, must have been due to something else than a "conspiracy" connected with the change in the government of Denmark in 1660.[578]

JAN LAURENS.

Jan Laurens, from Ribe, in Denmark, is on the list of soldiers who were to sail to New Amsterdam, April 15, 1660, on the

---

578 Theodore F. Chambers, The Early Germans of New Jersey, their History, Churches, and Genealogies, 1895, Dover. New Jersey, p. 487.

ship "de Bonte Koe." In a footnote the list says: Presumably some of these soldiers will be found missing. Whether Jan Laurens was among the missing, cannot be ascertained, as the sources reveal nothing more about him.[579]

SEVERYN LAURENSZEN.

Severyn Laurenszen, from Roskilde, in Denmark, was in New Amsterdam as early as 1656. On May 25, in that year, he married Tryntie Reynderts, of Hengel, widow of Arent Theuniszen.[580]

We meet him first as a soldier, then as a tavern keeper, finally as a farmer and public official.

On April 12, 1658, he was sentenced for theft. The sentence, as entered in the Records, reads: "Severyn Lourens, Lance Corporal, for theft to be stripped of his arms and publicly flogged and branded."[581]

He was committed to jail, but broke jail before the sentence of April 12 was executed. On May 28, 1658, he was pardoned and permitted to live on Long Island.[582] He returned to New Amsterdam and became a tavern keeper, in partnership with Jan Jansen Romeyn. On May 11, 1662, both he and Jansen were prosecuted for selling liquor during divine service.[583] On July 3, 1664, he was sentenced in court for "permitting persons to play nine pins on his premises on Sunday."[584]

On August 10, 1661, Laurenszen stood sponsor at the baptism of Adrian, a son of his partner, Jan Jansen, and wife, Marretje Adrians (Jeurians), from Copenhagen. (See article Marritje Jeurians. Part II.)

In November, 1661, Captain Post sued Laurenszen for "forty-one guilders, five stivers according to account." But Laurenszen's wife came forward and produced an offset account and "besides

579 Year Book of the Holland Society of New York, 1902.
580 New York Genealogical and Biographical Record, VI., p. 84.
581 Calendar of Historical Manuscripts, I., p. 194.
582 Ibid., I., p. 196.
583 Ibid., I., p. 237.
584 Ibid., I., p. 248.

this, some claim." The Burgomasters and Schepens referred the matter in question to Thomas Hall and Frerick Lubbersen to hear the parties, "to examine and decide their affairs, and if possible, reconcile them; if not, to report their decision to the Court."[585]

Under date of April 25, 1662, the court calendar stated that "Severyn Lauwersen and Jan Janszen van de Lange Straat" had a suit against Daniel Vervelen, and that both parties were in default. The suit seems to have been about a debt.[586]

On May 2, 1662, Johannes de Witt brought suit against "Severyn Lauwerens and Jan Janszen van de Lange Straat." He demanded of them two hundred guilders. They acknowledged the debt, but said that for the sum of one hundred guilders they gave an assignment to de Witt on Daniel Vervelen. De Witt, they claimed, was content with this. De Witt replied, he was satisfied only "if Vervelen paid it." The Court having heard the parties, ordered Laurenszen and Janszen to pay the two hundred guilders.[587]

On May 6, 1664, Laurenszen with five others appeared before the Director-General and stated that "the General has enclosed the Highway heretofore made use of and made another road, which is not passable in winter." The result of this visit was a promise of the General that he would "attend to it."[588]

The next notice of Laurenszen in the court records is under date of July 4, 1665: "Mr. Harmen Wessels entering requests, that the attachment issued by him on Jan Damen's goods in the hands of Severyn Laurensen, may be declared valid. Fiat quod Petitur."[589]

On October 3, 1665, the Court in New Amsterdam took notice of Laurenszen by deciding the following:

"Whereas, complaint has been made to us on the part of Wolphert Webber, that he has suffered much damage in his garden through the cattle of Severyn Laurenszen, with requests that some

585 The Records of New Amsterdam, III., p. 411.
586 Ibid., IV., p. 67.
587 Ibid., IV., p. 72.
588 Ibid., V., p. 52.
589 Ibid., V., p. 271.

persons may be appointed to inspect the same and estimate the damage, therefore the Major and Aldermen of the City of New York this day appoint and authorize Mr. Thomas Hal, Dirck Siecken, and Arien Cornelissen to inspect the aforesaid garden, to estimate the pretended damage and to determine how the same occurred, whether by imperfect fencing or otherwise, and if possible to reconcile parties; if not, to report their finding to the W. Court."[590]

In 1662, "Severyn Lourens, of Roodschildt in Denmark" and his wife made their joint will. "Her children were Reiner, Mary, and Hendrick Arents (Van Engelen)."[591]

On August 5, 1671, Severyn Laurenszen being a widower, married a second time. His second wife was Grietje Hendricks, widow of Focke Janszen, "both residing at the bowery."[592]

In 1672, the Court of New Amsterdam elected Severyn as overseer of fences and highways.[593]

HENDRICK MARTENSEN.

Hendrick Martensen (Hendrick Martensen Wiltsee), from Copenhagen, was in New Netherland before 1660. On January 10, 1660, he married in New Amsterdam, Margaret Meyers (Meyring, Meyrinck), widow of Herman Jansen and daughter of Jan Meyrinck.

Previous to this, he may have been for some time at Esopus, as he, on August 21, 1659, deeded property at Esopus to Lukas Dircksen.[594]

Shortly after his marriage he brought action, at New Amsterdam, against Herman van Borssum, demanding remuneration for damage to a canoe, which van Borssum committed by sailing against

590 Ibid., V., p. 295.
591 Year Book of the Holland Society of New York, 1900, p. 142. New York Colonial Documents, XIII., p. 74.
592 The Records of New Amsterdam, 1653 1674, VI., p. 335.
593 Ibid., VI., p. 374.
594 Munsell, Collections on the History of . . . Albany, VI., p. 154.

it with his boat. At the first hearing van Borssum denied that he
had done any damage. At the second hearing, the wife of Martensen appeared against him, declaring that he had stated that he
would let the canoe be repaired. Van Borssum admitted this, and
said he had stated this to prevent trouble. The court informed
him that it was better to let the canoe be repaired than to proceed
further, which would be more expensive. Van Borssum then
promised he would repair the damages. The court informed Mrs.
Martensen of this and "ordered her to be satisfied therewith to
prevent further costs."[595]

At the close of the year Martensen was at Esopus, or Kingston, where his daughter Sophia was baptized, December 11,
1660.[596] On May 2, 1661, he "drew a lot at Esopus: lot No. 2,
and was allotted same."[597]

He was at this time a soldier at the garrison on the Esopus.[598]
In the summer of 1663 he was in the Esopus war. He was captured by the savages and reported killed,[599] but this proved to be a
mistake, and he soon obtained his liberty.

On April 28, 1667, he signed, with other burghers of Wiltwyck, a document, stating that they had been in arms in the Brodhead mutiny, when Captain Brodhead had threatened to burn the
village.[600]

In 1673 Martensen petitioned the court of New Amsterdam to
render judgment in a matter, not known to us, regarding Staten
Island. This court, however, referred him "to the Court at Staten
Island to demand justice there from them, or otherwise to act as
he thinks proper; as this Court has no connection with that of
Staten Island."[601]

In early records, Martensen was sometimes called Wiltsee.
He is the ancestor of many families bearing this name, commonly
written Wiltsie. He had six sons: Martin, who was baptized in
Wiltwyck, April 3, 1667; Hendrick, baptized in New Amsterdam,

---

595 The Records of New Amsterdam, III., pp. 147, 153.
596 R. R. Hoes, Baptismal and Marriage Register . . . of the old Dutch
Church of Kingston.
597 New York Colonial Documents, XIII., p. 195.
598 Ibid., XIII., p. 202.
599 Ibid., XIII., p. 245.
600 Ibid., XIII., p. 414.
601 The Records of New Amsterdam, VII., p. 20.

HAFNIA METROPOLIS

COPENHAG
Original View by Johan Classen v
From J. A. Fridericia's Da
Det Nordiske

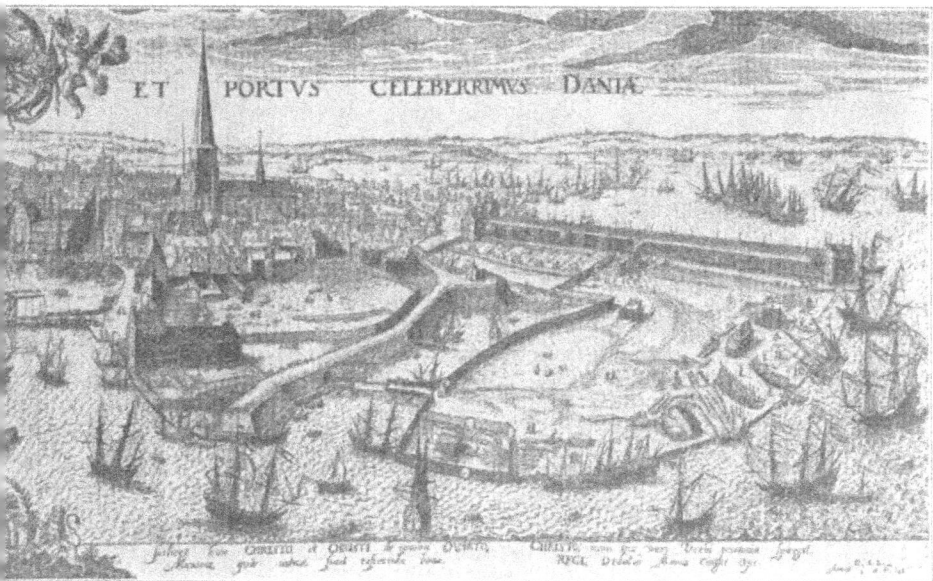

ET PORTVS CELEBERRIMVS DANIÆ

BOUT 1610.
yck, engraved by Johan Diricksen.
Riges Historie, 1588-1699.
, Copenhagen.

November 24, 1669; Meyndert, February 11, 1672; Teunis, January 10, 1674; Jacob, March 18, 1676. They all married and had families. Their posterity is now numerous, particularly in Westchester and Dutchess Counties.[602]

Of his daughters, Sophia was baptized in 1660 (see above); Jannetje was baptized January 7, 1663. One of the sponsors at this baptism was Marten Hoffman, a Swedish Lutheran. Barbar(a) was baptized March 1, 1665.[603]

PIETER MARTENSEN.

Pieter Martensen, from Dithmarschen, arrived at New Amsterdam in 1663, on board the ship "de Rooseboom," which sailed March 15, 1663. He was accompanied by his child, seven years old.[604]

In 1701 he seems to have resided in Albany.[605]

CHRISTIAN NISSEN.

Christian Nissen, Christian Nissen Romp, from Holstein, was in New Amsterdam as early as 1657. On February 4, in that year, he married Styntie Pieters, of Copenhagen.[606] He was a Lutheran by creed: he signed the petition of the Lutherans in New Amsterdam, October 10, 1657, requesting that the government might permit the Lutheran pastor Johannes Goetwater to remain in New Netherland instead of being deported.[607]

We find Nissen as sponsor at the baptism of several children in New Amsterdam. On January 27, 1657, he was sponsor for a child of Carl Margen and Cathalyntie Hendricks; November 6, for a child belonging to Gustavus Daniels and Annetje Loons;

602 Riker, Annals of Newtown, p. 372.
603 See Reference 596.
604 Year Book of the Holland Society of New York, 1902, p. 23.
605 New York Colonial Documents, IV., p. 989.
606 New York Genealogical and Biographical Record, VI., p. 85.
607 See note 42.

November 24, for a child belonging to a Dane, Christian Pieter-sen; April 4, 1659, for a child of Mathys Boone.[608]   On December 11, 1660, he was sponsor in Kingston, at the baptism of Sophia, the daughter of the Dane Hendrick Martensen.[609]

Christian and his wife had boarders for some time during their residence at New Amsterdam.   For on February 11, 1658, Nicolas Velthuysen was ordered by the court to pay Nissen for "board, drink, attendance and washing for Jan van Deventer's account 8 gl. per week, amounting for six weeks to fl. 48."*

On June 27, 1659, Nissen conveyed a lot in New Amsterdam to Gerrit Hendricksen.   The lot was "situate in the Marckvelt Steegh; bounded west by the house and lot of Frerick Aarsen; on the north, by the lane aforesaid; on the east, the house and lot of Nicolaas Boot; on the south, by house and lot of Teunis Tomassen Van Naarden.   In breadth and length, according to deed of October 25, 1658."†   Not much later Nissen moved to Esopus.   On March 28, 1660, he went as sergeant, with a company of seventy-seven men, to "Manathes."[610]

In 1661 he commanded the garrison at Wiltwyck (Kingston).[611]   New York Colonial Documents (II, pp. 453, 455, 463) give data as to how much powder his garrison at various intervals possessed.   The same work contains several communications from Nissen, addressed to Director Stuyvesant.[612]

Nissen was a faithful commander, and was held in esteem by the government, as is seen by the following letter of his to the Director and Council and by the action taken upon it.

Nissen's letter, written in June, 1662, reads as follows:

"To the Noble, Worshipful Director-General and the Honorable Council of New Netherland.   Shows with all due reverence Christian Nissen, chief sergeant in the service of your Hon. Worship that I have had charge in this quality for some time of the

608 Collections of the New York Genealogical and Biographical Society. II.
609 R. R. Hoes, Baptismal and Marriage Registers of the . . . Church of Kingston.
* The Records of New Amsterdam, 1653-1674. II., p. 329.
610 New York Colonial Documents, XIII., p. 158.
† Valentine, Manual of the . . . City of New York, 1865, p. 660.
611 Year Book og the Holland Society, 1897, p. 125.
612 New York Colonial Documents, XIII., pp. 191, 328, 367f.

garrison at the Esopus and find that my pay is not sufficient for my subsistence, to attend duly to my position and therefore I request that your Hon. Worships will please, to consider, that I need a little higher pay, and I do not doubt that after your Hon. Worships have taken it into consideration, they will favor me with higher pay. Which doing I remain Your Hon. Worships' servant Christian Niessen."

The Director and Council acted favorably on the request:
"The Director-General and Council considered the expenses which the petitioner must now and then necessarily incur in the discharge of his duties, and as the same have been attended to with great diligence and vigilance since his appointment, it is decided, That the petitioner shall henceforth receive twenty guilders monthly pay. Date as above [29. June, 1662].[618]

On August 19, 1663, Ensign Nissen was sent out with fifty-five men to certain corn plantations to look for savages who had been committing ravage and murder. Two months before this, he had evinced great courage in the war against the Indians. Of his forty-two men, one was killed, sixteen wounded.

Notwithstanding, Nissen, as little as any one else, could escape the censure of Director Stuyvesant, who sent him a reprimand at the close of the year, censuring him for disobedience of orders. It reads:

"Honorable, Valiant Sir: We are very much surprised by your improper disobedience in not carrying out our so plainly expressed orders and directions to send back the saddles, the surplus hand and side arms, not in use, the three bronce pieces and the old rope. Although we cannot, on account of the unfavorable season, correct at present your disobedience and disregard, as it ought to be done, yet we warn you not to disobey henceforth any of our orders upon so unfounded presumptions and made up pretexts, but to execute and obey them, as it is proper, else we shall be obliged to proceed with cashiering or otherwise according to circumstances. Meanwhile we command you herewith to send down the required things promptly, if the state of the weather permit, which is left to the judgment of the bearer. Closing here-

---

618 Ibid., XIII., p. 228.

with etc. Actum Fort Amsterdam December 19, 1663. To Ensign Christian Nissen."[614]

Evidently Nissen acted in good faith and knew better than the Director what was needed at Esopus.   He retained the confidence of Stuyvesant, however, and sent him a letter dated April 21, 1664, in regard to an Englishman who said that the English would possess New Netherland in six or eight weeks.[615]

The Englishman was not mistaken, for in September, 1664, New Netherland became the possession of England.

CLAES PETERSEN.

Claes Petersen came to New Amsterdam in 1660.   He was a soldier, "Adelborst"* from Dithmarschen, who left Holland by the ship "de Bonte Koe," which sailed April 15, 1660.   In the list of passengers kept by the ship, it is stated that he assigned two months' wages per year to Marritie Hendrixen, his betrothed.

He seems to have been in Esopus in 1663.[616]

---

614 Ibid., XIII., p. 320.

615 Calendar of Historical Manuscripts, I., p. 306.

* An Adelborst, as Dr. L. Daae says, was a soldier of the navy, who drew greater wages than the common file, received better treatment, and had better prospects of advancement.   Hence many young men of education and good family often started on their career as Adelborsts.   In the Introduction (in this volume) we have referred to the fact that the Dutch fleet had many Scandinavians in its service.   In 1665 the Norwegian hero, Curt Sivertsen Adelaer, was asked to accept the position of vice-admiral in the Dutch fleet. (Danske Samlinger, 2. Række, 5. p. 18.)

In 1672 Holland had a navy of 135 vessels manned by 20,738 men.   The navy and mercantile fleet must have had altogether 40-50,000 sailors.   Naturally a little country like Holland had to employ a great number of foreign sailors, many of whom were Danes and Norwegians.

Says the English writer Molesworth, in "An Account of Denmark in 1692": "The best seamen belonging to the King of Denmark are the Norwegians; but most of these are in the service of the Dutch, and have their families established in Holland."

Another English writer, criticising Molesworth's account, admits: "The Danes and Norse are very good seamen, the Dutch are mighty desirous of them, and consequently have several of them in their service; yet not so but that they would return upon occasion; and indeed all the seamen are so ready to be employed in the King's service, that there is no need of pressing to man the fleet." See "Animadversions on a pretended Account of Denmark."

616 Year Book of the Holland Society of New York, 1902, p. -4; 1897, p. 127.

ANNEKE PIETERS.

Anneke Pieters, from Holstein, widow of Jacques Kinnekom, was married November 22, 1652, in New Amsterdam, to Barent Jansen Bal, from Velthusysen in Benthem. Barent Bal's name is met with as early as 1640, when he was sponsor at a baptism.

On August 31, 1651, Remmert Jansen gave Barnt Jansen Bal and Hendrick Jansen lease of a bowery on the south side of Hans Hansen's brewery, called in Indian Rinnegackonck. See Calendar of Manuscripts, I., p. 55.

ELSJE PIETERS.

Elsje Pieters, from Holstein, is registered in the Church Record of the Dutch Reformed Church in New Netherland as Elpken Neven van Eckelvaer in Holstein. The transcriber, no doubt, had difficulty in reading the original. Elpken is a corruption for Elsje, Aeltie, or Heyltie. "Neven" represents an obstinate attempt to decipher Pieters or Peters. Eckelvaer is another corruption. Can it mean Eckernförde? "Elpken Nevens van Eckelvaer" was married, September 14, 1652, in New Amsterdam, to Albert Jansen. He was widower of Hilletje Willems. "Elpken" was widow of David Clement. At the baptism of a child of Jochem Kalder, February 9, 1653, Albert and his wife were sponsors. Her name is given in the records under that date as Heyltie Pieters.[617] Elsje is the name she is generally mentioned by in the Church Record.

Albert was a carpenter from Amsterdam. He was in New Netherland as early as 1642. On August 7, 1644, he is credited with 19½ day's wages at sixteen stivers a day for work done at the house of Domine Megapolensis in Albany.[618]

In 1643 he signed the resolution of the commonalty of the

---

617 New York Genealogical and Biographical Record, VI., p. 81. Ibid., V., p. 148.

618 Van Rensselaer Bowier Manuscripts, p. 830.

Manhattans; in 1654 he acted as sponsor at a baptism in New Amsterdam.[619]

He worked in 1653 for Harmen Smeeman, a Dane.[620]

He had property in New Amsterdam, in 1655, when he was taxed for fifteen florins.[621]   On February 28, 1658, he requested of the Court that, as he was about to build a small house and his lot was too little, an adjoining lot be granted him.   The Court granted him a lot next to that of Jannetje Bones, on condition of paying what it was valued at.[622]

He was doing carpenter work for a Mr. Stickely in 1658.   He seems also to have been tanning hides for upholstery.   In June Stickely brought suit against Albert for three hides.   Albert answered that he had made for Stickely two pillows and a bedstead, for which he was to have 500 pounds of tobacco.   The Court settled the dispute by ordering that Albert should pay Stickely what the hides weighed, in hides or beavers, on the condition that Stickely should give security to pay what he owed Albert.[623]

Albert and Aeltie had several children.

Albert Jansen was dead February 26, 1659, when guardians were appointed for his widow and the five surviving children, of whom four were girls, and one a boy.   The eldest child, Catryn, was born about 1651, perhaps her father was Aeltie's first husband. Gritie was baptized July 13, 1653; Elsje, July 8, 1654; Marritje, September 17, 1656; Jan, March 31, 1658.[624]

The fact that Jochem Kalder, his wife Magdalene Waele, and Annetje Jans were sponsors at the baptism of Albert and Aeltie's daughter, 1654, and that Albert and Aeltie (Heyltie Pieters) were present at the baptism of the daughters of Jochem Kalder, February 9, 1653, and September 17, 1656, shows that the two families were related, or had other ties in common, based on sympathy, nationality, or religion.[625]

---

619 New York Colonial Documents, I., p. 198.

620 The Records of New Amsterdam, I., p. 58.

621 Ibid., I., p. 371.

622 Ibid., II., p. 348.

623 Ibid., II., p. 406.

624 Year Book of the Holland Society of New York, 1900, p. 116.   Albert's wife is here called Aeltie.

625 Collections of the New York Genealogical and Biographical Society, II., pp. 33, 37, 43.

MARRITJE PIETERS.

Marritje Pieters was from Copenhagen. She was married, 1639, in New Amsterdam, to Jan Jacobsen of "Vrelandt," a brother of Cornelius Jacobsen van Vrelandt, alias Cornelius Jacobsen Stille. She seems to have been a relative of the famous Jonas Bronck or his wife.

The marriage contract between this Danish lady and her husband is the *earliest recorded instance of a marriage contract in New Netherland*. It is found in the New York Colonial Manuscripts, vol. I., page 163, and in New Jersey Archives, First Series, vol. xxii., page 20. The translation is by Mr. George R. Howell, at one time Archivist of New York. The contract bears the date of August 15, 1639, and reads thus:

"In the name of God, amen. Be it known unto all men that on the 15th of August in the year 1639, before me Cornelius van Tienhoven, Secretary residing in New Netherland on the behalf of the Incorporated West India Company, and the undersigned witnesses, appeared the worthy Jan Jacobsen fram Vrelant, future bridegroom, assisted by Marritje Peters from Copenhagen, his future bride, on the other part, and they the appearers declared that they had mutually resolved, engaged and agreed to enter together the holy state of matrimony, and that under the following nuptial contract, praying the Almighty God that his divine Majesty would be pleased to bless their future marriage and let it redound to his honor.

"First, in regard to the property which he, the bridegroom, shall leave behind, in case he come to die, whether movable or immovable, or such as may rightfully belong to him, it shall belong in free propriety to Marritje Pieters aforesaid, without any of Jan Jacobsen's blood relations having any claim thereto. On the other hand, if Marritje Pieters, the future bride, first happens to die, Jan Jacobsen shall, in like manner, own all her means and goods, whether movable or immovable, in free propriety, without his giving any account thereof to any of her blood relations. Provided always that he, the bridegroom, or she, the bride, aforesaid, whichever of them both come to live the longest, shall not possess the property longer than the day of his or her death, and then be partitioned and divided by the brothers or lawful heirs of him, the bridegroom, and Teuntje Jewriaens of [New] Amsterdam, or Jacob Bronc, her present husband, as heirs of Marritje Pieters aforesaid, each the just half.

"Thus done and executed in the presence of the undersigned witnesses in Fort Amsterdam, this day and year aforesaid.

"This is the + mark of
"Jan Jacobsen above named.

"This is the M mark of
"Maritje Peters above named.
"Claes van Elslant, witness.   Hermanus A. Booghardij, witness."

We know but little in regard to Maritje Pieters. It is probable that she was a guest at the parlor of the City Tavern, in New Amsterdam, on the night of March 15, 1644, where besides her husband, Dr. Hans Kiersted, Domine Bogardus, Nicholas Coorn, Gysbert Opdyck, and others were present with their wives, spending, as it seems, an agreeable evening together. But the entire gathering was put to flight by the brazen effrontery of Captain John Underhill.

M

Signature of Marritje Pieters.

"About an hour after supper there came in John Onderhil, with his lieutenant Baxter, and drummer, to whom . . . Philip Gerritsen [the owner of the parlor] said, 'Friends, I have invited these persons here, with their wives; I therefore request that you will betake yourselves to another room, where you can be furnished with wine for money.' They finally did so, after many words. Having been gone a short time, said Onderhil and his company, who had then been joined by Thomas Willet, invited some of our company, to take a drink with them, which was done. George Baxter, by Onderhil's orders, came and requested that Opdyke would come and join them,—which he refused. Thereupon he, Onderhil and his companions, broke to pieces, with drawn swords, the cans which hung on the shelf in the tavern; endeavoring by force, having drawn swords in their hands, to come into the room where the invited guests were. This was for a long time resisted by the landlady, with a leaden bolt, and by the landlord, by keeping the door shut; but finally John Onderhil and his associated, in spite of all opposition, came into the room, where he uttered many words. Captain Onderhil, holding his sword in hand,—the blade about a foot out of the scabbard,—said to the minister, as reported, whilst he grasped his sword: 'Clear out of here, for I shall strike at random!' In like manner, some English soldiers came immediately (as we presume, to his assistance), . . . Onderhil being then guilty, with his companions, of gross insolence."

Several officers and a guard from the fort were sent for. But this had no effect on the drunken English visitors. Underhill, when threatened that Governor Stuyvesant would be sent for, replied: "If the Director come here, t'is well. I had rather speak to a wise man than a fool." In order to prevent further mischief, the Dutch-Scandinavian crowd broke up. (Kiersted, Bogardus, Jacobsen had Scandinavian wives.)

Interesting as Marritje's marriage contract is, equally interesting is the Memorandum of the engagement of some farm laborers, including her brother-in-law, Cornelis Jacobsen of Mertensdyk, in 1632 (?) The Memorandum is in the handwriting of Kiliaen van Rensselaer:

[June 15, 1632?]

The following persons have been engaged as farm laborers for the term of four years commencing on their arrival on their farm in that country, on condition that they receive for the outgoing and return voyages a gratuity hereafter specified and on pain of all their monthly wages and effects if they leave their service [before the end] of their term, or if they obtain any furs of beavers, otters or like animals by trade, gift or exchange, which they have expressly agreed not to do; and in case they are asked by their farmer to do any other work besides farming, such as felling of trees or other work which they are able to do, they may not refuse it but must diligently and willingly do everything and also serve under such farmer as the patroon shall direct.

Hendrich frerixsen Van bunnick, 26 years old, shall receive 120 guilders a year and a pair of boots once in four years and as a gratuity for the passage 25 guilders.

Cornelis Jacopsen van Marttensdijck, 23 years old, shall receive 110 guilders and as a gratuity for the passage 25 guilders.

MEMORANDUM OF THE ENGAGEMENT OF FARM LABORERS, JUNE 15, 1682.

In handwriting of Killian van Rensselaer.

From Van Rensselaer Bowler Manuscripts, % of original size.

Cornelis thonissen van Meerkerc, 20 years old, shall receive
_{Can write a} 80 guilders and two pairs of boots, but if he behaves
_{little} well he shall receive the last year some increase and
as a gratuity 50 guilders.

_{as boy.} *Marcus Mensen van Cuijlenburch,* 17 years old, shall receive
40, 50, 60 and 70 guilders during the four years and as gratuity
18 guilders.
[Signed]

the mark of   the mark of

X   X

hendrick frerixsen   *Cornelis Jacopsen*

Cornis Thonis   the mark of

                                    X

                      Marcus Mensen

Gerrit de reus would like to have *Hendrick frerixsz, Cornelis thonisen* and *Marcus Mensen.*

Marritje's husband, it appears, was a brother of Secretary Cornelis Van Tienhoven, whose patronymic appeared in the name of Cornelis Jacobsen. Two brothers had the same name, according to J. H. Innes, "New Amsterdam and Its People," p. 313.

On August 15, 1639, Jonas Bronck leased some of his land for a period of six years to Marritje's husband and Cornelis Jacobsen Stille, her brother-in-law (not the secretary).

After the death of Bronck, his widow married Arent van Curler who sold the Bronck property to Jacob Jans Stoll, evidently a son of Marritje and her husband. The "Bronx" thus remained for some time in the hands of a person of Danish blood.

STYNTIE PIETERS.

Styntie Pieters, from Copenhagen, was the wife of Ensign Christian Nissen, to whom she was married February 4, 1657, in New Amsterdam. She and her husband were sponsors for several children in New Amsterdam. About 1660 they removed to Esopus, where Nissen was appointed commander of the garrison. (See article "Christian Nissen." Part II.)

CHRISTIAN PIETERSEN.

Christian Pietersen, from Husum, was in New Amsterdam as early as 1657, when he, on October 28, married Tryntie Cornelis, from Durgerdam in the northern part of Holland.[626] She was the daughter of Adriantje Walich or Walings and Cornelis Jansen Shubber. After the death of her father, her mother was married, in 1650, to Dirck Theunissen, a Norwegian. (See the article Dirck Theunissen. Part I.)

HUSUM, ABOUT THE CLOSE OF THE SIXTEENTH CENTURY.
From Braunius: Theatrum urbium, iv.

Christian and Tryntie had several children: Pieter, who was baptized, November 24, 1658, the sponsors being the Dane, Christian Nissen, and Marritje Cornelis; Marie, baptized, December 22, 1660; Cornelis, January 8, 1662; Paulus, June 22, 1664; Jacob, October 21, 1668.

Tryntie and her mother joined the Dutch Reformed Church between 1649 and 1660. Christian did not join it.

From the court records we obtain the information that Pietersen sued Jacob Eldersen, a Dane, August 28, 1658, for work

---

626 New York Genealogical and Biographical Report, VI., p. 86.

done in the latter's brewery. He demanded fl. 12:10 for "three days and two nights and one-fourth of a day's work earned in Jacob 'Wolfersen's' brewery." After the Court had heard both parties, Eldersen was ordered to pay Christian Pietersen (here called Barents) the demanded sum. Eldersen was slow in settling his accounts, and on September 10, 1658, Pietersen again brought the matter before the Court, whereupon the bailiff was instructed to collect the money from Eldersen.[627]

On November 22, 1658, Pietersen received the small Burgher Right, took the Burgher oath and signed an obligation to pay the Treasurer 20 gl. in beavers, within eight days.[628]

On August 31, 1660, Pietersen was made defendant in an action brought against him by Jan Janzen van Breestede. The latter demanded fl. 44 for rent due in May according to a lease which he exhibited in court. Pietersen replied that he had rented a house with a number of trees standing in the garden. But one tree had been taken from the garden, from which "he could have made money to the extent of three beavers." The court referred the matter to Pieter Cornelissen van der Veen and Isaac Grevenrat to decide the question between the parties and if possible reconcile them, "if not, to report to the Court." [629]

On October 4, 1661, Gerrit Hendricksen, of Hardewyk, deeded to Christian Pietersen "a lot south of the Marckvelt Steegh (Marketfield Street); bounded east by the house and lot of Nicholas Boot; south, by lot of Jacob Teunissen Kay; west, by the house and lot of Frerick Aarsen; and north, by the steegh aforesaid. On the north and south sides, 20 feet 3 inches; east side, 48 feet; west side, 47 feet 6 inches. On the same date Pietersen deeded this property to Jacob Leendersen Van der Grist (Valentine, Manual of . . . the city of New York, 1865, p. 684 f.).

On April 25, 1662, Nicolaas Meyer, a well-to-do citizen of New Amsterdam, formerly a resident of Hamburg, brought suit against Pietersen, demanding of him the balance of a note and book debt, amounting to the sum of 104 guilders and four stivers.

627 The Records of New Amsterdam, II., p. 428; III., p. 7.
628 Ibid., VII., p. 200.
629 Ibid., III., p. 196.

The defendant said that Meyer must deduct eighteen guilders for "a canoe and a half " of hewn stones, which he delivered him. Meyer acknowledged that he had received the stones, but said that there were but three carts full. The Court ordered Pietersen to pay Meyer the 104 guilders.

The case was again before the court May 23. Meyer exhibited the judgment which he had obtained against Pietersen and requested "fulfillment thereof, whereupon the Court ordered Pietersen to satisfy and pay Meyer the judgment . . . on pain of execution."[630]

On June 19, 1663, Isaack Grevenraat appeared in court against Pietersen. But the latter was on "public service," as his wife, who appeared for him, said. She requested time until the fair. The court ordered Pietersen to appear on the next court day. As Pietersen did not appear on that day, July 3, Grevenrat demanded that the attachment issued against him be declared valid. The Court concurred in the demand.[631]

The matter remained unsettled as late as February 14, 1665. For under this date the court minutes read as follows: " . . . Schout Allard Anthony, arrestant and pltf. vs. Christiaen Pietrs, arrested and deft. Pltf. says, it appears by Tonneman's book, that the defendant has violated an attachment prosecuted on the 2d. July 1663, by Isaack Grevenraat; demanding in consequence from the defendant the fine of sixty guilders with costs. Defendant says, as it was in the Indian war he was allowed by Burgomasters to go home on condition of appearing at the next court day, and in the meanwhile two Christians living in the village with him were killed by the Indians. Isaack Grevenraat also entering, states that the defendant was allowed to go away. The Officer replying says the deft. has not fulfilled the promise of his wife to appear on the Court day; and therefore the attachment is prosecuted and declared valid. Burgomasters and Schepens condemn the deft. to pay to the Officer the sixty guilders fine," unless he can prove, that he had the Burgomaster's consent to go.[632]

Pietersen was interested, it would appear, in the welfare and

---

630 Ibid., IV., pp. 65, 85.
681 Ibid., IV., pp. 259, 273.
632 Ibid., V., p. 186.

protection of wronged youth, though his effort, indicative of this, in 1671, was not crowned with success.

In May 1671 Abel Hardenbrook brought suit against Jan Roelofzen, complaining that Roelofzen "kept his runaway boy fourteen days." He demanded satisfaction for this. Roelofzen denied that he had detained the boy, but said he had given him lodgings for about eight days; after he had understood that the boy belonged to Hardenbrook he "brought the same himself to him." Christiaen Pietersen and Jochem Beeckman complained that Hardenbrook beat and treated the boy in such a way that he could not possibly live longer with him. The court thereupon discharged Roelofzen from arrest and ordered that the boy should remain with his friends until next court day, when the complaint on both sides, relative to the boy, should be further heard and decided.[633]

On the next court day Pietersen and Beeckman appeared as witnesses for the boy, whose name was Hendrick van der Borgh. Hardenbrook stated that he had hired the boy for the term of four years to learn the shoemaker's handicraft and he had now for divers reasons run away. The witnesses testified that Hardenbrook did not provide proper board for the boy, abused him, beat him, kicked him, so it was impossible for the boy to stay any longer with him. The Court after having heard the testimony, ordered that the parties on both sides should be released from each other, and that the boy should pay Hardenbrook "for board etc. to date hereof the sum of one hundred guilders zewant and settle the costs incurred herein . . .[634]

In the same year Assur Levy brought suit against Pietersen. But it appears that the latter was twice in default. The records do not state what the nature of the case was.[635] It was perhaps regarding commercial transactions. We have, it would seem, a similar case under an earlier date, to wit:

On May 24, 1663 "Hendrick Jans Spieringh of "Gemoenepa" made a declaration at the request of Jurian Hanel regarding commercial transactions with Christian Pietersen and a conversation regarding the same with Hans Dietrich. Witness Hendrick Louwersen Van der Spiegel."[636]

633 Ibid., VI., p. 284f.
634 Ibid., VI., p. 288.
635 Ibid., VII., pp. 302, 851.
636 Year Book of the Holland Society of New York, 1900, p. 156.

In 1662 Christian Pietersen seems to have lived for some time in Bergen, New Jersey. For in December, that year, he and other inhabitants of Bergen and Comunipaw petitioned the government to be excused from fencing in their land, as timber was scarce and the fence would therefore be very expensive.[637]

As late as 1675 we find him a settler in Esopus.[638]
We have two petitions from him at about this time, which show that he had outstanding accounts and that he again was, as his wife had testified in 1663, "on public service."

In 1674 he petitioned the Commandant and Court of Willemstadt (the new name of Albany) against Collector Kregier what Messrs. Lovlace and Lavall owed him. He was referred to the "Commissioners thereunto appointed to whom it belongs to examine the justice of his claim." He was at the same time ordered to pay the excise which he owed.[639]

Pietersen was more successful in his next petition, the nature of which we ascertain from the following action taken on it:

"On the petition of Christian Pietersen it is allowed that the little freight which will be earned in coming down and going back shall not be paid to the public treasury, but to him individually, inasmuch as he was pressed by the Commandant and Court of Willemstadt to bring down the Committees and French prisoners.[640]

Pietersen was listed in 1674 as possessing, in New Amsterdam, property, rated as "third class," on the present Stone Street, between Whitehall and Broad St. (Year Book of the Holland Society of New York, 1896) He died before 1686.

JAN PIETERSEN.

Jan Pietersen, a woodsawyer, from Husum, was in New Amsterdam about 1639. Under date of March 3, 1639, we have an indenture of Thomas Wesson to serve Jan Pietersen from Husum

637 New York Colonial Documents, XIII., p. 234.
638 Year Book of the Holland Society of New York, 1897, p. 127.
639 New York Colonial Documents, II., p. 687.
640 Ibid., II., p. 708.

for three years. Under the date of June 20, 1640, we find a receipt of Jan Pietersen of Husum for three mares and three milk cows which he hired from the West India Company.[641]

It seems that he married twice. The name of his first wife was Elsje. By her he had a daughter Neeltjen, who was baptized September 9, 1640; a son, Jan, baptized June 28, 1643; again a daughter, Annetje, baptized January 28, 1646.

After the death of his first wife, it would seem that he, on May 15, 1652, married Grietje Jans, of Groeningen.[642] By her he had a daughter Elsje, who was baptized, July 13, 1653.

On March 28, 1658, Nicasius de Silla sold to "Jan Pietersen, woodsawyer from Holstein a lot in the Sheep Valley, length on the east side seven running feet; on north eighty-nine, on west side, on the Prince Graght, twenty-nine, and on the south side ninety-four running feet." This would be on the east side of the present Broad Street, south of Exchange Place, says D. T. Valentine (1861).[643]

In 1659 Pietersen bought land of Symon Leen.[644]

On June 1 "Jan Pietersen Van Holstein conveyed to Thomas Wandel "a house and lot east of the Prince Graght; bounded north by house and lot of Fiscal De Sille; east by lot of said De Sille; south, by house and lot of Hermen Van Hoboocken; west, by the said Graght. On the east, 7 feet; on the north, 89; on the west, 29; on the south, 94." (Valentine, Manual of the . . . City of New York 1864, p. 664.)

Signature of Jan Pietersen van Holstein, 1659.

On August 22, 1659, he appeared before the Council stating that he had an account against the city for four guilders, "for riding timber." He was directed to take a note from the president and bring it to the treasurer.[645]

---

641 Calendar of Historical Manuscripts, I. The Records of New Amsterdam, 1658-1674, III., p. 88.

642 New York Genealogical and Biographical Record, VI., p. 81. Cfr. dates of December 18, 1672, May 16, 1678, February 8, 1680, in the Record of Baptisms of the Dutch Reformed Church in New Amsterdam.

643 D. T. Valentine, Manual of . . . the City of New York, 1861, p. 598.

644 The Records of New Amsterdam, 1658-1674, III., p. 88.

645 Ibid., VII., p. 231.

In 1661 Arent Cornelis Vogel brought suit against him. But as they both had accounts against each other, they requested arbitrators. The arbitrators, however, were not able to settle it that year, and in 1662 Vogel brought new proceedings against Pietersen for four guilders, eight stivers and eight pence — "and moreover a seven years cow and its increase." Pietersen's account against Vogel amounted to fl. 165,17:8 in beavers. He requested that the case might be finally disposed of by arbitrators under proper submission. The court appointed arbitrators to decide the case, and, if possible, to reconcile the parties.[646]

JAN PIETERSEN.

Jan Pietersen, from Dithmarschen, was a soldier whose name is on the list of passengers that sailed from Holland to New Amsterdam in "de Bonte Koe", April 15, 1660.[647]

MARRITJE PIETERSEN.

Marritje Pietersen, from Copenhagen, was married on July 28, 1641, in New Amsterdam, to Albert Pietersen of Hamburg, commonly known as Albert the Trumpeter, being a trumpeter in the service of the West India Company.[648]

On February 22, 1649, he bought, in New Amsterdam, a lot of Jan Corn(elis) van Hoorn. It was situate on the West side of the Graft between the lot of Frederick Lubbertsen and Conrate Ten Eyck: "breadth in front of the road or east 2½ rods and ½ a foot; in the rear on the west, 3 rods. Depth on the north, 7 rods, 2 feet; on the south, 7 rods less 2 feet." Albert built a house upon this lot and sold both to Reynhout Rynehoutsen, January 19, 1656.[649]

---

646 Ibid., IV., p. 168f.
647 Year Book of the Holland Society of New York, 1902, p. 14.
648 New York Genealogical and Biographical Record, VI., p. 88.
649 D. T. Valentine, Manual of the . . . City of New York, 1861, p. 582.

On July 1, 1652, he bought a lot on the north side of Prince Street, and about eighty-five feet east of the present Broad Street. Here, too, he built a house.[650]

In 1654 he asked for and obtained permission to sell beer and wine by small measure. It would appear that he also sold fish and perhaps other merchandise, like butter or pork.[651]

Marritje was several times in court. On November 9, 1654, she sued Maria de Truwe, demanding payment of fl. 3.11 for fish sold to her. Maria defended herself by saying that she had "sent the money by the servant, and it fell into the ditch." She had no more money for the time being, but promised payment at the earliest opportunity. Marritje was satisfied with this explanation, and the two women left the city hall reconciled.

Marritje was often obliged to visit the court in order to give her testimony in regard to the conduct of visitors who came to her husband's place "for beer and wine by small measure" or for merchandise.

She appeared in court on September 21, 1660, testifying in behalf of Jan Rutgersen, who was prosecuted for having struck the wife of Frerick Aarsen. The defendant "denied it, bringing with him Merritje Pieters, Albert Trumpeter's wife, as witness, who declares, that she did not see him strike Frerick Aarsen's wife." Grietje Pieters, Aarsen's wife, claimed, however, that Rutgersen had struck her, and "if she had not prevented it, he would have beaten in her brains." She now related the causes which gave rise to it. Marritje's testimony did not save Rutgersen, nor did Grietje Pieters, the wife of Aarsen, gain anything by using strong language. Rutgersen was fined six guilders; Grietje Pieters, three guilders "for her evil speaking."[652]

A week later Marritje appeared in court again, and this time her testimony saved her husband from a fine for selling fish on a Sunday morning.

The court records give this information concerning her testimony:

"[Tuesday, 28 September] . . . Schout Pieter Tonneman, pltf. vs. Albert Trompetter, deft. Pltf. says, that deft. sold fish on Sun-

650 J. H. Innes, New Amsterdam and Its People, p. 150.
651 The Records of New Amsterdam, I., pp. 261, 269.
652 Ibid., III., p. 215.

day morning, and that Resolveert Waldron has subjected him to the fine. Resolveert Waldron appearing in court declares he fined him because he sold fish on Sunday morning. Deft.'s wife appears in Court, says it occurred before the ringing of the bell." The Court dismissed the Officer's suit as the occurence took place before the preaching.[653]

Of other lawsuits which directly concerned Marritje's husband, we shall mention the following.

On November 1, 1660, "Johannes Nevius, rising in the court room of New Amsterdam prosecuted an arrest made on a tub of butter in the possession of Albert Trumpeter belonging to Jan Arcet alias Jan Coopal; having a claim thereon." The court declared the arrest valid.[654]

On September 16, 1664, Albert Trumpeter prosecuted "an attachment made on a hog." The Court also declared this attachment valid.[655]

On September 23, 1664, Marritje's husband prosecuted Daniel Tourner for taking a hog from Barent Island. Tourner, who declared he "thought it was his own, was ordered by the Court to make good the removed hog to Albert Trumpeter."[656]

On October 11, 1664, Marritje appeared in court protesting against a fine that had been imposed upon her husband. We know very little about the particulars. From the minutes we infer that Albert had been engaged in a brawl:

"Schout Pieter Tonneman, pltf. vs. Albert Trumpetter, deft. Pltf. demands from deft. pursuant to award of arbitrators, the sum of thirty guilders for a fine imposed. Deft.'s wife appearing says, she does not know for what the fine is to be given, as her husband was struck; admits to have demanded arbitrators to settle the matter in order to prevent further mischief, but is not content with

653 Ibid., III., p. 218.
654 Ibid., III., p. 243.
655 Ibid., V., p. 114.
656 Ibid., V., p. 117.

the award. The W. Court decree, as deft. is not content with the award of arbitrators, that the Officer shall enter his case anew and for this purpose summon the deft. again."[657]

Marritje and Albert had a child, Griet, who was baptized on May 24, 1649. They lived, in 1674, on the present William Street, between Hanover Square and Wall Street, then known as the Smith street. In 1679 their house was assessed at 4s.

In 1673, he sold the lot he had bought in 1652.

The deed of sale (Collections of the New York Historical Society for . . . 1913, v. XLVI., pp. 16f.) reads:

"Appeared before me Nicholas Bayard, Secretary of the City of New Orange the worthy Albert Pietersz Trompetter, burgher and inhabitant of this City, who in the presence of the subscribed Messrs. Schepens (by virtue of certain deed of Mr. Petrus Stuyvesant, dated July 1, 1652 & confirmation of the same by Col. Richard Nicolls under date of Feb. 14, 1667) declared to cede, transfer and convey in a right true and free ownership to and in behalf of Mr. Gabriel Minvielle, Merchant within this City, a certain his house & lot with everything on and in the same fixed to the earth and rights as the said Albert Pietersz has possessed and owned the same, as the said house and lot is fenced in, erected and confined, standing and situated within this city in the Sheep Meadow, now named the Prince's Street broad on the South side of the Street three Rods, one foot in the rear broad on the North side two rods and seven feet; long on the East side Nine rods seven feet and on the West side ten rods; all free and unencumbered without any charge neither resting on nor emanating from the same, excepting the Lord's right, For which said house and lot said Albert Trompetter acknowledged and declared to be well and thankfully satisfied and paid. Consequently said Albert Trompetter in behalf of the said Gabriel Minvielle declares to cede and convey all property right, claims and pretensions he has possessed in said house and lot, promising not to proceed nor cause to be proceeded against the same either in law or otherwise, pledging his person and goods, real and personal none excepted. In testimony of the truth the present has been subscribed to by grantor besides the Messrs.

657 Ibid., V., p. 184.

Schepens at New Orange on the island Manhatans, September 30, 1673. Guilain Verplanck.

"This is
made by
Pietersz
[alias]
himself.

the mark
Albert
Swart
Trompetter

Signature of Albert Pietersen, husband of Marritje Pietersen.

"In my presence
      "Epraim Herman
            "Clerk."

MICHEL PLES.

Michel Ples, from Holstein, came to New Netherland in 1658. He sailed on the ship "de Bruynvis", which left Holland on June 19, 1658. He was accompanied by his wife and two children, one of whom was four years old, the other an infant.[658]

CLAES POUWELSEN.

Claes Pouwelsen a mason from Dithmarschen, came to New Netherland in "de vergulde Otter", which sailed December 22, 1657.[659] He must not be taken for Claes Poulisen, who was taxed in New Netherland in 1655. It is possible that Claes Pouwelsen returned to Dithmarschen, and thence came a second time to New Netherland in the ship "de Pumerlander," which sailed October 12, 1662.[660] A Clause Pouwelsen took the oath of allegiance in 1664, when the English conquered New Netherland.

---

658 Year Book of the Holland Society of New York, 1902, p. 7.
659 Ibid., p. 6.
660 Ibid., 1902.

JURIAEN POUWELSEN.

Juriaen Pouwelsen was from Schleswig, Denmark. He came over by "den Houttuyn," which sailed from Texel, in June, 1642, arriving at New Amsterdam on August 4, 1642. He began to serve in the colony of Rensselaerswyck August 13, in the same year. He must have been quite young at the time, as he is referred to as Jeuriaen Poulisz Jongen (the boy). In July, 1644, he was a servant of a Michiel Jansz. He does not appear in the accounts of the colony of Rensselaerswyck after 1644.[661]

JONAS RANZOW.

Jonas Ranzow (Ranzo, Ranson, Rantson) ,from Holstein, was in New Netherland as early as 1659 or before. On April 12, in that year, he was sponsor, in New Amsterdam, at the baptism of Jannetje, a child of Peter Van Doren and "annetje Ranken" (perhaps a sister of Ranzow).[662]

In 1661 he was Corporal in the garrison on the Esopus. He paid in the same year excise on beer and wine.[663]

In 1663 he was an important member of the council of war in Kingston (Esopus).[664]

On September 21, 1664, he married in New Amsterdam Catharyntie Hendricks, daughter of Hendrick Hendricksen, from Erlangen, in Germany.[665]

Under date of September 30, in the same year, Nicholas Gosten brought suit against Ranzow. The charges are not specified in the minutes of the court. Ranzow was in default.[666]

In December Ranzow and his wife, and her parents were permitted, on their own request to leave New York for Europe.

---

661 Van Rensselaer Bowier Manuscripts, p. 828.
662 Collections of the New York Genealogical and Biographical Society, II., p. 52.
663 Year Book of the Holland Society of New York, 1897, p. 128. New York Colonial Documents, XIII., pp. 153, 201, 212.
664 Ibid., IV., p. 88.
665 New York Genealogical and Biographical Record, VI., p. 146.
666 The Records of New Amsterdam, V., p. 121.

Evidently the change in government caused many to return to Europe.

We append a copy of the pass which the Governor gave them.

"Whereas the Bearer hereof Hendrick Hendrickse van Erlanger hath requested of me Liberty to Transport himself, wife and Sonn in Law Jonas Ranzo, and his wife, unto Holland, these are therefore in his Ma*ties* name to require all Persons to permit and suffer the persons above said . . . to pass in the Ship Unity . . . unto any Port or Harbor of Holland.[667]

"Manhatans 7th day of Dec. 1664.

"'Richard Nicolls.'

HANS RASMUSSEN.

Hans Rasmussen, judging from the name, was a Scandinavian, probably a Dane. He served as a soldier in New Netherland, and the records state that in the year 1662 he was paid for a certain term of service Fl. 124. 15. 8.[668]

MATHYS ROELOFS.

Mathys Roelofs, from Denmark, arrived at New Amsterdam, with wife and child, in 1659. He sailed with the ship "de Trouw," which left Holland for New Netherland February 12, 1659. His child was at that time three years of age.[669]

In August, 1659, he acquired land in Esopus. At about the same time he joined with others in petitioning the authorities in New Amsterdam for the appointment of Rev. Bloem as a pastor in Esopus.[670] Two months later he and some other settlers in Esopus signed a letter addressed to Director Stuyvesant, stating

667 Colonial Records of General Entries, VI., 1664-65. In University of the State of New York State Library Report, 1898.

668 New York Colonial Documents, II., p. 182.

669 Year Book of the Holland Society of New York, 1902, p. 8.

670 New York Colonial Documents, XIII., p. 103.

that they were besieged by Indians at the Fort. He signed with mark.

We next find him designated in the muster roll as "Constable in the Netherland service."[671]

In May, 1661, he obtained a lot in Esopus.[672]

From the Baptismal Registers of the old Dutch Reformed Church of Kingston we learn that the name of Roelof's wife was Aeltje Sybrants, and that his son Sybrant was baptized in 1661 (the date is torn out of the Register). Among the sponsors at this baptism were three Danes, Christian Nyssen, Jan Pietersen, Jonas Ransou (Ranzow).[673]

Under date of June 7, 1663, an entry states that "two little boys of Mathys Roelofs were killed by Indians at Wiltwyck.[674] These boys must have been the infant Sybrant, and his brother who came over, with his parents, in 1659.

In April, 1664, Mathys Roelofs himself followed his little sons in death, being killed by Wapping savages.[675] His wife survived him.

JAN PIETERSEN SLOT.

Jan Pietersen Slot, the ancestor of the Slottes or Sloats of Orange County, New York, came over in 1650 from Holstein. He was accompanied by his two sons Johan and Pieter, who had been born in Amsterdam. He settled at Harlem, where he became prominent. He was a carpenter by trade. From 1660 to 1665 he served as magistrate. In 1662 he sold a house and lot to Dirck

---

671 Ibid., XIII., p. 119.
672 Ibid , XIII., p. 195.
673 R. R. Hoes, Baptismal and Marriage Registers of the old Dutch Church of Kingston, p. 2.
674 New York Colonial Documents, XIII., p. 246.
675 Ibid., XIII., p. 371.

Jansen, the Cooper. In 1665 he bought land at the Bowery in New Amsterdam. He acquired land in 1667 also. At about this time he moved to New Amsterdam, where he resided till 1686. He lived for a while in Wall Street. He died in 1703.[676]

His wife, Claertje Dominicus was a member (1686) of the Dutch Reformed Church in New Amsterdam.

JOHAN JANSEN SLOT.

Johan Jansen Slot came over with his father, Jan Pietersen Slot and his brother Pieter Jansen Slot, in 1650. His father was from Holstein, who before coming to New Netherland resided a while in Amsterdam, where his two sons were born.

On April 28, 1672, Johan married, in New Amsterdam, Judith Elswarts.[677] He made his residence in New Amsterdam. Some of his children removed to Hackensack. On November 10, 1676, he was assessed in the city of New York 12s. 6d. In February, 1677, he had a credit, on the books of the city of New York, of f70 in wampum.*

PIETER JANSEN SLOT.

Pieter Jansen Slot, a son of Jan Pietersen Slot, a Dane, came over with his father in 1650. He was born in Amsterdam, to which his father had immigrated.

On May 14, 1657, he bought fifty acres of land at Communipaw in Bergen County, New Jersey, on which he was located in 1665.

On August 22, he was sponsor for Jannetje, daughter of Francois Leerhie and Jannetje Hillebrants.

676 Tennis G. Bergen, Register of Early Settlers of Kings County, p. 264. J. Riker, Harlem, Its Origin and Early Annals, p. 217. Cornelius B. Harvey, Genealogical History of Hudson and Bergen Counties, pp. 19, 182.

677 Collections of the New York Genealogical and Biographical Society, I., p. 36.

* Minutes of the Common Council of the City of New York, I., pp. 32, 44.

On February 2, 1663, he married Maritie Jacobs Van Hoorn, or Winkle, of Bergen.[678]   He became a member of the Dutch Church.

In regard to the marriage festivities of Slot, Mr. J. Riker relates the following:

"It happened that Pieter Jansen Slot, son of the ex-schepen, was to wed a fair damsel of Ahasimus,* by name Marritie Van Winckel. The young roysters of the village hearing, on Friday, February 2d. 1663, that the bans had that day been registered, were jubilant over the news, and set to work,—it was an ancient rustic custom of fatherland, — to honor the happy Pieter by planting a May-tree before his door. Now some workmen in the employ of Mr. Muyden and others, in for ruder sport, not only raised 'a horrible noise in the village by shouting, blowing horns, etc., while others were asleep,' but proceeded to deck the May-tree with ragged stockings; at which, when discovered by Pieter, he was very wroth, taking it a 'a mockery and insult.' He at once cut the tree down, but the young men brought another to take its place; when, as it lay before the house, along came Muyden's men and hewed it in pieces. Not to be baffled, the young folk the same night procured and raised a third tree, which, however, shared the same fate.

"On Sunday morning, February 4th, Jan Pietersen, at whose house Pieter was staying and all this happened, made his complaint to Montagne, the schout; the masters also informing him that their men were plotting other mischief, but that they had no power to prevent it. The schout, now going thither, ordered the rioters to disperse; but they only defied him, and even threatened him with their guns and axes. Only more enraged, they gave the Sabbath to cutting down and burning the palisades around Jacques Cresson's barn. Next morning Jacob Elderts, who had lately bought a lot on Van Keulen's Hool, was engaged bringing thatch from Bronck's meadow. Before he had spoken "a single word" they caught and beat him, also wounding him on the head. In vain 'Meester Willem' who witnessed the assault, commanded them to desist. Perhaps it was to pay off Elderts for the death of their

678 Collections of the New York Genealogical and Biographical Society, I., p. 28.
   * New Jersey.

countryman Bruyn Barents, a cooper, five years before; perhaps not.

"The Schout, seeing that the rioters heeded not his authority, and apprehending further trouble, hastened the same day, to inform the Director, who with the Council, referred the matter to the Attorney-General to take further information about it."[679]

In 1671, Pieter Jansen sold the Bergen lands and removed to New Amsterdam, remaining there until 1677, when he removed to Esopus and followed his trade as a builder.

In 1673, after the Dutch regained possession of New Netherland, he requested of the magistrates of New Orange (= New Amsterdam) a lot.[680]

Pieter Jansen Slot had five children: John, born in 1665; Jacobus, 1669; Tryntie, 1671; Aeltie, 1678; Jonas, 1681. The descendants of these are thickly scattered over Rockland County, New York, and Bergen County, New Jersey.[681]

Pieter died in 1688. In 1692 his widow was married to Jean de Mareets.[682]

HERMAN SMEEMAN.

Herman Smeeman, from Dithmarschen, was in New Amsterdam as early as 1645 or before. On December 4, of that year, he married, in this city, Elisabeth Everts, the widow of Barent Dircksen.

On April 2, 1647, he obtained a patent of 23 morgens, 480 rods of land on the East river, "north of the West India Company's great bouwerey."[683]

On May 4, 1653, Michael Jansen conveyed to Smeeman "25 morgens of land with the house and all that is thereon." In the

---

679 J. Riker, Harlem, Its Origin and Early Annals, p. 196.
680 New York Colonial Documents, II., p. 631.
681 Harvey, Genealogical History of Hudson and Bergen Counties, p. 182.
682 Collections of the New York Genealogical and Biographical Society, I., p. 71.
683 Calendar of Historical Manuscripts, I., p. 874.

same year Smeeman leased 25 morgens, belonging to Olof Stevensen Cortland, at 38 guilders in annual rent.[684]

From the court records we glean the following in regard to Herman Smeeman. In February, 1653, he was sued by Sybout Clousen, who demanded the payment of six beavers, earned from Volckert Evertsen deceased, whose estate had gone into the hands of Smeeman, as heir. Evertsen seems to have been a relative of Smeeman's wife. Smeeman denied the debt on the ground that it had not been mentioned in former accounts or been talked of; and he demanded of Clousen a payment of thirteen beavers, according to judgment of the Court on October 7, 1652. The Court decided the case in favor of Smeeman. On the next court day Clousen brought his account books into court, and Smeeman now acknowledged that he had not paid for the coffin for the deceased. The Court, however, ordered that Clousen should swear to his accounts. If he could not swear to them, his demand was to be refused. Later Clousen swore to the truth of the statement, and Smeeman was condemned to pay for the coffin.[685]

On May 11, 1654, Smeeman petitioned the city council that he might retail wine and beer to the traveler, out of the city on his own farm, by paying the usual excise or the sum the Council and he could agree on. But the Council declared: "the petitioner can not have his prayer granted for sufficient reasons."[686]

On October 23, 1656, Jan Barentsen sued Smeeman for the sum of fl. 65.10. Smeeman acknowledged the debt and offered to pay, but said that Barentsen had "arrested his pease in the straw and therefore cannot thrash them to make money and pay the defendant." The court decided, after having heard both parties, that Smeeman should have "eight days from this date" to pay the defendant. But the "arrest" was declared invalid "as the defendant is a burgher here."[687]

On January 21, 1658, Michael Jansen brought suit against Smeeman. He demanded payment of the price of his bowery, "about the sum of fl. 900 in good pay, which one trader can pass

684 Ibid., I., p. 378.
685 The Records of New Amsterdam, 1653-1674, I., pp. 50, 52, 58.
686 Ibid., I., p. 197.
687 Ibid., II., p. 196.

off the other." Smeeman admitted the debt, and requested that the bowery be sold in order that Jansen might get his pay, as the bowery was mortgaged. The Court, however, ordered Smeeman to pay Jansen the sum demanded within one month's time.[688]

In 1654, Smeeman is mentioned as an administrator of some property, and in 1656 as guardian for six minor children of Aryantie Curn, widow of Cornelis Claesen Swits.[689]

Harmen Smeeman was one of the signers of the Lutherans' petition (165 f.), asking that the Lutheran pastor Goetwater might be permitted to stay in New Netherland, instead of being deported as the government had unjustly ordered.[690]

In 1661, Smeeman went to live in Bergen, New Jersey. Bergen obtained, on September 15, 1661, a patent of incorporation. It was called Bergen, after the town of that name in North Holland. Michael Jansen, Herman Smeeman, Casper Steinmets, and Tielman van Neck were the first magistrates of earliest court of justice erected within the limits of the present state of New Jersey.

In 1661 Smeeman and the three other magistrates of Bergen petitioned the Director-General and Council "that they may have a God-fearing man and preacher, to be an example to, and teach the fear of God in, the community of Bergen and its jurisdiction." They had passed a list for voluntary subscriptions towards paying the salary of a minister. Twenty-seven persons had voluntarily subscribed fl. 417, which sum would be the approximate annual salary of the minister. Smeeman himself subscribed fl. 25.[691]

Smeeman often acted as sponsor at baptisms in New Amsterdam.

On April 7, 1647, he was sponsor at the baptism of Aeltie, child of Hendrick Van Duisberg; July 4, 1649, at the baptism of Geertie, child of Cosyn Gerritsen; October 23, 1650, at the baptism of Christian, child of Claes Martensen; February 18, 1657, at the baptism of Christian, a child of Christiaen Barentsen and Jannetje

---

688 Ibid., II., p. 307.
689 Year Book of the Holland Society of New York. 1900, pp. 173. 112.
690 See reference 42.
691 New York Colonial Documents, XIII., p. 233.

NORTHEAST AND SOUTHEAST CORNERS OF BROAD STREET AND EXCHANGE PLACE, NEW YORK CITY, AT THE CLOSE OF THE SEVENTEENTH CENTURY.
From Valentin's History of New York.

Jans; Dec. 29, 1661, at the baptism of Marritie, child of Jan Lubbertsen; May 24, 1662, at the baptism of Johannes, child of Adriaen Hendrickszen and Gritie Warnarts; August 5, 1663, at the baptism of Caspar, child of Caspar Steenmuts; Dec. 22, 1676, at the baptism of Judith, child of Daniel Waldron and Sara Rutgers; October 11, 1676, at the baptism of Marritie, child of Hendrick Gerritszen and Marie Waldron; July 16, 1679, at the baptism of Annetje, child of Jan de Lamontagne and Annetje Josephs.[692]

After the death of his first wife, Smeeman married, on December 1, 1668, Anneke Daniels, the widow of Joseph Waldron. She was a member of the Reformed Church in New Amsterdam, in 1660. After the death of Smeeman, she was married, 1682, to Conraetd ten Eyck. She is sometimes called Annetje Dama.[693]

In 1674 Smeeman was listed in New Amsterdam as possessing property on the present east side of Broadway, between Beaver and Wall St., then known as a part of the Markfield and Broadway. His property was classed as "third class" and rated at $1000. (Year Book of the Holland Society of New York, 1896.) In 1677 this house was taxed 6s.

ROELOF SWENSBURG.

Roelof Swensburg appears to have been in New Amsterdam as early as 1661. On February 19, 1661, his widow, Styntie Klinckenborg, from Aachen, was married to Jan Doske, from Tongeren, a soldier. As the name indicates (Swensburg = Svendborg) Roelof Swensburg was a Dane.[694]

---

692 Collections of the New York Genealogical and Biographical Society, II.
693 Ibid., I., pp. 38, 51.
694 Collections of the New York Genealogical and Biographical Society, I., p. 27.

AELTIE SYBRANTSEN.

Aeltie Sybrantsen, the wife of Mathys Roelofs, from Denmark, came to New Netherland in 1659 by the ship "de Trouw". She was accompanied by her husband and her child, three years of age. It is probable that she was Danish, not Dutch. See article "Mathys Roelofs." Part II.

PIETER TEUNIS.

Pieter Teunis, from Flensborg, was among the soldiers listed to sail from Holland to New Netherland in the ship "de Otter," sailing April 27, 1660.[695]

ANDRIES THOMASEN.

Andries Thomasen, of Jutland, was in New Netherland about 1659. All we know about him is, that he fled from Fort Amstel to Maryland, in 1659, and that Vice-Director Aldrich wrote to Governor Fendall of Maryland, on June 25, of the same year, that Andries Thomase, of Jutland, Denmark, a soldier "has deserted and is skulking within your Honor's jurisdiction." He requested that he be sent back.[696]

JURIAEN TOMASSEN.

Juriaen Tomassen, from Ribe, arrived at New Amsterdam, by the ship "de Bonte Koe," which sailed from Europe on April 16, 1663. About ninety persons were on board on this voyage, one of whom was Jan Laurens, also from Ribe.[697]

---

695 Year Book of the Holland Society of New York, 1902, p. 15.

696 New York Colonial Documents, II., p. 64.

697 Year Book of the Holland Society of New York, 1902, p. 25. It has been claimed that this ship sailed from Ribe, Denmark. There is nothing that supports this contention, though it is a fact that Danish ships came to New Netherland as early as 1644. See New York Colonial Documents, I., p. 145.

Tomassen married on May 25, 1667, in New Amsterdam, Tryntie Hermans, by whom he had several children: Thomas, baptized January 28, 1668; Gerrit, September 27, 1670; Aeltje, December 21, 1672; Marritie, April 28, 1680; Harmen, October 21, 1682; Herman, December 8, 1686.[698]

On July 16, 1671, Thomassen acted as sponsor for Johannes, son of Jan Andrieszen and Grietje Jans; January 26, 1680, as sponsor for Gerrit, a child of Adriaen Pos and Catharina Geirits.[699]

Juriaen Tomassen died September 12, 1695. Some of his descendants are called Yereance or Auryansen (= Juriansen).

One of his descendants was Daniel van Ripen, a smith. He served as lieutenant in the army of George Washington. Later he became Justice of the Peace in the county of Bergen, N. J. He died in July, 1818. Another descendant, Reeltje van Ripen, was in 1814 married to John van Buskerk.

In Jersey City, N. J., one of the avenues bears the name of the pioneer immigrant from Ribe: "Van Ripen Avenue." It was here that Tomassen had his land.

TOBIAS WILBERGEN.

Tobias Wilbergen was in New Netherland as early as 1655. He married on July 4, 1655, in New Amsterdam, Hilletje Jaleff from 'Oldenburgerlandt'. In the marriage record it is stated that Wilberg was from 'Torreb' (Torup), in Jutland, Denmark.[700]

698 Collections of the New York Genealogical and Biographical Society, I.
699 Ibid., II.
700 New York Genealogical and Biographical Record, VI., p. 88.

Excursus.

I.

CHRISTIAN BARENTSEN.*

Christian Barentsen, who is sometimes called Christian van Hoorn in the documents, was probably a Scandinavian, a Dane (though we do not count him among our 188). A recent work on "Christian Barentsen Horn and His Descendants," by C. S. William, in treating of Barentsen takes "van Hoorn" as meaning that Barentsen was either from the city of Hoorn in Holland, or a descendant of the old Dutch Van Hoorn family.

It has been difficult for me to get away from the supposition that Barentsen is a Dane. Were he Dutch, it is strange that he both had a name so pronouncedly Scandinavian as, "Christian Barentsen," and that he signed the petition of the Lutherans in New Amsterdam in 1657. A Dutchman from Hoorn would in all probability have been adhering to the Reformed Church. Secondly, a Lutheran, from Dithmarschen, Herman Smeeman, stood, in the same year, sponsor at the baptism of Johannes, Barentsen's son. Thirdly, the names of his children appear to be those that a Scandinavian rather than a Dutchman would select, especially the name of Barent (Bernt).

As to the use of "van Hoorn," there is nothing to show that Barentsen ever used it himself. There are several places on the map called Horn: Horn, formerly a suburb, now a part, of the city of Hamburg; Horn in Lippe, Germany; Horn in Austria; Horn in Norway; Horn in Island, and Horn in Denmark.

---

* What we here state concerning Barentsen lies hard by the field of conjectural criticism, which is not without merits in genealogical research also.

It may be objected that these places are spelled Horn, and not Hoorn. But anyone familiar with the orthography in our early records will not take this objection seriously. Moreover, a town named "Horne" in Horne Parish (Ribe Amt), Denmark, is spelled Hornae and Hoorn about the year 1340 (J. T. Trap, Kongeriget Danmark, p. 74). "Van Hoorn" may mean any of the Horns mentioned, if they all existed in the days of Barentsen. We may leave the Horn in Lippe and Austria out of consideration, for if Barentsen were a German he would probably not have had the patronymic termination of "sen." Horn near Hamburg may be the place from which Barentsen came. This place was hard by the jurisdiction of the Duchy of Holstein, and not a few Danes were living in the vicinity of Hamburg. It is significant that Cornelius B. Harvey in "Genealogical History of Hudson and Bergen Counties" makes the statement — on what authority I do not know — that "Barent Christianse" (likely the same as Christian Barentsen) is from Holstein.

However, we need not exclude the Horn of northern Denmark as the original home of Barentsen, if it existed in the seventeenth century. The same may be said of Horn in Norway* and in Island. For early New York had immigrants even from Faroe Islands (Jonas Bronck), and probably from Spitsbergen.**

But may not "van Horn" have an entirely local meaning? May it not mean a pointed corner (spitzige Ecke)? Barentsen's lot and house in New Amsterdam — which he bought in 1657 — formed a pointed corner. What would be more natural, according to the usage of Scandinavians, than to call the resident on this lot Christian van Horn, or Christian from (or, at) the corner? The fact that Laurens Andriessen (who married Christian's widow), became later known as Laurens van Buskirk (from the church by or near the bush), shows how easily new names of local significance were invented and applied. Now Barentsen, to my knowledge, is not called "van Hoorn" before he had purchased the house and lot, just mentioned — in 1657.

Another solution, if the one given be too hypothetical: Barentsen may have got his name at the South River. See docu-

---

* Horn in Norway is not far from Brönnö in Helgeland. In older Norwegian, Horn signifies corner.

** Teunis Cornelise Spitsbergen, at Fort Orange (1661-1687).

ments published in William's book on Barentsen and dated Aug. 28, and Dec. 18, 1658; July 16, 1659; January 30, 1660.

To maintain, in view of the indefiniteness of the sources, that "van Hoorn" in the present instance must mean *either* a member of the Van Hoorn family or an immigrant from Hoorn in Holland would be just as faulty as it would be to contend that every one, with "van Bergen" attached to his name in the records of early New York, must be "from Bergen" in Norway, since there is no van Bergen family in that country. In fact, "van Bergen" in these records, when "Norway" is not added to it, may — and it often does — mean "from Bergen in Holland," "from Bergen in New Jersey," or "from Bergen in Germany."

The reader will pardon this digressive introduction to the record of Christian Barentsen. It shows how difficult it sometimes is to decide the nationality of early immigrants. Barentsen *may* have been a Dutchman, but this is only a possibility, not amounting to probability — not to speak of as an established fact.

As stated, he probably was a Dane. He married Jannetje Jans, by whom he had three children: Barent, Cornelis, Johannes Christense (New Jersey Archives, First Series XXI, p. 193). His second son, Cornelis, was baptized in New Amsterdam, August 3, 1653. Johannes or Jan was baptized, at the same place, March 18, 1657. Probably Annetje's fourth son Andries, baptized in March, 1659, also was by Barentsen (see article "Laurens Andriessen. Part II.).

Christian Barents was a carpenter. At various times he was appointed by the Court to inspect carpenter work.

In 1654 he was a partner of Auken Jans. These two had constructed a "sheet-piling" at the Graft but it had fallen down, caved in, in consequence of heavy rain and water. The Court summoned them, but being told what was the cause of the falling down, it agreed with the carpenters to pay them for reconstructing it, the sum of thirty-two guilders (besides providing two men as "diggers") on condition that all should be done and properly repaired. (The Records of New Amsterdam, 1653—1674, p. 23.)

On February 26, 1656, Barentsen and two others were appointed firemasters by the burgomasters of New Amsterdam — to inspect, whenever "they please, all the houses and chimneys in jurisdiction of the city and there to do for the prevention of fire what is necessary and to collect such fines, as are prescribed by the published orders and the customs of our fatherland." Most of the houses were built of wood, some were roofed with reed. The wooden and plastered chimney was not uncommon (l. c. 21f.).

Barentsen signed the Petition of the Lutherans in New Amsterdam (October, 1657), requesting that the government permit the Lutheran pastor Goetwater to remain in the country. (See note 42, Part I.)

Barentsen was engaged at South river (Delaware river) when he died, June (?) 26, 1658. On August 28, the court messenger handed a letter to the Council, communicating "the demise of Christian Barentsen." (See Year Book of the Holland Society of New York, 1900, p. 114.)

The Minutes of the Orphanmasters of New Amsterdam state (We quote from C. S. William's book):

"August 28, 1658, Orphanmaster Pieter Wolfersen Van Cowvenhoven produces a letter received through Court Messenger, Pieter Schabanck, which having been opened, was found to have been written and sent by the Hon. Alrichs from the South River and to report the death of Christian Barentsen Van Hoorn on the 20th of July, 1658, with a statement by inventory of his estate and request to assist his widow."

He had property. Under date of November 7, 1657, it is recorded that Cornelis Jansen Plavier, of New Amsterdam, acknowledged that he owes Barentsen 1233 guilders and 17 stivers purchase money of a house and lot at New Amsterdam, west of the broad "Heerewegh" bounded by the east and north side by the said "Heerewegh" and the city wall, to the west Do(mine) Drysius, to the south the house and lot of Jacob Vis and of the Company. Plavier mortgaged the lot. (Year Book of the Holland Society of New York, 1900, p. 167.)

Under date of May 3, 1658, we find an entry that Hendrick Hendricksen, a tailor, was indebted to Barentsen for the sum of 500 guilders, the balance of purchase money for a house and lot at New Amsterdam, near the land to the Gate, the Heerewegh to the west. Barentsen had bought it on August 1, 1657. Hendricksen mortgaged his house to him. (Ibid, p. 165.)

Barentsen's estate was sold to Solomon Hansen in January, 1660. It brought the sum of 574 guilders. The one who supervised the sale was Laurens Andriessen, who had married Barentsen's widow, December 12, 1658. (Ibid., p. 119.)

It appears that Barentsen had a grist-mill on the estate of his wife's father in the colony of New Amstel, and that Vice-Director Alrich, who governed this colony was concerned about the welfare of the widow of Barentsen. He wrote a letter to Director Stuyvesant, August 17, 1658, in which he asked the Director to help her and her affairs, recommending her to the orphan masters. He again wrote to Stuyvesant, September 5, 1858:

"In regard to the widow of Christian B[arents] as she desired beyond measure to go there and requested it within three days after her husband's burial by word of mouth and by writing, also that the property, which he left behind, might be sold immediately, all of which has been agreed to and permitted at her repeated instances or demands and arranged for the best of the heirs. so that they have been benefited more than usually by some presents or words of consolation, as your Honor will have seen from the transmitted letters and account and sale of the property, therefore there is no cause given the aforesaid widow to complain, but I only advised or proposed to her, that it would be for her best to remain in possession, she should be assisted in completing the mill, with the income of which through the grist she would be able to diminish the expenses and live decently and abundantly with her children on the surplus; besides that she had yet 3 or 4 good cows with sheep and hogs, which also could help her to maintain her family, she and her children should have remained on and in her and the father's estate, which was in good condition here, wherein the widow with the children could have continued reputably and in (good) position to much advantage: but she would not listen to advice . . . that she was to be restricted in her inclinations and wellbeing, which I shall never think of, much less do. This God may grant and give, and I will ask him to take your Honor and us with our families in his Almighty care and protection." (New York Colonial Documents. XII., p. 224.)

Jannetje may have been Norwegian. (See Laurens Andriessen. Part II.)

In the following excerpts which we quote from C. S. Williams, Barentsen is called "van Hoorn":

1) From the Records of New Netherland.

"December 18, 1658. Before the Board appeared Burgomaster Olaf Stevensen Cortlandt who is informed by the Orphanmasters, of the inventory of his property here, made by the widow, wherein differences appearing with which they do not know what to do, the widow of the said Christian Barentsen Van Hoorn, called Jannetje Jans, is called and asked whether the payment for the house near the Land Gate had been received; she answers, yes, by Hendrick Van Dyck who had Power of Attorney from her husband; asked about the payment for the house where Hendrick Hendricksen, the tailor, lives, she says not to have received it, but it is still due and charged.

"Jannetje Jans, widow of Christian Barentsen Van Hoorn, is ordered to send to the South River the last inventory made here, as they have the case in hand. She has asked the people on the South River to have the proceeds of the goods there forwarded to her, which was promised to her, if she can give bail or security; she is therefore advised to write to the South River that she will give security for the money and offers as such a house."

2) Letter to magistrate at the South River.
"Amsterdam, N. N.   July 16, 1659.
. . . .
"At the request of Lauwrerens Andriessen, drayer, who has married the widow of *Christian Van Hoorn,* deceased, at the South River last year, we inform you herewith that there are deposited in your Orphans Court the goods belonging to his children as paternal inheritance, while the children are here in this City, and we request, that following the usages of other places, said goods may be sent to the Orphans Court here.   You will find us in similar cases willing to reciprocate, with which we remain.
"Yours . . .
"By Order, J. Nevins, Secretary."

3)   "January 30, 1660. Laurerens Andriessen appearing declares not to have received more from the estate left by Christian Barentsen [Van Hoorn], deceased, his wife's former husband, than 574 Guilders from Solomon Hanzen.   He also says there are still

outstanding at the South River about 13 or 14 Guilders heavy money at the rate of ten heads of Wampum for one Stiver, and shows an account of the estate with what it owes and what is due to it. The Orphanmasters reply that a copy of the account shall be made by the secretary Nevins and the original shall be returned to him; they shall further order him to bring to the next session, the statement and inventory, shown to the Director-General and Council, with their marginal order thereon."

As we have seen, Jannetje did not remain long in her widowhood. Laurens Andriessen married her six months after the death of Barentsen and gave her such social advantages as she did not have in her first marriage nor could have had as a widow on the estate of her father.

In studying the genealogy of the Van Horn family, the descendants of Christian Barentsen, one will readily see that this family merits the predicate of distinguished.   To it belongs e. g. Robert T. van Horn (b. 1824) who founded, and for forty years, edited the "Kansas City Journal." He served in the Civil War and was member of Congress. Another distinguished member of this family was Wm. H. Carbusier, Lt. Col. U. S. Army, who also served in the Civil War. A third member is Alfred C. Johnson, who has been U. S. Consul in Germany.

II.

UNCLASSIFIED NAMES.

It is possible that the following persons in New Netherland were Danes (we do not count them among our 188 immigrants):

SIMON JANSEN ASDALEN.

Simon Jansen Asdalen, who in 1663 purchased a house and lot in New Amsterdam, was, if we can depend on the reading "Asdalen," either from Norway or Denmark. There is an Asdal in Nedenes Amt, Norway. It is spelled Aasdal in 1610, Asdahl in 1670, Asdal now. (Norway has also an Asdöl) The ending "en" is the definite article. Asdalen thus means: the bowery at Asdal. (Rygh, Norske Gaardnavne, VIII., p. 112):

There is also an Asdal (parish) in Denmark. In a niche above the main entrance to the leading manor building in this Asdal, one can see "Karl Pölses Fläsk," a shrunken ham-bone, which is referred to the legend about Karl Pölse of Asdal, who had a controversy with the lord of the manor of Odden. The two men, in order to settle the controversy, parted a hog. One part was hung up at Odden, the other at Asdal. He whose half-hog first decayed, was to stand confessed as the wronging party. Odden proved to be guilty, for Asdal's part of the hog is still on exhibition. Hence the saying: "Odden hin olde, Asdal hit bolde."

JOHN ASCOU.

John Ascou, who in 1661 hired a canoe from the Dane Pieter Kock, which he was sued for by Kock's widow, may have been from Askov, Denmark.

JAN SNEDINGH.

Jan Snedingh (Snedinck, Smedingh, Snediger) a tavernkeeper in New Amsterdam (1648), magistrate of the Midwout (1654), was possibly from the manor of Snedige, Denmark, that had been owned by families like the Grubbes and Trolles. He was married. When Nicolaes de Meyer sued him, 1658, for about 350 guilders, the wife of Snedingh appeared for her sick husband, who claimed he could not pay before the corn would be ripe. It was told in court that Mrs. Snediger, when requested to pay the plaintiff, had said, "Where there is nothing, Caesar has lost his right." In 1659 Snedigh sued Matthys Boon for "fl. 10., balance of fl. 14, one pair of stockings, one pair of shoes for his son's wages." In 1660 he sued the Swede (or Finn) Moenes Pietersen. He had hired a house from the defendant for twenty-four gl. a year. After six months he moved out. He paid thirteen guilders to Pietersen, who seized eleven guilders with Jan van der Bilt, Snedingh's money; he also let a new party move into the house. The court decided that Snedingh had a right to the eleven guilders. — Snedingh sold timber and kept boarders in 1660—1661. In 1663 he was sued for taking away bricks from the strand and removing them to his house. The Schout demanded that he "shall be condemned to go to prison and there to remain on bread and water for the term of one month or to redeem the same with a sum of 100 guilders with costs." Snedingh answered, he was innocent of having so done, as the bricks were not in a heap, but lay scattered around and that he saw some boys also there picking up bricks. He claimed therefore that he could not be fined. The court thought differently, and fined him twenty-five guilders.

HERRY ALBERTSE.

Herry (Harry or Hendrick) Albertse "van londen", who came over in 1639 and worked in Rensselaerswyck, is regarded by the editor of "Bowier Manuscripts" (pp. 609, 822) as being from London, England. But may not "van londen" signify "from Londenis," or still better, from "Londen" (south of Husum), places in Denmark and found on the map of Denmark in "Theatri Europæi. Pars V." (1647)?

HENDRICK HENDRICKSEN OBE.

Hendrick Hendricksen Obe, often mentioned in the Records of New Amsterdam 1653—1674, may have been from Oby in Denmark. (See map in Theatri Europæi. Pars V.") He was city constable in 1665, a juryman in 1667, collector of Excise in the same year.

JAN VOLKARSEN OLY.

Jan Volckarsen Oly, Notary in New Amsterdam in 1664, was probably from Oby in Denmark, "Oly" being, I conjecture, intended for "Oby."

Also the following names of persons in New Netherland lend themselves to favorable consideration by such as are desirous of increasing the list of Danish immigrants in early New York:

Hans Nicholaeszen, who had a child (Laurens), baptized in 1642, in New Amsterdam. The sponsors appear to have been Scandinavians.

One of these sponsors was *Hans Fredericksen,* a soldier, whose name seems to be *Norwegian* or *Danish.*

Another sponsor was *Christina Vynen.* It has been said that she was English, and that her real surname was "Fine." In the baptismal record (see under: Nicholaeszen, 1642), the word "engelsman" is appended to her name. No doubt "engelsman" here does not stand for "Englishman" but for Engel Mans, who was a Swedish woman, and sponsor at the same baptism.

Vynen — I take it — means the island of Fyen (or Fünen), Denmark. Christina often appeared as sponsor in New Amsterdam.

Rachel Vynen (1641) was likely her sister. Capt. *Francois Fyn,* (Ffyn), it would appear, was another relative of hers. He acquired land (Hog Island) near Hellegat, 1651; and 26 morgens at Long Island, 1656. He had a family.*

Of other persons with Scandinavian names in New Netherland, mention may be made of *Peter Hanse* and *Eerick Jansen.*

"Fyhn," "Fyen," "Fine" are names not infrequently met with in Danish and Norwegian genealogy. It is therefore not necessary to connect "Vynen" with the place-name in Denmark. However, as Guillaume Vigne, who had immigrated from Valenciennes, France, had two daughters called Christine (wife of Dirck Holgersen) and Rachel, it is possible that "Vynen" or "Fyn" is a corruption of "Vigne." In that case these names are French.

Hanse gave Jansen power of Attorney to receive moneys due him by the West India Company for service at Curacao (1649).

Jan Christiansen Andersen (1660) appears to be another Scandinavian.

Laurens Hansen and *Knut Mauritz,* who served as soldiers in New Netherland, resp. 1654 and 1660 (Esopus), and were, 1662 and 1674, in New Amsterdam, immigrated, it would seem, from Norway, Sweden, or Denmark.

Elling Morgen who about this time stood sponsor at a baptism is likely a Dane or a Norwegian.

PART III
SWEDISH IMMIGRANTS
IN NEW YORK
1630-1674

ANDRIES ANDRIESSEN.

Andries Andriessen was in New Amsterdam as early as 1655. He married, on October 17, 1655, in New Amsterdam, "Weiske" or Niesje Huytes, from "Coulum" in Friesland. The marriage record states that Andriessen was from Vesterås, in Sweden.

Only two days before his marriage, he was assessed six guilders at the house of J. V. Couwenhoven, where, it would appear, he was lodging.[701] Couwenhoven and his wife were sponsors at the baptism of Andriessen's first child, November 19, 1656. In the beginning of 1657, Andriessen and Couwenhoven were probably not so friendly as at the baptismal festivities. For Andriessen brought, in January, suit against Couwenhoven. We know nothing as to the particulars of the litigation.

In September, 1655, Andriessen bought a plantation and a house on Long Island, adjoining Hellgate. Perhaps he moved thither after his marriage.

The deed he received reads as follows: [702]

"Before me, Cornelis van Ruyven, Secretary, in New Netherland in the service of the General Priv. West India Company and before the undernamed witnesses, appeared the worthy Lieve Jansen of the one part, and Andries Andriesen from Vesterås in Sweden, of the other part.

"The abovenamed Lieve Jansen declared, that he has sold, and Andries Andriesen, that he has purchased a certain plantation belonging to the vendor, situate on Long Island, beyond the Hellgate, extending on the east side along Simon Josten's land, and on the west side abutting Juriaen Fradel's land, as large and small as appears by the groundbrief thereof, together with the house standing thereon, and all that is thereon constructed, built,

---

701 The Records of New Amsterdam, 1653-1674, I., p. 374.
702 New York Colonial Documents, XIV., p. 382.

set off or planted, and 13 hogs old and young, as seen by the purchaser. For which plantation and what is abovementioned, the purchaser promises to pay the sum of four hundred and ten guilders right down, to wit: 100 guilders in merchantable beavers and 130 guilders in good current wampum. The purchaser shall also pay all costs, which attend the sale and conveyance as well as those parties respectively pledge their persons and properties, present and future, submitting the same to all courts and judges.

"In testimony whereof this is signed by parties with the witnesses at Amsterdam in New Netherland the 10th of September Anno 1655.

"Lieve Jansen.

"This is the mark ☩ made by Andries Andriessen himself.

Signature of Andries Andriessen.

"By me, Stoffel Michielsen, as witness.
"In my presence, Cornelis Van Ruyven, Secretary."

Andriessen had several children. Andries, whom we have mentioned, was baptized November 19, 1656; Jacob, May 11, 1659; Tietie, March 31, 1662; Marritje, October 22, 1664; Huybert, November 20, 1667; Tietje, February 20, 1669; Huybert, December 28, 1672.[703]

He was deceased before February 23, 1682, when his widow was married to Jan Vinge, the widower of "Emmerens Van Nieuwerzhuys."[704]

There were several persons having the name of Andries Andriessen, in New York, in the middle of the seventeenth century. This makes it very difficult to trace the history of any one of these persons in particular. One was a mason (Metselaer), but he is not mentioned as such in the Records of New Amsterdam before 1666. One was a ship carpenter, who in 1660 married Anneke Salomon. Another was a skipper; still another a weighhouse laborer. We can not, therefore, state what was the trade of Andriessen of Vesterås, or Andries the Swede, as he was called

---

703 Collections of the New York Genealogical and Biographical Society. II.
704 Ibid., I., p. 25.

in December 1655, when Jan Rutgersen brought suit against him, as to the nature of which nothing is said in the court minutes. Perhaps he worked in the weigh-house.

ANDRIES BARENTSEN.

Andries Barentsen was in New Amsterdam as early as 1666. But nothing can be related of him beyond his marrying, on January 24, 1666, in New Amsterdam, "Grietje Cregires." The marriage record says, he was from Stockholm, and his wife from Amsterdam.[705]

There was an Andrew Barentsen in Bushwyck in March, 1662;[706] another, or perhaps the same one, in Kingston, in 1662. The latter was the husband of Hilletje Hendricks.[707]

DIRCK BENSINGH.

Dirck Bensingh (Benson) was a Swede who, after he had left Sweden, resided for some time in Groeningen and in Amsterdam, and thence sailed to New Netherland. On August 2, 1649, he bought a lot "situate northeast of the bastion" of Fort Amsterdam.[708] In the next year he bought another lot, on Broadway.

On June 21, 1651, he gave a mortgage to Fiscal Van Dyck, "of his house and lot on the east side of the Great Highway, Manhattan." [709]

In 1654, he went to Fort Orange. On June 29, 1654, he received a permit "to return up the river and attend to his business."[710]

He secured a lot in Fort Orange, upon which he built a house.

705 Collections of the New York Genealogical and Biographical Society, I., p. 31.

706 New York Colonial Documents, XIV., p. 511.

707 R. R. Hoes, Baptismal and Marriage Registers of the Old Dutch Church of Kingston, p. 2.

708 Calendar of Historical Manuscripts, I., p. 47.

709 Ibid., I., p. 86.

710 Ibid., I., p. 139.

He was a carpenter by trade, and worked on the new church in Fort Orange, built in 1656. In August, in the same year, he conveyed a parcel of land to the Reformed pastor, Johann Megapolensis: it was lying on the present west side of Broadway opposite Bowling Green.[711]

He must have made several journeys between Fort Orange and New Amsterdam. In November, 1655, he was to have appeared as defendant in a suit before the court of New Amsterdam. The court minutes, however, contain nothing specific about the suit, and merely state that "the defendant had departed in spite of arrest." John Kip was the plaintiff.[712]

In 1658, Bensingh loaned the deacons in Fort Orange 100 guilders.

He died February 12, 1659.

The wife of Bensingh was Catarina Berck (Berg). After the death of Bensingh, she was married to Harman Thomassen.

Of Bensingh's children, Dirck was born in 1650. He became a skipper on the Hudson, and lived in Albany. Samson was born in 1652. He set up a pottery in Albany, and was known as "Pottebacker." Johannes was born on February 8, 1655. He chose the vocation of innkeeper and went to Harlem. Catarina was born 1657. She married a physician, Reyner Schaets, and, later, Jonathan Brodhurst. Maria was born in 1659.

HAGE BRUYNSEN.

Hage Bruynsen (Brynson) was in New Netherland as early as 1646, when he entered the service of Burger Joris, a blacksmith at the Smith's Fly and owner of a grist mill at Dutch Kills.[713] Burger Joris was from Silesia, and his wife from Sweden. The church record says, she came from "Coinxte," in Sweden. Perhaps Hage was a relative of hers. Possibly they both came from the same place. Coinxte may be a corrupt reading (as is

711 D. T. Valentine, Manual of the . . . City of New York, 1861, p. 581.
712 The Records of New Amsterdam, 1653-1674, I., p. 400. See also J. Riker, Harlem, Its Origin and Early Annals, p. 426. Munsell, Collections of the History of Albany, IV., pp. 97, 278, 322.
713 J. Riker, Harlem, Its Origin and Early Annals, p. 236.

VEXIÖ, ABOUT 1700.

also Weische) of Vexiö, the place from which Hage Bruynsen came.

On March 23, 1653, Hage Bruynsen, from "Weische, in Smaaland, Sweden" married Anneke Jans of Holstein. (See article "Anneke Jans, of Holstein," Part II.)[714]

In 1653 he bought a house in New Amsterdam, apparently upon the site of No. 255 Pearl Street. This house is of some interest as the lodging place, in 1679, of the Labbadist missionaries, Danker and Sluyter. In October, of the same year, Bruynsen bought a house and lot in Beverwyck.[715] His wife was desirous of moving to this place, but a suit that she had brought against a Mrs. Abraham Genes, who she supposed had taken some napkins from her, detained her in New Amsterdam. For the Court did not allow her to go before she had settled with Mrs. Genes or prosecuted her suit against her.

By Anneke, Bruynsen had a son, Hage, who was baptized November 29, 1654, and married Geesie Schurman of New York, in 1681.

After Anneke's death Bruynsen married, on April 7, 1661, Egbertie Hendricks of Meppel, the sister of the wife of Cornelius Matthyszen, a Swede. By his second wife, Bruynsen had a son, Hermanus, who was baptized on January 24, 1662.

On February 16, 1654, Dirck Holgersen, a Norwegian, sued Bruynsen for payment of a certain lot. As Holgersen had not given the deed to Bruynsen, the Court ordered that the "plaintiff shall deliver the deed, and defendant shall then pay." [716]

On August 17, 1654, Bruynsen brought suit against William Harck, requesting that he might get back a canoe which Harck had taken away from him. This canoe Bruynsen had bought of the Indians "for a cloth coat, that cost him one beaver and one guilder, making in all nine guilders." Harck explained that he bought the same canoe of Indians, in presence of Govert Loockermans and that he gave fl. 11:10 for it, which canoe Harck's mate found, and took away as if it were his own." Harck offered to pay the half of what Hage Bruynsen gave for it. After the

714 New York Genealogical and Biographical Report, VI., p. 82. The famous singer, Christine Nilsson, was born near Vexiö.

715 E. B. O'Callaghan, History of New Netherland, II., p. 588.

716 The Records of New Amsterdam, 1653-1674, I., p. 161.

parties had been heard, the Court decided that Harck should be bound to restore the canoe to Bruynsen.[717]

When the city of New Amsterdam, in 1655, requested a voluntary contribution from its citizens, to defray the expenses of strengthening the fort around the city, Hage Bruynsen offered to work "three days at the city works."[718]

On October 23, 1655, he sued the Skipper of the "Spotted Cow" for taking away certain stones which he drew and had before his door, to repair the street. He requested the payment of fl. 6, as "he had worked for them two days." The skipper replied that he asked for the stones and was allowed to take them away without any payment being asked for them, being about ¼ ballast for a boat. The Court, after hearing both parties, condemned the skipper to pay to Bruynsen fl. 4 for the stone.[719]

On March 8, 1658, Bruynsen began a suit against Simon Joosten. He demanded the payment of the sum of fl. 88., the balance of an obligation of the year 1655 "exhibited in court proceeding from three ankers of brandy sold him, defendant, with interest thereon and costs of suit." Joosten admitted the debt, and said that he had offered Bruynsen tobacco in payment, but that he would not accept it. Bruynsen explained that the tobacco was not good. The Court after hearing the parties, decided that Simon Joosten should pay Bruynsen according to obligation, with costs of suit.[720]

On March 28, 1658, Bruynsen and Dirck Holgersen appeared in court and said that Bruynsen requested his lot to be "set off." The magistrates answered that the surveyor should be ordered to "measure off their share for parties and to satisfy parties."

In April Bruynsen sued Holgersen. He demanded that he might set off his place, which he had bought of Holgersen. The burgomasters informed the Court concerning the inspection taken by them of the ground in question, also concerning the contract made thereof and that "Holgersen cannot fulfill it." The Court therefore allowed Bruynsen to set off his ground as Holgersen had no ground to make a common passage.[721]

On November 4, 1659, Bruynsen was sued by Jan Snedigh.

717 Ibid., I., p. 227.
718 Ibid., I., p. 370.
719 Ibid., I., p. 386.
720 Ibid., II., p. 351.
721 Ibid., II., pp. 366, 368.

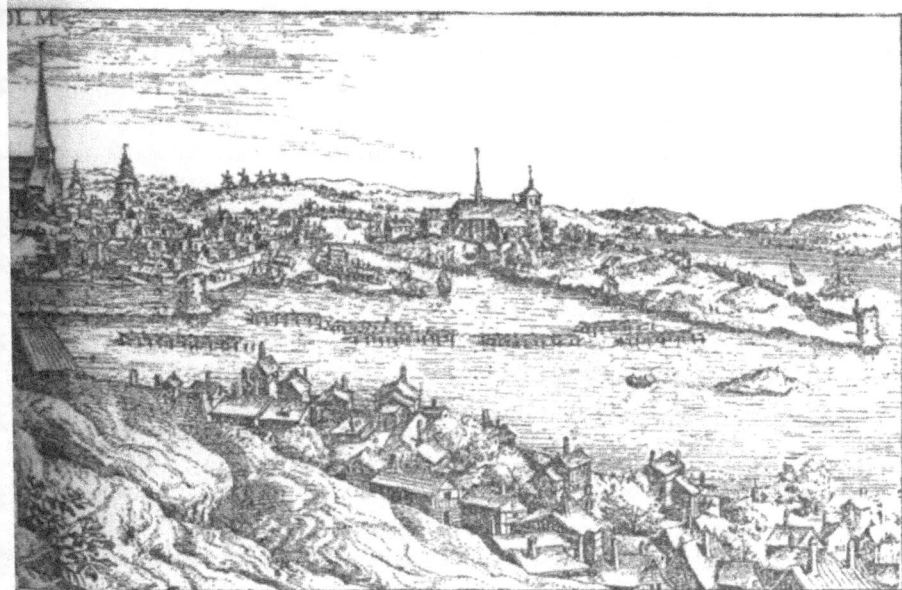

THE NORTH ABOUT 1600.

Brum urbiam, iv.

who said that Bruynsen had seized his money, three guilders, in the hands of a farmer, on Jacob Hayens (Hey) land. Bruynsen said that if Snedigh had paid what he owed him, this would not have happened. Snedigh replied by stating that the claim of Bruynsen against him concerned also his comrade, and he had paid for him. Bruynsen rejoined that "he agreed for it with the plaintiff." After the Court had heard both sides, it ordered "the plaintiff and his comrade to give the defendant each thirty stivers."[722]

On June 1, 1660, Govert Lookermans sued Bruynsen for cutting sod from the best of his land. He demanded an indemnification of fifty guilders. The Officer, as guardian accordingly demanded "the fine according to placard." Bruynsen replied that he did not know whose land it was. A week later, however, he was condemned by the Court to pay the fine according to the Placard "at the discretion of the officer."[723]

On September 19, 1662, James Davidts brought suit against Bruynsen for demanding too much for wages. Bruynsen had fastened a "piece of a mizzen mast and half a hatch" and was not content with a rix dollar, the sum Davidts had offered him. The Court then asked Bruynsen how much he demanded. He replied, a pair of cargo-shoes or ten guilders in seawan. The Court then ordered Davidts to pay Bruynsen, "for wages, six guilders in seawan; wherewith he should be content."[724]

On July 3, 1664, when Bruynsen's son by his first wife was about ten years old, Bruynsen himself and Dirck Jansen, who was the brother of Bruynsen's wife, appeared before the orphan masters' court, in regard to the boy. Dirck Jansen said he would take care of the boy without charge. Dirck was one of the guardians of young Hage. The other guardian, Cornelis Janszen Clopper, consented to this arrangement.[725]

On September 22, 1668, the Court at New York made provisions for the administration of the estate of Bruynsen, deceased. The records state: "On petition of Dirck Jans, Jan Adams and Cornelis Mattysen, next of kin of the deceased Hage Brynsen, requesting in substance that they the petitioners may be authorized with a fourth person, to take the estate left by the abovenamed

722 Ibid., III., p. 72.
723 Ibid., III., p. 173.
724 Ibid., IV., p. 136.
725 Year Book of the Holland Society of New York, 1900, p. 126.

Hage Brynsen and to administer it for the advantage of the interested; is apostilled as follows:— In case no administrator has been appointed by the will of the deceased, the petitioners with Sieur Jacob Kipp are authorized as curators, to administer the estate left by the late Hage Brynsen for the advantage and greatest profit of the interested, provided they shall render to the orphan court of the city due account and explanation; and those of the Haerlem court are ordered to hand over the goods of the deceased to said curators." [726]

In January, 1669, the curators sued Martin Hoffman, a Swede, for fl. 735 seawan arising from an unpaid bill of exchange of fl. 200 Hol[ds] according to an agreement with Bruynsen. Hoffman was condemned to pay the bill and costs.[727]

JAN CORNELISSEN.

Jan Cornelissen, of Göteborg, in Sweden, was in New Netherland as early as 1668. On May 11, 1668, he married, at Kingston, Willemtje Jacobs, widow of Albert Gerritsen.[728] He was deceased before December 24, 1679, when Willemtje was married to Jan Broersen Decker, widower of Heltje Jacobs.[729] The marriage register says that Cornelissen and his wife were "married by the Honorable Justice."

JAN DAVIDSEN.

Jan Davidsen appears to have been in New Netherland as early as 1663, serving in the "second Esopus war" at Kingston.[730] He had some experience as an Indian interpreter. On June 18, 1676, he married, in New Amsterdam, Jannetje Jans. The mar-

726 The Records of New Amsterdam, 1653-1674, VI., p. 148.
727 Ibid., VI., pp. 153, 167. See articles "Cornelis Matthysen," Part III; "Direk Jansen," Part II.
728 R. R. Hoes, Baptismal and Marriage Registers of the Old Dutch Church of Kingston, p. 502.
729 Gustave Anjou, Ulster County Wills, I., p. 30. See article "Jan Broersen," Part II.
730 New York Colonial Documents, IV., p. 51.

riage record states that he was from Sweden. Jannetje was the daughter of Jacob Loper, a Swede. (See article "Jacob Loper," Part III.)

After his marriage, Davidsen seems to have resided in New Amsterdam, where all his children were baptized: Marie was baptized May 2, 1677; Jan, May 29, 1680; Margariet, November 5, 1681; David, March 31, 1683; Pieter, February 3, 1686.

On January 9, 1679, Davidsen and his wife were sponsors at the baptism of Lucretia, daughter of Jan Corneliszen and Helena Hendricx. They were sponsors in 1681 also; and in 1697, at the baptism of Jacob, son of Dominicus Poulse and Dorothe Wil lems.[781]

EVERTJE DIRCX.

Evertje Dircx was in New Amsterdam sometime before 1656. She may have immigrated to New Sweden, and thence to the Manhattans. All we know about her is gleaned from an entry dated October 26, 1656:

"As complaints have been made against Evertje Dircx, a Swedish woman . . . that she has been in bad repute for a long time already, therefore in order not to involve her in a public scandal, she was told to transport herself within eight days from the Manhattans either to Long Island or to the South River. wherever it might suit her best, without delay."[782]

ROELOF DIRXSZ.

Roelof Dirxsz arrived at New Amsterdam in 1659. He was from Sweden. He came over in "de Otter," which sailed on February 17, 1659. One Sweris Dirxsz (Severus Dircksen) from Sweden was on board the same ship. Perhaps they were related.[783]

781 Collections of the New York Genealogical and Biographical Society, I., II. Year Book of the Holland Society of New York, 1904, p. 49.
782 New York Colonial Documents, XII., p. 181. Cfr. Calendar of Historical Manuscripts, I., p. 176.
783 Year Book of the Holland Society of New York, 1902.

SWERIS DIRXSZ.

Sweris Dirxsz came to New Netherland in 1659. He was from Sweden. He came over in "de Otter" which sailed on February 17, 1659.[734] In the court records of New Amsterdam he is called Severus Dirckszen. With two others he appeared, on March 28, 1662, as witnesses for a Geertje Teunis, who had been accused of tapping on the day of General Fast, March 15. Dirckszen and his companions testified that she did not tap on the day of General Fast when they were at her place. After hearing the parties concerned, the Court dismissed the case, but ordered that a negro who had falsely accused Greetje Teunis should be imprisoned.[735]

BARNT EVERSEN.

Barnt Eversen was in New Netherland as early as 1658. He was from Stockholm, Sweden. All we know about him is found in the court minuets of New Amsterdam, where we have the following statement, dated September 17, 1658.

"Jan Rutgerzen, pltf. vs. Mr. Allerton, deft. Pltf. again demands from deft. payment of the sum of fl. 121.6 for two obligations executed by Pieter Janzen of Frederickstatt and Barent Eversen of Stockholm, for which the deft. has signed as bail to pay him. Deft. says, he will prove, that the abovenamed Pieter Janzen of Frederickstatt and Barent Evertsen of Stockholm had determined to run away from the ship; maintaining therefore he is not bound to pay. The Court orders the deft. to give security for the monies, and to prove within three weeks that the abovenamed Pieter Jansen of Frederickstatt and Barent Eversen of Stockholm were willing to run away from the ship." [736]

734 Ibid., 1902, p. 10.
735 The Records of New Amsterdam, 1653-1674, IV., p. 56.
736 Ibid., p. 10.

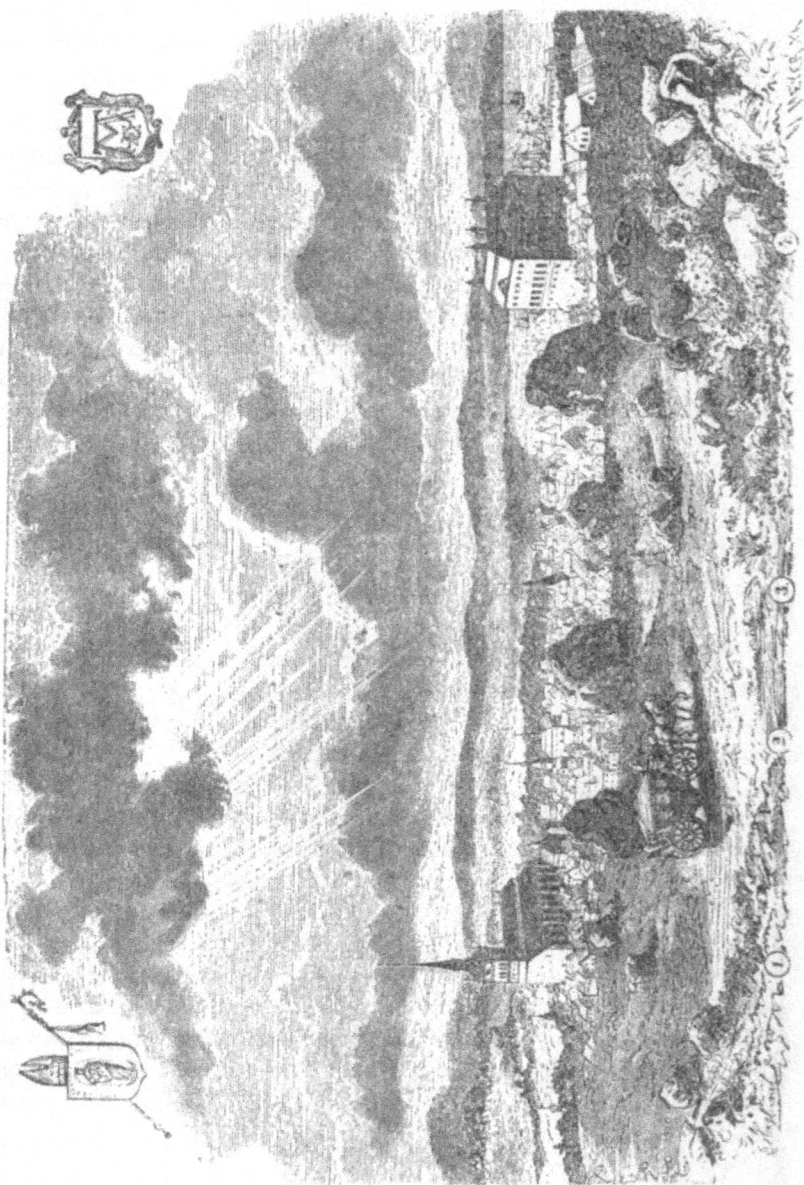

VESTERÅS, ABOUT 1600.

JAN FORBUS.

Jan Forbus (Forbis, Forbish) was in New Netherland as early as 1638. The marriage record of the Dutch Reformed Church in New Amsterdam states that he was from Vesterås, in Sweden. He married, December 7, 1642, in New Amsterdam, Margaret Frankens, who was from "Löster" (Leicester?), in England[737] About 1644 he acquired a parcel of land on Long Island. It lay close to the land that Claes Carstensen, a Norwegian, which he acquired shortly afterwards or perhaps already possessed. In 1644 he gave Claes Carstensen a note of 150 guilders purchase money, "balance due on plantation."

On May 15, 1647, he obtained a patent for sixty-five morgens, on Long Island, on East river.[738]

In 1649 he sold seventy five morgens to a Norwegian, Pieter Jansen Noorman. This land was formerly occupied by Claes Carstensen, David Andriesen and George Baxter.

He had not formally conveyed it to Jansen as late as 1658. Jansen, on the other hand, had not paid him. A litigation about some other matter caused this negligence to be discussed in court. The Court accordingly sent a letter to Forbus, February 7, 1660, ordering him to convey the land in question to Pieter Jansen "and in default thereof to bear all costs that may accrue thereto."[739]

After 1680 Forbus took up about 400 acres on the Raritan, about twenty miles above Amboy.[740]

Under date of July 19, 1662, we find Forbus and his wife acting as sponsors at the baptism of a child belonging to William Solby (Salby).

On May 20, 1666, Forbus made his will: "I, John Forbus, of Flushing, do make my wife Margaret Forbes, my sole heir and executor of my estate. To be for her sole use and for heirs."

On August 28, 1682, "Letters of administration on the estate of John Forbus of Flushing were granted to his wife Margariet."[741]

---

737 New York Genealogical and Biographical Record, VI., p. 85.
738 New York Colonial Documents, XIV., p. 69.
739 See articles "Claes Carstensen," "Pieter Jansen Noorman."
740 Teunis G. Bergen, Register . . . of the Early Settlers of King's County, p. 113.
741 Collections of the New York Historical Society: Abstract of Wills, I., pp. 469, 119.

WILLIAM GOFFO.

William Goffo arrived at New Amsterdam in 1663. He came over in the ship "de Bonte Koe," which sailed on April 16, 1663, for New Amsterdam. In the list of passengers on board this ship, his name is given as "Guilliam Goffo [in credit account: Gouffon], from Sweden."[742]

ANDRIES HANSEN.

Andries Hansen, or Andries Hansen van Schweden [Sweden], was in New Netherland as early as 1660. We find him at Fort Orange in that year, when he and another Swede, Dirck Hendricksen, signed a document. His surname is sometimes given as Scherf, Sharp, Scharf (also Barheit). His name appears in a list of soldiers at Esopus, March 28, 1660.

On January 28, 1663, Jan Andriesen and Andries Hansen offered themselves as "sureties and principals for the presence of Rutger Jacobsen," the husband of Tryntie Jans, a Danish woman. Hansen put his mark to the document.[748]

$$+$$

Signature of Andries Hansen.

Andries Hansen was married to Gerretie, daughter of Teunis Teunissen Metselaer. He made his will in 1685.

He had two sons, Johann and Gysbert, who settled at Kinderhook and had large families.

In 1683 Andries Hansen was a member of the Church of Jesus Christ at New Albany.[744]

---

742 Year Book of the Holland Society of New York, 1902, p. 25.
743 Documentary History of New York, XIII., p. 153. Pearson, Early Records of Albany . . ., p. 281.
744 Ibid., p. 44. Year Book of the Holland Society of New York, 1904.

DIRCK HENDRICKSEN [BYE].

Dirck Hendricksen [Bye] (alias De Sweedt) seems to have been from Göteborg, in Sweden.[745] In 1660 he was a member of the company of soldiers staying at Esopus.[746] Under date of August 27, 1660, we have a document to which he and Andries Hansen affixed their names as witnesses.[747]

Dirck Hendricksen Bye made Esopus or Wiltwyck his permanent home. He was one of the burghers at that place who signed a document, April 28, 1667, stating that he and other burghers had been in arms during the Brodhead mutiny. Captain Brodhead had threatened to burn up the village.[748] The document was presented to a court held at Esopus to investigate the troubles caused by and on account of Brodhead. Among other matters it was revealed that George Porter, a soldier, "coming in the barn of Pieter Hillebrandt's and finding there Dirck Hendrix, took his sword and thrust the same through the said Dirck Hendrixe's breeches." [749]

On May 31, 1671, Dirck Hendricksen is mentioned in a document as the possessor of land in the neighborhood of another Swede, Andries Hansen (Sharp).[750]

A document of 1676 states that the wife of Dirck Hendricksen was Sarah Verhaele. By this document Hendricksen conveyed a lot to Pieter Du Moree. The wording was as follows: [751]

"Appeared before me, Robert Livingston, secretary, etc., and in the presence of the honorable commissaries, etc., Mr. Philip Schuyler, and Pieter Winne, Dirk Henderickse Sweedt, who declared that he in true rights free ownership, has granted, conveyed and transferred by these presents, to and for the behoof of Pieter Du Moree, for a certain lot of land lying behind the Kinderhoeck; to the west of the kil, to the south of Jan Martensen, to the east of Jan Martensen, and that free and unencumbered, with no claim standing or issuing against it, excepting the Lord's

---

745 Munsell, Collections on the History of Albany, IV., p. 87.
746 New York Colonial Documents, XIII., p. 153.
747 Pearson, Early Records of Albany . .., p. 281.
748 New York Colonial Documents, XIII., p. 414.
749 Ibid., VIII., p. 407.
750 Pearson, Early Records of Albany, p. 484.
751 Ibid., p. 123f.

right, without the grantors having the least claim any more upon the same, and acknowledging himself fully satisfied and paid therefor, the first penny with the last, giving therefore *plenam actionen cessam,* and full power to the aforesaid Pieter Du Moree, his heirs and successors or those who may hereafter acquire title from him, to do with and dispose of the aforesaid lot as he might do with his patrimonial estate and effects; promising to defend the same against claims and charges, which may hereafter arise and are lawful, and further, never more to do or allow anything to be done against the same, either with or without law, in any manner whatsoever, under obligations as provided therfor by law.

"Done in Albany, the 7th of March 1676.

"This is the mark of Sarah + Verhaele, wife of Dirk Hendriks.

"Philip Schuyler,

"Pieter Winne,

"In my presence,

"Ro. Liviningston, Secr."

JAN HENDRICKSEN.

Jan Hendricksen was a Swede, whom we find as party in a suit noted in the court minutes of New Amsterdam under date of November 29, 1655. Isaac Hansen brought this suit against him. But both were in default.[752] Jan Hendricksen may be the same person as John De Sweet, of Flushing, whom John Kip, on October 20, 1661, sued for the recovery of a canoe.[758]

MARTIN HOFFMAN.

Martin Hoffman (Martin Hermansen Hoffman) was in New Netherland as early as 1657. We find him in Esopus, where he in

---

752 The Records of New Amsterdam, 1658-1674. I., p.410.
758 Calendar of Historical Manuscripts. I., p. 280.

1658 joined with other residents in warfare against the Indians. In 1659 he was a member of a company of soldiers. The Ensign of the Fort reported, September 29, 1659, to Director Stuyvesant that 'on the twentieth Marten Hoffman and other alarmed" him and the guard, whereupon he sent out nine or ten men to see what was to be done.[754]

Hoffman was born about 1625 at Reval, in Esthonia, which from 1561 to 1710 belonged to Sweden. Hoffman, no doubt was a Swede, though the name is also German. He was interested in getting aid from the Swedes on the Delaware: In 1672 he made a journey from Albany to the Swedish settlement in Delaware to collect money for the Lutheran church in Albany. Racial rather than creedal affinity likely determined this action.

He was a saddler by trade. He spent some of his time in New Amsterdam, some in and about Albany. In 1660 he stood sponsor in New Amsterdam at the baptism of a child belonging to Jan Woutersen and Arentje Arets. In 1661, his name occurs in the Directory of New Amsterdam, which states that he was living in De Heere Straat. He was paying taxes on his house.

In 1662 we find him living in Beverwyck. He occupied at the beginning of that year a house belonging to Jan Lambertsen of Bergen.[755]

In 1663 he was again at New Amsterdam. His house on De Heere Straat was, in 1665, assessed for one guilder.[756]

He sold it in 1669 to John Manning.[757] After 1670 or 1672 he seems to have lived in Albany, following his occupation as a saddler though he was no mean adept at auctioneering.

He contracted two marriages. His first wife was Lysbeth Hermans of Oertmarsen in Overyssel, whom he married in Brooklyn, April 22, 1663.[758] His second wife, whom he married, May 16, 1665, in New Amsterdam, was Emmerentje DeWitt of "Esens in Embderlandt."[759]

By his first wife he had no children.

754 New York Colonial Documents, XIII., p. 115.
755 Pearson, Early Records of Albany, p. 299.
756 The Records of New Amsterdam, 1653-1674, V., p. 221.
757 Ibid., XI., p. 190. Pearson, Early Records of Albany, p. 127.
758 Collections of the New York Genealogical and Biographical Society, I., p. 28.
759 Ibid., I., p. 30.

By his second wife he had five: Annetje, baptized March 1, 1665; Marritje, baptized December 12, 1666. The date of the birth or baptism of his other three children is not given. Their names were Zecharias, Nicolaes ,Taatje.

In January, 1665, a Freryck Gysberzen van den Bergh prosecuted a suit in the Court of New Amsterdam against Hoffman. He demanded of him forty four guilders "balance per account for rent and consumed drink." Hoffman replied that the plaintiff took no cognizance that one Claes Pietersen occupied the house with him. He offered to pay his share. The court decided that Hoff-

REVAL, ABOUT 1600.

man should pay the plaintiff half the rent "and the remaining two guilders for the wine he drank."[760]

On September 19, 1665, Hoffman brought suit against Jan Hendricksen van Gunst for having done damage to his boat, which he had hired to him on the express condition that it should be returned uninjured. Hendricksen claimed, however, that the "rigging belonging to the boat was rotten and worn." The Court ordered that Hendricksen should repair the boat, and that arbi-

---

760 The Records of New Amsterdam, 1653-1674, V., p. 177.

trators should see what damage it suffered during the time the defendant had it, and if possible reconcile the parties.[761]

Hoffman had also some dealings with his countryman Hage Bruynsen, whom he owed 735 florins at the death of the latter (1668).[762]

In 1669 he was sued by Arent Jansen Moesman because he had sold his house to Captain Manning, without regard to the mortgage, dated November 19, 1664, which Moesman had in it. The Court accordingly condemned Hoffman to pay the debt to Moesman, within three months' time, with costs.[763] Captain Manning later brought another suit against Hoffman.

On December 18, 1670, the wife of Hoffman appeared in court in a suit which William Merit had brought against him, charging him for freight on goods brought from Delaware. She asked that hearing might be postponed until the return of her husband from Albany.[764]

In 1671 Hoffman was sued by a Lutheran pastor in New Amsterdam, Jacob Fabritius, for defamation. Fabritius had very little of character. There was no end to his quarrels. The Court ruled in this case, as it did in two other suits, which Fabritius had brought against other persons: "The difference being about defamation, the court ordered these causes to be thrown out of court, they being found only vexations."

In the same year Hoffman sued Jan Roelofsen "Seubringh" for the payment of a debt of one hundred guilders sewan and 400 lbs. of tobacco. He had warned the plaintiff three times to come to New Amsterdam from Flatbush to pay what he owed. Hoffman won the suit.[765]

In January, 1672, Hoffman, who was a Lutheran, got a pass from the governor of New York, to go to Delaware to collect money towards erecting a church for the Lutherans in Albany. In Delaware there were many Lutherans, especially in the Swedish settlement. Hoffman, being a Swede, no doubt was well qualified to solicit funds among his countrymen.[766]

In 1672 he bought a lot in Albany, which he, on December,

761 Ibid., V., p. 292.
762 Ibid., VI., p. 153.
763 Ibid., VI., p. 190.
764 Ibid., VI., p. 264.
765 Ibid., VI., pp. 318, 318.
766 Ecclesiastical Records of the State of New York, I., p. 622.

1676, sold, with house on it, to Cornelis Cornelisen van der Hoeve.[767]

Hoffman was still in Albany in 1678.

Of Hoffman's children, Annetje married, January 4, 1702, Hendrik Pruyn.

Zacharias, married, 1706, in the Reformed Dutch Church at Kingston, N. Y., Hester, a daughter of Jacobus Bruyn, from Norway, and Gertruy Esselstein. He lived at the old homestead at Shawangunk until 1744, when he died. He had several children: Zacharias, Jacob, Geertruyd, Ida, Janneke (who married William Rosenkrans), Margaret.

In 1716 he was captain of a Company of Militia in Ulster County.

The third of Hoffman's children to marry, was Nicolaes. He married Jannetje Crispel, a Huguenot, born 1686. He acquired, like his brother, Zacharias, much property. He, too, commanded as captain a company of the Ulster County Regiment at Kingston in 1717. He was trustee of the town of Kingston, and deacon of the Reformed church. Nine children were born in this marriage.

The last of Hoffman's children was Tjaatje who, 1697, married, at Kingston, Everhardus Bogardus. He was born 1660. They had six children.

The Hoffman family numbers preachers and lawyers, statesmen, authors, college presidents. One of the family was engaged to marry Washington Irving, but died in her eighteenth year. Another, The Hon. John Thompson Hoffman, was Governor of the State of New York.

Members of the family are found intermarried with families of Benson, Livingston, Brinckerhoff, Du Bois, Ogden, Vredenburgh, Verplanck, Beekman, Schuyler, Provoost, Storm, Van Cortlandt. Some of the Roosevelt and the Rosenkrans families are related to the Hoffmans.

The "Genealogy of the Hoffman Family: Descendants of Martin Hoffman" was published in 1899, — a book of almost 550 pages. It contains the arms of the family, many portraits, including the portrait of Martin Hoffman himself.

---

767 Pearson, Early Records of Albany, p. 148.

CATRINE JANS.

Catrine Jans, of Helsingborg, in Sweden, was in New Nether land as early as 1656. She seems to have been a resident in the Swedish colony on the Delaware, which at about this time was annexed to New Netherland. We mention her here, because she figures in a marriage contract. It might be compared with the marriage contract in which a Norwegian woman, Eva Albertse was a party, or with that of the Danish woman Marritje Pieters, the earliest recorded instance of a marriage contract in New Netherland. (See Part I., article "Albert Andriessen"; Part II., article "Marritje Pieters.").

"To-day, date as below, appeared before me, A. Hudde, Secretary at Fort Casimir on the South-River, appointed by the Hon*ble* Mr. Peter Stuyvesant and High Council, residing at the Manhattans, in presence of the undersigned witnesses, the worthy Jan Picolet, a native of Bruylet in France with the maiden Catrine Jans, born in Elsenborgh in Sweden. Together and each for him or herself they have made, of their free, preconsidered and unbiased will and deliberate opinion a promise of marriage, under the condition that on account of special reasons the marriage solemnization should be delayed, until a preacher came here. And Jan Picolet promises faithfully to Catrine Jans to keep the aforesaid engagement unbroken, likewise Catrine Jans promises in the same manner to adhere steadily, firmly and inviolably to the promise of marriage made to Jan Picolet, to which end we, the engaged, submit ourselves, each individually, to such punishment, as is ordered by law for convicted adulterers, if one of us or both should retract the foregoing promise or violate or break it. We bind us, for the vindication and satisfaction of justice, to keep ourselves pure and undefiled in our engagement, until the complete consummation of the marriage, as decency and the laws of our magistrates require it. We declare by signing this, that we, for further confirmation of this our foregoing promise, place our persons, goods, movable and immovable, now belonging or hereafter coming to us, all under the control of the pertinent laws. In attestation of the truth we have signed this without reservation or deceit.

"Done at Fort Casimir, this 24th of February of this Year 1656 on the South River of New Netherland.

"Jan Picolet
her
"Catrine + Jans."
mark

Mr. William Nelson, editor of New Jersey Archives, First Series, Vol. XXII, comments upon this document after this fashion:

"On the 24th of the following May the contracted couple appear before the Council, when Jan requests in writing and verbally, that he might be discharged from his promise of marriage, made to the aforesaid Catrine Jans on January [?] 24, 1656, and that the same be declared null and void. He had asked her, he said, 'with serious intention, upon honor and faith, to be his wife, and that he did not know else, but that she was a virtuous girl.' About a month after, to his direct question, she assured him to that effect, and 'they would have been married if a preacher had been at hand.' It subsequently became evident that she was not as she pretended to be. Catrine then confessed to the Council that in the fall of 1655 she had been engaged to a soldier. . . The Commissaries adjudged that she had gone 'outside of her first betrothal, from which she had not been released, neither by the death of the bridegroom nor by other lawful reasons, and had by her second betrothal deceived the plaintiff, contrary to the written law,' and they gave judgment that the aforesaid Picolet be released from his betrothal and marriage contract and they declared the same null, ineffectual, of no value and as if the same had never been made,' passed, written nor signed.' They moreover condemned Catrine to appear in Fort Casimir, and there, before the Council, to release the plaintiff and with bent knees to ask the pardon of God and justice and promise henceforth to behave as a virtuous woman. On June 16th the couple once more appeared before the Council, and having heard the above [given] judgment, 'the parties giving each other the right hand, discharged one the other legally before the Council of the promise of marriage.' "

Catrine shortly afterward, on December 24, 1656, was married to Lauritz Pietersen, from Leyden, aged twenty-three years, she being only nineteen.[768]

BARENT JANSEN.

Barent Jansen, or Barent Jansen Blom, from Sweden, was one of the early settlers in New Netherland. He was born in 1611 in Stockholm, and not, as Riker says, at Ockholm (in Schleswig). The marriage record of the Dutch church in New Amsterdam states that both he and his wife, Styntie Pieters, whom he married September 15, 1641, were from Stockholm.[769]

He was for some time overseer of Van Twiller's farm on Ward's Island. He was known as "Groot Barent," the Barent of huge proportions. He removed to Brooklyn in 1652, after van Twiller was discharged by the government.

On January 23, 1652, Barent bought of Peter Linde twenty morgens of land on the shores of Long Island, between the lands of Andries Hudde and Claes Jansen Ruyter,[770] near the Wallabout, where he lived till he died.

Two islands were named after him, Great Barent's Island, and a smaller adjacent one, Little Barent's Island.[771]

Barent Jansen died June 5, 1665, from a stab wound in the side given by Albert Cornelis Wantenaer, and at once fatal. Riker says that as Albert set up the plea of self-defense, the Court of Assize, at his trial, October 2, convicted him only of manslaughter. He was "then and there burnt in the hand according to law"; the further penalties, which were the loss of his property and a year's imprisonment, being remitted by the government.

By his wife, Barent had two sons, Jan, born 1644 and Claes (Nicolaes), born 1650; likewise two daughters, Engeltje, born 1652, and Tutie, born 1654.

Engeltje was married to Adam Vrooman, of Schenectady. Tutie was married to Lembert Jansen Van Dyck.

---

768 New Jersey Archives. First Series, vol. XXII., p. xxxi; New York Colonial Documents, XII., pp. 154, 156.
769 New York Genealogical and Biographical Record, VI., p. 34.
770 Calendar of Manuscripts, I., p. 100.
771 J. Riker, Harlem, Its Origin and Early Annals, p. 127.

Jan, surnamed Barentsen Blom, became a farmer at Flatbush. He married Mary, a daughter of Simon Hansen.

Claes married, 1685, Elizabeth, daughter of Paulus Dircksen and widow of Paulus Michielse Van der Vort.[772]

Regarding the wife of Barent Jansen, we can add only this: On March 11, 1646 ,she was sponsor at the baptism of Annetje, daughter of Jochem Kalder. (See article Jochem Kalder. Part I.)

JAN JANSEN.

Jan Jansen, of Göteborg, Sweden, was in New Amsterdam as early as 1651. On September 9, in that year, he got a mortgage in the house of the Norwegian Roelof Jansen Haes. On May 11, 1654, he brought suit against Claes Jansen Ruyter and Harmen Douwesen. But both he and the defendants were in default. On October 12, 1654, the case was tried. Jan Jansen demanded fl. 329, balance of a note signed by Claes Jansen Ruyter and Harmen Douwesen, dated September 4, 1651, with interest on it from August 1, 1652, to the time of payment. The payment should be made "in beavers," according to the obligation. Ruyter acknowledged the debt, but said that Jan of Göteborg "was satisfied with tobacco," which he, Ruyter, had promised to deliver on first opportunity. The Court, after hearing the evidence, disposed of the case by condemning Ruyter to pay the obligation "in beavers." [773]

On July 16, 1654, Jan Jansen of Göteborg, mate of the ship "Conick Salomon," about to return to Holland, "conferred powers of attorney upon Dirck Van Schelluyne, to collect for him certain money owing to him by parties in this country."[774]

Jan Jansen may have returned to Europe; if so he came back again; for he was a resident of New Amsterdam as late as 1667. On July 2, 1667, Johannes d'Wit brought suit against him, but he was in default. The Court then ordered that the "defendant shall within the term of twenty-four hours give security for his appearance at the next court day."[775]

---

772 Ibid., p. 128.
773 The Records of New Amsterdam, 1653-1674, I., pp. 196, 251.
774 Year Book of the Holland Society of New York, 1900, p. 174.
775 The Records of New Amsterdam, 1653-1674, VI., p. 81f.

GÖTEBORG, ABOUT 1700.

PIETER JANSEN.

Pieter Jansen, from Stockholm, in Sweden, was in New Netherland as early as 1658.[776]   He appears to have lived in Albany.

CORNELIS JURRIAENSEN.

Cornelis Jurriaensen appears to have been a Swedish soldier from Winseren (Vintjern?), in Sweden.   In the New York Colonial Documents (II., p. 64) it is stated that he had fled from Fort New Amstel to Maryland, in the year 1659.   Another Swede, Hans Roeloff, seems to have been his companion in the flight.   The Vice-Director Alrich informed Governor Fendal, of Maryland, about this flight, and requested that Jurriaensen and his companion be sent back.

JACOB LOPER.

Jacob Loper was a Swede, from Stockholm, who settled in New Amsterdam about the year 1647.   For some time he had held a naval appointment in the Dutch service.   He had been captain lieutenant at Curacao.[777]

On June 30, 1647, he married, in New Amsterdam, Cornelia Melyn, the eldest daughter of Cornelius Melyn.   Melyn was one of the leading men in New Amsterdam, a friend of the Dane Captain Jochem Pietersen Kuyter, and, like him, an outspoken critic of Director Kieft's administration.   We have related about Melyn's being deported from New Netherland, in company with Kuyter, and that he returned.   (See article "Jochem Pietersen Kuyter," Part II.)   But Melyn's entire family suffered for many years on account of the malignant disposition of the officers of the West India Company towards him.   Loper, his son-in law, felt

---

776 Munsell, Collections on the History of Albany, IV., p. 89.
777 New York Colonial Documents, I., p. 358.

it only too keenly. On June 14, 1649, he presented a petition to proceed to the South River of New Netherland and sail there with a chartered sloop and goods. He was refused, however, to trade on South River. The Council resolved, "Whereas said Loper has married the daughter of Cornelis Melyn and having regard to the dispatch of the Lord Mayors, dated January 27, 1649, the request cannot be granted." To this resolution the following is appended in the minutes of the Council: "Mr. Duncklage is of the opinion that Loper's petition can be granted, provided he do nothing to the prejudice of the Company. La Montagne has scruples in the case, in consequence of the dispatch of the Lord Mayors. Bryan Nuton idem." [778]

Melyn had made, July 11, 1647, a deed of his house in Broad street to his daughter Cornelia. According to J. H. Innes, it appears to have been a two-story house of small size, in all probability built of brick. It seems to have been situated in the easterly half of the present Broad Street, midway between Pearl and Stone streets. Here Loper and his wife lived.

They had two children, Jacob, who was baptized in the Dutch Church, October 25, 1648, and Janneken, who was baptized October 30, 1650. Jochem Pietersen Kuyter was one of the sponsors of Janneken. Loper himself was sponsor, September 15, 1650, of Jacobus, a son of Jan Martyn. [779]

Loper was deceased before April 7, 1653, when his widow was married to Jacobus Schellingen of Amsterdam.

In regard to the inheritance of Loper's children, the following documents may give us an insight into the administrative minutes of New Amsterdam.

"In Amsterdam in N: Netherland the 22d January 1658.

"Whereas the contract made between the Burgomasters and the Orphan Masters relative to the house and lot of the children of Jacob Looper, deceased, situate on the *Heeren Graght,* which was written by the former Secretary Timotheus de Gabry, is lost, the Burgomasters therefore resolved to order a certificate of said contract and to write a letter concerning it to the late Secretary; but the order for the certificate is deferred and the letter reads as follows:—

---

778 Ibid., XII., p. 50f.
779 Collections of the New York Genealogical and Biographical Society, I.

"To Sieur Timotheus Gabry.

"A⁰ 1658, this 25. January in Amsterdam in N: Netherland.

"Honble Discreet and good Friend, Health.

"These serve to let your Hon^r know, that the Burgomasters of this City have enquired through me their Secretary for the contract made with the Orphan Masters of this City, respecting the house and lot of the children left by N. Looper, deceased, which stood by the *Heeren Graght* next to the house and lot of Jochim Pietersen Cuyter, deceased, which was written by you; and whereas the abovenamed have need of the aforesaid contract, and do not find it either among the papers lying at the City Hall, nor at the Secretary's, nor is it registered, which seems strange to their Worship's; they, therefore, request, should the abovementioned contract be accidentally among your papers, that you would please to send it over by first opportunity; or should it not be among your papers to advise us, where it may, to the best of your recollection, be found, as much is depending on it. Which expecting we commend you as well as friends in general to the merciful protection of the Most High. Your sincere friend

"Joannes Nevius.

"By order of the Burgomasters of the City aforesaid."[780]

The son of Captain Jacob Loper, Jacob, did not possess the comforts of his rich married sister. For in the beginning of 1677, he had a dwelling house that lacked chimneys. It is mischievously said, that there is a state in the United States where house-chimneys are such luxuries that every man possesing a house with two chimneys is called "colonel." If New York had resembled this state in the seventeenth century, it would have been difficult for Loper's son to perpetuate the title his father had. For the son's name is found in the following curiously spelled document, written under English rule. It shows he had a house without a chimney, and reads:

780 The Records of New Amsterdam, 1653-1674, VII., p. 168f.

BROAD STREET, 1642.
From "Historic New York." Edited by M. W. Goodwin.
By Permission of G. P. Putnam's Sons, New York.

City off
New Yorke

ATT a meetinge att Mr Mayo^rs house the
28th day of ffebruary 1676[-7]*

Before Nicho Demyer Mayo^r
    Mr Thomas Gibbs deputy Mayo^r
    Mr Stephanus Van Courtland ⎫
    Mr Johannes De Peister   ⎬ Aldermen
    M^r ffrancis Rumbolt   ⎪
    Mr Thomas Snawsell   ⎭

Persons that haue no Chimneys or not fitt to keepe fire in
    Claus Ditlos noe Chimney
    Adam Miller the Like
    Cobus de Looper the Like
    John Penacooke the Like
    Peter Powell the Like
    ffredrick the Shoemaker the Like
    Jacob the Jew the Like
    Sibrant Jansen the Like
    Clem^t Salmon the Like
    Isack Molyne not fitt to keepe fire in
    John the Glass maker noe Chimney
    Arien hee not fitt to keepe fire in

Beinge Returned as aboue by Robt Whitte Constable

ITT IS ORDERED that all and Euery the Pson & Persons
aboue menconed shall build or Repayre his or their seu^rall and

* Minutes of the Common Council of the City of New York, 1675-1776, I., pp. 42f.

In new style the date would be February 18, 1677. Protestant Netherlands ended the old style Friday, Dec. 21, 1582. It began the new style next day, Saturday, Jan. 1, 1583. The Records of the Dutch in New York accordingly follow the new style, which we, as much as possible, have followed in the present volume. Norway and Denmark introduced the new style in 1700. Sweden gradually adopted the new style after 1696, by making no leap-year after 1696 until 1744, by which plan 11 days were dropped. England ended the old style on Wednesday, Sept. 2, 1752, beginning the new on the following Thursday, Sept. 14, 1752. Columbus discovered America on Friday, Oct. 12, 1492, O. S. By N. S. this event happened Oct. 21. George Washington was born Friday, Feb. 11, 1732. We celebrate his anniversary Feb. 22, omitting eleven days.

In changing Old Style to New Style nine days must be omitted for the period beginning March 1, A. D. 1400, and ending March 1, 1500. Ten days must be omitted for the period March 1, 1500, to March 1, 1700; eleven days for the period March 1, 1700 to Sept. 2, 1752.

The first of January is the beginning of the historical year. But for many centuries the Ecclesiastical, or Legal, og Civil year obtained, beginning March 25. March would thus be the first month in the year. September the seventh (septem); October, the eighth (octo); November, the ninth (novem); December the tenth (decem); January, the eleventh; February, the twelfth.

The observance of the historical and civil year caused doubledating to be resorted to, as e. g. in the New York document given above.

Respectiue Chimneys in his and their houses wthin the Time or Space of Three months next after the date hereof Vpon paine that hee or they that shall neglect Soe to doe shall depart their houses and not bee suffered to Liue in the same they not only Endangeringe their owne houses but alsoe their Neighbours to be burnt by fire &c.

Jannetje, the daughter of Loper, was married, 1676, to Jan Davidsen, a Swede, residing in Albany. (See article Jan Davidsen, Part III.)

After the death of Davidsen, she married, on June 5, 1681, Hendrick Beekman, first son of Wilhelmus Beekman. Hendrick Beekman's grandmother was a Slagboom, probably Danish. (See article Teuntje Jeurians. Part II.)

Hendrick, became Justice of the Peace, of Ulster County, N. Y., 1684.

By Jannetje (Joanna Lopers) he had three children: William, who died in Holland; Catharine, born 1683, married three times, died 1745, leaving no children; Cornelia, born 1696, married Gilbert Livingston.

Gilbert's father, Robert Livingston, was the founder of the distinguished Livingston family in America. Robert Livingston was wealthy. In 1685 he purchased about 160,000 acres of land, extending along the eastern shore of the Hudson for about twelve miles. He became known as first Lord of Livingston Manor.

For genealogical data see Wiliam B. Aitkin, "Distinguished Families in America descended from Wilhelmus Beekman and Jan Thomasse Van Dyke." (1912).

JONAS MAGNUS.

Jonas Magnus, from Sweden, was in New Amsterdam about 1660. In November, of that year, he brought suit against Mons Pietersen, also a Swede or a Finn. But both were in default. Nothing is said as to the nature of the suit.[781]

---

781 The Records of New Amsterdam, III., p. 289.

On January 31, 1665, Cornelius van Ruyven sued Jonas Magnus. He demanded an attachment to be declared valid, and that the "officer be authorized to put the defendant in prison, whenever he comes hither." The Court finally declared the attachment valid, "authorizing the Officer to imprison the defendant on his coming to New Amsterdam."[782]

A Jan the Swede, mentioned in a court transaction in December, 1653, is likely another person.[783]

ENGELTJE MANS.

Engeltje Mans was one of the early residents in New Amsterdam, where she was married, December 18, 1639, to Burger Joris. In the marriage record it is stated that she was from "Coinxte," in Sweden.[784] Can this mean "Vexiö," from which Hage Bruynsen (a Swede, who worked for Joris) came?

An entry in the Church Book of the Dutch Reformed Church in New Amsterdam, 1639.

Burger Joris was in New Amsterdam in 1637 and was secured as smith in the colony of Rensselaerswyck, where he worked until sometime in August, 1639, when he moved to Manhattan. His original home was in Hirschberg, in Silesia.[785]

In 1641 he built one of the first dwelling houses, if not the very first, in New Amsterdam, east of the present Broad Street upon Hoogh Straet. He sold it, December 17, 1644, to Cornelis Melyn. It was situated on a plot of about 135 English feet frontage.[786]

---

782 Ibid., V. p. 179.
783 Ibid., I., p. 143.
784 New York Genealogical and Biographical Record, VI., p. 33.
785 Van Rensselaer Bowier Manuscripts, p. 815.
786 J. H. Innes, New Amsterdam and Its People, pp. 104, 128.

On April 28, 1643, he received a groundbrief for sixty acres of land on Mespath Kill.[787]   The deed reads, according to Collections of the N. Y. Historical Society, XLVI., p. 100f.:

"We, Willem Kieft Director General and Councillors for the High Mighty Lords States General of the United Netherlands, his Highness of Orange and the Hon. Heeren Managers of the privileged West India Company, residing in New Netherland, Make known and declare by these presents that on this underwritten date we have granted to Burger Joorissen a lot situated on the bank of the East River on the Island Manhatans to the East of the Fort, extending to the East eleven rods and to the North ten rods, being an uneven square amounting to one hundred and ten rods of land; with express conditions and stipulations that he, Borger Joorisen, or those acquiring by virtue of this present his right, shall acknowledge the aforesaid Heeren Managers as his Lords and Patroons under the Sovereignty of the High Mighty Lords States General, and here their Director and Councillors to obey in everything as good inhabitants are bound to do; and provided he, Burger Joorisen further submits to all such charges and duties as have already been imposed or shall yet be imposed by the Hon. Heeren.   It is also stipulated that Burger Joorissen, in one or two years time, on the said lot on the strand shall yet cause to be built a good house.   Therefore conferring upon said Burger Jorissen, or those entering upon his right in our stead real and actual ownership of said lot, granting him by these presents absolute and irrevocable power and authority and special order to build on, inhabit, and use said lot, as he might do with other his patrimonial lands and possessions, without we grantors, in our aforestated quality, having, reserving or retaining any the least share, ownership or authority in the same, but in behalf of as above from now on and forever renouncing everything, promising further firmly, irrevocably, and unbreakably to observe and carry out this their Conveyance, all under pledge as expressed by law; without guile or craft this has been subscribed by us and confirmed with our seal in red wax, in Fort Amsterdam April 28, 1643, New Style. Was signed Willem Kieft.

---

787 E. B. O'Callaghan, History of New Amsterdam, II., p. 582.

A. House belonging to Cornelis van Tienhoven. B. House belonging to Adriaen Vincent. C. The old Bark Mill. D. House of Carel Van Brugge. E. House of Wessel Evertsen. F. House of Rutger Jacobsen, who married **Tryntie Jans,** a **Danish** woman. G. House belonging to Richard Smith. H. House belonging to Burger Joris, who married **Engeltje Mans,** a **Swedish** woman.

"By order of the Hon. Heeren Directors and Councillors of New Netherland.
                              "Cornelis Van Tienhoven
                                        "Secretary.
    "Lib A. fo. 58.
    "A true Copy.
"David Jamison
"Endorsed in Dutch
"Grant of Burger Jorison, of the 28th April 1643."

On January 20, 1644, he bought a lot in New Amsterdam;[788] likewise in September, the same year, a "house, garden and brewery," which had been the property of Hendrick Jansen.[789]

As intimated, Joris was a smith (hoefsmid) by occupation, but being a thrifty man he was soon in position to engage in other pursuits.

He was the owner of a sloop, with which he occasionally made a trading voyage up the Hudson river.

He often appeared in Court. He was independent, and wanted everything his own way. In 1664 when the English conquered New Netherland he raised such an uproar — he was a great "swearer" — about the ears of the timid spirits, that the surrender to the English was delayed for several hours.

We meet his wife quite often as sponsor, for instance as early as 1642, for a child of John Suycker and for one of Hans Nicholaeszen. In the baptismal record, giving the name of the sponsors at the baptism of Nicholaeszen's son, her name is apt to be overlooked. The record says "engelsman," which some have taken for "Englishman," and for being in apposition with the name of Christina Vynen, another sponsor, who thus has been erroneously considered as English. (See Excursus, "Unclassified Names, B. in Part II). No doubt "engelsman" here refers to Engeltje Mans.

D. T. Valentine, who speaks of the boisterous way of Burger Joris, regards Engeltje as one of the "notable women of olden times."[790] A statement of J. H. Innes would indicate that she was not unequally yoked with her husband:

788 Ibid., II., p. 583. Year Book of the Holland Society of New York, 1902, p. 124.
789 Calendar of Historical Manuscripts, I., p. 29.
790 D. T. Valentine, Manual of . . . the City of New York, 1855, p. 521.

"Engeltje appears to have been a vigorous old lady of some-what masculine disposition. She was frequently, as witness or litigant, before the Court at the Stadt Huys, where she was much dreaded on account of her loquacity, the magistrates being forced to protest against her upon their minutes, as being addicted to, 'an outpouring of many words'."[791]

She appeared in court on January 24, 1656, producing a de-claration of what was left on her husband's bowery. Thomas Griddy, who had lived there, was the cause of her presence in court. He brought the suit against Joris.[792]

In November, the same year, she appeared again in court for her husband, who had sued Cornelis Van Tienhoven;[793] likewise in December, when a case between her husband and another German, Hans Vos, was to be tried.[794]

On January 29, 1657, she sued Geertie Jacobsen, wife of Geurt Coerten ,for having circulated a false report about her. She demanded proof of any dishonor or "in default thereof, that deft. be punished therefor as an example to others, as the Court deems proper." Geertie explained that she did not disgrace Engeltje with what she had said, declaring she knew no dishonor of the plaintiff. "The Schout as guardian of the pltf. concludes that deft. be condemned to ask pardon of God, Justice, and the wronged party in Court, and be moreover amerced in a fine at the discretion of the Court." The Court now declared that Geertie "shall demand pardon of God, Justice, and the wronged party and further declare that she knows no dishonor of her, and moreover be fined ten guilders for the Honble. Schout." Geertie complied with this verdict, and added that she "is thankful for impartial law."

Under the same date the court records relate the following in regard to a suit instituted against Engeltje by Jacob Strycker:

"Pltf. says that they (pltf and deft.) disagree about a beast; and whereas the deft. says that he, pltf. asserted, she and the Honble. Silla acted and complotted together, demands that she, deft. shall acknowledge the same or deny having said so.

791 J. H. Innes, New Amsterdam and Its People, p. 234.
792 The Records of New Amsterdam, 1653-1674. II., pp. 13. 23.
793 Ibid., II., p. 222.
794 Ibid., III., p. 94.

Deft. answers, that pltf. has said, that she and Honble Silla acted together. Honble. Silla being present, standing up, declares himself a party, and says if the Deacons can prove, that it is their beast, that the same falls to the Church. Deft. Engeltje says, that the beast in question was last Thursday taken from her stall. The Deacons answer, they are ignorant of it. And whereas the Honble. Silla, as party, being asked for proof, that it is the beast of the Poor, says he can give no other proof, than that John Snediger's wife should have said, the beasts, belonging to the Poor, should have a cut like a half moon on the ear. Parties being heard, and the court having examined the proofs, produced by the Deacons, of those, who had raised the cow from a calf and also, who wintered it last year, decide that said proof is sufficient and that, consequently, the cow in question belongs to the Poor and therefore commission the Hon: Willem Beeckman and Jan Vinge to tax the costs incurred by deft. and if parties think they have any particular difference, they may institute their action therefor."

Burger Joris received, in 1658, a distinction that was given to very few in New Amsterdam, that of the great Burgher's right, in spite of his having violated various ordinances of the city. He

Signature of Burger Joris, 1659, husband of Engeltje Mans.

had e. g. recived from a Hendrick Jansen a brew-house, and began to sell beer without paying excise tax. He was prosecuted for this in 1646. He denied the general charge, but admitted that three half-barrels were drunk in his house "with some company"! He was provoked at the ado made about the matter and threatened to "cut a slice" of the fiscal. The aggrieved fiscal brought suit against him, whereupon he appeared before the Council and begged pardon of the officer. But the fiscal insisted that Joris should be fined. Arbitrators were appointed. However, their work proved to be in vain. They reported to the Council that Joris "made game of them." The Council finally took the affair in hand, and fined Joris 60 guilders. Upon his addressing that body in a derogatory manner, it ordered him "to remain four and twenty hours in chains."[795]

In 1654 Joris established a mill upon his bowery, for a long time it was called the "Burger's Mill." In the same year, when it was planned that new streets should be made in New Amsterdam, and that one street must pass through the garden of Joris, he determined to sell the house in which he had been living for fourteen years. He sold it 1655. The street was laid out the next year and received the name Smith Street (Smee Straat) from the blacksmith (Joris), whose land it ran through. Later it was named William Street.

About 1660 Joris sold off in small parcels all of his land remaining upon the west side of this street. His later house, the site of which is covered by New Cotton Exchange was at the eastern corner of William and Stone streets, and here he resided during the remainder of his stay in New Amsterdam.

In the early part of the eighteenth century, this house became of interest as being the residence and place of business of William Bradford, the first established printer in New York; here, in 1725, is supposed to have been issued the first number of the 'New York Gazette,' the pioneer newspaper of the City."[796]

Joris left New Amsterdam about 1664 and took up his residence upon his Long Island bowery. Here, too, he proved himself a man of considerable prominence. He was one of the patentees named in the Nicol Patent (Cfr. Collections of the New York Historical Society XLVI., p. 80f.) of the town of Newton, and one of the several commissioners appointed in 1670 to lay out and regulate roads in that town.

Joris and his wife had many children. Catharyn was baptized December 16, 1640; Maryken, December 14, 1642; Joris, July 28, 1647; Janneken, January 30, 1650; Hermanus, March 3, 1652; Elsje, December 7, 1653; Claes, June 17, 1657; Lysbeth,

---

795 J. H. Innes, New Amsterdam and Its People, p. 231.

796 Ibid., p. 234. Valentine, Manual of . . . City of New York, 1865, pp. 665, 666.

May 18, 1659; Johannes, February 16, 1661; Elias, April 2, 1664.[797]

The sons took the patronymic Burger. They were repeatedly called to assist the civil government in the township in which they resided.

Burger Joris died in 1671, at his farm on the Dutch Kills.

In 1674, his widow lived in New Amsterdam in her house rated as "second class" and valued at $1,500, on the present Old Slip, between Stone and Pearl St., then a part of the street called Waterside. Sometime before 1683, she purchased the house of Richard Smith upon Hoogh Straet (now No. 56 Stone Street). Here she resided for many years, with her sons Hermanus and Johannes. They appear as members of the Dutch Church in the list of 1686. Both Engeltje and her husband had joined this Church before 1660.

Engeltje Mans attained a great age. She was still living in 1701.

CORNELIS MARTENSEN.

Cornelis Martensen, from Sweden, was in New Netherland in 1655. A notice in the Calendar of Historical Manuscripts states that "Dirck Michielsen, a Finn, and Cornelis Martensen, a Swede, were, on July 31, 1656, ordered discharged from confinement on a charge og giving beer to Indians." Their plea was ignorance of the law.

In New Amsterdam such pleas were listened to. September 21, 1656, Martensen petitioned for the "restitution of wine seized by the Fiscal in 1655." It would appear that the order of July 31 gave Martensen the courage of asking for "restitution." of his confiscated liquor.[798]

Cornelis Martensen must not be confounded with Cornelis Martensen of Steenwyck, likewise residing in New Amsterdam.

797 Collections of the New York Genealogical and Biographical Society, II., pp. 11, 14, 22, 27, 31, 36, 46, 53, 60, 72.
798 Calendar of Historical Manuscripts, I., pp. 171, 174.

Donabat huic opera,
Hieronymus Scholeus.

STOCKHOLM, SEEN FOR
From Braunius:

STOCHOLM

E SOUTH, ABOUT 1600.
trum urbium, iv.

CORNELIUS MATTHYSEN.

Cornelius Matthysen, or Nels (Nelis) Matthysen, was from Stockholm, in Sweden.[799]   He must not be taken for his contemporary countryman in Delaware, Nils Matson.

Cornelius Matthysen was in New Amsterdam as early as 1658. Under date of August 12, 1658, he brought suit against Cornelius Janzen, a woodsawyer, demanding "the sum of fl. 128.4 balance as appears by account exhibited in Court." Janzen was angered and denied that he owed so much.   He accused Matthysen of being "a thief, saying he stole a crow-bar from the General and sold it to little Abramje; moreover, advised him to steal his timber from the General and sell it; offering to prove it."   No decision was given then; and in September Matthysen requested that the account between him and Janzen might be taken up by arbitrators. On November 7, the same year, Matthysen obtained judgment against Janzen.[800]

On February 26,, 1661, Cornelis Matthysen and Barentje Dircks of Meppel were married in New Amsterdam.

He was one of the founders of Harlem (1661), where he was well esteemed.   "By occupation a carpenter and timber-hewer, he was the first tenant of the land first known as the Church farm, from which he cut and cleared the primeval forest trees."   His lease on this property expired in 1668, when he left the town and bought a small place at Hellgate Neck, Newtown.

The Court minutes of New Amsterdam have on record several cases which are suggestive of the troubles of a pioneer timber-hewer in New Netherland when it was a question of delivering timber "at its proper time" and "of the right measure."   We have mentioned one case, where Matthysen was a litigant, we shall mention another:

In November, 1664, Matthysen started suit against Denys Isaacksen, claiming that he bargained with him for some timber for the sum of fifty-five guilders. He demanded the half of this. Isaacksen, however, claimed that he had bargained for the timber

---

799 New York Genealogical and Biographical Records, VI., p. 148.
800 The Records of New Amsterdam, 1658-1674, II., pp. 418, 422; III., pp. 4, 19; V., p. 245.

for skipper Claas Gangelofzen Visser, and had spoken to him about it, further that Matthysen had not delivered the timber either at its proper time nor of the right measure. The Court, after having heard the parties, appointed two men to arbitrate the case.[801]

On June 12, 1666, Matthysen was elected by the Court of New York as one of the Overseers of New Haerlem. He had been nominated by the inhabitants of New Haerlem. His office was for one year. It had jurisdiction in all cases up to fl. 200.

Matthysen's oath was as follows: "You solemnly swear in the presence of almighty God, that to the best of your knowledge and with a clear conscience, according to the laws of this government and without regard to person, you will in all cases up to 200 fl., brought before you, maintain law and justice; you will as much as possible, endeavor to further the welfare of your village and inhabitants. So help you God."[802]

Matthysen, it appears, was a relative of Hage Bruynsen. For in a petition, September 22, 1668, he and two other men requested the Court that it would appoint the petitioners, who were "next of kin of the deceased," and a fourth person to take the estate left by Hage Bruynsen, of Sweden. The petition was granted.[803]

In 1673 Matthysen and Christina Lourens requested by petition that they might be granted the proprietorship of a "piece of land called Pattry's Hook, situated between Lewis Morris's land and the Two Brothers." The government, in acting upon this petition, ordered that it "be for the present declined." [804]

Matthysen sold his property at Hellgate to Thomas Lawrence, and obtained a grant of sixty acres at Turtle Bay, in 1676. This he sold to Joh. Pietersen. He perhaps went to Hackensack (as did his family) after 1681.

He had children: Mathys, Hendrick, Anna, Maria, Catherine, Sarah, and Rachel.

Mathys was baptized December 18, 1665; Hendrick, Decem-

---

801 Ibid., V., p. 152f.
802 Ibid., VI., pp. 15, 21.
803 Ibid., VI., p. 147.
804 New York Colonial Documents, II., p. 643.

ber 5, 1669; Catharine, February 19, 1676; Sarah and Rachel. twins, December 23, 1681; Anna ——? Maria ——?

Sarah was married to Jacob Matthews, Maria to Samuel Hendricksen, both of Hackensack.

Mathys (surname: Cornelissen) married Tryntie Hendricks, 1692. He died at Hackensack, 1743—8. His descendants retained the name of Cornelissen.[805]

HENDRICK OLLOFSEN.

Hendrick Ollofsen (de Sweet — the Swede) was in New Amsterdam about 1655. On March 8, of that year, he was sued by William Hallett, who demanded payment of fl. 177. A week later Ollofsen replied in court that Hallett's claim and account were not correct. He requested proof from Hallett, and would pay the sum if proof was forthcoming. On the other hand, he demanded damage for what Hallett's cattle had done to his plantation in turnips, pumpkins, tobacco, maize, etc., the extent of the damage to be determined by the Court. The Court ordered the parties to settle their claims before arbitrators. Ollofsen chose Jan van Leyden to arbitrate. The court minutes state that Ollofsen was a Swede, but convey no information as to which part of Sweden he came from.[806]

BRIETE OLOFS.

Briete Olofs (Brielle Oule), from Göteborg, Sweden, was in New Amsterdam as early as 1656. She may have immigrated to New Sweden and thence to New Amsterdam. On August 5, 1656, she was married in New Amsterdam to Pieter Corneliszen of Varberg in Sconia, a Dane. He was later — perhaps on account of his wife — known as Pieter Corneliszen the Swede. (See article

805 J. Riker, Harlem, Its History and Early Annals. p. 229. Harvey. Genealogical History of Hudson and Bergen Counties, p. 45.
806 The Records of New Amsterdam, 1653-1674, I., p. 296.

"Pieter Cornelissen," Part II.) A daughter, Margariet, was born to them in 1657. She was baptized April 15, in the same year.[807]

Pieter was deceased before December 1666, when Jan Jacobsen, a Frieslander, informed the orphan masters that it was his intention "to marry Briete Olofs, widow of the deceased Pieter Cornelissen Sweet." Focke Janzs and Cornelis Aerts were appointed guardians. Jan Jacobsen married Briete, December 4, 1666.[808]

Upon becoming widow for the second time, Briete was married to a German, Gabriel Carbosie, who was born in Lauffen near Manheim and was widower of Teuntie Straelsman, whom he had married in 1657.[809]

Briete Olofs must not be taken for Helena Olofs who, like Briete, was married to a Jan Jacobsen.

STYNTIE PIETERS.

Styntie Pieters, from Stockholm, wife of Barent Jansen Blom, also from Stockholm, was in New Amsterdam as early as 1641 or before. (See article "Barent Jansen," Part III.)

MONS PIETERSEN.

Mons Pietersen (Mons Pietersen Staeck) was either a Swede, or a Finn, from Åbo, Finland. He was one of the founders of Harlem. He owned a house in New Amsterdam in 1660, as is shown in a notice in the court minutes. Under date of April 13, 1660, the minutes report: "Jan Snedingh, pltf. vs. Moenes Pietersen, deft. Pltf. says he hired a small house from deft. for 24 gl. the year and has occupied it half a year; is on a bowery, where he is going to live the half year and that others reside in the house;

807 Collections of the New York Genealogical and Biographical Society, II., p. 45.
808 Year Book of the Holland Society of New York, 1900, p. 128.
809 J. Riker. Harlem, Its Origin and Early Annals, p. 376.

and he paid the defendant thirteen guilders and that the defendant has seized eleven guilders with Jan van der Bilt; asks why he has done so? Answers, for the remaining rent. Defendant is asked, if the others have gone to dwell in the house with his consent? Answers, Yes. Burgomasters and Schepens having heard parties decree, as the defendant allowed others to reside in the house, that, in that case he has no claim on the plaintiff. Therefore the plaintiff may receive the money from Jan van der Bilt."[810]

In November, 1660, "Jonas de Sweet" (Jonas the Swede) brought suit against "Moens de Sweet" (the Swede). But the defendant, who can be no other than Mons Pietersen, was in default. Nothing is said as to what was the nature of the suit.[811]

On January 24, 1663, Mons Pietersen married, in Brooklyn, Magdalentje Van Tellickhuysen. She was widow of Adam Dircksen from "Colen" of New Haerlem, and was sometimes called Magdaleentje Lamberts; she had come from Steinfurt, Germany.[812]

Pietersen had taken part in laying out the village of Harlem. At first he rented a house and a bowery. He soon disposed of these and entered into a "three years' partnership, January 17, 1662, with Jan Cogu, from whom he received the half of his allotment of land with house, barn, etc., for 125 guilders and the balance in cash . . . With farm and lime kiln, with a canoe valued at fifteen guilders, and the herding to attend to, they also engaged, August 22, 1662, to work Tourner's land, already under the plough." Cogu died about the time the partnership expired, February 1, 1665.

Mons Pietersen held minor offices in the town of Harlem. He was an unlettered man, but by nature gifted. Riker says, "Much reliance was placed upon his judgment; yet strong drink often made him abusive and violent and this failing marred his whole life."

In 1665 heavy penalties were imposed on Pietersen by the court in Harlem. This may have caused him to leave Harlem. He re-

810 The Records of New Amsterdam, 1658-1674, III., p. 158. The marriage register states that Pietersen was from "Arbon in Sweden."
811 Ibid., III., p. 289.
812 New York Genealogical and Biographical Record, VI., p. 145. Year Book of the Holland Society of New York, 1897, p. 140.

moved to Elizabethtown, New Jersey, "taking his lumber thither in a canoe, aided by Gillis Boudewyns." Here Mons took the oath of allegiance, on February 19, 1666.

We shall let the court minutes of New Amsterdam speak in regard to his standing in court:
[October 3, 1665]
"Jan Montagne, Moenes Pietersen and N. Verneltje, pltfs. vs. Daniel Terneur. Pltfs. communicate in form of complaint, that a dispute arose a while ago between them and the defendant (all inhabitants of N. Harlem) on account of deft.'s dog having bitten one of the pltf.'s Montagne's pigs; concerning which the deft. summoned them before the constable and Commissaries of N. Haerlem, who condemned the pltf's severally on the 28th September last in a fine of one pound Flemish for the benefit of the poor. Deft. delivers in copy of aforesaid judgment and maintains that the same was justly pronounced and delivered. He requests therefore that the same be approved of. The Mayor and Aldermen having heard parties' verbal debates, and the produced judgment being examined, they approve and ratify the same, and for reason condemn each in his costs.[818]

This case was of little account. Far more serious and, as above intimated, likely determinative for Pietersen's leaving Harlem, was his beating of a herdsman and threat to treat the town constable in a similar manner.
The version of the Court minutes dealing with this matter is as follows:
"Resolveert Waldron, Constable at N. Haerlem, pltf. vs. Moenes Pietersen, deft. Pltf. says, that deft. has been condemned by the Court of Haerlem in a fine of one hundred guilders for and because he had sorely beaten the herdsman of said village, named Jacques, according to the declaration thereon being, but in place of satisfying said judgment he threatened to treat the Constable in a like manner; requesting approval of said judgment, etc. Deft. denies that he beat the abovenamed Jacques the herdsman or threatened the Constable, etc. Jacques the herdsman appearing in person declares, that the defendant struck him, because he had driven the deft.'s oxen with the young cattle of the whole village

---

away from the milk cows; proving the same by a declaration made to this effect by Joost Oplines (Oblinus). The Mayor and Aldermen having heard parties, condemn the deft. first the fl. 100 according to the previously rendered judgment approving the same, and further, to be imprisoned until he give security for his (good behavior) and to demean himself as becomes an honest inhabitant."[814]

As we have already noticed, Pietersen was a resident of Elizabethtown in 1666. "Within ten years he went to the Swedish Colony at Upland, Penn., and got land at Calkoen Hook, where he was yet living in 1693."

"Too often mastered by his bad habit, once for scolding a magistrate, he was fined 1000 guilders, but the fine was remitted at the request of the injured party, upon Monis asking pardon for his abuse, and pleading that he said it 'in his drink.' His native frankness and good sense disarmed resentment, and, despite his weakness, won respect. His sons, Peter, Matthew, and Israel are understood to have been the ancestors of the Stuck family." [815]

SIMON DE SWEEDT.

Simon de Sweedt was in New Amsterdam about 1661. As the name indicates, he was from Sweden. What we know about him is due to the following notice in the court minutes of New Amsterdam:

[January 25, 1661]. Jan Janzen van de Langh Straat, pltf. vs. Simon de Sweedt, deft. Pltf. demands from deft. twenty five guilders balance of a piece of land sold him for ninety guilders. Deft. says, that pltf. cannot deliver him the land. Pltf. replies, that he sold the deft. the land as he bought it and that deft. had sold the piece of land back to the man, from whom he bought it. Deft. rejoins, that the pltf. had promised him a ground brief, which pltf. denies. The Court refer the matter in dispute to Cornelis Aarsen and Peter Stoutenburgh to reconcile parties if possible as

---

814 Ibid., V., p. 297.
815 J. Riker, Harlem, Its Origin and Early Annals.

regards the piece of land in question, if not to report their proceedings to the Court." [816]

HANS ROELOFF.

Hans Roeloff, from Stockholm, was a soldier, in service of New Netherland, who fled from Fort New Amstel to Maryland in the year 1659, as per New York Colonial Documents, II., p. 64. Another Swede, Cornelius Jurriaensen (See article "Cornelius Jurriaesen," Part III.) seems to have been his companion in the flight. In the years 1659-1662 a "Roelof Swenske" (Roelof Swede) is listed among the soldiers receiving pay in the military service at Fort Amstel in New Netherland. (Ibid., II., p. 179.) Whether he is the same person as Hans Roeloff can not be definitely stated.

CLAES DE SWEET.

Claes de Sweet (the Swede) was in New Amsterdam about 1655. The words "de Sweet" indicate that he was from Sweden. We know nothing of him beyond what can be inferred from the court minutes of New Amsterdam:

On June 14, 1665, Marritie Jorisen prosecuted a suit against Andries de Haes, and said that de Haes had scolded her as a whore, and her husband as a rogue, in the presence of Claes Michelsen and Claes de Sweet.

July 5, 1655, she "sustained by these two witnesses that de Haes had used abusive language against her and her husband." Andries de Haes objected, that the two witnesses were servants of Marritie Joris. She replied that they were not her servants. De Haes acknowledged that as she said she was not indebted to him, — he replied, "Whores and knaves act so." He now declared before the court that he knew the plaintiff and her husband as honest

---

816 The Records of New Amsterdam, 1653-1674, III., p. 251. Is he the same person as Simon Hansen?

and decent man and wife, and that the words had been expressed in haste. The Court condemned de Haes for his calumnies in a fine of six guilders for the behoof of the deaconry of New Am sterdam, and dismissed the plaintiff's claim.[817]

ROELOFF TEUNISSEN.

Roeloff Teunissen was a seacaptain from Göteborg, in Sweden, who settled in New Amsterdam about 1651. In 1651 he had found employment in the Dutch service, and was then "Master of the ship the Emperor Charles". In New Amsterdam he was a neighbor of Dirck Holgersen, a Norwegian. He bought, on September 18, 1651, Holgersen's original house on a parcel of ground in Smit's Vly. This house had been built by Holgersen about the year 1649. It must have stood upon the whole or a part of the site of the modern building, No. 259 Pearl Street. Roeloff Teunissen resided there till 1657, when he sold the premises to Jan Hendricks Steelman (J. F. Innes, New Amsterdam and Its People, p. 323f.). Teunissen and Steelman must have had busi-ness transactions with each other before. For, on March 8, 1655, Jan Hendricksen Steelman was sued by Jacobus Bakker on account of some property. But Steelman answered "in writing, showing by letter from Roeloff Teunissen to Sieur Schrick (a German), and bill of sale, dated July 4, that he lawfully bought" the property in question.[818]

---

817 Ibid., I., p. 322.

818 Ibid., I., p. 296.

Note: The early records of New Netherland probably present less difficul-ties for tracing Swedish names than the Danish or Norwegian. In the preface we have mentioned Jan Swaen, whom a Scandinavian would take to be Swedish, as a negro. He is sometimes called Swaen Janse. According to Bergen's "Early Set-tlers of Kings County," he came from Luane, to this country in 1654. When Cor-nelius B. Harvey's "Genealogical History of Hudson and Bergen Counties, New Jersey," states that Jan Swaen was a Swede, this depends on reading "Stockholm" for "Stockem" (?). In the church register of New Amsterdam, it is stated that Jan Swaen was "van Stockem in landt van Luyck" (—Liege or Luttich). This was another person.

Eldert Engelbertszen, who in 1656 married Sara Walker, of Boston, is men-tioned by Riker as a Swede. He came, however, from Eland in East Friesland.

Retrospect.

More than a century has passed since an American man of letters, Washington Irving, whose parents were immigrants from Great Britain, wrote what is known as the Knickerbocker History of New York. This burlesque was produced not long after he had recovered from his depressed state of mind, caused by the death of a young lady he was to marry, Mathilde Hofmann, a descendant of a Swedish immigrant Martin Hoffman, whom we have treated in this volume. Washington Irving never married. He remained true to the memory of his early attachment.

Had he been equally faithful in writing the history of New York, we should not have had the Washington Irving school of writers which has done sorry work in distorting the history of the Empire State. This school, says Mr. J. H. Innes. "has done so much to propagate false and unworthy notions of New Netherland History." It is to be lauded that Mrs. Van Rensselaer shows, in her large work on New Amsterdam, an undisguised and proper contempt for these notions; but it is to be deplored that they are almost daily propagated by teachers of literature who in all seriousness recommend "Diedrich Knickerbocker" as a guide in colonial history. Any one familiar with the authentic records of New Netherland will, upon taking Irving's farcical "History" in hand, immediately see how utterly fantastic, even anachronistic, his descriptions are, and how willingly the author yielded to a bias that might be looked for in older English descriptions of the nearest Teuton neighbor across the channel or his offspring on this side of the Atlantic.

Washington Irving was born in New York. He was an American by virtue of his birth on American soil, not by virtue of having English speaking parents. He would have been no less American if his parents had come from Holland, or if he had been born in Sweden, or if he had come over to our country as a "foreigner" and naturalized as a citizen.

It is not pedigree that makes a man an American. Politically he may be an American, but in other respects something else. But politics is not everything. Philip Schaff used to say that he was a Swiss by birth, a German by education, an American by choice. But that does not mean that he renounced his German education in favor of the American. For he considered the former quite superior. It is conceivable that a person may be politically an American, though biologically a Greek, intellectually a German, religiously a Russian, aesthetically an Italian, and recreatively an Englishman.

Nor is it language that makes a person an American. A free country like Switzerland does not discriminate against its citizens because they speak French and not German, or German and not French.

Nor do customs make a man a citizen. The Bavarian does not regard the Mecklenburger as un-German or unpatriotic, though he has some different customs.

It is not easy to define an American. He is not an Anglo-American in the sense that he discriminates against the Dutch-American or the German-American or the Scandinavian-American. Biologically, or racially, he may be a hyphenated American, and as such make use of the hyphen, prefixing Irish, Danish, Swedish, English, etc., to his "American." But the biological factor, as an authority on Sociology proper, Dr. J. H. W. Stuckenberg, says, is not one of the *social* forces that go to make up society. The American is above all a cosmopolitan; that is he is, or should be, removed from the clannishness that regards the naturalized citizen as an inferior because he speaks another tongue or has antecedent spouses who were born under another flag than the stars and stripes. The true American shows the same kind of consideration for the immigrants of the twentieth century as Mr. Theodore Roosevelt and Rev. Dr. David Burrell do in their speeches on the Dutch immigrants, before the Holland Society of New York. This society, founded in 1885 for historical and social purposes, includes only direct descendants in male line of the Netherlanders by birth or adoption who immigrated before the final establishment of English dominion 1674—75. As many of the Scandinavians treated in the present volume must have been Netherlanders by adoption before they came to America, not a few of their descendants are eligible to membership in this organization.

At its banquet in 1903, Dr. Burrell, in speaking of the Dutch fathers of early New York, said:

" . . . Our Dutch fathers were not aliens; they were not refugees; they were never foreigners in any sense; they came here to be Americans, and they were Americans from the first moment when they set foot on the soil of the New World. They were never hyphenated Americans, and they are not hyphenated to this day. I remember when Romulus founded Rome he had a lot of heterogeneous people gathered around him, and they were very much like the population that comes to us from every quarter of the world to-day in the steerage of all the ships. He gathered them around him, and, as he dug the foundation of the ancient city, he required every man among them to take from his neck a little bag of earth which he had fondly brought from his own fatherland, and empty the bag of earth and say, 'civis romanus sum.' That is the only qualification for American citizenship, and our forefathers set the example."

Practically the same thought was expressed seven years before by Mr. Roosevelt, who, like Dr. Burrell, is of Dutch ancestry. Mr. Roosevelt addressed the Society as follows:

". . . I am glad to answer to the toast, "The Hollander as an American." The Hollander was a good American, because the Hollander was fitted to be a good citizen. There are two branches of government which must be kept on a high plane, if any nation is to be great. A nation must have laws that are honestly and fearlessly administered, and a nation must be ready, in time of need, to fight, and we men of Dutch descent have here to-night these gentlemen of the same blood as ourselves who represent New York so worthily on the bench and a Major-General of the Army of the United States.

"It seems to me, at times, that the Dutch in America have one or two lessons to teach. We want to teach the very refined and very cultivated men who believe it impossible that the United States can ever be right in a quarrel with another nation — a little of the elementary virtue of patriotism. And we also wish to teach our fellow citizens that laws are put on the statute books to be enforced; and that if it is not intended they shall be enforced, it is a mistake to put a Dutchman in the office to enforce them.

"The lines put on the programme underneath my toast begin: 'America! half-brother of the world!' America, half-brother of the world and all Americans full brothers one to the other. That is the way that the line should be concluded. The prime virtue of the Hollander here in America and the way in which he has most done credit to his stock as a Hollander, is that he has ceased to be a Hollander, and has become an American, absolutely. We are not Dutch-Americans. We are not "Americans" with a hyphen before it. We are Americans pure and simple, and we have a right to demand that the other people whose stocks go to compose our great nation, like ourselves, shall cease to be aught else and shall become Americans."

We shall not quote the entire speech. But we wish to quote what the American press often has overlooked in referring to this speech. For Mr. Roosevelt said more than this. We put it in italics:

"And further than that, we have another thing to demand, and that is that if they do honestly and in good faith become Americans, those shall be regarded as infamous who dare to discriminate against them because of creed or because of birthplace."

He adds: " . . . These, then, are the qualities I should claim for the Hollander as an American: In the first place that he cast himself without reservation into the current of American life: that he is an American, pure and simple, and nothing else. In the next place, that he works hand in hand and shoulder to shoulder with his fellow Americans, without any regard to differences of creed or to differences of race and religion, if only they are good Americans. . . . " (Year Book of the Holland Society of New York, 1896.)*

The words of these two descendants of Dutch immigrants — incidentally Mr. Roosevelt styles himself a Dutchman — also apply to the Scandinavian immigrants of early times. They were

* The recent discussion about the hyphenated Americans (cfr. Scotch-Irish, Canadian-French) is not responsible for my quoting Burrell and Roosevelt. Seven years have passed since I transcribed their speeches before the Holland Society with the view of incorporating them in the present volume.

good Americans because they were good Scandinavians. And they had something to their credit that the New Netherland government did not have. They were tolerant of the established Dutch Reformed church, and still maintained that they had a right to assemble for worship according to their *own* creed, the Lutheran. The government of New Netherland was intolerant of Lutherans, Quakers, Independents, Mennonites and Catholics. The Dutch in early New York were not quite as tolerant as Mr. Roosevelt's speech makes them appear. This part of his speech has therefore been criticised, and Mr. Roosevelt has accepted the criticism with good grace, stating he was glad that we were now enjoying religious liberty in a broader sense than that which obtained in early New York.

But, in order to be just to the Dutch, how much toleration could be expected of any people of the seventeenth century? Holland (and Turkey) was then the only European power that sanctioned the toleration which now prevails in nearly all modern states. But even Holland did not know religious liberty and equality as we know it to-day.

Notwithstanding, New Netherland was more democratic than Virginia or New England. The mixture of many nationalities — more than twenty — in the Dutch province broadened the democracy of the population, in strong contrast to the clannishness of the neighbors north and south. New England paid deference to blood, education, wealth, social distinction. On the list of Harvard College the students were ranked not alphabetically but according to their social standing, a system that persisted until 1773. The title of Mr. is prefixed to only eight names out of 231 on a list of persons that took the freeman's oath in Connecticut in 1650—1660.*

The nobility in New Netherland, as such, played no role in the development of the national spirit. "Only three or four scions

---

* The conventional usage which does not allow that the honorific prefix "Reverend" by immediately followed by a surname (Rev. Jones), but insists that it should be immediately followed by a Christian name (or initials) or instead by a title (Rev. John Jones, Rev. J. Jones, Rev. Mr. Jones), is rooted in the class distinction which prevailed in the 17th century in places like Connecticut, where, as we have seen, only eight names out of a list of 231 freemen were entitled to the prefix "Mr." Naturally, an English parson was Master or Mister by tacit consent, as "Mr." (formerly Sir) was a translation of "dominus," a title that the parsons in England had used for a long time. When "Reverend" came to be habitually used of the parochial clergy of the Church of England—and that was since the end of the 17th century—the clergyman became, among the few "Misters," the "Reverend Mister." "Reverend was not the property of the Anglican clergy alone. It was also applied to the priest (Roman Catholic) and the minister (Dis-

of the old Netherlands aristocracy ever saw its shores;" and only one nobleman from Scandinavia, a Dane.

It is true that the records of ancient New York are richly sprinkled with the particles "van" and "de". But "van" was not the same as the German "von". It meant *of* or *from*. Thus, Vandeventer meant "from Deventer." "Van Buskirk" was added to the name of Laurens Andriessen, a Dane, to show that the Laurens Andriessen meant was the one living by the church (kerk) in or near the woods (bosch). Van Hoorn could mean "from the city of Horn" but also "from or at the *corner*." Nor was "de" indicative of aristocracy. It was nothing but the article *the*. Pieter Andriessen de Schoornsteenveger, a Dane, was Pieter Andriessen the chimneysweep (p. 156). Dirck de Noorman was Dirck the Norwegian (p. 73). Simon de Sweedt was Simon the Swede. Laurens de Drayer was Laurens the turner (p. 153).

The feeling of the New Netherlanders was no more aristocratic than the blood. Every citizen was in theory at least a "full brother" to every other citizen irrespective of language or nationality. The Scandinavians intermarried among the Germans, and

senter), though an attempt was made in the English court to prohibit the use of "Reverend" on a tombstone of a Wesleyan minister.

To speak of a Scandinavian, a German, or a Dutch Lutheran pastor of the seventeenth century as a "Reverend Mister" is anachronistic. For the Lutheran view of the ministry, as then held, was decidedly democratic as compared to that of the Anglican Church or to that of the Dissenters, who followed Calvin and adhered more or less to the English class distinction. More democratic than these were the Dutch Reformed. The Dutch Reformed were often at one with the Lutherans in putting the prefix "Reverend," without further ado, immediately before the clergyman's surname. The "Ecclesiastical Records of the State of New York," (I-VI., 1901ff.), edited by Mr. Hugh Hastings, State Historian of New York, use "Rev. So-and-So" and "Rev. Mr. So-and-So" indiscriminately, e. g.: Rev. Polhemius, pp. 317, 326, 337; Rev. Wellius, p. 376; Rev. Goetwater, preface xx; Rev. Blom, p. 464; Rev. Drisius, Rev. Schaats, p. 605; Rev. Weeksteen, p. 764; Rev. Dellius, pp. 845, 880, 893; Rev. Selyn, p. 851; Rev. Varick, p. 1067; Rev. Voskuil, Rev. Klingant, Rev. Groenewegen, Rev. Elias, p. 1183; Rev. Freerman, p. 1140; Rev. Leydt, p. 3862; Rev. Ritzema, p. 3886; Rev. Kalkoen, p. 4026; Rev. Leadley, p. 4049; Rev. Kuyper, p. 4119; etc.

Those who condemn this use of "Reverend" without a titular appendix as inconsistent with the English idiom, should register their grievances with the State Historian of New York.

But it is not in the official translation of the Dutch Reformed Documents alone, that "Reverend" is used in this unceremonious manner. The Minutes of the Twelfth Session of the "Evangelical Lutheran Synod of West-Pennsylvania," Gettysburg, 1836, register ministers like Rev. Heim, Rev. Heyer, Rev. Yeager, Rev. Stroh, Rev. Lochman, Rev. Martin, Rev. Oswald, Rev. Moser, Rev. Keyl, Rev. Gottwald, Rev. Anspach, etc. The Minutes of the same Synod for the year 1860 speak, e. g. of Rev. Ide, Revs. Berry, Gotwald, and Guss.

This conventional latitude of the New York Dutch Reformed, and the West Pennsylvania Lutherans also appears in Rev. J. C. Jensson's (now Roseland) "American Lutheran Biographies," Milwaukee, 1890.—a large work of some 900 pages: Rev. Albrecht, p. 23; Rev. Andersen, p. 35; Rev. Ansbach, p. 39; Rev. Dahl, p. 153; Rev. Dietrichsen, p. 163; Rev. Eberhardt, p. 181; Rev. Eggen, p. 184; Rev. Goetwater, p. 213; Rev. Haupt, p. 309; Rev. Kuhl, p. 439; Rev. Mechling, p. 507; Rev. Paulson, p. 581; Rev. Preus, p. 595; Rev. Reck, p. 607; Rev. Ruth, p. 629; Rev. Telleen, p. 798; Rev. Kildal, p. 890; Rev. Lenker, p. 891.

Finally a testimony from the official weekly paper of the "General Synod" of the Evangelical Lutheran Church in the United States of America," "The

the French, but especially among the Dutch.   A Scandinavian intermarriage with the English belonged, however, to the exceptions.

For example, Hans Hansen, from Bergen, Norway, married the daughter of a Walloon father and a Parisian mother.   The ancestor of the American Vanderbilts married, as his first wife, Anneken Hendricks, also from Bergen, Norway.   Laurens Pietersen, a Norwegian, married a lady from Germany.   Anneke Jans, the famous Norwegian lady from Marstrand was married, as widow, to a Hollander, Rev. Boghardus.   Engeltje Mans, of Sweden, was married to a German.   Hage Bruynsen, of Denmark, married a Swede.   That a Dane married a Dane, a Norwegian a Norwegian, a Swede a Swede, was rather uncommon.   Intermarriage was the rule.   And remarriage was the rule among widows and widowers.   Many married for the third time.   In the days of Lovlace, one man, a German, is mentioned as being the fourth husband of his first wife, and the third husband of his second wife whose forebears had been a Dane and a Hollander.   Briete Olofs, from Sweden, married in succession a Swede, a Frieslander,

Lutheran Church Work and Observer'' (Harrisburg and Philadelphia), in the last issue of the year 1915. This paper mentions on p. 2, Rev. Cannaday, Rev. Spangler, Rev. Dunkelberger; on p. 15, Rev. Botsford; on p. 16, Rev. Richard.

All this proves conclusively that ''Rev. Mr.'' is not universal usage. And as shown, it owes its origin to a social classification, which obtains no longer. We say Bishop Ball and Doctor Hall, Professor Hart and Dean Hort, without a ''Mr.'' either prefixed or affixed. Why, then, should not ''Reverend Jones'' be treated in the same way? Some may object, ''Reverend'' is an adjective, the other prefixes mentioned are nouns. But why should ''Reverend'' perpetually remain an adjective or be a mere appellative petrifaction, excluded from the laws of evolution, since it is used as a noun in many sections of our country, notwithstanding the conservative label it has been given by the dictionary. To illustrate, the Greek word ''Christos'' (anointed) was at first an adjective. Later it became also a proper noun. Now, ''Reverend'' as a honorific prefix has gone through a similar development. It is well known that ''The'' as a sine qua non prefix to ''Reverend'' is no longer insisted upon in sections where provincial standards have given way to broader views. And what is there to hinder the ''Mr.'' from following suit as a conventional, but provincial and undemocratic drag, that the doctor and professor has dismissed. We have no ''Dr. Mr.'' and no ''Prof. Mr.''

Perhaps it would be well to dismiss ''Reverend'' entirely as the stereotyped style for clergy, substituting ''Pastor'' or another equivalent. Certain Ministerial Associations have tabood it. And they have been wise in so doing,—just as wise as Sir William Ramsey, who has dropped ''Saint'' as the prefix to the apostle Paul.

Says this distinguished English professor in ''The Teaching of Paul in Terms of the Present Day'' (1913): ''I have intentionally avoided using the honorific prefix ''St.'', which places Paul on a conventional pedestal, and obscures the man, the missionary, and the teacher. It has in English lost entirely its original force in Greek usage. In Greek we use ho hagios (the holy) with the names of angels and archangels and the spirit of God, and so in Latin sanctus; but in English the convention would not allow St. Raphael, St. Michael, or St. Spirit.''

I, too, have intentionally avoided using in the present work ''Rev. Mr.'' as prefix to the surname of ministers. At best ''Rev. Mr.'' can be only on par with ''Rev.'' The address ''Rev. Jones,'' whether English or not English, solves a dilemma when one does not know if ''Rev. Jones'' (Christian name or initials unknown) is a man or a woman (there are several hundred ordained lady preachers), a ''Mr.'', a ''Mrs.'', or a ''Miss.'' (See my article ''Pastor or Minister?'' in the ''Lutheran Observer.'' Vol. LXXVI., No. 10. (Philadelphia, 1908).

and a German. Divorce suits were few in number, fewest among the Scandinavians.

The matrimonial democracy of the parents was perpetuated by the children, and these were many. The Norwegian-French marriage of Hans Hansen, of Bergen, gave life to nine children. The Norwegian-Dutch marriage of another Norwegian from Bergen, Herman Hendricksen, resulted in ten children. The German-Norwegian matrimonial alliance of Dr. Kierstede and Sara Roelofs, from Marstrand, enriched the population of New Amsterdam by half a score. The marriage of Bording, a Dane, with a Hollander increased his family by ten. Thomas Fredricksen, a Dane, and his wife, from Holland, were parents of eight children. Martin Hoffman, a Swede, had by his second wife, who was German or Dutch, five children. Burger Joris, a German, married a Swedish lady and had ten children.

In business affairs, racial differences were as little in evidence as in matrimony. It was not uncommon for Scandinavians to be in partnership with Dutch or Germans.

As Dutch was spoken by the majority, this language played much the same role among those who were not of Dutch blood as English plays to-day among our city immigrants from foreign lands. Those who did not speak Dutch belonged to the exceptions. And up to the time of the American Revolution, New York city remained a characteristically Dutch-German-Scandinavian city in custom and feelings. It is related that travelers noticed the un-English aspect and atmosphere of the place. Notwithstanding, New York was distinctively American. And taking its rank as a fullfledged city as early as 1653, when it had no rival in the English colonies, it is the oldest of American cities, as well as the greatest. As the Scandinavians did not have Scandinavian churches, schools, and papers, they must have learnt Dutch more rapidly than the immigrants of to-day acquire English.

The factors at work in retarding the learning of English to-day in various rural sections of our country were much the same as those which made the Dutch in New York and the Germans in Pennsylvania slow in turning to English. They were in no hurry to bid adieu to the continental tongues.

Says Mrs. Van Rensselaer: "For two or three generations

even a colloquial acquaintance with the English tongue was not universal on Manhattan; and all through colonial times the English speech of its people was very corrupt, for a large proportion of them heard only Dutch in the family, the church, and the school. The Reformed church permitted no English sermons to be preached from its pulpits until 1764 and did not abolish Dutch sermons until the end of the century; no master taught English in its school until 1773 and the first who taught it exclusively took charge in 1791."

The Dutch language had the same hold on the population of Manhattan as the German on that of Pennsylvania. As late as 1783 a motion was made in the legislature of Pennsylvania to the effect that the official language of the state from then on should be German. The motion was lost by a majority of one vote, and this vote was cast by a German.

There is indeed nothing particularly commendable in an exclusive adherence to the language of one's forefathers when expediency demands a greater command of the tongue that is spoken by the majority of the land. On the other hand, there is nothing supremely heroic in renouncing, perhaps denouncing, the language of parents or grandparents to the exclusive cultivation of the official language of the land. Emerson's rule to read nothing but English, to read even the classics of foreign nations only in English translation, is, to say the least, fully as much at fault as was the attitude of the older Dutch and German pioneers towards English. An asset of the Jew is his linguistic ability. Even a man so remote from commercial motives as Paul of Tarsus knew several languages: Hebrew, Aramaic, Greek, and probably Latin. The sudden growth of Germany as a commercial power at a time when the routes and markets of commerce were pretty well established, is, in no mean degree, due to the stress which that country lays on the study of languages. The educated American and his insular cousin the Englishman are linguistically no match for the cultured Dane or Dutchman of Europe. As for the Dutch, the Scandinavians, and the Germans in our country, they are as a rule bilinguals. As such they can appreciate the spirit of America's greatest poet, Longfellow, who after finishing college spent many years in studying foreign languages.

But — to give our digression a point. American citizenship

is not inconsistent with paying homage to a tongue that is not English. For otherwise American citizens must cease blaming, for example, Germany for forcing German upon the Danes of Schleswig-Holstein, and Russia for Russianizing Finnland and compelling the Poles to speak Russian. America, the new home of many tongues, should be fully as democratic as was imperial Rome, where perhaps almost three fourths of the population spoke Greek, but only a little more than a fourth knew Latin. The Apostle Paul, one of the greatest organizers that history knows, a cosmopolitan in the best sense of the word, a traveler that visited Spain as well as Eastern Antioch, — separated from each other by the distance of some 3000 miles — was probably better at home in Greek and Hebrew than in the official language of the land which had bestowed upon him the rights of Roman citizenship. But — to come nearer to our age, our America of to-day should be fully as democratic on the language question as was ancient New York.

Respect for foreign speech is a twin brother of respect for colored race. And here, too, New Netherland teaches the modern American a lesson, especially such as discriminate against negroes and Indians.

As to the New Netherlanders' treatment of the Indian, Mrs. Van Rensselaer says: "In general the Dutchman tried to treat the Indians well. By nature they were more gentle than the Puritan Englishman; they did not share his hatred and contempt for aliens and heathen; and they were more strongly inclined by their social needs to a friendly policy. . . . In theory at least the Hollander considered the Indian a man like himself with analogous rights."

This statement applies equally well to the Scandinavian immigrants. One of the first among them to remonstrate against Governor Kieft for his unfair treatment of the Indians, was the Dane Jochem Pietersen Kuyter. The signing of a treaty of peace between the government and an Indian tribe took place at the house of another fairminded and democratic Dane, Jonas Bronck (p. 179). Leading interpreters of Indian in New Netherland were Claes Carstensen (p. 51) and Sara Roelofs (p. 106), both Norwegians; and Jan Davidsen, a Swede.

To keep or sell natives of the soil as slaves was never sanctioned in New Netherland by law, by custom, or by public opinion. But a few Indian slaves were introduced from foreign parts, and two governors saw fit to export a few captives in a time of war. The Norwegian woman Sara Roelofs (107) mentions in a will her "Indian, named Ande," whom she gave to one of the sons she had by her first husband, Dr. Kierstede from Magdeburg. But she, the excellent Indian interpreter, may have proved a good mistress for Ande, who served under English — not Dutch — rule.

The Indians adopted Teutonic names, for example, Hans, Hendrick. Some of them joined towards the close of the century the Dutch Reformed church. But no special effort was made by the New Netherlanders to carry on any missionary enterprise among them, such as the Swedish minister John Campanius planned in the Swedish settlement at the Delaware. Rev. J. Campanius, who was born in Stockholm about 1601, was in New Sweden from 1643 to 1648. His home was at Tinicum Island, nine miles south-west of Philadelphia. He translated Luther's Small Catechism into the language of the Delaware Indians. The translation antedates that of Eliot's Indian Bible.* It was, however, not published until 1696. Its pages alternate with Swedish and Indian. (A copy of it is found in the archives at the Theological Seminary, Gettysburg, Pa.; in the Library of Congress; and in one of the libraries in Philadelphia.)

Commercially the red men were outwitted by the Europeans. It suffices to point to the negotiation which resulted in their sale of Manhattan, 24,000 acres, for $24, or $120 in present value. But they also knew how to strike a bargain as they attempted to do, when they captured Pieter Andriessen, a Dane, and demanded a high ransom. The greatest weakness of the Indian was his liking for fire-water. The government was obliged to issue several ordinances prohibiting the sale of liquor to him.

Less deference was paid to the negro. The blacks were bought and sold as slaves. But slave-traffic as such was not indulged in. There never were many slaves in New Netherland until after the first conquest by the English. The first that came directly from Africa arrived in 1665, about a century after the first English slave ship carried off from Africa its cargo of

---

* The first edition of the entire Bible printed in the New World in a European language was the German Bible of 1743, from Sauer's press, Germantown, Pennsylvania, with 1272 pages, quarto form. No Bible had been printed in the English language in the colonies before the German Bible of 1743.

vendible natives. Sir John Hawkins, later vice admiral of the Armada, owned the ship, whose name of "Jesus" harmonized but poorly with its mission to Africa in 1562.

The Netherlanders employed the negroes as house servants They could not chastise them without permission of the magistrate. Manumission was an easy matter and quite inexpensive. The husband of Ciletje Jans, Danish, united with two other men to liberate a slave. They had to pay ten pounds sterling. Pieter Andriessen, from Denmark, kept negro slaves, one of whom displayed on a certain occasion that well known but unaccountable weakness of a black man in the presence of chickens which often leads, and then did lead, to pleadings in the court. Pieter Jansen, from Norway, seems to have had a negro slave. And Sara Roeloefs, Norwegian, owned several slaves. She mentions them in her will: a negro boy Hans; "a little negress called Maria"; a negro boy, Peter; two negresses Susannah and Sarah. Marritje Janse, likewise from Norway, owned a slave, "a negro boy," whom she bequeathed to her son.

In those days it was not considered wrong even for churches to own slaves. One of the Swedish Lutheran congregations in the settlement at the Delaware owned a negress called Peggy. She was servant at the parsonage. Ministers could come and go. But she had to remain. However, she had a mind of her own. She got so stubborn at last that the congregation sold her for $25.

Some of the negroes in New Netherland joined the church. A negro with the sonorous sounding name of Franciscus Bastianzen joined the Dutch Reformed church in 1674. In the year following, also his wife Barbara Manuels, "Negerinne," joined it. Two other negroes belonging to this church were Claes Emanuels and Jan de Vries. Several blacks had Teuton names, e. g. Swaen Janse, Anna Jans, Emanuel Pietersen, Lucas Pietersen, Andries de Neger. Slaves from Africa were called Angola slaves. They were thievish and lazy. African nativity was sometimes indicated by names like Jan Van Angola Neger, Dorothea Angola Negerinne. The oft repeated statement that a negro was the official hangman of New Amsterdam is a fiction.

We have thus far considered the attitude of the Dutch and Scandinavians in their matrimonial and business relations to one another and in their general relation to colored races. We shall now consider to what extent the Dutch were willing to give the Scandinavians a share in the administrative affairs of the colony. Was democracy as evident in this field as in others?

Now, the Scandinavians had not left their native or adopted land because of religious or political discontent or for the lack of industrial opportunity. They came to New Netherland voluntarily, being recruited for the service they might render the West India Company. Some even brought their wives and children along, though the large majority married in the New World. They came by way of Holland, commonly from Texel. Originally they may have started out from harbors like Bergen, Copenhagen, Göteborg. Their sojourn in Holland lasted perhaps for a few weeks or even for years. They were their own masters. Thus being more or less acquainted with Dutch institutions, it was not difficult for them to assimilate with the Dutch in New Netherland; whose language, closely related as it is to Danish, Norwegian, and Swedish, they easily acquired. Dutch was in those days the language of commerce. Even the instructions on the Danish men-of-war were printed in Dutch for some time during this period, not because the Danish fleet was manned with more Dutchmen than Danes, but because Dutch was pre-eminently the language of the sailors, and there were a good many sailors of foreign speech in the Dano-Norwegian navy, as there likewise were many Danish and Norwegian sailors with the Dutch fleet.

New Amsterdam was visited quite early by Scandinavian ships, but it does not appear, that they carried immigrants direct from Scandinavian harbors. Holland's harbors were then for Scandinavian immigrants what English harbors have been for them in the nineteenth century: the passengers went off one ship in order to get aboard another. This accounts for the fact that Scandinavian passengers, as the rcords show, came over by Dutch ships, for example, "de Eendracht," "Rinselaers Wijck," "de Rooseboom," "de Bruynvis," "de Statyn," "de Trouw,' "de Moesman," "de Bonte Koe," "den Houttuyn," "de Leide," "de Vos," "de vergulde Bever," "de Otter," "de vergulde Otter." "De Brant von Trogen" carried Jonas Bronck, the Dane, to our shores. It was a private ship. "Het Wapen van Noorwegn" (The Arms of Norway) is mentioned several times in the records. Jan Jansen, a Swedish immigrant was mate of "de Coninck Salomon." Roelof Teunissen, another Swedish immigrant, was master of the ship

"Emperor Charles."   Skipper Syvert van Bergen, probably Norwegian (p. 145), was commander of "Broken Heart."

The Scandinavians were always eligible to public offices in New Netherland.   As early as 1632 two Norwegians, Roelof Jansen and Laurens Laurensen were schepens in the region about Albany.   The Dane Jochem Kuyter was, as we have shown elsewhere, successively a member of the Board of Twelve men, Board of Eight Men, and Board of Nine Men.   And in 1653, when he died, he was schepen.   Though the West India Company stated in 1653 that the officials in New Netherland ought to be "as much as possible of the Dutch nation" on the ground that they would give the most satisfaction to the people at large, yet no discrimination was ever made against Scandinavians.   They continued eligible also after 1653.   For example. Claes Bording, the Dane, was several times nominated for the office of schepen.   Matthys Roelofs, Danish, served as constable.   Smeeman and Laurens Andriessen, Danes, were magistrates of the court of Bergen.   The Dane Jan Broersen was magistrate of Horly and Marble in 1674.   Dirck Holgersen, the Norwegian, was magistrate of Bushwyck in 1681.   Matthysen, the Swede, was overseer of the court at Harlem, and Jan Pietersen Slot was magistrate in the same village from 1660 to 1665.

Among those appointed by the Governor to positions of trust was Roelof Jansen Haes, a Norwegian.   He was Receiver-General of Excises in 1647 at a salary of fl. 480.   [The Schout-fiscal received fl. 920, the Secretary fl. 632, the commisary and bookkeeper fl. 800, the preacher fl. 1400.]   The salary that Haes got was considered by the Company as an evidence of Governor Stuyvesant's "good knowledge of his (Haes') honesty."   Some of the Jansens, from Bredstedt in Denmark, were inspectors of staves or firewardens.   Also Christian Baerents, probably a Dane, was firewarden.   Dirck Holgersen, from Norway, was "city carpenter."   The Scandinavians, however, did not acquire the political influence of their German cousins who came from the commercial centers of what the Records designate as the "Kayserreich."   They did not ascend to the top of the political ladder as Nicholas de Meyer. from Hamburg, who was mayor of New York city in 1676; or as Jacob Leisler, from Frankfurt am Main, who became lieutenant-governor of the entire province.   On the other hand, the Scandinavian women, especially the Norwegian, constituted a good part of the New Amsterdam aristocracy.

Before considering the status and influence of the women, a word might be said in regard to Scandinavians as soldiers. The first soldiers came to New York in 1633. But the professional soldiers were too few in number to give adequate protection to the citizens, who therefore organized themselves into private military companies. Among the Danish immigrants serving in military capacity were Ensign Nissen, distinguished for his "great diligence and vigilance"; John Ranzow, corporal; Sybrant Cornelissen, barber surgeon; also Pieter Laurenszen Kock, sergeant; Jan Laurens; Severyn Laurensen; Hendrick Martensen; Jan Pietersen; Hans Rasmussen; Andries Thomassen. On the whole they seem to have had a good record, though Thomassen deserted; and Severyn Laurensen, Lance Corporal, was stripped of his arms, publicly flogged and branded because of theft.

Among the Norwegian soldiers were Laurens Andriessen, who was wounded in the war against the Indians, and whose shoes during his state of helplessness on the battlefield were pulled off by a soldier comrade and sold for whisky; also Roelof Jansen Haes, who fought the Indians in 1643. Andries Pietersen was another soldier. And Dirck Holgersen, though advanced in years, was ensign of the local militia at Bushwyck in 1689.

Among the Swedish soldiers were Dirck Hendricksen Bye and Cornelius Jeuriansen, who deserted. Jacob Loper, from Sweden, who had ben captain lieutenant at Curacao, in the navy was no doubt an expert in military as well as in naval matters.

The enemy that these Scandinavian pioneers had to encounter in battle was the Indian, the Englishman, and the Frenchman. The Indian outbreaks at Manhattan, the massacres at Esopus and Schenectady bear testimony to that.

But what sheds lustre upon the Scandinavian in New Amsterdam was less the martial bravery of the men than the quiet influence of the women.

Tryn, or Catharine, Jonas from Marstrand, Norway, was the first midwife of New Netherland. She was paid from the public purse, and certainly earned what she got by her patient waiting upon the sick.

A daughter of hers was Anneke Jans, of New York fame, who married the Dutch pastor, Rev. Bogardus. She was the first woman in the city of New York to marry a minister. By her husband she inherited land that to-day is rated at some $300,-000,000, being in the very heart of New York city. The descendants of Anneke Jans, from the Norwegian fishing-town of Marstrand, are very numerous and very wealthy.

A daughter of Anneke augmented the New Amsterdam aristocracy by marrying Dr. Kierstede, a German physician. He was the first permanent physician in the city of New York. The first recorded coroner's inquest ever held in that city was conducted by Dr. Kierstede and two assistants.

Another daughter of Anneke, Fyntie, was married to a magistrate of Albany, an expert at estimating Indian money.

Her third daughter, Katrina, was married, first to the Vice Director of Curacao; then, as a widow, to a wealthy merchant, later mayor of New York. Katrina's daughter, Elizabeth, was married to the son of Augustyn Herrman, from Prague, who became the owner of some 30,000 acres of land.

But midwife Tryn Jonas had also another daughter and another grandchild who became the wives of distinguished men. Her daughter Marritje was married first to the leading shipwright of the colony; and later to Govert Loockermans, one of the wealthiest men in the province. Marritje's daughter, Elsie, was first married to a Dutchman, a schepen of New Amsterdam; as a widow she became the wife of Governor Jacob Leisler, mentioned in the text books on United States history as the one who called the first colonial Congress.

Another famous woman was Engeltje Mans, from Sweden, the wife of Burger Joris, who was one of the Great Burghers and a schepen. By his determined attitude he delayed by several hours the surrender of New York to the English. He was a smith. But this "smith, a mighty man was he." Tryntie Jans of Denmark was married to a magistrate of Rensselaerswyck, and her sister became the wife of a capitalist. Eva Albertse, Norwegian, was married to Anthony De Hooges, superintendent of the colony of Rensselaerswyck; and later to a sheriff of Ulster County. Marritje Pieters of Copenhagen married the brother of the Secretary of the colony. Her marriage contract is the first instanced marriage contract in New Netherland (1639). It is given on page 257 in this work.

Incidentally it might be mentioned that Hans Hansen, of Bergen, married the first girl born of European parentage in New Netherland; and that Dirck Holgersen, another Norwegian, married the sister of the first boy born of white people on the same soil. Holgersen was thus the brother-in-law of the Secretary of the colony.

These marriages went far to strengthen the ties already formed between Scandinavians and Dutch, and to make those characteristics count which were more peculiar to the pioneers from Denmark, Norway and Sweden than to those from Holland.

As law-abiding citizens, the immigrants from northern Europe stood in the front ranks. As industrious men and women they were excelled by none. They were determined, aggressive in their efforts to secure religious liberty, fearless in defending their rights. But they were also mindful of their duties, and reasonable in their dealings with other nationalities and races. Their women were active in commercial life as shopkeepers, as farmers and even traders in the wilderness. Sarah Roelof's ability to speak Indian was not acquired by living in a town. Like their Dutch sisters, the Scandinavian women pleaded their own cases in court, had power of attorney in their husband's absence. They were thus more emancipated than their good sisters of the New England states.

Woman's equality in court, especially in matters of pleading, was due to the fact that Law in New Netherland was inexpensive, for it was common sense. There were no lawyers in this province, only notaries whose assistance was invited in framing legal documents. The local government was fashioned after that of the cities of Holland, where even the smallest village had its elected judiciary of five or seven schepens. The schepens in the villages of New Netherland were usually four in number. They and the burgomasters formed the court. The schout was the sheriff or prosecuting attorney. When not acting as prosecutor, he could preside over the court. The presiding officer was to see that justice was done to the litigants concerned, in getting at the evidence pro and con. The court often referred the litigants to arbitrators. The cases in which the Scandinavians figure were mainly civil cases, which were referred to arbitrators or settled by mutual agreement or by the wronging party's paying a small fine begging pardon of God and man etc. The criminal code was lenient as compared with that of European states. One of the severest verdicts rendered was the one that sentenced the Dane Laurents Duyts to "have a rope tied around his neck, and then to be severely flogged, to have his right ear cut off, and to be banished for fifty years." Mild in comparison was that which was rendered against Jacob Eldersen, also a Dane, who, more by accident than by intent, caused the death of a fellow cooper. He was condemned to pay 100 guilders and costs. Amusing indeed was the verdict rendered against Hans Hansen from Bergen, who was charged with having aided in smuggling. The Court considering that he had been "for fourteen years a respectable resident of New Amsterdam" dismissed the charge "on condition that he beg pardon of God and the Court."

We look in vain for any hardened criminals among the Scandinavians in New Netherland. When the lawsuits to which they were a party, did not concern the payment of debts, fulfillment of contracts, they commonly dealt with sins of the tongue. Mere trifles — a dog biting a hog — were sufficient to create litigation. And few were those whose names never figured in the courts. Deference was paid to none. The Lutheran pastor Fabritius, likely a Pole, had his actions sifted in court by Marritje Jeurians, Danish. And Hans Pietersen, a Norwegian, sued the Swedish Lutheran pastor Lars Lock, of the Swedish settlement at the Delaware, for "the recovery of a mare."

As a rule it was differences between employer and employee, between creditor and debtor that occasioned most of the suits. And considering the various vocations of the litigants, there arose from time to time various matters that called for adjustment by the Court.

What were these vocations?

We have first the farmers who had let a part of their land and were looking for stipulated returns. A majority of the inhabitants owned farming land and farmed, though they had learnt one or more trades. Some of them worked in saw mills and grist mills. The Norwegians, especially, proved themselves experienced hands in sawing lumber. The forests and waterfalls of Norway had offered abundant opportunity for those millers that were not used to the windmills of Holland. Laurens Andriessen, Norwegian, operated "two large sawmills," run by a "powerful waterfall." Another Norwegian, Laurens Laurensen, owned a saw mill. Jan Pietersen, a Dane, was a woodsawyer. Also two other Danes, Pieter Jacobsen and Volckert Jansen, operated mills.

Not a few owned yachts and boats, and were engaged in fishing, freighting lumber and other merchandise on the Hudson, or the Delaware. Laurens Laurensen, Norwegian, used several yachts for timber transport. He also built yachts for the market. One of them "Swarten Arent" (Black Eagle) was valued at fl. 1400. Hans Carlsen, Norwegian, sailed a large boat and employed hired men on it. Christian Pietersen, a Dane, plied his boat up and down the Hudson. The Swedes Jan Jansen and Roelof Teunissen commanded larger ships. Danes like Bording, Kuyter, Bronck were experienced navigators. Norwegians like Albert and Arent Andriessen were used to the seas. The great ship "New Netherland," built at Manhattan, was the work of Scandinavian carpenters, engaged by Pieter Minuit. It was of 600 to 800 tons burden, fitted to carry thirty guns. "It was one of the largest merchantmen afloat, and not for two hundred years was another as large launched in the same waters. Sent at once to Holland and employed in the West India trade, everywhere it excited wonder by its size and by the excellence and variety of timber used in its construction." (Mrs. Van Rensselaer). Among the early ship carpenters was Hans Hansen, from Bergen; and Tymen Jansen, husband of Marritje Jans, from Marstrand.

Among the general carpenters, mention can be made of Dirck Holgersen, a Norwegian; Jan Pietersen Slot, a Dane; Dirk Bensingh, a Swede. The latter worked on the New Church at Fort Orange. A number of houses in New Amsterdam were built by Scandinavian carpenters. Among the masons were Danes like Marten Harmensen and Claus Paulson. Laurens Andriessen, Danish, was an expert at the lathe. Pieter Andriessen, another Dane, was a professional chimney sweep. Hage Bruynsen, Swede, had worked as a smith. Marcus Pietersen, Norwegian, was a cobbler. But he quarrelled with his master, Jochem Beckman, and nicknamed him "black pudding."

Some were "jack-of-all-trades."

Not a few were coopers, brewers, and tavernkeepers. Volckert Jansen, a Dane, had a brewery. The Danes Jacob Eldersen and Thomas Fredricksen were brewers and coopers. The Danes William Adriaensz, Jan Jansen, and Frederick Hendricksen were coopers. Claes Claesen, Norwegian, was versed in "brandy-making" and "beer-brewing." Pieter Kock, Pieter Andriessen, Severyn Laurensen, Danes, were tavernkeepers.

Apparently the Danes were more concerned about liquor than were the Swedes or Norwegians. But it would not be fair to stamp them as worse than the Dutch. Drunkenness, says Mrs. Van Rensselaer, was everywhere the great sin of the Dutch.

Every one drank beer, wine, and whisky at this period. Water was the only alternative. Tea, coffee, and chocolate were all unknown until the close of the seventeenth century. Beer was served at every meal. This explains why many were brewers. The coopers were in demand, because liquor in those days was not bottled but kept in casks and kegs. As for the taverns, they served as hotels, restaurants, clubhouses, news-exchanges.

Twelve tavernkeepers were counted in New Amsterdam in March 1648. But only one of them was a Scandinavian, Pieter Andriessen. The city numbered in the same year seventeen tapsters. Rev. J. Backerus wrote regarding them in a letter of September 2, 1648, to the Classis at Amsterdam:

"The congregation here numbers about 170 members. Most of them are very ignorant in regard to true religion, and very much given to drink. To this they are led by the seventeen taphouses here. What bad fruits result therefrom, your Reverences will readily understand. . . . If you could obtain from the Hon. Directors an order for closing these places, except three or four, I have no doubt, the source of much evil and great offense would be removed."

Nine years later, the number of tapsters in New Amsterdam had increased to twenty-one. But none of them were Scandinavians.

That liquor was freely indulged in on festive occasions, may be inferred from what happened at the German-Norwegian wedding of Dr. Kierstede and Sara Roelofs, when Governor Kieft took advantage of the alcoholic hilarity of the guests and induced them to subscribe toward the building funds of the church. They competed with one another in subscribing sums that made their hearts ache when they on the next day realized how generous they had been.

Not infrequently quiet gatherings at the taverns would be subjected to the same treatment as that which an Englishman, Captain John Underhill, proferred to a company of guests who had been invited for a social time at the chief tavern of the town. Five of the leading citizens of New Amsterdam and their wives, three of whom were Scandinavians, were being entertained one evening by the host, when Captain Underhill rushed in and threatened dire destruction if he did not have things his own way (p. 258). The guests were sober, but the Captain who has been called one of "the right New England military worthies" failed sadly in this respect, and therefore broke up the party. His conduct, it seems, was on par with his spelling. He spelled by ear. It has been pointed out that in his letters to Winthrop he invented 'favarabell,' 'considderachonse,' 'menchoned,' and 'ling-grin,' wrote that the 'last chip' which had 'arifd' from England was 'but nine wicks in her viagse,' and described John Browne as a 'jentiele young man, of gud abilliti, of a louli fetture and gud behafior.'

But to change the subject from tavern to church (as Governor Kieft did at the wedding), it must be stated that no less than five of those who signed the petition of the Lutherans at New Amsterdam in 1657 (requesting that Rev. J. Goetwater might remain in the country as a Lutheran minister) were brewers. There were twenty-four signers in all. Five of them were Scandinavians. Of these five, one was a brewer, Jacob Eldersen. As for the effort of the Lutherans to get denominational recognition in New Amsterdam see Appendix IV. Suffice it here to mention that Laurens Andriessen, from Norway, defied Governor Stuyvesant by giving Rev. Goetwater lodging at his house for an entire winter. In denominational matters the Scandinavians co-operated with the Germans more than with the Dutch.

Turning our attention, from the more or less public affairs, to the homes, we inquire, How did the homes of the Scandinavian immigrants look?

The present volume contains several views conveying an idea of the houses they lived in. They present the houses of Roelof

Jansen Haes, Sara Roelofs, Christina Capoen (wife of Jacob Haes), Anneke Jans, Jochem Kuyter, Jacob Loper, Engeltje Mans. The views date from 1652, when New Amsterdam had about 100 houses. The dwellings were not large. Even Secretary Van Tienhoven lived in one not larger than thirty feet long and twenty feet wide.

It would be interesting to have a view of the dwelling of Jonas Bronck. It was a stone house, covered with tiles. Among other things it contained an extension table, around which such people dined as were no strangers to table cloths and napkins, alabaster plates and silverware. It contained other articles that may have been stored in different rooms; for example, a Japanese cutlass, two muskets and three guns, a black cloth mantle, some satin suits, four tankards with silver chains, etc. Bronck's library collection was perhaps the most interesting object in the entire house, being the first known library in New York. It consisted of twenty bound volumes in Danish, Dutch and Latin, including a Danish Calendar, a Danish Child's book, a Danish Law book, a Danish Chronicle, Luther's whole catechism, a Lutheran hymnal, a German Bible, Calvin's Institutes; also seventeen books in manuscript, and a number of pictures. This library, of which the inventory was taken in 1642, was a trifle larger than those that were owned by Danish ministers at that time. Bronck was a God-fearing man. He called his house Emmaus, and his motto was "Ne cede malis" (Do not yield to misfortunes). His name is perpetuated in the Borough of Bronx, New York City.

Among the names of the old Scandinavian immigrants none are so well known in New York to-day as Bronck and Anneke Jans. We know but little as to how Anneke lived. In her will she makes mention of some beds and silver mugs. Her daughter Sara speaks of silver spoons; perhaps they were inherited from the mother. Anneke's sister makes mention of gold earrings, a diamond rose ring, the Great Bible, silver spoons, a silver chain with keys, a silver chain with a case and cushion, and a silver bodkin.

The houses of the Scandinavian immigrants were doubtless modestly furnished, perhaps much like those of the immigrants from Holland, the kitchen being the living room.

We will not venture to describe the bill of fare. The New

Netherlanders had no difficulty in obtaining fruit and vegetables. The wild strawberry and wild grapes grew in abundance. The potato which as late as 1616 was a rare dish on the table of French royalty, was no stranger to New Netherland, one of whose citizens went by the nickname of Potato: Hendrick Claesen Pataddes. There was plenty of game: pigeons, partridges, venison and wild turkey. Fish was a common dish, including lobsters a foot and a half long. Marritje Pietersen, of Copenhagen, was frequently visited when people were in want of fish. At her place, fish and beer could be obtained at all seasons not proscribed by law. She made it a point of honor not to sell fish on Sundays "after the ringing of the church bell."

Among the articles imported from Europe, mention can be made of the Edam and Leyden cheese, salt and vinegar. Van Rensselaer sent his colony such merchandise as Flemish stockings, linen underwear, watertight leather shoes, blankets (green and white), soap, dishes, winnowing baskets, gunpowder, firelocks, canvasses, axes, Norwegian files, and "Norwegian kerseys". The ship "The Arms of Norway" had on one occasion so much of these and kindred articles, that the sailors protested against sailing, not being willing to take the chances of reaching the New World with the entire cargo.

The medium of exchange among the settlers of New Netherland was not gold, silver, or copper. Nor was it in any marked degree naturalia. It was Indian money called wampum, the Indian name for it. It consisted of beads of two colors, white and black. The white "were made from periwinkle shells, the black which were twice as valuable, from the dark spot at the base of the shells of the clam. Both kinds were about as thick as a straw and less than half an inch in length. They were drilled and polished. For use as currency they were strung on deer sinews or strands of fibre and then measured by the span or cubit." Wampum, as the English called it, or zeewant as the Dutch called it, was the only legal tender between individuals. Debts of thousands of guilders were discharged with this kind of money. Of course these beads were never sent to Europe. As an expert in the value of this shell money, the records mention Pieter Hartgers, husband of Fyntie Roelofs, a Norwegian.

As to recreation, skating and sleighing must have been quite common in their season. But the modern buggy ride, for example, was unknown. Only utilitarian carts were built, none for comfort. Horseback riding and boat riding must have been an every day occurence. New Amsterdam had a number of "porters" or carmen. One of them was Jan Carelsen, fro Norway. The celebrations of Christmas, New Year, and Mayday was not much saner than some modern fourth of July celebrations.

As for the intellectual status of our pioneers under the Dutch dominion, it must have been on a fairly high level. Some of the early documents are drawn up in Latin. Kuyter no doubt knew this language. Bronck was versed in this and in several other tongues. Three other Scandinavians, whom we have noticed, were versed in the Indian languages. Doubtless all the Danish, Norwegian and Swedish immigrants spoke at least two tongues, their native language and the language of their adopted country. And as the mastery of one of the Scandinavian languages means also the ability to understand the other two languages, — the Scandinavians could boast of four tongues to the Dutchman's one. Of course, none of the pioneers from the north made any attempts at writing literature. Even among the Dutch immigrants there was none that wrote with literary intent, and only three that wrote poetry: Jacob Steendam, Nicasius de Silla, and Domine Sellyn. Whatever printing the New Netherlanders needed, was done in Holland, which at that time occupied the same position as Germany does now, printing more than the remaining countries taken together.

As to the marks used in signing documents, they are in many cases inconclusive as proofs of inability to write. We know many plain people who prefer to put a mark on a paper instead of writing their names in full, and that not because they do not know how to write, but because they think they can not write a fair hand. Anneke Jans appears to have written a mark when it did not suit her to write her name. Jan Broersen appears to have had a good hand, and yet he made use of a mark (see p. 155). The cases of Hans Hansen, Laurens Pietersen, and Dirck Holgersen are more doubtful. Hansen's "H" is sometimes constructed on the vertical order, and sometimes on the horizontal (p. 59). Laurens Pietersen sometimes wrote his "P" upside down (p. 130).

Dirck Holgersen showed manifest improvement in his respective marks of 1651, 1658, 1661 (p. 69). At least they were more ingenious than the mark of the ancestor of the Vanderbilts, which mark "resembles a window sash — with four panes of glass." (p. 61.)

But no matter what the immigrants were educationally, they were a thrifty people who chose, of their own accord, to settle in our country, to take upon themselves the burdens of pioneer life. With their fellow citizens of New Amsterdam they share the honor of having been the first "to put on American soil the public school." They also deserve honor for the firm stand they took in championing, against a majority, the rights of religious liberty; in protecting a man whom the government exiled because he was a Lutheran minister; and in promoting such a spirit of voluntaryism that one of their numbers, a Dane, willed — what was unheard of in those days — a legacy to a modest church which had been obliged to beg the English government, no less than the Dutch, for permission to exist: he thus set a good example for his brethern whose ideas of giving was what could be expected from men that had been trained in the "established church."

And where are the descendants of the nigh 200 Scandinavian immigrants? By birth or intermarriage they are connected with well known families whose branches extend over the entire United States.

The first of the *Putnams* in America married the daughter of Arent Andriessen from Norway.

The *Bradts* of New York are descendants of the same Andriessen.

The first of the *Vanderbilts* married Anneken Hendricks. from Bergen, Norway.

Her daughter — half Dutch, half Norwegian — was married to Rem Remsen, a German, the progenitor of the *Remsen* family.

The American *Rosenkrans* family are descendants of Herman Hendricksen of Bergen. Best known among these is *General William Stark Rosecrans,* Brigadier General of the Regular Army in the Civil war, afterwards U. S. Minister to Mexico, later Congressman from California, and first Register of the Treasury under President Cleveland.

Related to Anneke Jans, of Marstrand, Norway, are the families of *Bayard, De Lancey, De Peyster, Governeur, Jay, Knickerbocker, Morris, Schuyler, Stuyvesant, Van Cortland,* and *Van Rensselaer.*

The *Van Buskirks* are descendants of Laurens Andriessen from Holstein. Among these is the first American-born Lutheran minister in the United States, and Dr. John Alden Singmaster, President of the Lutheran Theological Seminary at Gettysburg, Pa.

The *Broncks* are descended from Jonas Bronck, the Dane from Faroe Islands. His grandson was a lieutenant in the army, his great-grandson was a major; and another great-grandson served as major and lieutenant colonel, as member of the New York Assembly, and as New York State senator.

Descendants of the daughter of Tryntie Jans, Danish, are the *Bleeker* family.

The ancestor of the *Wilsies* is Hendrick Martensen, a Dane.

The *Van Ripens* are descendants of Juriaen Tomassen from Ribe, Denmark.

Member of the Swedish *Hoffman* family are intermarried among the families of *Benson, Verplanck, Beeckman, Benson, Livingston, Brinckerhoff, Du Bois, Vredenburgh, Provoost, Storm, Ogden, Van Cortland, Schuyler.*

Some of the Rosenkrans and the *Roosevelt* family are related to the Hoffmans. Hon. John Thompson, once Governor of the state of New York, was a descendant of Hoffman. The Hoffman family numbers statesmen, preachers and lawyers, authors and college presidents. Mathilda Hofmann, one of the family, was, as has already been referred to, engaged to marry Washington Irving.

The *Stuck* family is descended from Mons Pietersen.

There is Swedish blood in the *Melyn* family.

The *Burger* family is originally Swedish on the mother's side, German on the father's.

The *Livingston* family has Swedish blood by the Lopers, the granddaughter of Captain Loper marrying the son of Robert Livingston, who as first Lord of the Livingston Manor owned 160,000 acres of land.

A descendant of *Jacob Bruyn* of Norway served several terms in both branches of the New York state legislature and was for many years an associate judge in Ulster county.

A descendant of *Andries Andriessen* represented the county of Albany in the provincial assembly.

By intermarriage there is also Scandinavian blood in a branch of the *Van Buren* family, to which Van Buren, once United States President, belonged.

The Dows are descendants of Volckert Jansen, a Dane.

Descendants of Christian Barentsen, who was in all probability a Dane, were Robert T. van Horn who founded and, for forty years, edited the "Kansas City Journal"; and Wm. H. Carbusier, Lt. U. S. Army, later a member of congress,

AND SO FORTH.

Appendix I.

SCANDINAVIANS IN MEXICO AND SOUTH AMERICA, 1532–1640.

Probably the first Scandinavian in America was *"Jacob from Denmark."* In 1532 he was in Mexico, and is counted among the Augustinian monks who in that year went thither. The catholic historian, P. Wittman, quoted in Dr. Chr. H. Kalkar's "Den Christelige Mission Blandt Hedningerne" (1879), says that Jacob from Denmark was related to the Danish royal family, "which has remained faithful to the church of the fathers" (Roman Catholic).

Another Scandinavian who came to the New World in the sixteenth century was *Christian Jacobsen,* a Danish explorer. He was born in Copenhagen, 1528, where he studied theology. He went to Peru in 1551, and served in the civil wars of that country. At the advice of a cousin he entered the Roman Catholic Church in order to get an appointment in the army. In 1557 he went to Chili. In 1565 we find him in Buenos Ayres. Thence, sailing again for Peru, he settled in Lima, where he devoted his leisure to literary labors and where he died in 1596. See Appleton's Cyclopedia of American Biography.

Jens Munk, born 1579, in Barbu, near Arendal, Norway, was destined to try the hardships of South America as well as of Canada. His father was a Danish nobleman, who had lived for many years in Norway, an able soldier and mariner, but despotic in rule, and licentious in life. His son Jens inherited the father's ability in commanding the seas, but was his opposite in life and character. At the age of twelve Jens Munk began his life as a sailor. He went to Oporto to learn the Portuguese language, he then hired out on a ship sailing for Brazil. After great difficulties he arrived at Bahia, where he for some time worked for a shoe-

JACOB JENSSØN NORDMAND.
From ''Norges Historie,'' IV., by Prof. Yngvar Nielsen.

FRIGATE ''DEN NORSKE LØVE'' (THE NORWEGIAN LION).
Model in Ivory, by Jakob Jenssön Nordmand, 1654.
From ''Norges Historie,'' IV., by Prof. Yngvar Nielsen.

maker and a painter, and was at length initiated into the merchant's business. After having, through a bold deed of his, saved some Dutch merchants from an attack planned against them by some Spaniards, he was obliged to flee from Bahia. He returned to Europe in 1598. He got a ship of his own in 1605, and was appointed captain in the Danish fleet in 1611. Eight years later he was requested by the king of Denmark to take the charge of an expedition, whose object was the discovery of the way to China through what was then known as the Northwest passage. See Appendix II.

Jacob Jenssön Nordman (1614—1695), a Norwegian who was noted for his carving in ebony, spent five years in Brazil as a soldier in the service of the Dutch. Returning to Norway about 1640, he was appointed constable at Akerhus, and served in the war against Sweden. In 1648 Frederik III., king of Denmark and Norway, became acquainted with him, and later appointed him instructor of the royal family. He taught both the king and the queen, and other members of the family, to carve. He carved beautiful pieces in ebony, now preserved at Rosenborg, Copenhagen. His most finished production is his grand model, in ivory, of the frigate "Den norske löve" (The Norwegian lion).

Appendix II.

SCANDINAVIANS IN CANADA, 1619--1620.

The first arrival of Scandinavians in Canada took place in 1619. Christian IV., King of Denmark and Norway, being desirous of sending an expedition to discover the way to China through the "Northwest passage," requested Captain Jens Munk, who has been mentioned above, to take charge of it. The expedition, when leaving European waters, consisted of sixty-four men, forty-eight of whom were on the ship "Enhiörningen," and sixteen on a smaller ship "Lamprenen."

Captain Munk and his crew sailed from Copenhagen, May 9, 1619. Two days later, the log records, one of the sailors jumped overboard and drowned. A week later, because of a leak in one of the ships, it was found necessary to lie over for five days in Karmsund, Norway, where three new men were added to the crew.

They passed the Shetland Island and Faroe Islands, Cape Farewell, crossed Davis Straits, entered Frobisher Bay, then Hudson Straits. In July they came to Salvage Islands, where they met some Eskimos . After sailing around for some time in Ungava Bay, they re-entered Hudson Straits, and crossing Hudson Bay, which Munk called Mare Christian, the crew landed, on September 7, 1619, at the mouth of Churchhill River.

Meantime he had lost, on August 8, one of his crew, Anders, from Stavanger, Norway, who was buried in Haresund (Icy Cove). And before he left winter quarters, the rest of his crew perished, save two with whom he started and completed his return voyage to Europe, reaching Norway on September 21, 1620.

Munk had taken possession of the new land, in the name of his king, calling it Nova Dania. Due to the intense cold, massive snow drifts and lack of proper equipment for living in such frigid regions, the crew could not obtain fresh food by hunting. They had no snow-shoes or "ski." They had very little fur clothing. They were thus compelled to spend their time on and near the ships, without sufficient exercise and without proper food. The never-varying fare of salt meats brought on scurvy. Every week witnessed several deaths. The conditions aboard the ships were frightful. In the annals of polar travelers the experience of the Munk expedition is one of the most terrible. On February 25, Munk had twenty-two dead, on April 10, forty-one, on June 4, sixty-one.

First on June 18, the ice gave way to the ships. With extreme difficulty, Munk and his surviving crew of two got the lesser ship,

MAP OF CAPTAIN MUNK'S SAILING ON HUDSON BAY, 1619.
From Jens Munk: Navigatio Septentrionalis.

on June 26, ready for sailing. On July 16, they left what may be called the first Scandinavian, we may also say, the first Lutheran cemetery in North America. For almost all of the mariners were Lutherans by faith. They even had in their midst Rev. Rasmus Jensen from Aarhus, Denmark, who preached his first and last Christmas sermon in America on Christmas day, 1619.

Jensen died on February 20, the following year. The first Lutheran minister in America lies buried in Canada.

Captain Munk has left us a book which describes his journey

to and from Hudson Bay: "Navigatio Septentrionalis," 1624, edited and published anew by P. Laurissen (Copenhagen, 1883. An English translation has been made for the Hakluyt Society). From this carefully kept book, or Relation, as Munk calls it, we see the piety of the author and learn when and under what circumstances the several members of the expedition died.

At least two of the crew were English, the mates William Gordon and John Watson (died May 6, 1620). Less than a dozen may have been Germans and Swedes. At least twelve were Norwegians, while the majority were Danes.

CAPTAIN MUNK'S WINTER QUARTERS IN "NOVA DANIA (CANADA).
From Jens Munk: Navigatio Septentrionalis.

The Norwegians were:

Anders Staffuanger (d. Aug. 8, 1619, seaman).

Laurids Bergen (d. Feb. 5, 1620, seaman).

Hans Skudenes (d. March 1).

Christoffer Opslö (Oslo, d. April 5, chief gunner).

Oluff Sundmöer (d. April 24, mate to the captain of the hold).

Halffward Brönnie (d. April 27).

Thoer Thönsberg (d. April 28).

Anders Marstrand (d. May 3).

Morten Marstrand (d. May 4, boatswain's mate).

Suend Marstrand (d. May 12).

Erich Hansen Li (d. May 19). Munk says, Li "had been very industrious and willing and had neither offended anyone nor deserved any punishment. He had dug many graves for others, but now there was nobody that could dig his, and his body had to remain unburied."

Knud Lauritzsen Skudenes (d. in May).

Of the Danes we give these names:

Jens Helssing (d. Jan. 27, seaman).

Rasmus Kiöbenhauffn (d. Feb. 17).

Rev. Rasmus Jensen (d. Feb. 20, minister).

Jens Borringholm (d. March 1).

Erich Munk (a nephew of the captain, d. April 1).

Mauritz Stygge (d. April 10, lieutenant).

Peder Nyborg (d. in May, carpenter).

No doubt also the majority of the following are Danes:

Hans Brock (d. Jan. 23, 1620, second mate).

Oluff Boye (d. March 8).

Anders Pöcker (d. March 9).

M. Casper Caspersen (d. March 21. He was probably a German surgeon).

Povel Pedersen (d. March 21).

Jan Ollufsen (d. March 25, skipper), navigating officer of *Enhiörningen*.

Ismael Abrahamsen (Swede ? d. March 29).

Christen Gregersen (d. March 29).

Suend Arffuedsen (d. March 30, carpenter).

Johan Pettersen (d. March 31, second mate. He was buried in the same grave with Erich Munk).

Rasmus Clemendsen (d. April 5, mate of the chief gunner).

Lauritz Hansen (d. April 5, boatswain).

Anders Sodens (d. April 8).

Anders Oroust (d. April 16).

Jens Bödker (d. April 16).

Hans Bendtsen (d. April 17).

Oluff Andersen (d. April 17, servant).

Peder Amundsen (d. April 19).

Morten Nielsen, Butelerer (d. April 28, butler).

Jens Jörgensen (d. May 12).

Jens Hendrichsen (d. May 16) "skipper," master of *Lamprenen*.

On the fourth of June, Munk gave up all hope of life. We give below the entry which Munk on that day made in his book. We accompany it with a facsimile of a page of his manuscript, which is preserved in the University Library of Copenhagen.

"On the 4th of June, which was Whit-Sunday, there remained alive only three besides myself, all lying down, unable to help one another. The stomach was ready enough and had appetite for food, but the teeth would not allow it; and not one of us had the requisite strength for going into the hold to fetch us a drink of wine. The cook's boy lay dead by my berth, and three men on the steerage; two men were on shore, and would gladly have been back on the ship, but it was impossible for them to get there, as they had not sufficient strength in their limbs to help themselves on board, so that they and I were lying quite exhausted, as we

THE MUNK EXPEDITION.

had now for four entire days nothing for the sustenance of the body. Accordingly, I did not now hope for anything but that God would put an end to this my misery and take me to Himself and His Kingdom; and, thinking that it would have been the last I wrote in this world, I penned a writing as follows:

(FACSIMILE OF MANUSCRIPT OF CAPTAIN MUNK. LIBRARY OF THE UNIVERSITY OF COPENHAGEN.)

In print the above given writing appears thus:

"[Efterdi at Jeg nu icke haffuer
forhaabning at kunde leffue]
her hoss beder Jeg Nu for guts skuld om
Naagen Krestne Menisker hender hied
att kome att die Met Arme Legom
med die Andere som Nu her hoss findes
udi Jorden wille Lade Kome, och tagendis
lön aff gud i hemelen. Och att dene

min Relasion Maate blifue Min Naad
dig here och Koning tilstelet
thie det er sanferdigt Alt huad i
hrude findes Ord for ord skreffuet paae
Att Min fatig hustru och bören Maatte
Nyde Min Ynkelige Affgang Noget gaat
Att, her med Alluerden gode Natt och min
Siel i det Euige Rige: Jens Munk"

. . . . .

We append this translation:

"Inasmuch as I have now no more hope of life in this world, I request, for the sake of God, if any Christian men should happen to come here, that they will bury in the earth my poor body, together with the others which are found here, expecting their reward from God in Heaven; and, furthermore, that this my journal may be forwarded to my most gracious Lord and King (for every word that is found herein is altogether truthful) in order that my poor wife and children may obtain some benefit from my great distress and miserable death. Herewith, good-night to all the world; and my soul in the eternal kingdom.

"Jens Munk."

Munk concludes his "Relation" with this prayer:

"*O Almighty, Eternal God*, Gracious Father, and Heavenly Lord, who hast commanded us to call upon Thee in all necessity and adversity, and also dost promise that Thou wilt graciously hear our prayer and save us, so that we may thank Thee for Thy loving kindness and Thy wonderful acts, which Thou doest towards the children of men: I have now, on this long and perilous journey, been in danger and necessity, in which I have nevertheless experienced Thy gracious help and assistance, in that Thou hast saved me from the ice bergs, in dreadful storms, and from the foaming sea. Thou wast my chief pilot, counselor, guide, and compass. Thou hast led and accompanied me, both going and coming. Thou hast led me out of anxiety, disease, and sickness, so that by Thy help I have regained my health, and have returned to my native country, which I entirely believe to be Thy doing. Nor has it been accomplished by my own understanding or providence, wherefore I humbly and heartily give thanks to Thee,

O Thou my gracious Father. And I pray that Thou wilt give
me grace of Thy Holy Spirit, that I may henceforth be found
thankful to Thee in word and deed, to Thy honor and glory, and
for the confirmation of my faith with a good conscience. To
Thee, O Holy Trinity, be Praise and Thanksgiving for ever, for
these and all Thy benefits.

"To Thee alone belongs all Power and Glory
"for ever and ever
"*Amen.*
"Isaiah, Chap. xliv.

"Fear not, for I have redeemed thee. When thou passest
through the waters, I will be with thee, that the rivers shall not
drown thee."*

---

* The passage is Isaiah xliii, 1, 2. The translation differs slightly from the
English version.

In the "Lutheran Observer" (Philadelphia), Dec. 27, 1907, I have related
about the articles in the American press which have dealt with the Munk expedition.
Rev. Rasmus Andersen, of Brooklyn, New York, deserves the credit of having called
attention to the fact that there were Scandinavians in Canada as early as 1619-20.
The best from his pen on this subject is found in "Teologisk Tidsskrift," I., 26ff.
(1899), Decorah, Iowa. His article is a digest of the Munk journal in the edition of
1883. Neither he nor the other American writers, however, have used the carefully
edited English edition of the Hakluyt Society. The present writer has consulted
both editions.

Appendix III.

SOME SCANDINAVIAN IMMIGRANTS IN NEW YORK IN THE EIGHTEENTH CENTURY.

As this volume makes no pretensions to go beyond the seventeenth century in its treatment of Scandinavian immigration, it is almost needless to state that the following is nothing but the result of incidental jottings on the part of the writer. He is confident that the sources of the eighteenth century contain much data for those who go to them with the express purpose of writing on Scandinavian immigration to our country after the year 1700.

The Swedish immigrants are so numerous that the registering of their names in this appendix cannot be attempted. The Swedish colony in America lost its independence, but its settlers and their descendants attracted new immigrants from Sweden. The history of Delaware, New Jersey, and Pennsylvania cannot be treated judiciously unless due notice be given to the Swedish element that helped to colonize and develop these states. The material for a detailed presentation of early Swedish immigration is not confined to American sources. Much of it is in foreign archives.

A people that has given us the "Records of the Gloria Dei Church, Philadelphia," (Extracts translated in "Pennsylvania Magazine of History and Biography," II); "The Records of Holy Trinity (Old Swedes Church), Wilmington, Del.," 1697—1773 (translated for and published by the Historical Society of Delaare, 1890); Thomas Campanius "Kort Bescrifning om Provincien Nya Swerige uti America," 1702 (translated 1834); Johannes Dan, Swedberg "Dissertatio Svionum in America Colonia," 1709; Tobias E. Björck "Dissertatio gradualis de Plantatione Ecclesiae Svecanae in America," 1731; A. Hesselius "Kort Berettelse om Then Svenska Kyrkios närwarande Tilstand i America 1725;

Israel Acrelius "Beskrifning Om De Svenska Församlingars Forna och Närwarande Tilstand Uti Det saaKallade Nya Sverige," 1759 (translated 1874); Carl K. S. Sprinchorn's "Kolonien Nya Sveriges Historia," 1878; Prof. C. T. Odhner's "Kolonien Nya Sveriges Grundläggning 1637—1642," in "Historisk Bibliothek. Ny följd, 1876"; Otto Nordberg's "Svenska Kyrkens Mission vid Delaware i Nord-Amerika," 1893 — such a people, on their native soil or in America, are certainly not wanting in materials for presenting the history of Swedish immigrants from 1638 to the American Revolution.

Americans of Swedish ancestry have translated and supplemented the data given by the above mentioned writers. It suffices to mention the interesting articles contained in the Pennsylvania Magazine of History and Biography I; II, 224f.; 341f.; III, 402f., 409, 462ff.; VII; VIII, 107f.; XVII. Consult also Proceedings of Delaware County Historical Society, I, 269; Proceedings of New Jersey Historical Society, III; etc. All this before the year 1900.

The present writer was making a study of these books or treatises and of other pertinent works with a view to writing a history of the Swedes in America in the seventeenth century. He then learned that another was covering the same ground. Thereupon he turned his attention to Scandinavian immigration to New York, an almost entirely unexplored field. Whatever data he saw fit to publish regarding the Swedes at Delaware are contained in "The Lutheran Observer," Philadelphia, 1907 and 1908.

This explains why he finds it inexpedient to include the Swedes in this appendix: They have been, and are being, treated by competent writers like Dr. Amandus Johnson.

It is different with the Danish and especially with the Norwegian immigrants. They are comparatively few and unknown. Many Danes came to the Moravian settlement in Pennsylvania in the eighteenth century. They have been ably dealt with by Prof. Vig in "Danske i Amerika," and we shall therefore not attempt to treat them, and several other Danish immigrants of the eighteenth century mentioned by him, here. Mr. Torstein Jahr has also treated this field in an interesting manner and, moreover, included Norwegian immigrants who joined the Moravian colony, foremost of whom was perhaps Hans Martin Kalberlahn, a surgeon from Trondhjem, Norway.*

What we give in the following is nothing but a few items, which, so to speak, have been "gathered by the wayside" and not noticed by others.

FROM REV. JUSTUS FALCKNER'S CHURCH RECORD.

With the year 1700 we date the arrival of Justus Falckner, born 1672 in Saxony, to New York. In 1703 he was ordained by Swedish ministers in Gloria Dei Church at Wicaco. He was the first Lutheran minister ordained in America, moreover the first Lutheran minister in this country to publish a work on religion. The hymn "Auf, ihr Christen, Christi Glieder," published in the Halle Gesangbuch of 1697 is from his pen. It has been translated into English, "Rise ye children of Salvation," and, by Brorson, into Danish, "Op, I Christne ruster eder!" Falckner was not minister only of the Lutheran churches in New York and Albany, but of all the churches on the Hudson river, which he visited on a circuit. From the church register, which he kept, we give the following data:

Oct. 12, 1707, he married "Peter Johansen, at house of Faes Vlirboom, N. Y., born at Bergen, Norway, and Maria, daughter of Pieter Lassen Brower's dau. beyond the Highland."

Oct. 10, 1708, "in our church at N. Y. b(aptized) last summer beyond the Highlands, Johannes, y. s. of Pieter Norman and wife Maria. Witnesses: Jacob Jacobsen Halenbeck and Gertruyd Vasen Vlierboom has told me that she stood up as god-mother, signed

---

My source for this is Holand's "De Norske Settlementers Historie," which refers to "Decorah-Posten," Sept. 9, 1904.

See also Moravian Emigration to Pennsylvania (1734-1765) by John W. Jordan, in "The Pennsylvania Magazine for History and Biography," 1909.

The "Pennsylvania Archives," XVII., ff., no doubt contains names of many Scandinavians who came to Pennsylvania in the eighteenth century. Thus the name of Andries Evie (Evje), a Norwegian, who came to our country in 1728. It is found in the original list of passengers aboard the ship "Mortonhouse," commanded by John Coultas, and sailing in August, 1728, from Deal, near Dover, England. The Englishman promptly changed "Andries Evje" into "Andres Ente."

It would appear that Andries' wife and children (wife, Elisabeth, age 28; children, Lisabeth, Katrina, John, age 8, 8, 6 respectively) followed him four years later, sailing from Rotterdam, on the ship "Samuel," of London (commanded by Hugh Percy). "Evje" has on this trip across the ocean become "Evy."

(Rev) M. C. Knol (The entry in parenthesis was in a different handwriting.)

April 18, 1710, "at our meeting at the house of Peter Lassen beyond the Highlands b. March 11, 1710, Catharina y. d. of Peter Jansen Noorman and wife Maria. Witness I, Justus Falckner, the pastor, Cornelia Lassen.

April 30, 1713. "At the house of Pieter Lassen in the Lange Rack beyond the islands the following: Elisabeth b. last summer in Dutchess County, child of Andreas Pick and wife Veronica. Witnesses: Pieter Jansen Norman, and in his place Johannes Milltler, and Mary Jansen Normans."

*

Jan Denemark was married in New York, by Falckner, June 13, 1704, to Maria Ten Eyk.

Frans Mulder, from Holstein, was married in New York, Sept. 30, 1705.

Johan Volckertsen Van Husum was married, Nov. 25, 1705, in Albany, to Engel Jansen.

Maria Denemarke was married in New York, July 26, 1707, to Arie Affel.

Jan Thomas Vos "young man from Denmark," was married in New York, Dec. 9, 1711, to Willemyntie Brouwer.

Christopher Dennemarcker and Christina Elisabeth, his wife, had their child Anna Dorothea, baptized by Falckner, Feb. 7, 1714, in "Rosendak in Sopus" (Esopus).

Laurens Ruloffsen, born in Copenhagen, 1689, residing at Raritan was married by Falckner, May 16, 1715, to Catharina Schumans, daughter of Herman Schuman, a German. Catharina was born 1695, died 1776. They had children: Laurents, baptized March 27, 1716, and Roelof. Roelof had many children: Laurence, John, Christian, Lea, Isaac, Anna, Abraham, Henry, Elisabeth.

These were Norwegians or Danes.

Falckner's record contains also Swedish names:

*

On Sept. 14, 1704, Pieter Harlandt, young man of Gothland, Sweden, married Catarina, young daughter of Samuel Beeckman, "Voorleser" of "our church at N. Y."

On April 20, 1707, Jurgen Woll, from Wiborg, Sweden, married Altje Browers of Roanes.

On July 29, 1726, Jan Pell, born at Stockholm, married Jannetje Browers, "both living at New York."

The Church Record kept by Justus Falckner has been published in Year Book of the Holland Society of New York, 1903.

A MUSTER ROLL OF MEN RAISED AND PAST MUSTER FOR THE PROVINCE OF NEW YORK.*

Sybriant Adrian, ship carpenter from Norway, age 27, 5 feet, 7 inches tall, fair complexion, light hair, blue eyes, enlisted, April 28, 1759, in the company commanded by Captain Richard Smith (Another source says Captain Hardenbuck).

Albert Egeles, sailor, from Norway, age 33, enlisted June 10, 1760, his company going to Canada.

Dennis Anderseon, mariner from Norway, age 22, 5 feet, 5½ in. tall, enliste din company of Captain Deforest.

Conrad Cor, mariner from Norway, age 35, stature 5 ft. 7½ in., enlisted, in May, 1761, in company of Lt. Welsh.

Hans Jacobsenborg, mariner from Norway, age 30, stature 5 ft. 9½ in., blue eyes, brown hair, brown complexion, enlisted in county of New York March 27, 1762.

---

* Collection of New York Historical Society, XXIV. Report of the (N. Y.) State Historian, 1897. Col. Series II.

John Christian Enevoldsen, age 36, born in Denmark, stature 5 ft. 7 in., brown complexion, sandy hair, eyes do., cordwainer by trade, enlisted in New York City for Captain Richard Smith's Company April 26 (28), 1759.

Albert Thomas joined the same company April 23, 1759. He was born in Denmark, 24 years of age, 5 ft. 7 in. tall, of light complexion, blue eyes, smith and mariner by trade.

John Frederick Mattheson, blacksmith, joined Smith's company April 16, 1659. He was born in Copenhagen, age 24, stature 5 ft. 7 in., of brown complexion, brown hair, brown eyes.

John Henry Brown (Bower) enlisted with N. Y. Provincial troops, Company of Captain R. Livingston April 16, 1659. Brown was born in Denmark, 44 years of age, stature 5 ft. 5½ in., of brown complexion, brown hair, blue eyes. By trade, a mason.

Andries Andries, born in Copenhagen, joined Captain Moore's Company, April 20, 1759. Age 28, stature 5 ft. 7 in., of brown complexion, brown hair, blue eyes. Mariner.

Paul Sanders, born in Denmark, mariner (miner?), age 28, stature 5 ft., "round face," light hair, blue eyes; was member of a company of soldiers, 1758, in Westchester County.

Johannes Hogoland, sailor, from Denmark, age 28, stature 5 ft. 9½ in., joined Captain Deforest's Company, May 25, 1761.

Appendix IV.

GERMAN IMMIGRANTS IN NEW YORK, 1630–1674.

In the Preface to our work it is shown that, judging by Prof. Flom's scholarly "A History of Norwegian Immigration" and by Mr. Holand's more popular "De norske Settlementers Historie," the immigration of Scandinavians to New York in the seventeenth century must have been practically (and professionally) a *terra incognita* as late as 1909, when these authors published their works.

Much the same may be said in regard to the German immigration to New York during the Dutch rule, if we judge by Prof. Albert Bernhardt Faust's (Cornell University) "The German Element in the United States," published in the same year. This standard-work, submitted in a contest to the Germanic Department of the University of Chicago, obtained for the author the first prize, $3000, given by Mrs. Catherine Seipp, of Chicago. Excellent as Prof. Faust's work is, it makes only two statements that might permit of a conclusion as to the numerical strength of the Germans in New Netherland.

The first is this:

"There were Germans in the Dutch settlement of New Netherland, and among them two who were second to none in moulding the destinies of the colony. The one was the first governor of New Netherland, Peter Minuit, and the other the first governor of New York to represent the popular party, Jacob Leisler."

The second reads:

"Dwelling with the Dutch settlers of New Amsterdam, there was undoubtedly quite a sprinkling of Germans. A good example is that of Dr. Hans Kierstede, who came from Magdeburg in 1638 with Director Kieft. He was the first practising physician and surgeon in that colony. He married Sarah Roelofse, daughter of Roeloff and Anneke Janse, the owner of the Annetje Jans farm on Manhattan Island."

The latter statement is somewhat hypothetical. The former is rather indefinite. They offer nothing tangible for answering the question, How great was this sprinkling? Professor Faust makes mention of no other Germans in New Netherland than Minuit, Kierstede, Augustin Herman, and Leisler. Though his treatment of Minuit is as elucidating as his description of the activities of Leisler is sympathetic, he fails to call attention to German leaders like Schrick, Ebbing, Van Beeck, Burger Joris, and Nicholaes De Meyer the burgomaster of New York city in 1676.

This criticism does not aim to detract anything from the value of Prof. Faust's splendid contribution to the history of the German element in our country. Its object is merely to indicate that the German immigrants in New York 1630—1674 have received no more attention than the Scandinavian.

As the background for a treatment of these German immigrants would be much the same as what our volume outlines in treating the immigrants from the Scandinavian countries, we venture in the present Appendix to register the names, with more or less pertinent data, of some 180 immigrants from various cities and districts of Germany, including a few from Switzerland and Austria. The list does not claim to be exhaustive. A more extended examination of the sources will increase the number of names, and, of course, add to the data, which I have collected, but of which I here present only a part.

Prof. Faust states a fact when he says that October 6, 1683, is "the date celebrated by all Germans in America as the beginning of their history in the United States." But we believe that the history of the Germans in the leading state of the United States begins (like that of the Scandinavians) more than a half century earlier.

Long before 1683, scores of places in Germany were represented in New Netherland and registered in the records of the Empire State.

It is as if a part of the history of the Middle Ages and the era of the Reformation passes in review before us when the records present names as these: *Aachen, Stade, Fulda, Wrede,*

*Wesel, Eisleben, Mansfeld, Magdeburg, Worms, Jena, Augsburg,
Nürnberg, Hesse, Zürichsee, Bern, Mülhausen, Münster, Tübingen,*
They are suggestive of the coronation of emperors, of monastic-
ism; of a forerunner of the Reformation; of the history of Luther
and diets; of a Philip of Hesse; of Zwingli; of the Peasants' War
and the Anabaptists; of the theological efforts of Andrea to restore peace among contending theologians.

And what a variety of associations are connected with names
like *Bremen, Hamburg, Lübeck, Cologne, Frankfurt am Main,
Berlin, Königsberg, Wolfenbüttel, Erlangen, Giessen, Berg, Bonn,
Bocholt, Borken, Brunswick, Emden, Ems, Elberfeld, Elsfleth,
Falkenburg, Gemen, Herborn, Hirschberg, Hammelwarden, Jever,
Johannisberg, Lauffen, Lemgo, Lippstad, Kremmen, Mannheim,
Osnabrück, Rodenkirchen, Soest, Struckhausen, Xanten;* and
*Baden, Berg-Cassel, Cleves, East Friesland, Jülich, Oldenburg,
Waldeck, Westphalia.* Even *Transylvania* and *Prague* are repre-
sented, and the name "Das 'Kayserreych'" is not failing.

But enough. These places together with the one hundred and
eighty men and women who represented them in New Netherland
before the close of the Dutch Dominion on American soil are sufficient to merit at least the brief treatment that is accorded them
in the present Appendix, which endeavors only to call attention to
the fact that the Germans, no less than the Scandinavians, were
by no means a *quantité négligeable* in the history of New York,
1630—1674.

Like the Dutch, the Germans and Scandinavians are Teutons.
They have the same civilization. And yet, so far as New York is
concerned, the German and Scandinavian immigrant in the seventeenth century had more in common with each other than with
the Dutch:

First, the majority of the German pioneers had the same
creed as the Scandinavian: They were Lutherans.

Secondly, in number they were inferior to the Dutch, who
had some reason for priding themselves on being natives from
what was then the most flourishing state in Europe. Moreover,
these sons of Germany, Sweden, Denmark, Norway were not so
apt as the Dutch immigrants to overlook difficulties and expect
immediate rewards.

What Mr. J. K. Riker says of the pioneers of Harlem also holds true, it would seem, of the entire population of New Netherland: "Though the Dutch and French elements were dominant in giving tone to the community, the Scandinavians and Germans, few in number . . . were second to none for sterling common sense, while foremost to bear danger and hardship, to wield the axe whose ring first startled the slumbering forest, or to turn the first furrow in the virgin soil."

Mr. Riker's contention is supported by the court records. They reveal that the German and Scandinavian element on the whole showed a greater respect for law and order than the more adventurous elements from Dutch- and French-speaking Netherlands of Europe.

As to the creedal factor, the Scandinavians were Lutherans "by birth" so to speak. Their native states recognized no other creed than the Lutheran. As this creed was not tolerated by the Governor and Council of New Netherland, who were bent on keeping the Reformed creed (especially the canons of the Synod of Dort) the state religion of New Netherland, — the Scandinavians , in their efforts to get religious liberty, received allies in the Lutheran immigrants from Germany. The majority of these German pioneers were Lutherans of the seventeenth century type; though not a few of them, coming from the western part of Germany, were Reformed or Roman Catholic.

Settled in New York, a number of these Lutherans, both German and Scandinavian, joined the Reformed church. They intermarried among the Reformed. But the large majority adhered to the "faith of their fathers," even if this adherence at times savored of "zeal without knowledge." This majority had a common enemy in the politico-ecclesiastical measures of the Governor and Council, and found little or no sympathy with the Dutch colonists, who in ecclesiastical matters were of the same cloth as Stuyvesant. In fact, the *Dutch* Lutherans in early New York were hardly in evidence. The story that the oldest Lutheran church in New Netherland was Dutch, lies hard by the realm of myths.

The first Lutheran church in New Netherland was cosmopolitan;* perhaps better, essentially German-Scandinavian — with

* I have made this statement before: in Ruoff's "Volume Library," p. 404; "Realencyclopädie fuer protestantische Theologie und Kirche" v. XXIV, 588 (Leipzig, 1913), edited by Albert Hauck.

emphasis on German. It is significant that the petition of the Lutherans in New Amsterdam, 1657, requesting that Rev. Goetwater
be permitted to remain in New Amsterdam, appears to have been
signed by *sixteen* Germans, *five* Scandinavians and *three* Hollanders. (pp. 37 fl.)

It is also significant that the Reformed preachers in New Amsterdam expressly mention *Paul Schrick,* from Nürnberg, as the
leader among the Lutherans (p. 88) ; *Pieter Jansen* as a "northern
er," "stupid" enough to take sides with the Lutherans in discussing baptism (p. 87) ; the Norwegian, *Laurence Noorman,* as a
Lutheran sponsor and as the host who for a winter concealed the
Lutheran minister on his farm (p. 39) when the government had
ordered him to go into exile ; and *Magdelene Kallier* (-Waele),
a Scandinavian woman, as a godparent. These preachers do not
complain, however, of Dutch Lutherans. And the records tell
nothing about squabbles between Dutch Reformed preachers and
Dutch Lutheran laymen, though they do not fail to set forth the
dispute, in 1680, between Rev. Gideon Schaets, Dutch Reformed
minister of Albany, and Meyndert Fredricksen, a *German* Lutheran.

Does not this indicate that the Dutch Lutherans, in proportion to the German and Scandinavian, were too few in number or
too much wanting in aggressiveness?

And, does not the presence of a man like Jan Goetwater as
the first Lutheran minister in New Amsterdam indicate the pre-
ponderance of the German element in the church he was to serve?
The Reformed preachers at times called him "Goetwater," though
"Gutwasser" was the form he used in signing his name. Was
"Goetwater" his real name? If so, "Gutwasser" is a Germaniza-
tion of it, showing that strong German influences likely were at
work in the circle he was sent over to serve. It is more probable,
however, that "Gutwasser" is the original; and that the bearer
of this name was a German, who was at home in the Dutch
language as well as in his native tongue. The Consistory of Amsterdam presumably acted according to the desire of Paulus
Schrick and his countrymen when they sent over to New Netherland a preacher, who probably was of German extraction, but
could preach in Dutch.

As has been indicated in various places in our book, the Lutherans in New Netherland were not allowed the exercise of

public worship according to the dictates of their conscience or in harmony with their creed. It was the policy of the new government whose subjects they were to make and keep the Reformed "religion" the religion of the entire province.

This policy was not a new one. In 1638 the government proclaimed that "every man shall be free to live up to his own conscience in peace and decorum; provided he avoid frequenting any forbidden assemblies or conventicles, much less collect or get any such." This proclamation was confirmed, in reality explained, in the West India Company's New Charter of Patroonship, 1640, which specified that "no other religion shall be publicly admitted to New Netherland except the Reformed, as it is at present preached and practiced by the public authority in the United Netherlands."

The Council waived this, however, so far as the English were concerned. It proclaimed in 1641 that the "English shall have free exercise of their religion." It also decreed when New Sweden was conquered, 1655, that the Swedes living there should be permitted to adhere to the Augsburg Confession and to have their own minister. But these concessions were dictated by policy, and not by principle.

The English Independents were as little recognized as were the Lutherans. The "fate" of the Independents was also the "fate" of the Lutherans, Mennonites, Quakers and Catholics. Stuyvesant and his predecessors in office were not able to comprehend the spirit of liberty, which found such energetic spokesmen as Gustavus Adolphus and Oliver Cromwell.

And therefore, even as late as February, 1656, the Director-General and Council regarded it as their duty to decree the following:

"The Director General and Council have credibly been informed, that not only conventicles and meetings are held here and there in this Province, but that also unqualified persons presume in such meetings to act as teachers in interpreting and expounding God's holy Word without ecclesiastical or temporal authority. This is contrary to the general political and ecclesiastical rules of our Fatherland and besides such gatherings lead to troubles, heresies and schisms. Therefore to prevent this the Director General and Council strictly forbid all such public or private con-

venticles and meetings, except the usual and authorized ones,
where God's reformed ordained Word is preached and taught in
a meeting for the reformed divine service conform to the Synod
of Dort and followed here as well as in the Fatherland and other
reformed churches of Europe, under a fine of 100 pounds of
Flemish to be paid by all, who in such public or private meetings,
except the usual authorized gatherings, on Sunday or other days
presume to exercise without due qualification the duties of a
preacher, reader or precentor and each man or woman, married
or unmarried, who are found at such a meeting, shall pay a fine
of 25 pounds Flemish [= $60.00]. The Director General and
Council do not however hereby intend to force the consciences,
to the prejudice of formerly given patents, or to forbid the preaching of God's holy Word, the family prayers and divine service
in the family, but only all public and private conventicles and
gatherings, be they in public or private houses, except the already
mentioned usual and authorized reformed divine service. In
order that this order may be better observed and nobody plead
ignorance thereof the Director General and Council direct and
charge their Fiscal and the inferior Magistrates and Schouts, to
publish it everywhere in this Province and prosecute the trans-
gressors, whereas we have so decreed it for the honor of God,
the advancement of the Reformed service and the quiet, unity and
welfare of the country in general.

"Thus done etc., February 1, 1656."

The Directors in United Netherlands were not altogether
pleased with this placard, and still less with Stuyvesant's enforcing
of it. For, according to a letter of the Directors, in June of the
same year, Stuyvesant actually committed some Lutherans to
prison. It reads:

"We would have been better pleased, if you had not published
the placard against the Lutherans, a copy of which you sent us,
and committed them to prison, for it has always been our intention, to treat them quietly and leniently. Hereafter you will therefore not publish such or similar placards without our knowledge,
but you must pass it over quietly and let them have free religious
exercises in their houses."

The sources accessible to us do not give the names of these
prisoners or help us to establish the accuracy of the statement in

regard to any imprisoning of Lutherans. Perhaps the Directors in United Netherlands were laboring under some misapprehension. The probability, however, is that Stuyvesant did what the letter claimed he did. It suffices to mention his subsequent treatment of Rev. Goetwater.

The Lutherans in New Amsterdam, while obediently acting upon the prohibitive order of February, 1656, received word from their friends in United Netherlands (who had interceded for them there with the Directors of the West India Company) that the Directors "in a full meeting" resolved that the doctrines of the Unaltered Augsburg Confession should be tolerated in the West Indies and New Netherland "under their jurisdiction, in the same manner as in the Fatherland, under its excellent government."

The Lutherans in New Netherland informed Stuyvesant and the Council in regard to this, October 24, 1656, praying "that henceforth we may not be hindered in our services. These with Gods blessing we intend to celebrate, with prayer, reading and singing, until, as we hope and expect, a qualified person shall come next spring from the Fatherland to be our minister and teacher, and remain here as such."

But the Council at New Amsterdam would make no concession, and simply reiterated that no one should be prevented from having family worship. Public worship was to remain under the same restriction as before.

Meanwhile Rev. Jan Goetwater arrived in the summer of 1657. But the Reformed pastors sent in to the Burgomasters and Schepens their objections against his taking up any pastoral work among the Lutherans in New Netherlands. Among the objections were these:

If the Lutherans should have public worship, the result would be "great contention and discord" not only among the inhabitants and citizens in general, but also in families, "of which we have had proofs and complaints during the past year. For example, some husbands have forced their wives to leave their own church, and attend their conventicles." Secondly, the numbers of hearers in the Reformed church would be "perceptibly diminished. Many of that persuasion [Lutheran] have continued attentive hearers among us, and several have united themselves with our church.

These would separate themselves from us." Thirdly, "the treasury of our deacons [the poor fund] would be considerably diminished, and become unable to sustain the burdens it has hitherto borne," as "there is no other means provided for the support of the poor, save what is collected in the church." Fourthly, "if the Lutherans should be indulged in the exercise of their (public) worship, the Papists, Mennonites and others would soon make a similar claim. Thus we would soon become a Babel of confusion, instead of remaining a united and peaceful people. Indeed it would prove a plan of Satan to smother this infant rising congregation, almost in its birth, or at least to obstruct the march of truth in its progress."

The Burgomasters and Schepens were pleased with these arguments, and adopted measures accordingly. They summoned Rev. Goetwater. They charged him not to hold any public or private religious exercises in New Amsterdam, and informed the Director General and Council of what their views were and what they had done. This latter body and Stuyvesant ratified their action, and requested them strictly to enforce the placard of February, 1656. Goetwater got orders to leave the country.

The Reformed ministers now sent a report, Aug. 5, 1657, to the Classis of Amsterdam, stating that they could not have believed that the Directors in United Netherlands should have permitted the Lutherans to have public worship. But they were disillusioned when Rev. Goetwater arrived, as they wrote, "to the great joy of the Lutherans, but to the special displeasure and uneasiness of the congregation in this place; yea, even the whole country, including the English, were displeased." They urged that Goetwater, "the snake in our bosom", be sent back to Holland.

It was now that the Lutherans sent in their well known petition of Oct. 10, 1657, so often referred to in this volume, and given in full on page 37 ff. The Reformed ministers later claimed that this petition was "signed by the least respectable" of the Lutherans, and that "the most influential among them were unwilling to trouble themselves with it."

Their petition of October 10, followed by a letter from Rev. Goetwater to the Director General and Council, proved to be in vain. Goetwater was again commanded to leave the country.

But he was in no hurry to depart.

He remained during the winter of 1657—58 at the farm of a Norwegian. (See p. 39.) His opponents, the Reformed minister wrote that Goetwater, instead of returning to Holland "went out of the city and concealed himself with a Lutheran farmer during the whole winter," where the congregation "supported him at the rate of six guilders ($2.40) per week. On the fourth of August last, when we celebrated the Lord's Supper, they made a collection among themselves for him. The Fiscal was again directed to arrest him, and compel him to leave by one of the earliest ships. In the meantime the Lutherans came and represented to the Director-General that their preacher was sick at the farmer's, and besought the privilege of bringing him within the place for treatment. This was granted them. The Fiscal was at the same time empowered to watch over him, and when well again to send him to Holland. Whether on his recovery, he will return or conceal himself again, time must show."

The Council not long thereafter, on November 11, 1658. passed a resolution, that Goetwater "remain in New Amsterdam until otherwise directed." He did not preach, however.

Stuyvesant did all in his power to make Lutheran preaching in New Netherland an utter impossibility. In 1662 he again published a proclamation against the preaching of any other than the Reformed doctrine "either in houses, barns, ships or yachts, in the woods and fields."

Not before the English conquered New Netherland, in 1664, did the Lutherans in this colony get a "charter," granting them the right of free and public exercise of divine worship according to their conscience; provided they would "not abuse this liberty to the disturbance of others . . ."

This "charter" was far from implying complete parity. It did not mean autonomy. And when the Dutch, in 1675. reconquered their territory, the Lutherans were legally in the same position as before, petitioning anew for permission to exercise public worship. But the Dutch government proved more liberal now than before. It permitted the free exercise of worship to the Lutherans (September. 1673), but forbade, in March, 1674, Jacobus Fabritius, Lutheran pastor from Grosglogan in Silesia. to act as clergyman for a year, because he had solemnized a marriage, without having been lawfully authorized to act as clergyman. This attitude to a clergyman that in 1669 had received permission from Governor Lovelace to become pastor of the Lutherans in New York and Albany, shows that the Dutch government was in continuity with itself, though it was trying to follow a more lenient policy than before. Fabritius, who preached in Dutch, but seems to have been a Pole, had already at the outset proved himself a troublesome clergyman, quarreling with his parishioners and the state authorities: he had domestic troubles, and now and then got drunk. He was obliged to resign in 1670, and became the pastor of the Swedes on the Delaware. But his weakness is no excuse for the sentence imposed upon him by the restored Dutch rule under Colve.

After the restoration of the English rule, in 1674, the Lutherans enjoyed their rights as before. Fabritius, however, fared no better. The Swedish and Finnish Lutherans at Cranehook remonstrated against him in August, 1675, because they could not understand his language. In September, in the same year, the English government again suspended him "from exercising his function as a minister, or preaching any more within this government either in public or private." The reason for this suspension was his "irregular life and conversation."

The treatment of Rev. Goetwater by the Dutch Government, the sad experiences with his successor who was morally unfit for his position may have discouraged the Lutherans, and caused that a number of them joined the Reformed church. Meanwhile the differences between the Reformed and Lutherans were gradually disappearing in the consciousness of the common people, though the problem of election caused ill feeling among members of the respective denominations as late as 1680.

Later, when James II. ascended the throne of England, the fear that Catholicism would become a power in the colonies drew the contending Protestants in New Netherland closer together. And the spirit of Protestantism, whether originally imbibed from the Lutheran "doctrine" or from the Reformed "religion" or both, was at the close of the century so strong that the attempt to make even the Episcopal church the state church of New York proved abortive.

This is not the place to indulge in denominational polemics. But the fact that Germans and Scandinavians played an important role in the life of our present metropolis is a factor that must be reckoned with in considering the religious developments in early New York.

As for the political influence, it suffices to point to a Dane like Captain Kuyter, to Germans like Mayor Nicholas de Meyer and Governor Jacob Leisler.

We can not here discuss the social, economic, and industrial assets of the early German immigrants. The list * of names immediately following may throw a little light on these and kindred questions. For us it is sufficient to point out the Germans in polyglot New Netherland, and to assist in giving an impulse to the study of the German element in the United States prior to 1683; yes, prior to 1674, when the Dutch rule, excellent as it was in many ways, gave way to the rule that was to obtain for a whole century but ended in the American Revolution.

LIST OF GERMAN IMMIGRANTS IN NEW YORK
1630—1674.

Jan Adamsen (Metselaer-Messler) was born at *Worms,* Germany, 1626, died 1696. His name appears in the court records of New Amsterdam in 1656. In 1665 he lived in Marketfield Alley. In 1669 he was one of the curators of the estate of Hage Bruynsen, a Swede (p. 306). His sons, Sebastian, Dirck, Abraham, Isaac were born in 1658, 1661, 1662, 1678 respectively. Of these, Abraham married, 1694, Harmetje Gerrits.

Barent Andriessen, from *Wrede* in Westphalia, married, in 1654, Elken Jans "van Voorden, int Graefschap Zutphen." They lived in New Amsterdam. Two years later, Andriessen was dead, the widow having married Thomas Franszen, of Boston.

Hans Albertsen, from *Brunswick,* got land in September, 1656, near Roelof Jansen de Haes, a Norwegian, in New Amsterdam. In 1658 he is mentioned in the court records, as a witness in a lawsuit.

---

* Immigrants from Schleswig and Holstein have been treated in Part II.

Harmon Arentsen was in New Amsterdam in 1644 (or earlier), when he was thirty-eight years old. He was from *Bremen.*

*

Jan Barentszen, of *Lübeck,* married in New Amsterdam, 1685, Maryken Jillis, widow of Robert Rotges. In 1694 he married Marritie Webbers.

Meyndert Barentszen, from *Jever,* in *Oldenburg* married in New Amsterdam, June 6, 1659, Anneke Cornelis. In October, 1657, he signed the petition of the Lutherans, requesting that Rev. Goetwater be retained as a Lutheran pastor in New Amsterdam. He was a cooper, and had several hired men. In 1665 he lived in Smith Street. He got the small burgher's right in New Amsterdam, 1657. He had children.

Paulus van der Beeck, from *Bremen,* married, 1644, in New Amsterdam, Maria Thomas, widow of Willem de Cuper. In 1657 he was farmer of weigh scales; in 1660 farmer of burgher excise of wine and beer. In his official capacity he was often in court, prosecuting. He owned several lots in New Amsterdam. In 1662 he let a contract for a house "40 ft. × 20 ft. × 6 ft." He was one of the leading citizens in New Amsterdam.

Cornelis Beckman, from Stift *Bremen,* married, in 1665, in New Amsterdam, Marritje Cornelis, widow of Hans Ketel, or Hans Christiaenszen. She was from Flensburg (p. 185).

Jochem Beeckman was in New Amsterdam in 1639 or before. He was a cobbler by trade. He had a quick hand and a ready tongue wherewith to defend himself, what brought him several times into court. His wife was a faithful ally in matters of self-defense. He was in all probability a German, as he is seen to have associated much with Germans, being frequently called in as sponsor in German families. In October, 1657, he signed the petition of the Lutherans that they might retain Rev. Goetwater as Lutheran pastor in New Amsterdam. He had a house and lot on the east side of Heere Graft, "to the North of Pine St., to the East the house and lot of Jacobus Baker, West the said Gracht." He had children.

Christina Bleyers, from "Stoltenon" in *Lüneburg,* was married, Jan. 17, 1659, in New Amsterdam, to Pieter Hendricksen Christians, from Denmark (p. 186).

Adam Brouwer Berkhoven immigrated to New Netherland from *Cologne,* in 1642. He married Mag(reta) Jacobs Verdon. In 1677—80 he and his wife were members of the Dutch Reformed Church at Brooklyn.

Matys Blanjan (Blanchan), from *Mannheim,* is mentioned in the records of New Amsterdam in 1662, when reference is also made to his son-in-law. Matys Blanjan jr. married in Kingston, N. Y., 1679. As there were in New Amsterdam several Frenchmen from Mannheim, Matys may have been one of them. He was a Protestant.

Jan Bosch, from *Westphalia,* arrived at New Amsterdam, by the ship "de Vos," which sailed from Texel, August 31, 1662. When the English Governor, in 1665, desired to billet off soldiers, Bosch claimed he could not receive soldiers, as "he has no bed" for them.

He is mentioned in the court records as late as 1674. He was dead before May, 1679, when his widow, Rachel Vermelje, married Dirck Wesselsen, from Arnhem.

Adam Bremen, from *Aachen,* sailed for New Amsterdam Dec. 23, 1657, by "de Jan Baptiste." His wife, Elsie Barents, and a servant girl followed in 1663, by "de Bonte Koe." He was dead before 1670, when his widow married Marius de Vos.

Aeltie Van Bremen is mentioned, in 1668, in the records of New Netherland. She is probably the woman who was married, 1643, at New Amsterdam, to *Pieter Collet,* from *Königsberg.*

Michiel Bronval is listed among the passengers, who were to sail for New Netherland, by "de Bonte Koe," April 15, 1660. He was from *Berg-Cassel,* and probably sailed as a soldier.

Albert Buer, from *Jülich,* sailed for New Amsterdam, April 8, 1662, by the ship "de Hoop."

Johannes Burger, from Gemen (*Münster*) is mentioned in the records of New Amsterdam in 1663.   In 1691 he married Helena Turck.

*

Claes van Campen, of *Oldenburg,* is designated as a farmer boy in the records of New Netherland, 1660.

Matthys Capito, surnamed Boon, Bon, Bontze, was probably from *Bonn,* Germany.   In August, 1650, in New Amsterdam, he married Elsje Pieters, from *Hamburg,* widow of Hans Webber. Capito signed, in October, 1657, the petition of the Lutherans in New Amsterdam, requesting that Rev. Goetwater be allowed to remain as their pastor.   In 1659 Capito was commissary at South River.   After about the year 1660 he was secretary of the village of Esopus, mustermaster, secretary of the council of war (Indian wars were waged).   He was schout of Wiltwyck, Dec. 1663— April, 1664.   The name "Capito" is a Latinization of "Köpfel." Capito's wife was killed and burned in the Indian war at Esopus. 1663.   He died about 1667.   His name often occurs in the records of New Netherland.   He figured frequently in the courts.   He had at least one child: Hendrick, born in 1653.   A letter of Capito, June 29, 1663, to Gov. Stuyvesant and the Council of New Netherland, speaks of his poverty after he had lost all he had in the war.   It reads:

"Gentlemen. Whereas I, your Hon. Worships' humble petitioner have also been brought to ruin during these late troubles in the village of Wiltwyck, caused by the savages, not having lost only my dear wife, who was killed by the barbarians and then burned with the house, to which they set fire, but in the same fire also all my moveable effects, that nothing else is left to me, but my honest name. Now, as I need during my further life, for covering my body and keeping clean, some linen and cloth, which at present cannot be obtained here, and which, even if it were to be had here, I cannot pay for, therefore I am compelled to turn to your Hon. Worships, in pity of my distressed circumstances and misery; (you) will please to assist me and provide me with low-priced clothing, to-wit, some cheap plain cloth for a suit of clothes and what is needed for it, two or three store-shirts or linen to make them, one or one and a half els of linen for handkerchiefs and nightcaps, a blanket and enough coarse linen for a straw tick and a pillow, two pairs of Icelandish socks and a pair of shoes—and charge these goods according to their prices to my account. I promise to make it good to your Hon. Worships as soon as I can, and as with God's blessing I shall have again prospered somewhat. Not doubting that I expect to receive them by the first opportunity, because my needy circumstances require them, closing with greetings, I commend your Honr. Worships to the Almighty's protection, wishing and praying sincerely, that the good God will save your Honbl. Worships and us all from all such and similar misfortune and troubles while I remain Mateus Capito."

Gabriel Carbosie (Carpesy), born in *Lauffen,* near Mannheim, married, in New Amsterdam, 1657, Teuntje Straelsman. He later married Briete Olofs, a widow, from Sweden (p. 340).

Wolfgang Carstensen, soldier, from *Wolfenbüttel,* married July 3, 1660, in New Amsterdam, Elsje Jans Bresteede, widow of Hendrick Jansen.

Jan Christiaen (De Jon Christiaen), from *Germany,* was in New Netherland in April 1660.

Dirck Claeszen, from *Bremen,* married, in November, 1650, in New Amsterdam, Aechtje Jacobs (Van "Hertogenbusch"). He seems to have been a potter.

Valentine Claesen, from *"Saxenlant,* in Transylvania," married, April, 1662, in New Amsterdam, Maritje Beest, from "Cuylenborg." In 1673 he was Schepen of Fordham village. As Riker says, the Valentines of our country are not descendants of Benjamin Valentine, a French dragoon in French military service in Canada, but from Valentine Claesen.

Jan Van Cleef (Cleves) was in New Amsterdam as early as 1653, when he was twenty-five years of age. In company with Titus Cyre he bought a horsemill belonging to Jacob van Couwenhoven. He later became the sole owner of it, but soon sold it, what brought on considerable litigation in the court.

Ulderick Cleen, [Uldrich Klein], from *Hesse,* married, in July, 1641, in New Amsterdam, Afje Pieters, of Amsterdam. They had at least one child, baptized in 1642.

Cornelis Jansen Clopper, from *Kloppenborg,* petitioned, in 1655, the council of New Amsterdam for permission to tap. It appears that he had just returned from Brazil to New Amsterdam, where he had resided before he went to South America. He had been "driven away" from Brazil. He was a smith, and had hired workmen. In 1660 he acquired a parcel of ground in Smith's Valley. He served on the jury in 1667.

Johannes Clute came to Beverwyck about 1656 from *Nürnberg.* He was commonly called captain and was held in esteem by the Mohawks. He was a trader and large land-holder in Loonenburg, Niskayuna, and Albany. His name was sometimes spelled

Cloete. There were many in early New York who had the name Clute. Johannes died about 1684.

Hans or *Jans Coenratse* was from *Nürnberg*. He is mentioned in the records of New Netherland in 1660.

Hendrick Coenratse, from *Bonn*, was in New Netherland in 1660.

Pieter Collet, from *Königsberg* "in Pruysen," married, in August, 1643, in New Amsterdam, Aeltje Jans, from *Bremen*, widow of John Cornelisen, of Rotterdam. He signed the well-known resolution adopted by the Commonalty of Manhattans in October, 1643. He had a child baptized in December, 1644.

Jan Cornelissen de Ryck was probably a German. He married in May, 1658, in New Amsterdam, Marritje Gerrits. They had children. The Jan Cornelissen who, in October, 1657, signed the petition of the Lutherans, in New Amsterdam, to retain Rev. Goetwater as pastor is possibly Jan Cornelissen de Ryck. In 1671 Cornelissen was overseer of Roads.

Hendrick Corneliszen Van Valckenburg was, judging by the name, from *Falkenburg* in Germany, not far from Jülich. In May, 1650, he married, in New Amsterdam, Marie Bowens, from London. He seems to have been a rope maker.

Lambert van Valckenburch was in New Amsterdam as early as 1644, and received a patent of land there, March 16, 1647. He removed to Fort Orange. See Plate facing p. 62.

Jan Coster [Köster], of *Aachen*, bought a lot in Beverwyck in March, 1661. In 1669 he was called Jan van Aecken.

Barent Court [Coerten] "van Rhenen" in "Stift *Münster*" married in December, 1664, in New Amsterdam, Anna Jans, widow of Andries Spiering. He joined the Dutch Reformed Church in 1666. In 1686 his wife was Christina Wessells. They lived on High Street. His property in this street was, in 1674, valued at $8000.

Michael Croes, from *Danzig,* married in June, 1661, in New Amsterdam, Jannetje Theunis.

Coenraet Croos, from *Switzerland,* was among the soldiers to sail, April 15, 1660, by "de Bonte Koe," for New Netherland.

*

Hans Diederick, of *Isleven* [Eisleben] married, in New Amsterdam, 1664, Grietje Warnaerts, widow of Adriaen Hendr. Zips. In 1673 he was elected Lieutenant at the nomination of the town of Bergen, N. J. In 1684 he appears as a witness in a lawsuit.

Carsten Dircksen, from *Bremen,* a shoemaker by trade, got the small burgher's right in New Amsterdam, in 1657.

Jan Dircksen, from *Bremen,* was in New Amsterdam as early as 1639. In 1643 was skipper of a vessel, receiving orders from Kiliaen van Rensselaer. His wife was Tryntie Anders. They belonged to the Dutch Reformed church in New Amsterdam, and had a child baptized in February, 1644. In 1665 it appears that he had a scow, on which he employed hired men and took passengers. Dircksen was a "tar of the old sort," who loved strong drink and took pleasure in striking terror into his servants.

Lucas Dircksen, from *Berg,* Germany, was one of the signers of the Lutheran petition in October, 1657, in New Amsterdam. His wife was Annetje Cornelis. They had several children. Dircksen came to New Netherland in 1652 or before. In 1654 he was given a license to retail beer and wine. Up to that time he seems to have been employed as a soldier. His business brought him a number of times into court, — to collect an account or to be fined for tapping after the hours of closing. He seems to have resided for some time at South River, where he possessed a house.

Hans Dreper, or Draper (Drapier) was no doubt a Teuton. His signing the Lutheran petition in October, 1657, for retaining Rev. Goewater in New Amsterdam, and again a Lutheran petition at Albany, in 1673, seems to indicate that he was from Lutheran Scandinavia or Lutheran Germany. He was probably a German.

In 1654 he had a son baptized in New Amsterdam, and two years later a daughter. His wife was Marritie Pieters [also called Margritie Jans]. In October, 1656, Dreper requested by petition leave to tap beer and wines. The petition was granted. He had several lawsuits, prosecuting people for board and drink. He was often fined for using unbecoming language, and at one time even imprisoned for six weeks on bread and water. Also his wife was given to petty quarreling.

*

Hieronymus Ebbing, from *Hamburg*, married, in 1659, in New Amsterdam, Johanna de Laet, widow of John de Hulter. They had several children. Ebbing was for many years church warden of the Dutch Reformed church at New Amsterdam. In 1658 he supervised the paving of Brewer St. with cobblestones as an "ornament and for the use of the city." He was curator of the estate of the Dane Jochem Pietersen Kuyter. In 1658 he was made Great Burgher. He was elected schepen of the city in 1661, and was often re-elected. He had the title of Sieur. In 1665, living at Brewer Street, he was assessed fl. 4; only nine other citizens paying so high a tax. In 1670 he was juryman, and in 1673 was nominated burgomaster, but not elected. He often served as arbitrator in disputes.

Harmen Eduardsen (Eduwarsen) signed the petition of the Lutherans of New Amsterdam, 1657, to retain Rev. Goetwater. Eduardsen was probably a German. In 1662 we find him in Bergen, New Jersey, where he, in company with Laurens Andriessen Boskerk (p. 152) and others, subscribed money to defray the salary of a preacher. He owned some sixty-nine acres of land in Bergen. In 1674 he acquired land on Staten Island at the mouth of "Kill von Koll."

Elbert Elbertsen (Eldert Engelberts) from an island off the coast of East Friesland was at Midwout in 1654 or before. In March, 1656, he married, in New Amsterdam, Sarah Walker, of Boston. Their daughter Anna Maria was born in December of the same year at Maspeth Kills. Elbertsen was one of the "good men" in an arbitration suit in 1656, the other arbitrator being Domine Megapolensis. Riker's History of Harlem registers Elbertsen as a Swede. The spelling Engelberts would point to Swedish antecedents. It is probable though that, coming from East Friesland, he was German.

Lucas Eldertsen, from *Jever,* was in New Netherland as early as 1643, when his name occurs in the records of the colony of Rensselaerswyck. He was in New Amsterdam 1646. In 1649 he was given power of attorney by Jan Lawrensen Appel to collect money due at South River, when he is called "the worthy Luycas Eldertsen from Jeveren." In 1654 a son of Eldertsen and his wife, Annetje Jans, was baptized in New Amsterdam, and a daughter in 1656. In 1657 we find him as laborer at the weigh house. In the same year he signed the petition of the Lutherans requesting that Rev. Goetwater be retained as Lutheran pastor. In 1661 he was in Beverwyck. His widow married, in May, 1666, Laurens Jansen Van Wormer, a Hollander. Eldertsen seems to have been a person of quiet disposition, though he often appeared in court.

*

Hendrick Folckertsen, born in 1634, married Feb. 26, 1655, at New Amsterdam, Geertie Claes. He was from *Jever.* He acted as sponsor in 1654. In 1674 he is mentioned in the court records as intending to make a voyage to the West Indies. Folckertsen and his wife had at least one child.

Jurian Fradel, from *Moravia,* acquired sixty-nine acres of land at Long Island in September, 1644. A year later he, as the "husband of the widow of Hendrick Hendricksen," acquired some more land. He had a child baptized in New Amsterdam in 1653. Judging by the court records, he was a dealer in tobacco.

Arent Francken, a baker from *Jever,* arrived at New Amsterdam by the ship "de Trouw," which sailed February 12, 1659.

Carsten Frederickse, from *Jever,* a brother of Meyndert Fredericksen (see below), was a smith by trade (master smith). With his brother he had a smith shop in Albany; he owned also a lot on the north corner of Broadway and State Street. He was deacon of the Dutch Lutheran church, in the same city, 1680.

His wife was Tryntie Warners. They made a joint will July 1, 1689, which mentions their four children.

Meyndert Fredericksen, from *Jever*, married, in August, 1655, in New Amsterdam, Catharyn Burchart (Burger); and secondly, in 1663, Pietertje Teunise Van Vechten. They lived in the city of Albany. He was a smith and had together with his brother Karsten, a smith shop on the north corner of Broadway and Spanish (later Hudson) St. He was sometimes designated as "armorer to the fort." He was elder of the Dutch Lutheran church in Albany in 1680. In 1673 he signed a petition of the Lutherans, requesting in "their own and in the name of their congregation of the Augsburg Confession at Willemstadt (Albany) . . . in substance free exercise of their religious worship, without let or hindrance, to the end that they may live in peace with their fellow burghers. . . ." They had enjoyed religious liberty under the English rule, but the Dutch, on reconquering New Netherland in 1673, were less liberal. However, the local Dutch government ordered, on receipt of this petition: "The petitioners are granted and allowed their aforesaid request on condition of comporting themselves peaceably and quietly without giving any offence to the congregation of the Reformed Religion, which is the State Church (de hooft kercke)." In 1701 Meyndert signed another Lutheran petition addressed to King William III.

Meyndert and his wife were zealous defenders of Lutheranism, manifesting, however, a zeal which was deficient in knowledge, as will be seen from the minutes of the Extraordinary Court held at Albany in March, 1680. The problem of election occupied the lay Lutheran mind of our country even as early as the seventeenth century. It assumed such importance in the mind of Meyndert that he and his wife quarreled with the Reformed minister.

"The Court met at the request of Domine Gideon Schaets (Dutch Reformed minister at Albany) accompanied by the W. Consistory, who complains that Myndert Frederickse Smitt came to his house and told him, the Domine, never to presume to speak to any of his Children on religious matters; and that he, the Domine, went sneaking through all the houses like the Devil; adding, Our Domine (meaning Domine Bernardus, Minister of the Lutheran Congregation) does not do so.

"Domine Schaets further complains that Myndert Frederickse's wife grievously abused and calumniated him behind his back at Gabriel Thomson's house, as an old Rogue, Sneak, etc., and that if she had him by the pate, she should drag his grey hairs out of it; which the Domine offers to prove by witnesses.

"Whereupon Myndert Frederickse and wife are sent for to Court, and Domine Schaets' accusation is read to Myndert, who denies it all, declaring that he has not given the Domine an ill word.

"Pietertje, wife of Myndert Frederickse, denies having abused Domine Schaets as a rogue and sneak; but that the Domine hath abused her Religion as a Devilish Religion.

"Hend. Rooseboom sworn, says that he was at Gabriel Thomson's last Monday when Pietertje, Myndert Frederickse's wife, entered, and wishing to go away, was called back by Gabriel, and conversing on the subject of Domine Schaets and her daughter, she said,—What business hath Domine Schaets to question mine daughter? To this Gabriel said—Why should he not do so? The Domine does well to question people. Whereupon Pietertje said, Domine Schaets, the old Rogue and Sneak; had she been by she should have caught him by the grey pate—adding he ought to look to his daughter, the W. . . . .e, and take care of her—To which Gabriel replied, Meutie, why say that and scold the Domine so? who answered him—You d . . . . dog! you protect your w . . . . . and knaves.

"Cornelis Teunise Swart, being sworn, says, he was also at Gabriel Thomson's last Tuesday, when Pietertie Myndert Frederickse's wife came in and enquired for her daughter, who not being there, she was going away, but Gabriel called her back and said—sit a while, Meutie; and being in conversation about Domine Schaets' wishing to question her daughter, she said she had, herself, a teacher to do so, that if she had the old rogue, she would take him by the grey pate, and further knoweth not."

"Mr. Sheriff Pretty requests their Worships that he may act herein, to institute his action, at a more convenient period.

"The W. Court postponed the matter to the next Court day to act on the merits. Meanwhile if parties can be reconciled, (through Respect for the Divine) they were particularly recommended to do so, saving Sheriff's action and costs."

On the next day the Court met again, when:

"Myndert Fredericksen and his wife appear before their Worships of the Court, requesting that they may be reconciled in love and friendship with Domine Schaets, as they have been with Gabriel. Whereupon their W. recommended him to call Domine Schaets, which being immediately done;

"Domine Schaets appearing before their Worships is asked—if he were willing to be reconciled with the aforesaid persons? who answers, Yes, on the condition that they both acknowledge him an honorable man, and that they know nought of him except what is honest and virtuous (always excepting the Dispute, out of which this Case arose, namely—Universal Grace—being no political question)*, also the Sheriff's claim.

"Whereupon Myndert aforesaid and his wife acknowledge the Domine in open Court to be an honest man,† and they know nought of him except all honor and virtue and are willing to bear all the costs hereof, also to settle with the Sheriff.

"N. B. It is settled by And. Teller and for six Beavers and six cans of wine!" (Ecclesiastical Records of the State og New York, I., p. 737f.)

In his will, 1704, proved May, 1706, Meyndert mentioned his "house and lot hard by the church in Cow St. (now Broadway), Albany, his garden behind the fort, and personal property, including a great silver tankard, a church book with silver clasps and chain, a silver tumbler, marked F . . . He had four children.

* This is explained by the following testimony in another case—"Hans Dreper further says that Gabriel's wife stated that Domine Schaets said at her house that whoever taught that Christ died alike for all men, taught a false and devilish Doctrine.
† The Domine's daughter was not without blame. Though unmarried she was the mother of a child by van Curler.

Cornelis Gerloffs, a tailor from *East Friesland*, came to New Amsterdam in 1661 by the ship "Gulden Arent," which sailed January 1, of that year. However, he had lived in New Amsterdam before, as the court records indicate.

Claes Gerritsen, son of Gerrit Lubbertsen, from *Wesel*, came to New Amsterdam by the ship "het Gekruijste Hart," sailing April 17, 1664. In 1671 he worked as a hired man.

Otto Grimm, from *Bremen*, married, in September, 1664, in New Amsterdam, Elsje Jans, widow of Elbert Jans. In the documents he is styled "captain at arms." In 1671 his wife, called Elsie Grimm, was sued by Jochem Beeckman. The records do not give any details as to this suit, only stating that, "Parties agreed." In 1674 Grimm's house in the present Broad St. was valued at $1,000.

Margaret Grootjen, from *Aachen*, married on June 11, 1660, in New Amsterdam, Barent Christoffelszen Cruydop, widower of Ursel Coenrats.

*

George Hanel, one of the signers of the petition of the Lutherans in New Amsterdam, 1657, requesting that Rev. Goetwater might be permitted to remain in the country as Lutheran minister, was probably a German. He is also later mentioned in the records of New Netherland, even as late as 1663. In the court records he is called Jurien Hanel. A "George Hans [Holmes]" signed the Resolution of the Commonalty of Manhattan, 1643. Is he George or Jurien Hanel?

Hendrick Hansen arrived in New Netherland in 1663, by "de Rooseboom," which sailed March 15, 1663. In the passenger's list it is said that he was "from *Germany*." Was he the mayor of Albany in 1698?

Jan Harberding [Harpendinck], from "Boeckholdt" [Bocholt] in Westphalia, married, in December, 1667, in New Amsterdam, Mayken Barents, from Harlem [New York?]. He was a shoemaker by occupation. In 1674 his property on the north side of the present Stone St., between William and Broad St., was valued at $3,000. He joined the Dutch Reformed church in April, 1664.

Johannes Hardenbroeck, from *Elberfeld,* arrived, with his wife, Urseltje Duytman, and four children, in New Netherland by the ship "de Trouw," which sailed January 20, 1664. The children were eight, six, five and three years old respectively. In 1665 he lived at the Prince Graft, in New Amsterdam. He became a prominent man in this city, often serving on the jury. An Abel Hardenberg (Obel Hardenbroeck), often referred to in the court records, and a well-to-do person, was possibly a relative of Johannes. The latter, it seems, was also ensign of the militia. He joined the Dutch Reformed church in 1686.

Melem Harloo, from the province of *"Middelsaxen,"* married in July, 1644, in New Amsterdam, Elsje Jans, widow of Jan Pietersen.

Frederick Harmenszen, from *Bremen,* was a member of the Dutch Reformed Church in New Amsterdam in 1649.

Hans Jacob Harting, from *Bern,* Switzerland, married in July, 1668, in New Amsterdam, Gertje Lambertsen Mol.

Claes Hayen, from *Bremen,* sailed for New Netherland in the ship "de Bonte Koe," April 15, 1660. He was an "Adelborst." He married Marritje Claes.

Cornelis Hendricksen, from *Ens* [Ems?], was probably a German. He came to New Netherland in "de Vergulde Bever," which sailed May 17, 1658.

Gerrit Hendricksenz, from *"Waerdenbroeck" in Cleves,* married in 1654, in New Amsterdam, Hermken Hermans, widow of Wilhelm Jansen. Gerrit acquired land in the vicinity of New Amsterdam as early as 1646. In 1663 he acquired land on the Schuykill. In 1658 he was farmer of excise in New Amsterdam, which office he continued to hold for several years. As such he often appeared in court to transact business. He was deceased in 1671.

Hendrick Hendricksen, from *Westphalia,* came to New Amsterdam by the ship "de Rooseboom," which sailed March 15, 1663. There were many Hendrick Hendricksens in New Amsterdam, including an Irishman. One was a drummer, another a tailor, a third a soldier, etc. To find the data for each particular person bearing this name in ancient New York, is a hopeless task.

Hendricks Hendricksen, from *Erlangen,* was in New Amsterdam in 1664 (or before), when he is mentioned as plaintiff in a court proceeding. In the same year his daughter Catharyntie was married to Jonas Ranzow, of Holstein (see p. 273). A Hendrick Hendricksen signed the Lutheran petition of 1657, requesting that Rev. Goetwater be permitted to stay in the country as Lutheran minister. Was it the one from Erlangen?

Huybert Hendricksen, from *Rodenkirchen* (near Cologne), married, January, 1656, in New Amsterdam, Marritje Hendricks Van Norden in East Friestland. They had several children. In 1663 he brought suit against Francis de Bruyn for tobacco. In 1665 he lived in Brewer St. He was still living in 1672, when he stood sponsor for a child belonging to John Otten.

Jan Hendricksen, from *Strückhausen,* in Oldenburg, acquired land in New Castle, in September 1656.

Juriaen Hendricksen, from *Osnabrück,* was at New Amsterdam as early as 1639. He seems to have been a carpenter. He is frequently mentioned in the records. In 1662 he went to Holland.

Marritje Hendricks "Van Norden" in *East Friesland,* was married January, 1656, in New Amsterdam, to Huybert Hendricksen, from Rodenkirchen.

Marten Hendricksz, from *Hamelwörden* [Hammelwarden], near Freiburg on the Elbe, Hanover, came to New Netherland on "den Harinck", July 7, 1639, and was engaged for six years as a farm hand in the colony of Rensselaerswyck.

Augustine Herrman, born in 1621 in *Prague,* Bohemia, came to New Amsterdam in 1643. He was the son of Augustine

Ephraim Herrmann and of Beatrice, a daughter of the patrician family of Redal. His father, a Protestant, was an honored citizen and merchant in the "Kohlmarkt," but was outlawed because of having been involved in certain political affairs; he then removed to Amsterdam. The son was highly educated, spoke several languages. By profession he was a surveyor. Tradition says that he took part in the Thirty Years' War before settling in New Amsterdam. He seems to have been employed as a clerk by the West India Company, frequenting the South River Country before 1643. He married in 1651, in New Amsterdam, Janneken Varleth (from Utrecht). On his own declaration he was the "first beginner" of the important traffic in tobacco between Virginia and New Amsterdam. "On his farm, near the site of the Astor Library of later years, he seems to have experimented successfully with the cultivation of indigo."

He was a member of the first "Board of Nine Men." Stuyvesant used him on many important embassies, the one of 1659, when he went to Virginia to clear the government of New Netherland from the charge of exciting the Indians against the English, becoming the occasion of his settling in Maryland.

He drew a map of the state of Maryland for Lord Baltimore, which was highly praised for its exactness, the first of its kind and printed in London in 1673. A copy of it is contained in the Grenville collection in the British Museum, adorned with Herrman's autograph and portrait. In payment for it he received a large grant of land, at the head of Chesapeake Bay, now in Cecil and New Castle Counties. This grant together with other grants he received from Lord Baltimore amounted to 30,000 acres. It was known as the Bohemian Manor. Herrman removed from Manhattan to this new manor with his family in 1661. His son Ephraim married a woman of Norwegian blood (p. 103). Both father and son were for some time interested in the project of the Labadists to found a colony. Augustine Herrman gave them a grant of land, a step which he later was sorry for. He cursed his son for becoming a Labadist.

In 1663 (1666?) Maryland by an act of legislature naturalized Augustine Herrman and his two sons — "the first act of the sort known to have been framed in any of the colonies."

Augustine kept a journal, parts of which have been preserved. Augustine's wife was a member of the Dutch Reformed church in New Amsterdam. But his name does not appear as a communicant.

Roeloff Hermansen, from *Germany,* and his wife came to New Netherland by the ship "de Vos," which sailed Aug. 31, 1662.

Barent Holst, from *Hamburg,* arrived at New Netherland in the spring of 1663 by "de Rooseboom." He was at Esopus in 1666, died 1667. A Laurents Holst figures in the court records of New Amsterdam 1668—71. Was he a brother of Barent? Could he have been a Dane? Laurents Holst and wife Hilletje Laurents were members of the Dutch Reformed church in 1686.

Adriaen Huybertsen, from *Jena,* was in New Amsterdam as early as 1660. If there were not two persons in this city by this name, he is the Adriaen Huybertsen who worked for Swartwout in Rensselaerswyck in 1637. A person by his name is mentioned in the records as fencing in farms, navigating yachts. In 1663 he was a widower, with three children. He lived in 1665 at High Street, New Amsterdam.

Reyner Van Giesen, was, judging by the name, from *Giessen,* Germany. He was in New Amsterdam in 1670.

*

Geertje Jacobs, from *Stettin,* was married, October 13, 1647, in New Amsterdam, to Geurt Coerton, from "Northhuysen in Gelderlandt." In 1657 Engeltje Mans, a Swedish woman, was fined 10 guilders for calumniating Geertje Jacobs, a woman "whom nobody would suspect." However, Geertje herself could vie with Engeltje in circulating gossip.

Herman Jacobszen, a soldier from *Emden,* married, in January, 1660, in New Amsterdam, Weyntie Martens.

Jan Jacobsen, from *East Friestland,* came to New Netherland, with wife and two children, in "de Rooseboom," which sailed March 15, 1663. He is sometimes called Intje Jacobs in the records.

Mrs. Jan Jacobsen (see above), coming, in 1663, to New Amsterdam, from *East Friesland*, in company with her husband was probably a German.

Pieter Jacobsz, from *East Friesland*, came to New Netherland by the "Bonte Koe," which sailed April 15, 1660.

Aeltje Jans, from *Bremen*, was married, in August, 1643, in New Amsterdam, to Pieter Collet, from Königsberg. Prior to this marriage she was the widow of John Cornelisen of Rotterdam.

Hilletje Jaleff, from *"Oldenburgerlandt,"* married, on July 4, 1655, in New Amsterdam, Tobias Wilbergen, from Torup in Denmark (p. 283).

Barent Jansz sailed from the Texel by "de Eentracht", March 21, 1630, arriving at New Amsterdam, May 24, of the same year. He was from "Esen" ("Desens" = the man from Esens) that is *Esens,* in East Friesland. He sailed as farm servant of Brant Peelen (from Nykerck), of the colony of Rensselaerswyck. His name does not occur in the records of this colony after 1634. He was probably the first German settler in New Netherland.*

Evert Jansen, from *Emden*, married, July, 1644, in New Amsterdam, Susanna du Trieux. He acquired a lot in 1647, another

---

* Arriving by the same ship and at the same time as Barent Jansz were Pieter Hendricksz and Rutger Hendricks, both from Soest. Whether from Soest in the province of Utrecht or from Soest in Westphalia, is not stated.

There were in New Netherland before 1630 people from Germany, concerning whose nationality nothing definite can be said:

Hendrick Christiansen van Cleef (Cleves) may have been a German. He was a mariner. In 1610 or 1611 he and another mariner, Andriaen Block, chartered a ship and visited Manhattan. He later made several voyages to New Netherland, where he served for a time as factor for merchants in Holland. Late in 1614 or early in 1615 he erected the first building in New Netherland of which any valid record remains. It was, says Mrs. Van Rensselaer, a little fort or blockhouse placed upon Castle Island, which, close to the western shore, is now within the limits of the city of Albany. It was built for defense and for the storage of furs. It was protected by two large and eleven smaller cannon, and was thirty-six by twenty-six feet in size, surrounded by a stockade fifty-eight feet square and a moat eighteen feet broad. It was called Fort Nassau. Jacob Eelkins was in charge of its little garrison of ten or twelve traders during Christiansen's absences. Hendrick Christiansen was killed by an Indian.

Peter Minuit, the first General Director of a self-governed New Netherland, was also from Cleves (Wesel). Prof. Faust claims that he was a German. Mrs. Van Rensselaer says, he was of French Huguenot extraction. He arrived at New Amsterdam in 1626. It was he who bought from the Indians the Island of Manhattan for sixty Dutch guilders. Under his rule New Netherland got self-government, however, under the patroon system. This system aroused a great deal of opposition, because the patroons became manor lords, who carried on colonization as a private affair. Minuit was recalled in 1631. He left the colony in a prosperous condition in 1632. Later he became leader of the Swedish colonization at Delaware, and built Fort Christina, where he died and was buried in 1641.

lot in 1652 at Beverwyck. His name often occurs in the church registers of New Amsterdam. He died in 1655.

Evert Jansen, from *Jever,* became a small burgher in New Amsterdam, 1657. He was either a shoemaker or a ferryman.

Gerrit Jansen, from *Oldenburg,* lived at the Manhattans as early as 1635. In 1632 he had been foreman at the farm of Van Rensselaer. About 1639 he married. He had several children. He acquired ninety-two acres of land at "Pannebackers Bou" in 1646.

Harmen Janzen, from *Hesse,* married, on December 11, 1650, Maria Malaet, Angola (Mulatto?). Janzen was well versed in the Indian language. He removed to Esopus in 1661. There were two Herman Janzens in New Amsterdam. The one from Hesse probably signed the Lutheran petition of 1657, regarding Rev. Goetwater.

Hendrick Jansen. from *Jever,* acquired fifty acres of land, August 25, 1654, on Long Island, near Hellegat. A Hendrick Jansen Smith, secured a lot in New Amsterdam as early as 1644. Was he the Jansen from Jever?

Hendrick Jansen, from "Aschwaerde in't Stift *Bremen"* married, September, 1652, in New Amsterdam, Magdaleen Jans van Swol. He seems to have been a mariner, being in 1648 at Fort Nassau on the South River, 1655 at Fort Cassimir. He was a member of the Lutheran church on the South River, and requested in 1675, that two congregations, established under the Lutheran pastor Fabritius, be confirmed. A Hendrick Jansen was member of Jacob Leisler's council in 1689—90. Was he the one from Bremen?

Hilletje Jans, from *Oldenburg,* was married, October, 1652, in New Amsterdam, to Ide [?] Corneliszen Van Vorst. In 1662 she was unjustly arrested for having baked a quantity of biscuits in order to sell them. She proved, however, that she had done it for "her lying in," and was acquitted. Her husband owned land at Schreyer's Hook in 1664. He is also mentioned in the records as late as 1674.

Jan Janszen, from *Tübingen*, married June, 1649, in New Amsterdam, Baertje Hendricks Kip, from Amsterdam. A Jan Jansen signed the petition of the Lutherans in New Amsterdam, 1657. Was it the one from Tübingen?

Netter Jansen, from *Emden*, came to New Netherland by "de Trouw", which sailed February 12, 1659.

P. Jansz, from *Brunswick*, acquired fifty acres of land in October, 1653, at Catskill, and twelve more, in November of the same year. Is he and Pieter Teunizs from Brunswick (see art.) the same person?

Rem Jansz, a smith from *Jever* in Oldenburg, was in New Amsterdam as early as 1638, and owned land on Long Island in 1643. In May, 1650, he leased a garden near the church yard of Ft. Orange. He is the common ancestor of the Remsen family, one of whom has been president of the Johns Hopkins University.

Gertruy Jochems, from *Hamburg*, came to New Netherland by "de Trouw," which sailed February 12, 1659. She had two children along. She was the wife of Claes Claesen, from Amersfoort, who had already emigrated.

Barent Joosten, from "Wiltmont in *Embderlandt*," married, in December, 1658, in New Amsterdam, Sytie Laurens, of Long Island. She was the daughter of Laurens Pietersen, a Norwegian. Barent had several children. In 1664 he was a magistrate.

Jacob Joosten, from *"Moesel, Graach"*, in Germany, was in New Amsterdam in September, 1662 (or before), when he is mentioned as a widower.

Pieter Jordaensen, from *Lübeck*, married, July, 1642, in New Amsterdam, Catharine van Coesvelt.

Burger Joris, from *Hirschberg*, Silesia, was in New Amsterdam in 1637. For some time he worked in the colony of Rensselaerswyck. In 1639 he removed to New Amsterdam, where he, the same year, married Engeltje Mans, of Sweden (p. 329).

Burger Joris was a smith. He was one of the few inhabitants of New York who got the great burgher's right (1658). He was prominent in public life.

*

Jan van Kalcker, presumably from *Kalkar*, in Cleves, was in New Amsterdam in 1653, when he is mentioned as party in a lawsuit.

Hendrick Karstens was born in 1610, in *Oldenburg*, Westphalia. Not long thereafter his father removed to Amsterdam. Hendrick went to sea, married in 1644 Femetje Coenrats, from Gronningen. Soon after the birth of their first child they came to New Amsterdam. They took up land at Harlem. Karsten is regarded as one of the founders of Harlem. Besides being a sailor, he was a mason.

Abraham Kermer, from *Hamburg*, married, December, 1656, at New Amsterdam, Metje Davids, from Arnhem. They had several children. In 1665 they lived near the "City Wall," in New Amsterdam. In the same year they promised the government to lodge soldiers in their house. Kermer is mentioned in 1674 as sueing one Jan Raye. Metje joined the Dutch Reformed church in 1677. Abraham joined it in 1678. They lived at that time in Niew Street.

Jochem Kettelheym (Kettel), from *Kremmen*, near Stettin, Pomerania, came to New Netherland by "den Houttuyn," which sailed August 4, 1642. He worked, 1646—48, in Van Rensselaer's colony (Vlackte). He leased a farm, 1649, formerly occupied by Simon Walichs. In 1661 the records show that he resided in New Amsterdam, where he owned a house.

Hans Kierstede, from *Magdeburg*, was one of the earliest surgeons and physicians in New York. As early as 1638 he held the position of official surgeon of the West India Company. He married, June, 1642, at New Amsterdam, Sara Roelofs (p. 105), daughter of the Norwegian couple, Roelof Jansen and Annetje Jans. The present work contains an illustration showing the house of Hans Kierstede and his wife. Hans first joined the Dutch Reformed church, January 11, 1664, the church which had been served by Rev. Bogardus, the step-father of Kierstede's wife.

Jochem Kierstede, from *Magdeburg*, a brother of Hans Kierstede, secured land in New Netherland in 1647. Not long there after he perished in the wreck of the "Princess."

Styntie Klinckenborg, from *Aachen*, was first married to Roelof Swensborg, from Denmark, who died in New Amsterdam. In February, 1661, she married again, in New Amsterdam, Jan Doske, a soldier from Tongeren.

Frans Krieger, from *Borken* (in Westphalia or in Hesse), married in February, 1660, in New Amsterdam, Walburg de Silla, from Maestricht.

Barent Jansen Kunst deeded, on October 13, 1662, to Albert Coninck, half of his house and lot in New Amsterdam. The other half was owned by Claes Carstensen, a Norwegian. Kunst was a German (p. 52).

*

Jan Jansen Lammertsen, from *Bremen*, came to New Netherland by "de Bever," which sailed May 9, 1661. In 1663 and later we find him in Albany. A Jan Lammertsen [and his wife, Gretie Jans] joined the Dutch Reformed church in New Amsterdam. October 7, 1663.

Jeurian Jansen, from *East Friesland*, married June 1, 1658, in New Amsterdam. He was a cooper.

Magdalentje Lamberts "Van Tellickhuysen," of *Steinfurt*, in Münster, was married in 1661, at New Amsterdam, to Adam Dircksen "Van Colen op N. Haerlem." She was later (1663) married to the Swede (or Finn), Mons Pietersen, from Abo.

Laurens Laurenszen, from *Bremen*, married August 25, 1669, in New Amsterdam, Hilletje Gerrits, widow of Gerrit Hendricksen.

Jacob Leisler, the best known German in New Netherland in the seventeenth century, came to New Netherland in **1660,** sailing as a soldier, by the Otter (April 27). In the ship's list of passengers he is called "Jacob Leyseler, from Franckfort," probably Frankfurt am Main, to which his father, a clergyman, had been driven by persecution from the Palatinate. On April 11, 1660, he married Elsje Tymens, who had Norwegian blood in her veins, being a niece of the famous Anneke Jans, from Marstrand, Norway (pp. 113 f.) He acquired his wealth through trade with the Indians, becoming one of the richest men in New York. In 1689 he bought a piece of land, the present site of New Rochelle in Westchester County: it was a humanitarian venture in behalf of the Huguenots who had come to New York. He was a champion of civic and religious liberty. "When, in 1675, Governor Andros fined a number of burghers because of their opposition to popery, Leisler refused to pay, preferring imprisonment to the renunciation of his principles. At another time, when a poor Huguenot family landed in New York and were to be sold as redemptioners, he instantly paid down the sum demanded for their transportation, thus delivering the refugees from years of servitude." (Prof. A. B. Faust.)

When Gov. Nicholson had to flee from the country, Leisler was appointed by a committee on safety commander-in-chief of the fort and of the city, until the arrival of the new governor from England. He was finally appointed, by the same committee, supreme commander of the province. As such he made complete reports to King William, to whom he was as loyal as to the Protestant cause. On December 11, 1689, he assumed the command as lieutenant-governor. Some of the old aristrocrats were his enemies. They were captured and sentenced to death. But they sued for mercy, and Leisler pardoned them

In the course of events, they caused his ruin. Had he "employed the thorough methods of the revolutionary dictator, he would have destroyed his enemies while they were in his power, and thereby forever ended their opportunities for doing harm. This act of grace on the part of Leisler, while it elevated him as a man, was undoubtedly a political mistake." (Faust).

Meantime he was master of his enemies at home. But there were more powerful enemies abroad. The French in Canada, aided by Indians, planned to attack New York by way of the Mohawk valley and Albany. The massacre of Shenectady, often referred to in this volume, was the result. The fort was burned, the occupants were slain or taken prisoners. Albany, which formerly had refused to recognize the authority of Leisler, now recognized it. He fortified the city, and his enemies fled to the New England states.

As he perceived the value of co-operative action, he invited the governors of Massachusetts, Plymouth, East and West Jersey, Pennsylvania, Maryland, Virginia to a common congress at New York. They were to discuss plans of resisting the enemy.

The congress met on May 1, 1690. New York, Massachusetts, Plymouth, New Jersey, and Maryland took part. It was the first congress of American colonies, the first of a series that was to culminate in the Continental Congress and deliver America from England.

Owing to jealousies and misunderstandings among the leaders, the plans that were accepted, were only in part carried out. Canada was to be conquered. But the colonies failed in their attempt on land and sea. Leisler's enemies attempted to make him responsible for the failure.

He was arrested by his old enemies. They charged him with rebellion. He was convicted of high treason, and was condemned to death. His judges, conducting a sham trial, were Bayard, Nicolls, Philipse, Van Cortlandt and four Englishmen who had just arrived from England.

Leisler and his son-in-law, Milborne, an Englishman, were executed on May 16, 1691. A judicial murder was thus committed. But the English Parliament later reversed the attainder against Leisler and Milborne, and restored to his heirs his property, which had been confiscated by the crown.

In 1698 the remains of Leisler and Milborne were taken from the burial-place under the gallows to the cemetery of the Dutch Church (in the present Exchange Place). This removal was an occasion of much solemnity, 1500 persons taking part. "Prominent contemporaries in other colonies regarded the execution of Leisler as eminently unjust, Increase Mather, for instance, declaring that Leisler was 'barbarously murdered'."

Leisler, as Prof. Faust says, was conspicuous for unquestioned honesty and integrity, unflinching firmness and energy.

Of Leisler's daughters, Hester married Rynders, a Dutchman. Mary, widow of Milborne, married Abraham Gouverneur, a person of brilliant attainments. "Mary's son, Nicholas Gouverneur married Hester's daughter, Gertrude Rynders; and a son of this marriage, Isaac Gouverneur, was the grandfather of Gouverneur Morris, one of the ablest members of the convention that framed the constitution of the United States."

Mrs. Van Rensselaer's "History of the City of New York" gives about 200 pages to the treatment of Leisler.

Johannes Levelin, from *Mülhausen,* came to New Netherland by the ship "de Bonte Koe," which sailed April 15, 1660. He embarked as a soldier.

Conraet Locker, from *Nürnberg,* was among the soldiers who were to embark for New Netherland on "The Otter," which sailed April 27, 1660.

Hendrick Loef, from *Fulda* in Thuringia, married November, 1657, at New Amsterdam, Geertje Hendricks, from Zutphen. They had children. Geertje, after the death of Loef, married Caspar Luttuer, from Augsburg.

Ulrich Lupold (Leopoldt), from *Stade* in the diocese of Bremen, became Van Dinclages successor as schout-fiscal in New Amsterdam. In 1638—1639, while in the colony of Rensselaerswyck, he corresponded with the patroon Kilian van Rensselaer, who was in Amsterdam.

Caspar Luttuer, from *Augsburg,* a soldier, married in July, 1664, in New Amsterdam, Gerritje Hendricks, widow of Hendr. Loef, from Fulda, in Thuringia. She was from Zutphen.

Christian Luyersen (Carsten Luurzen), from "Ley in't Stift van *Bremen"* married, in 1665, in New Amsterdam, Anna de Vos. He joined the Dutch Reformed church April 6, 1664. He was a tanner and shoemaker.

*

Hans van Mansvelt (from Mansfeld) was in New Amsterdam as early as 1642 or before, when he had a son (Pieter) baptized.

Tryntie Martens, from *Aachen*, was married in 1658, in New Amsterdam, to Paulus Pietersen, of the diocese of Cologne.

Adolf Meyer, from *Westphalia* ("Ulfen" or "Ulsen"?), was one of the founders of Harlem in 1661. He married, in the spring of 1671, in New Amsterdam, Maritje Ver Veelen. She joined the Dutch Reformed church in December, 1673. He joined it March 1, 1674. They had ten children. Adolf had two brothers, *Andrew* and *John Meyer* who also immigrated to America.

Martin Jansen Meyer, from *Elsfleth* in Oldenburg, was a resident of Amersfort, Long Island, 1653, where he was magistrate for some years. He was a smith. In 1662 he married, in New Amsterdam, Hendrickje Hermans. They owned a house and lot in Sheep's Lane, worth about $2,150. They were Lutherans. Martin signed a Lutheran petition in 1674. They made a joint will in 1693, which was proved in 1714. Their daughter, Elsje, born in 1663, married Burger Myndertsen, smith, probably a son of Meyndert Frederickse, from Jever. Martin and Hendrickje had nine children.

Nicholas De Meyer, from *Hamburg*, was one of the most prominent among the Germans in New Amsterdam, becoming mayor of the city in 1676. The New York Genealogical Record (IX., 16) well says: "Perhaps no class among the early residents of New Amsterdam was more distinguished for the rapid strides they made to wealth and social distinction in their adopted home, than those who came from the old commercial cities of Germany. The most prominent representative of this class, which includes, among others, the heads of Van der Beeck, Santfort, Ebbing, Leisler, Schrick [They are all treated in the present Appendix] was Nicholas De Meyer."

Mr. J. Riker, in his book on Harlem [city of New York] calls Nicholas De Meyer a Dane since his native city of Hamburg was claimed by the Duchy of Holstein. In all probability De Meyer was German. In the records he is often called Nicolaes van Holstein. He and his descendants seem to have preferred the ordinary appellation of De Meyer (= steward or farmer).

He settled in New Amsterdam about 1655, marrying on June 6, 1655, Lydia van Dyck, daughter of the ex-fiscal Hendrick van

Dyke. He engaged extensively in trade. In less than twenty years he became next to Fredrick Philipse the wealthiest inhabitant of the city, his fortune being equalled only by that of one person, Cornelius Steenwyck. De Meyer was elected schepen in 1664, alderman 1669—1670, again in 1675. In 1676 he was appointed *Mayor of the city*.

He joined the Dutch Reformed church in 1660.

His wife died in 1687, leaving Nicholas five children, the eldest of whom, William de Meyer, became a prominent citizen of Esopus and Kingston in the present county of Ulster. Nicholas married again: Sara Kellenaer, a widow. He died in 1690.

Jan Meyndertss, a farmer from *Jever*, came to New Amsterdam together with his wife by the ship "de Trouw," which sailed February 12, 1659. His wife was Belitje Plettenberg.

Marie Moores, from Aachen, came to New Amsterdam by the ship "de Trouw," which sailed December 22, 1659.

*

Pieter Van Oblinus, from *Mannheim*, married, in 1685, in New Amsterdam, Cornelia Waldron. He joined the Dutch Reformed church in 1681. Was he of French descent?

*

Evert Pels, from *Stettin*, Pomerania, came to New Netherland in "den Houttuyn," in 1642. He was accompanied by his wife and a servant. He was a brewer, and was engaged to brew beer in the colony of Rensselaerswyck. He moved to Esopus in 1661. We find him later as a contractor for the building of sloops. His widow, Breektje Elswaerts, married again in 1678.

Albert Pietersen, "Trompeter," from *Hamburg*, married in 1641, in New Amsterdam, Marritje Pietersen (see p. 268).

Annette Pieters, from *"Brutsteen in Duytsland,"* was married August 18, 1641, in New Amsterdam, to Laurens Pietersen from Tönsberg in Norway (p. 129).

Elsje Pieters, from *Hamburg*, widow of Hans Webber, married, in August, 1650, in New Amsterdam, Matthys Capito, a German. She was killed and burnt in the Indian War of 1663.

John Pietersen, from *Lübeck*, married, in September, 1676, in New Amsterdam, Mary Brouwers, from Gauwanes.

Paulus Pietersen, from "Merven" in diocese of *Cologne*, married in 1658, in New Amsterdam, Tryntie Martens, from Aachen. They had several children.

Pieter Pietersen "van *Bremen*" acted as sponsor in New Amsterdam in 1663.

*

Oben (Abel) *Reddenhasen* [Reddinhaus], from the Principality of *Waldeck*, married December 28, 1641, in New Amsterdam, Geertie Nannincks, widow of Van Tjerck Hendricskszen. They had children. As late as 1686 his wife is mentioned in the records (Geertruy Riddenhar). He died before August 2, 1644, when his widow sold her house in New Amsterdam, at the corner of the East River and the present Broad St.

Andries Rees, from *Lippstadt*, was one of the signers of the petition of the Lutherans at Amsterdam, 1657, requesting that Rev. Goetwater be permitted to remain as Lutheran minister in the city. His wife was Ciletje Jans. Their son Johannes was baptized in New Amsterdam on April 26, 1656. Andries, on his arrival at New Amsterdam, was probably a soldier. In June, 1657, he was promoted to "the rank of a cadet." When the government desired to billet off soldiers in 1665, Andries, being approached, said he could take no soldiers, because he "is afraid of being robbed!" He was engaged in tapping in 1660 and afterwards, being several times arrested for tapping and playing at nine pins on holidays. When arrested in 1663, he admitted that he had "tapped on Sunday," but "after the preaching," what he was entitled to. Moreover, he did "no business during the week." He was liberated. In 1674 he had property on the present William St., between Hanover Square and Wall St., then known as Smith St.

Hendrick Jansen Reur, from *Münster*, Westphalia, was appointed court messenger in the colony of Rensselaerswyck in 1651. He died before February 4, 1664, when his household effects were sold at auction.

Jan Riet, from *Bonn*, was listed among the soldiers who were to sail to New Netherland by "The Otter," April 27, 1660.

Robbert Roellants, from *Berlin*, is mentioned at various times in the early records of New Amsterdam. He appeared as sponsor in 1658, arbitrator in 1661. By trade he was a carpenter. He had contracted to build a house for Pieter Kock (p. 236).

Lysbeth De Roode, from *Danzig* (wife of John Salme) and her child, three years old, came to New Netherland by the ship "de Trouw", which sailed January 20, 1664. Six months later her daughter Sara was baptized in New Amsterdam.

Daniel Ruychou (Ritsco?), from *Danzig*, married, August 26, 1661, in New Amsterdam, Catharyn van der Beeck.

*

Adam van Santen [Xanten] came to New Netherland, accompanied by his wife and two children, in "de Bruynvis," which sailed June 19, 1658.

Jacob Abraham Santvort, from Germany, came over in 1661 in "de St. Jan Baptiste." He became one of the leading men in New Amsterdam. By trade he was a tanner. His first wife was Zybe Ariaens. In 1677 he married Magdalentje van Vleet, from Bremen. In 1674 his property on High St., was valued at $5,000.

Symon Scholtz (Schultz) came to New Netherland in the ship "de Vos," which sailed August 31, 1662. He was from *Prussia*.

Paulus Schrick, from *Nürnberg*, was the leader of the Lutherans in New Amsterdam, as is seen by a letter of August 28, 1658, from the Reformed pastors in that city to the General Director and Council (see p. 88). In 1654 he was in Holland, representing the Lutherans and requesting the consistory to send over a Lutheran pastor. He lived a part of the time at Hartford. He and a number of other "colonists" from New Amsterdam were the earliest settlers of Hartford, being there before the English. The first notices of Schrick in New Amsterdam is on August 28, 1651, under which date Laurens Cornelis van der Wel gave a promissory note to him, for fl. 361.58; again on Dec. 24, 1651, when he appeared as a sponsor at the baptism of Warnar, a son of Henrick Van Diepenroeck. Schrick was a merchant and free trader, a man of wealth. On October 29, 1652, he obtained a deed from Claes Jansen van Naerden of a lot in Pearl Street, New Amsterdam. He acquired four acres of land at "The Kolck," in October, 1653; again four acres at the same place, in 1662. He is one of the few in the records of New Amsterdam who are styled "Heer" or "Sieur." A notice of July 19, 1653, states that he had money coming in Germany. This may have been the prime cause of his sojourn abroad in 1654—1655, when he visited the Lutheran consistory in Amsterdam.

Schrick married on November 29, 1658, in New Amsterdam, Maria Varleth, widow of Johannes van Beeck. She belonged to the aristocracy of the city. She had six brothers and sisters: 1) Nicholas, who married Anne Stuyvesant; 2) Janneke, married to Augustine Herrmans, a German from Prague; 3) Anna, wife of George Hawke; 4) Catharyn, wife of Francis de Bruyn; 5) Sarah; 6) Judith, wife of Nicholas Bayard.

Schrick had two children, Susanna and Paulus, who were born at Hartford. But both children were baptized in New Amsterdam on the same day, September 2, 1663. Schrick died in the same year. His widow married a third husband in 1664, William Teller.

Hans Schröder, from *Mansfeld*, married, as widower, Aug. 25, 1641, in New Amsterdam, Aeltje Jans. His first wife was Lysbeth Jans.

Jan Hermanszen Schut, an "Adelborst," from *Lübeck*, married, December 26, 1649, in New Amsterdam, Margreta Dircx (Denys?), a widow. They had a daughter, Fytie, baptized in 1651. Schut seems to have traded at the Delaware river. He was killed about 1651, when his widow married Jan Nagel. There was also another Schut in New Amsterdam, a Williamse Schut who acted as sponsor in 1642.

Claes Claesen Sluiter, from *Oldenburg,* was in New Netherland in 1679 (or before), when he married at Kingston.

Lucas Smith [Schmidt van Jehansberch] (van Coerlant), from *Johannisberg* in the district of Gumbinnen, in East Prussia, arrived at the Manhattans, on "den Conick David," Nov. 29, 1641. He at once entered the service of Domine Bogardus. In August, 1642, he began working in the colony of Rensselaerswyck as a farmhand and clerk. In 1646 De Hooges testified in writing that Smith was an especially pious, faithful and honest young man.

Annetje Sodelaers (Sedelaers or Sylers) from *Königsberg,* in Prussia, married, Nov. 20, 1660, in New Amsterdam, Jan Sprongh, from Bon in the province of Drenthe. Mr. Bergen's Book on Kings County, N. Y., says that she came from "Connex in Bergen, Norway." This is erroneous. Jan and Annetje had several children. The records mention an Annetie Jacobs Sprongh as being dead in October, 1670, when her widower, Matthyas de Haert, married again. Was she the wife of Sprongh, or his sister? Bergen says that Annetje Sodelaers, as widow of Sprongh, was married to Claes Teunisse Clear, in September, 1694.

Caspar Steinmetz, a German, possibly from *Berlin,* was in New Amsterdam in 1648 or before. In 1653 his wife is mentioned as having worked for Judith Verleth. Steinmetz had nine children. In 1655 he petitioned for leave to "tap beer and wine for the accommodation of the burghery and strangers," which petition was granted. In 1665 he hired his house as a city school for fl. 260 a year. However, he had trouble in collecting the rent. He removed to Bergen, N. J., where he became magistrate. In 1674 he signed a petition of the Lutherans. He died in 1702.

Johan Steffen, soldier, from *Herborn,* in Prussia, came to New Netherland on the ship "de Moesman," which sailed March 9, 1660.

Engelbert Sternhuys, a tailor, from *Soest* in Westphalia, came to New Netherland on the ship "de Moesman," which sailed April 25, 1659. He died in 1678.

Harmen Stepfer, from the Duchy of *Cleves,* came to New Netherland by the ship "de Trouw," which sailed Dec. 23, 1660. In 1662 he is called Steppe or Stegge in a deed by which Pieter Jansen (see p. 81), Norwegian, portioned off a lot for him.

Hartwick Stoeff, from *Lübeck,* arrived at New Amsterdam on the ship "Draetvat" in the spring of 1657.

Jacob Stoffelszen, from *Zürichsee,* Switzerland, came to New Netherland in the spring of 1639. In 1643 he is mentioned as purchasing a boat from Jacob Couwenhoven; in 1653 as the step-father of Annetie Cornelissen Van Vorst, whom Pieter Kock (see art. p. 233) sued for breach of marriage contract. In 1654 Jacob sued Ide [?] van Vorst, his stepdaughter, "who lays claim to half a negro." Jacob thought he should be entitled to look upon the negro as his own property. Incidentally we learn that it was a habit to give negroes as presents to the bride at weddings. Ide got two at her wedding. Jacob had a brother, Reyer, who is mentioned by the pastors of New Amsterdam as singing "German songs on shipboard" (p. 88). On August 17, 1657, Jacob married a second time: Trintje Jacobs, widow of Jacob Waelingen, from Hoorn.

Reyer Stoffelszen, a brother of Jacob Stoffelszen, was from *Zürichsee,* Switzerland. He was a smith. He was at New Amsterdam in 1638, and succeeded Burger Joris, of Silesia, as smith of Rensselaerswyck in 1639. He does not appear in this colony after 1647, but is mentioned in the records of New Amsterdam in 1653. He was dead before 1660, when his wife, Geertje Jans, was widow. A letter of the Reformed pastors in New Amsterdam, Megapolensis and Drisius, Aug. 23, 1658, says that Paul Schrick, the leader of the Lutherans in that city took Reyer to be a Lutheran "because he sang German songs on shipboard on the way to Holland." (p. 88.) This must have been about the year 1654 when Schrick visited Holland and Germany. Reyer's wife was a member of the Dutch Reformed church in 1686. She was then living at the "Deacon's House for the Poor," in Broad St.

Hendrick Sweterinck, soldier, from *Osnabrück,* was among the passengers to embark for New Netherland, by the ship "de Bonte Koe," which sailed April 25, 1660.

Herman Theuniszen, from Zell in *"Münsterland,"* married, April 19, 1654, in New Amsterdam, Grietje Cosyns. In 1659 he worked for Augustine Herrmans, from Prague, as "his farmer." Herman had several children.

Pieter Teunisz, from *Brunswick,* is first mentioned in the colony of Rensselaerswyck under date of March 28, 1648, as taking with him cattle and implements to Catskill. In 1652 and 1653 he and John Dircks of Bremen were summoned before court to settle accounts. He is also mentioned in the Albany records as late as 1684—85.

Willem Janzen Traphagen, from *Lemgo,* in Lippe, widower of Jutge Claes Groenvis, married, June, 1658, in New Amsterdam, Aeltje Dircks, from Steenwyck. By her he had a son, Johannes, who was baptized April 9, 1659. He married a third time: Joosje Willems. Rebecca who was born in this marriage was baptized at Brooklyn, Feb. 9, 1662.

*

Nicholas Velthuysen, or Langvelthuysen, from *Lübeck,* was in New Amsterdam in 1650 or earlier. He was married twice. His first wife Janneke Willems died in April, 1659, leaving children. In June, of the same year, he married Aeltje Lubberts, widow of one Bickers. Five months later they separated. He beat her, "could not live with her." He was engaged in many brawls, what his vocation, that of a tapster, invited. About 1660 Velthuysen "absconded." It was decided that his estate should be sold. In 1662 a conversation was reported as having taken place in February, 1660, on board a ship, that Velthuysen had died on a trip to "Genee."

Johannes Verveelen had property in 1674 in New Amsterdam, on the present Broad St., on South William St. and Broad St. It was valued at $3,000. In 1667 he was constable of N. Harlem, also overseer of the N. Harlem court. In 1671 he was appointed constable and clerk of Fordham. Before 1664 he and his wife Anna Tjersvelt [Jaarvelt] joined the Reformed church.

The *Verveelen* family of New Amsterdam is of German stock

with infusion of French, as Riker, the historian of Harlem, says. It came from Amsterdam.

Johan Verplanck, a smith and baker, sailed as a soldier to New Netherland by the ship "de Bonte Koe," on April 15, 1660. He was from *Bonn* "above Cologne," as the passenger list states. In 1663 Sussana Verplancken and a child one and a half year old came to New Amsterdam. Was she a relative of Johan?

Magdalentje van Vleet, from *Bremen,* was married, in 1677, in New Amsterdam, to Jacob Abraham Santvort, a German.

Hans Vos, from *Baden,* came by "den Houttuyn," August 4, 1642. He worked in the colony of Rensselaerswyck. Soon after his arrival he was appointed court messenger in the colony, a position for which he was reappointed several times . In 1658 he appeared in court in New Amsterdam, though his residence was given as Fort Orange. In 1659 he had a contract on Burger Joris' [from Silesia] bowery. He was married. In 1661 he was deputy officer at the prison in New Amsterdam. In 1675 he is again mentioned as being at Esopus.

Thomas Vorst, from *Bremen,* came to Netherland by the "Otter," which sailed April 27, 1660.

Jan Vresen, "Adelborst," from *Hamburg,* embarked for New Amsterdam in the ship the "Otter," which sailed April 27, 1660. He was accompanied by his wife and two children, respectively eleven and nine years old. A Jan De Vries, and wife [name not given] joined the Dutch Reformed church in 1677.

Jan Vreesen, from *Hamburg,* came to New Netherland in "de Statyn," which sailed Sept. 27, 1663.

*

Jan Barentsz Wemp, nicknamed Poest, was in the colony of Rensselaerswyck as early as 1643. He had charge for some time of a saw- and grist-mill, and leased land 1647—1654. Poesten Kill is named after him. He was born about 1620, probably in *Germany.* "Wemp" would suggest that he was from Vemb [Incorrect for Vem: J. P. Trap] in Denmark, but his real surname was Wimpel. A silver cup of 1657 bears the name Jan Barensen Wimpel. "The New York Genealogical and Biographical Record," XXXV., 190 f., claims that he was from Germany, adducing as proof that "Wämpel" appears as a surname in *Bavaria*, 1604. "Vimpel," can be Danish, meaning, pennant. Wemp became one of the proprietors of Schenectady. His wife was Marritie Meynderts. They had six children. Wemp died in 1663. His widow married Sweer Teunis Van Velsen. Both were slain in the massacre of Schenectady in February, 1690.

Anneke Wessels van Colen [Cologne] was married, April 19, 1654, in New Amsterdam, to Hendrick Gerritszen "Van Nes in Embderlandt." He was a tailor.

David Wessel, who signed the petition of the Lutherans, in 1657, requesting that Rev. Goetwater might be permitted to remain in New Amsterdam as a Lutheran minister, was probably a *German*. His name as well as his close association with Germans, and his creed would indicate that. He was at Midwout in 1654; acted as sponsor for a child of Andries Rees, a German, in 1656. His wife was Tietje Gomme(ls). Their daughter, Amelia, was baptized July 4, 1660. Wessel was a turner. He lived, in 1665, on the Heere Graft in New Amsterdam.

Jochem Wessel (Backer) was probably a *German*. He obtained a lot in Beverwyck in April, 1651. He was a baker. He married Gertuy Hieronimus. They had several children. In 1674 he signed a petition of the Lutherans at Willemstad requesting permission to bury their dead. As it was, they were employing their own sexton, and were obliged to pay the Sexton (Aansprecher) of the Reformed Church besides.

Vrit (?) *Wessel*, who signed a Lutheran petition in 1674, in the capacity as elder or principal of the "Augsburg Confession here" (Bergen, N. J.) was possibly a *German*.

Wessel Wesselsen, from *Münster*, came to New Netherland by the ship "de Hoop," which sailed on January 12, 1661. A person by this name is mentioned as deceased Feb. 14, 1661. A

Wessel Wesselsen is mentioned as living at Esopus in 1667, and as having a wife called Maria ten Eyck, 1672.

Jacob Barents Weyt, from *Cologne,* was a member of the Dutch Reformed church in New Amsterdam in 1649.

Hendrick Wierinck, from *Wesel,* came to New Netherland in the ship "d'Eendracht," which sailed April 17, 1664.

Geertruyd Willekens, from *Hamburg,* widow of Hendrick Gulick (Gülch, near Cologne), was married, in September, 1653, in New Amsterdam, to Claes Claesen Smitt, from Amersfoort.

Hendrick Willemse, who signed the petition of the Lutherans in New Amsterdam, 1657, requesting that Rev. Goetwater might remain in the city as Lutheran preacher, probably was a *German.* He is mentioned as early as 1648. He owned a house at the N. W. corner of the present Bridge and Broad Street. He was a baker, was appointed inspector of bakeries in 1663. He was later appointed overseer of streets. About 1670 we find him in Albany. In 1671 he and other Lutherans signed a petition complaining of their minister. His daughter, Geesje Hendricks, married Dirck Jansen van Cleef (Vanderclyf, probably from Alphen, in Brabant). Geesje had six daughters, most of them married persons of English descent.

Reinert Willemszen, from *"Oldenburgerland,"* married, April 10. 1660, in New Amsterdam, Sussanna Arents. In 1655 the property of a Christian Jacobsen Backer of Sont was at his house. Willemszen was a baker, became Schepen and Firewarden of New Orange [New York] in 1673. His property on the present south side of Stone St.. between William and Broad Street was valued at $6,000.

Barnt Wittenhooft, tailor, from *Münster,* came to New Netherland by "de Trouw," which sailed March 24, 1662.

*

Andrew Christian Zabriski, came to New Netherland by "de Vos," which sailed Aug. 31. 1662. In the ship's list of passengers he is called "Albert Saborsiski, from Prussia." He was the progenitor of a prominent family of New York. Tradition says that he was a Pole. He may have been a German of Polish extraction. He had been intended for the Lutheran ministry, but as the authorities sought to force him into the army, he came to New Netherland.

SUPPLEMENT.

FORMER DUTCH COINS, WEIGHTS AND MEASURES AND THEIR EQUIVALENTS.

(From Van Rensselaer Bowier Manuscripts, p. 847 ff.)

Coins.

stuiver	$0.02
schelling (6 stuivers)	.12
gulden ⎱ (20 stuivers)	.40*
Carolus gulden ⎰	
goud gulden (1⅘ guldens)	.56
rijksdaelder (2½ guldens)	1.00
ducaton (3 guldens, 3 stuivers)	1.26
pond Vlaamsch (6 guldens)	2.40

Weights.

Amsterdam ons	1.085 ounces (avoirdupois)
Amsterdam pond (16 onsen)	1 pound, 1.36 ounces (avps.)

Linear measures.

Rhineland duim	1.03 inches
Rhineland voet	12.36 inches
Rhineland roede (12 voeten)	12.36 feet
Amsterdam duim	1.013 inches
Amsterdam roede (13 voeten)	12.071 feet

Square measures.

Rhineland morgen (600 square roeden)	2.103 acres
Amsterdam morgen (600 square roeden)	2.069 acres

---

* In New Netherland one guilder beaver was worth $0.40. One guilder sea-want was worth one-third of a guilder beaver. A good merchantable beaver skin was worth from $3.20 to $4.00.

SUPPLEMENT.

Liquid measure.

anker   10.128 gallons (wine)

Dry measures.

schepel   ⎱ 0.764 bushel (wheat)
             ⎰ 1.29 bushels (salt)
zak   3 schepels
mudde   4 schepels
last   36 zakken or 82.512 bushels
ship's last   3.71 cubic yards, 2½ tons burden

www.ingramcontent.com/pod-product-compliance
Lightning Source LLC
Chambersburg PA
CBHW030633270326
41929CB00007B/54